LANDMARK COLLECTOR'S LIBRARY

SHROVETIDE FOOTBALL
AND THE
ASHBOURNE GAME

LINDSEY PORTER

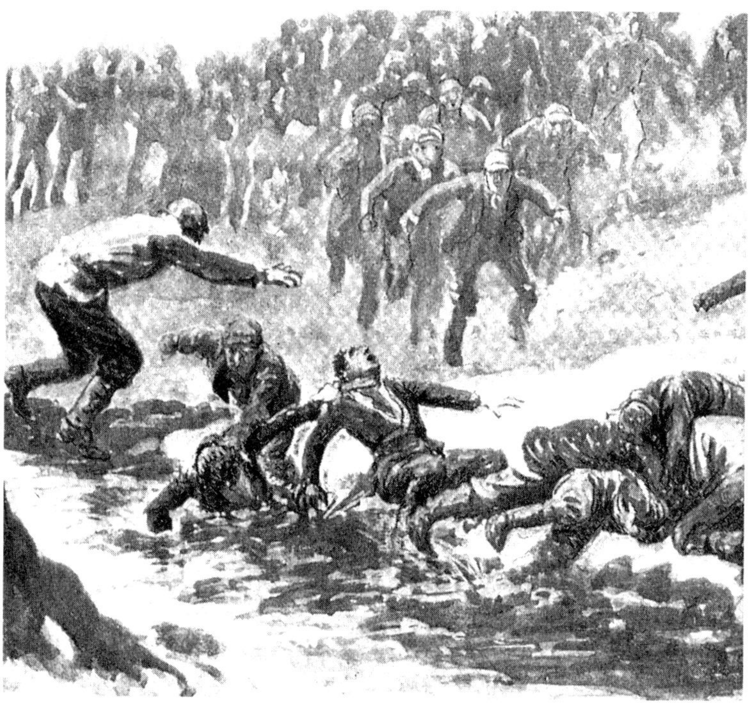

LANDMARK COLLECTOR'S LIBRARY

SHROVETIDE FOOTBALL
AND THE
ASHBOURNE GAME

Lindsey Porter

Landmark Publishing

Published by
Landmark Publishing Ltd
Ashbourne Hall, Cokayne Avenue
Ashbourne, Derbyshire DE6 1EJ England
Tel: (01335) 347349 Fax: (01335) 347303
e-mail: landmark@clara.net
web site: www.landmarkpublishing.co.uk

ISBN 1 84306 063 9

© Lindsey Porter 2002

The rights of Lindsey Porter as author of this work
have been asserted by him in accordance with the Copyright,
Design and Patents Act, 1993.

All rights reserved. No part of this publication may be reproduced,
stored in a retrieval system or transmitted in any form or by any means,
electronic, mechanical, photocopying, recording or otherwise without
the prior permission of Landmark Publishing Ltd.

British Library Cataloguing in Publication Data: a catalogue
record for this book is available from the British Library.

Printed by CPI, Bookcraft, Midsomer Norton, Somerset
Design: Ashley Emery
Cover: James Allsopp
Production: Lindsey Porter

Front cover: Simon Plumbly being escorted to the plinth to start the Ashbourne game,
Shrove Tuesday, 2002. Back cover: Paul Harrison goals at Clifton, 2000.
Page 3: Goaling at Sturston Mill, Ashbourne, 1907

Picture credits:
H. Alcock, Ashbourne News Telegraph, T. Baker, Mrs M. Brown,
H. Connell, M. & P. Cust, Derby Evening Telegraph, A. Henstock,
L. Porter, A. Smith, Mrs M. Winstone

Contents

	Introduction to the First Edition	7
	Introduction to the Second Edition	9
1	Shrovetide Football before 1800	14
2	Shrovetide Football in the 19th Century	30
3	Gazetter of Shrovetide Football Games & Ball Customs	39
4	Ashbourne Royal Shrovetide Football: Early Days	44
5	Difficult Times	59
6	Game Reports 1892-1949	76
7	Game Reports 1950-2002	141
8	Traditions & Reminiscenses	196
9	Surviving Games at Shrovetide	202
	Appendices	204
	Roll of Honour	214
	Chronology	221
	Index	224

There's a town called the Gateway to Dovedale
And early every year,
Men gather in the Green Man bar
To drink their rum and beer.

They play a game of football there,
They play it through the street.
The men they are a rugged crowd
And very hard to beat.

Shrove Tuesday and Ash Wednesday,
These days are always set
To play a game of football
Through sunshine, snow and wet.

They carry a chosen one shoulder high,
Until they reach Shaw Croft.
They sing *The Queen* and *Auld Lang Syne*,
Then the ball is tossed aloft.

All barriers are broken then,
Religions, races too,
To try and hold that wonderous ball,
Robed in red, white and blue.

It's sometimes up and sometimes down,
As they play there in the street,
And neither one will give way,
Or ever show defeat.

The day goes on and the night air cold,
As slowly they leave the town
To fight through hedgerow, sludge and brook,
Till that mill wheel is found.

Then out of dirty pockets wet,
A coin is quickly tossed.
Men walk away, no luck that day,
For them the game is lost.

The victor he rejoices,
His friends stand by his side.
With the ball tucked underneath his arm,
Into Ashbourne town they stride.

Men gather in the Green Man bar
And tales are told that night,
Of Royal Shrovetide football
And how they won or lost the fight.

So don't decry our ancient game
And never show defeat.
Let's see our children's children
Play Shrovetide in the street.

Recited by Don Lowndes at the Ashbourne Shrove Tuesday lunch when he turned up the ball in 1974

Introduction to the First Edition

It is surprising that no history of Ashbourne's Royal Shrovetide Football game has been written before. For me, association with the game has been confined to that of a curious bystander – glad to see the custom continuing but quite happy to stand on the sidelines and watch. I never appreciated that the mass play actually included an element of strategy, with runners quietly waiting, anticipating movement and placing themselves accordingly. Nor did I fully realise the spirit of the players – for their own side of course, but more importantly, for the game itself.

Older players, content to leave the rigour of play to younger men (and the occasional woman), help to maintain the dignity of the game – particularly at the Shrovetide luncheons. Perhaps it is just as well that the lunches provide an opportunity for this – there is precious little dignity in the hug. This spirit for the 'old game' is nothing new of course. It came very much to the fore during the 31 years spanning the prosecutions – 1860 to 1891 – although the threat of prosecution continued for much longer. The annual appeal prior to turning up the ball to keep the ball out of the streets continued well into this century.

Although I have written in the region of twenty books, none have given me the sense of interest and even excitement as this has. Principally, it was due to the uncovering of so many forgotten details about the game. It did however, involve many hours of my spare time searching old newspapers for reports. It is all too easy to miss something, and I wonder still whether some vital information was missed as I scanned page after page of newsprint. The early records of the Royal Ashbourne Shrovetide Committee (herein after referred to as the Committee) were destroyed in a fire and so the newspapers remain the principal source of information. It has proved interesting to see how much detail quoted about the game is inaccurate. From Glover, writing in 1829, to recent newspaper reports and the annually produced Roll of Honour: the passage of time has brought a veil of obscurity across the true history.

It is this adaptability of the game over the last two centuries which has been its strength. In fact without the willingness to change, the game would not have survived. There is nothing new in changes to the 'rules'. In fact there is little which does appear to be new. Players travelling to the goals seems unfair to those in possession, who know they cannot do the same. Yet it was happening a century ago with the 4.20pm train to Clifton being used for the same purpose!

This book essentially falls into two parts – the history of Ashbourne's Royal Shrovetide Football game up to 1891 and the period after that up to 1992. The Ashbourne News was formed in 1891 and reports about the game are much more detailed from then onwards. In fact, all the years since 1891 are covered in some detail. I recognise it is easy to become repetitive and I have tried to avoid this whenever I can. I have also mentioned some of the players. This has been arbitrary in many cases and I hope that the players who are not mentioned are not aggrieved by this. I often had only an abstract report to go on and had to recognise the demands of limited space. For future historians or those interested in particular features, I have quoted (freely) reports used in the text. Consequently AN, AT, ANT, DM, DA and a date refers to the date of the *Ashbourne News*, *Ashbourne Telegraph*, *Ashbourne News Telegraph*, *Derby Mercury* and *Derbyshire Advertiser* in which the report can be found. For convenience, I have also added a cronology and an updated Roll of Honour. In the latter, many changes are from early years and it even excludes an alleged 1902 Sturston goal which did not occur! I do not claim that this is accurate, but it does represent what the papers reported.

What then of the future of the game? It seems fairly clear that, so long as the players want it, the game will go on and on. Trespass and vandalism seem to be the biggest dangers. Wanton disregard by spectators of other peoples' property is a mindless act, which can easily cause bad feeling towards the game. Again it is nothing new. A visitor from The Potteries once insisted on climbing a fence near the church field when the adjacent gate was open. He got his come-uppance by falling off and breaking an arm.

The police seem tolerant of the obstruction to the highway for which we must be grateful. However, although it was police action that resulted in the prosecutions, it was originally as a result of action initiated by Ashbourne magistrates. They wished to remove play from the streets and Mr Frank of Ashbourne Hall deliberately tried to stop play altogether. Remember, damage caused during trespass may result in a civil action against the trespasser, but that really isn't the point. It is the damage to the goodwill towards the game that may endanger its future.

Looking back, as well as to the future, it is clear that the game is an essential part of Ashbourne's heritage. It would be gratifying to see plaques erected at memorable locations and to commemorate both the game and the tenacity of those who risked prosecution and imprisonment in order to protect it. A suitable location would be on the Haig Bar, to commemorate the days when the ball was thrown up at the Bull Ring and also thrown out of those premises by Mrs Woolley in 1860. Another good location would be on St John's Hall where the 1860 Court hearings were held. It was here that it was decided that the playing of the game in the streets constituted an offence.

Finally, an appeal. There is little early anecdotal evidence of the actual play: who was in the game; notable things that happened and never got reported. In a hundred years time, a future historian will say the same thing unless current players – young and old – record things they remember about the game and its players. Everything needs keeping in a central source, along with a collection of as many photographs as possible, especially of the early years of photography. Perhaps the Committee could address this matter on behalf of us all.

I wish to acknowledge the tremendous help I have received from Mr Brian Vertigen and Carol Frost of the Burton Mail Group (who own the *Ashbourne News Telegraph*) and Miss Silvia Bown of Derby Local Studies Library. Also Mr John Gadsby, recent past-Chairman of the Committee, who gave me a great deal of support and encouragement. He also allowed me to use material from his booklet on the game in my section on traditions and lent me photographs. My wife Stella put up with my demands on her time. She not only typed the manuscript but shared all the details of my discoveries and coped with my absence from domestic life while the research and writing were pursued. John Hanson helped by providing match reports of recent years. The research on Mrs Woolley and her family was done by George Shaw. Photos have been provided by *The Burton Mail*, Peter Breheny, Alan Harrison, Yvonne Hithersay, Hulton Picture Library, Chris Sowter and Mary Winstone. The Committee agreed to my request for a joint photo and Vince Ferry allowed the use of copyright material. Stuart Avery provided his cartoons which form part of the luncheon menus. Tonya Monk edited the text and John Robey handled the design and production. A big thank you to you all.

Many of the reports have been paraphrased although some detail is quoted extensively, especially in 1922 and 1928. The Burton Mail Group gave specific permission for this and without it, the production of this book would not have been possible. Finally, although I live in Clifton I hope all Up'ards will think my work is unbiased and forgive me if they think differently.

Lindsey Porter
Clifton, Ashbourne. 1992

Introduction to the Second Edition

Enjoyment for the Common Folk

This book stemmed from the fact that I throw very little away. Having married initially in 1968 and subsequently remarried, the presence in my hand of the parish magazine of Leek Parish Church for June 1968 seemed to reveal more patience from my second wife than it did reveal an understanding by me that the document had reached its dump-by date. Rather than throw it away, I was about to give it to a son with equal patience as a recipient of all his father's unwanted effects. A final perusal of the contents revealed quotations from the church records at the end of the 17th Century. One of them didn't exactly rivet me, but it more than caught my eye. It read '1697, Spent on Shrove Tuesday in securing the church from the Rabble, 2/-'.

Having produced nearly 100,000 words of text on the Ashbourne Shrovetide mass football game it set me pondering. At perhaps 6d per man for half a day, that would mean the vicar had needed four men to protect his church, maybe more. Not from football, I reasoned, but from what? The rabble, the vicar had noted. But why? Until about that time, I later found out, churches had often been used for cock fights in the chancel. Presumably the vicar had gone off the idea. Thinking about the matter, it sowed the seed of looking at Shrovetide events and especially Shrovetide football in general. By such strange beginnings my passion for the Ashbourne football game grew to investigate the festivity as a whole. My wife, despite being a passionate supporter of Ashbourne's football game, thought I was nuts to do the first book....

The festivities of Shrovetide are traditionally held to have been a last fling before the austerity of Lent. However, such a simplistic explanation masks the true reasons which are much more complex. It may have been a means for the housewife to use up her eggs, flour etc in pancakes rather than watch them deteriorate during Lent but the other reasons for playing games, sport or otherwise enjoying oneself are not so simple.

In fact the Shrovetide customs and festivities before the Industrial Revolution mirrored the course of British domestic history. Following the mechanisation of the economy, social order changed in many ways and the Shrovetide traditions fell a victim to it. Only in a few places did the ancient festivities and customs continue to become, in most instances, an anachronism in a changing world. But continue they have done, often without any regard as to why they were introduced or for what purpose. Some are really fashionable, like the Olney Pancake race, which has become an international event, adapting in spectacular style to using modern communications to see how the companion race progressed in Kansas. Others, such as the witch listening at Teddington is a harmless pursuit whose meaning has long since been forgotten. Cock fighting, dog and cock throwing have hopefully all ended but the game of mass football continues in various parts of the country. Only in Ashbourne, does the main form of the game, mass football formerly known as hug ball, continue.

Even here, in a game that knows no dignity once play commences, civic pride and some basic rules have been added to the ancient custom in an endeavour to mould it in some ways to match the requirements of an age different to that existing in former times. Perhaps the biggest change has been that the invitation to start the game is now the highest honour the town can bestow. It is a measure of how the festivity has changed since the 19th century.

This book looks not only at the Ashbourne game, but examples of Shrovetide football elsewhere in the country. The first edition of this official history of the Ashbourne Game (1) has been extended to bring it up to date, covering all the years to 2002; additional research found since the first edition of 1992 has been incorporated and a good measure of photographs added as well. After the first edition was published, some players remonstrated that match details were incorrect. Well, it was produced as reported at the time. Some of the reports have been altered accordingly. To all those who have helped and put up with my questions with resolute patience, I express my gratitude.

Shrovetide games tended to differ from place to place as this book graphically shows. These differences created, over the passage of time, distinctive customs and even different names for an inherently similar pursuit. One has to look no further than the very name Shrovetide. One Cumbrian librarian told me that 'there never were any Shrovetide customs in Scotland.' Indeed there were not, but there were plenty of Fasten E'en customs, the name by which the festival is known in that country.

In the times between the medieval period and the early Industrial Revolution, social unrest was a fear of civic authorities. Clearly there were times when the prospects of it were greater than at other periods. Walvin has suggested that the opportunity to have 'a blow out' allowed a safety valve to release pressure under circumstances where it was clearly known that it would be for one day only. He contends that from the 13th to the 19th Century, football was regarded as a violent game. It was an occasion for settling old scores, displaying prowess, testing strength and so on. Moreover, it was a game which came perilously close to testing the limits of the social control exercised by local and national governments. (2)

As Malcolmson put it: 'Civil and ecclesiastical discipline often had to be defended against the counter-morality of popular sports and festivities'. (3) Malcolmson's work is recommended as a good introduction to the subject. He goes on to say that:

"in a world which lacked effective policing systems, and in which the control of men in authority was often uncertain and tenuous, public turbulence, even in the pursuit of pleasure, was a volatile and potentially threatening force. To allow the common folk to have their day, to permit them to rule the streets and public space, through their boisterous enjoyments, if only for a day, was to turn the world upside down. But such outbursts were permitted on the strict understanding that the status quo returned the following day. Games played on Shrove Tuesday seemed to fit this pattern, and from the sixteenth century onward they were synonymous with a flurry of communal, turbulent pleasures; animal sports, cock fighting – and football. The cultural habits of the people were, however, shaped by local forces; their pleasures and games tended to be specific and very parochial."

This was all very well, but the Puritan movement, which had emerged in the reign of Elizabeth, during the 16th Century found objection with a lot of sports and pastimes. Their belief was that such activities could only be acceptable if the scope and end of them was that God was honoured in and by them. It is not known if the mayor of Chester who tried to stop the football match in 1533 was a Puritan, but one of his successors, who stopped the wakes pageant in 1599, was described as 'a godly and zealous man'.

Malcolmson makes it clear that the pressure ancient customs were subject to where the will of the Puritans held sway (and remember, they ruled the nation under the Commonwealth):

"For these 'preciser' sort of people the traditions of popular leisure were objectionable on a number of grounds: they were thought to be profane and licentious – they were occasions of worldly indulgence which tempted men from a godly life; being rooted in pagan and popish practices, they were rich in the sort of ceremony and ritual which poorly suited the Protestant conscience; they frequently involved a desecration of the Sabbath and an interference with the worship of the true believers; they disrupted the peaceable order of society, distracting men from their basic social duties – hard work, thrift, personal restraint, devotion to family, a sober carriage. 'Any exercise', declared Phillip Stubbes [writing in 1583] 'on the sabaoth (sic) or any other day else, is wicked, and to be forbidden'." (4)

However, it is, thank goodness, not easy to overcome the will of the majority on something as personal as how they are to enjoy themselves:

"A large number of people, including many farmers, parsons, and country gentlemen, retained a basic sympathy (or at least tolerance) for the established recreational customs. These were men of moderate or conservative disposition whose moral outlook was relatively worldly and permissive. After the Restoration, with many elements of Puritanism discredited and condemned, the strength of these traditionalist convictions in English society was considerably enhanced. Moreover, many men of property were themselves attracted to and involved in the customary recreational practices. They supported cock-fighting with enthusiasm and patronized those athletic sports which readily allowed for gambling; they celebrated some of the major holidays and helped to support certain local festivities which were customary in their own communities. In general they were fairly well disposed towards worldly pleasures 'taken in moderation', and their disposition served to restrain and counteract the influence of puritan reform." (5)

Malcolmson goes on to quote examples of customs being held on Oak Apple Day (the birthday of King Charles II and the date of his restoration). It is probable that the Ashbourne Shrovetide football match is an example of the introduction of a festivity following the Restoration, for Charles Cotton wrote :

'Two towns that long that war had raged, Being at football now engaged'. (6)

However, the occasional breaches of public order, both on the occasion of Shrovetide and at other public holidays, have given us records which are often all we now know of these festivities being observed by the lower orders and tolerated by the gentry at large, if not by the Puritans. At an early period attempts were made to introduce more order into some of our growing towns. The attempt to ban mass football in Chester in 1533 is perhaps the best known example. There are fewer records of attempts to suppress a custom in the rural areas.

The Industrial Revolution brought with it the need for a new social order, growing towns and less opportunity or tolerance for the ancient customs. Football had become marginalised. At best tolerated for centuries and often banned by royal decree it had become a spent force towards the end of the eighteenth century. However, it was recognised that it was a useful means of keeping the lid on the powder kegs which existed in some of our public schools. Walvin records that at Winchester between 1770 and 1818, there were six outbursts of pupil violence and order had to be restored on the last occasion by the militia with fixed bayonets. Similarly at Rugby, the Army had to be called in to the school to put down a riot in 1797.

Football games became established as a means of channelling youthful exuberance and gained in popularity. This in turn lead to the establishment of football clubs and eventually the Football Association. This move clearly marginalised mass football as a sport to be played as an old established custom only. Walvin's excellent book is recommended for its succinct appraisal of early football history, much of which is of interest but not directly relevant to this study. Ashbourne Grammar School permitted Shrovetide Football amongst its pupils. It is interesting to speculate whether the town had two games or whether the school was responsible for its survival in the 18th Century. At some point it is quite possible that the school game became the town's boys' game.

Whatever the festivity, the attempts to maintain public order amongst the lower classes and the fear of the upper classes of the consequences of public unrest saw the introduction of measures aimed at strengthening public control. Cock fighting, bull baiting etc were banned by Act of Parliament. *The Highways Act, s. 35, 1835*, allowed magistrates to prosecute for the obstruction of the highway with a fine of up to 40s 'for playing at football or any other game on any part of the said highways, to the annoyance of any passenger' and the *Police Act, 1840* gave the magistrates (i.e. the local gentry) the opportunity to enforce their will where football or other violent customs were concerned. Some customs were banned by Act of Parliament and this included at least one Shrovetide custom when the Whipping Toms were banned under the *Leicester Improvement Act, 1846*. Between 1840 and 1860, there was a concerted attempt to rid the country of many customs deemed no longer acceptable. Bushaway lists several examples and has written a good account of how our ancient customs were suppressed. (7) Although many went in the mid-19th Century, he does also show that many had gone before that too.

It could be said with some conviction that Shrove Tuesday was a public holiday we gave up. This is not strictly true, for it was never a Bank Holiday in the true sense, although banks presumably found it safer to shut in the interests of security than risk an unruly mob at the door. Even today, Ashbourne banks shut in the afternoon of Shrove Tuesday and Ash Wednesday, although this may have as much to do with the lack of custom as the worry about security. The ringing of the Pancake Bell may have called housewives to the hearth with a pan and their eggs etc, but it also signalled to many apprentices and schoolchildren the beginning of a half day's holiday. In Ashbourne, the local children still have a different mid-term holiday during Lent to the rest of the county schools. Their break coincides with Shrovetide, recognising the inevitability of mass truancy and an empty school in the event of conformity being introduced. Even the holiday developed its own, separate traditions, such as barring the schoolmaster from school on Shrove Tuesday, etc. This practice continued well into the 20th Century at Tideswell in Derbyshire, although in later years it was children late for school who were barred out. (8)

However, the idea of apprentices having half a day off did not auger well with the wave of new industrialists keen to meet targets and delivery dates. In a sense this was nothing really new, for the need to gather the harvest had clearly been recognised for generations. In 1671, for instance, a man was prosecuted for bull baiting, not because the sport was thought to be cruel, but on the grounds that it was harvest time and he caused 'divers labourers and other poore persons to leave their work.' (9) It would be interesting to know how many customs fell victim to 'progress' in this way. In more rural communities these pressures were not so acute, especially where the tradesman and the new middle class supported the festivity. This is one of the main reasons why the Ashbourne game survived. It would also be interesting to know the extent that more benign customs were introduced, which did not interfere with the new social order and the pressures of the factory system. The re-introduction of the Derbyshire well dressing custom mentioned in Chapter 3 may have been part of this, however indirectly. Customs introduced as an alternative to Shrovetide Football hardly ever survived.

Nonetheless, Walvin contends that the overworked, exploited apprentices, often harbouring a range of grievances, posed a threat of unruliness that often erupted into outbursts of radical agitation. If Shrovetide gave an opportunity for such outbursts to be restricted into some kind of annual institution (whether football or not), it could be tolerated. He makes the point though that football was, for centuries, often uncontrolled and spontaneous, sometimes threatening and always a matter for unease for men worried about the problems of civil order and social stability. Therein lay the demise for many unruly pursuits during the course of the 19th Century.

No complete appraisal of our custom of Shrovetide football has been made and this study takes us only so far down the road towards that. However, such a study can only be complete with a thorough trawl through all the ancient domestic records that chart the thousand-year history of our islands since the Conquest. Nonetheless, sufficient survives for us to glean an indication of the widespread popularity of the pursuit and set the Ashbourne game in that context. This study of folk-culture does not try to bottom the reason why such means of enjoyment were started or for what rationale they continued. Surely the need for local pleasure needs no justification. It is, however, sometimes interesting to view what we did within the framework of how other people viewed it at the time and what we think of it now.

For those only interested in the game in general, the amount of material in this book on the Ashbourne game will seem out of proportion. No apology is given for that: this book is primarily aimed at those who play in and those that follow the hug of Ashbourne's Royal Shrovetide Football.

My wife thinks that maybe now this book is finished, I'll have more time for domestic duties. She believes that Ashbourne football, together with the rabble of 1697 in Leek, have a lot to answer for. I hope you think that her patience has been justified.

Since the publication of the first edition, several people have helped significantly to further my knowledge of the game. I thank them all and hope they will not mind if I single out a few for particular praise: Tim Baker, Alec Smith, Janice Carruthers of Derby, Mathew Alexander of Guildford plus Mr J Black of the Burton Daily Mail Ltd, who own the *Ashbourne News Telegraph,* for the use of their photographs.

Lindsey Porter
Ashbourne, 2002

References

1. Porter, L., *Ashbourne Royal Shrovetide Football*, 1992, privately printed
2. Walvin, *The People's Game*, 2nd edit, 1994, pp12/15
3. Malcomson, RW., *Popular Recreations in English Society, 1700-1850*, 1973, pp5/6
4. ibid, pp6/7
5. ibid, pp13/14
6. Cotton, C., *Burlesque on the Great Frost*, see J Beresford, ed., *Poems of Charles Cotton*, 1630-1687, republished in 1923
7. Bushaway, *By Rite: Custom, Ceremony and Community in England 1700-1880*, 1982, pp238-79
8. For a photograph of this custom, see *The Spirit of Tideswell*, Hill T., and Black P, 2001, p154
9. Malcomson, op. cit., p25

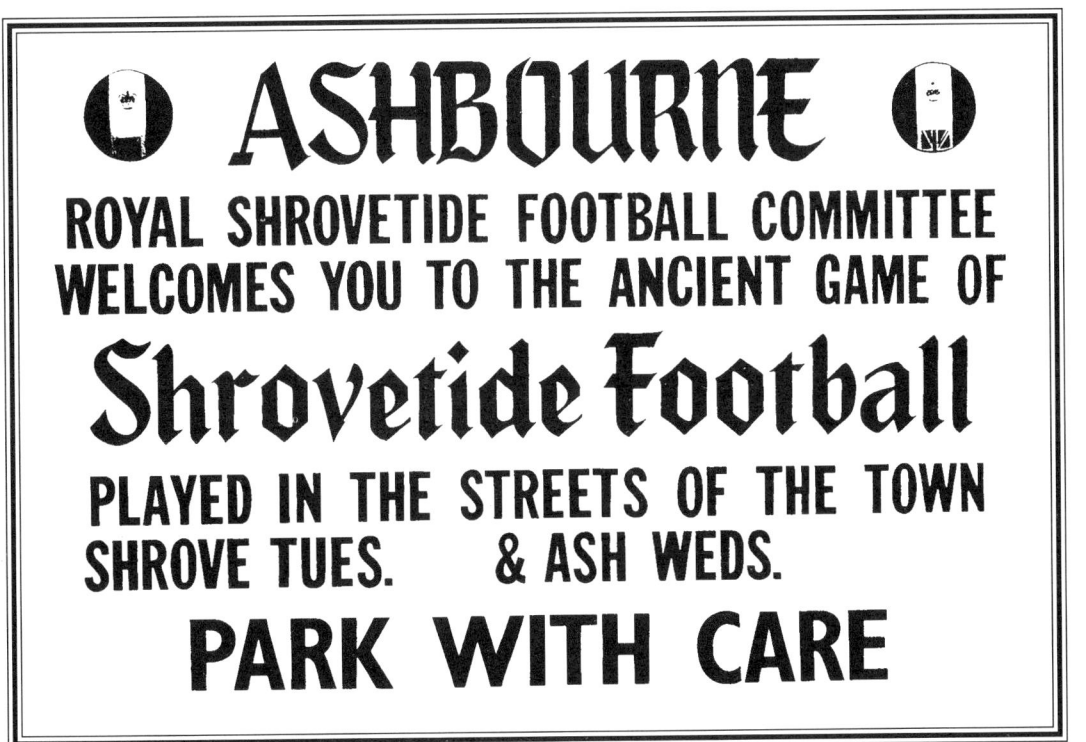

ASHBOURNE
ROYAL SHROVETIDE FOOTBALL COMMITTEE
WELCOMES YOU TO THE ANCIENT GAME OF
Shrovetide Football
PLAYED IN THE STREETS OF THE TOWN
SHROVE TUES. & ASH WEDS.
PARK WITH CARE

Street signs like these herald the two days of play in Ashbourne

SHROVETIDE FOOTBALL BEFORE 1800

Perhaps the most physically challenging of all Shrovetide pastimes was mass football. Some of the variations of the game were (and indeed still are) pretty innocuous but hug ball was definitely not in this category. Clearly a large gathering of people determined to move a ball in opposite directions creates a challenging environment. It brings (or chiefly brought) out the best and the worst of human spirit and endeavour.

The gathering together of lots of people in an unordered way gave the potential for the more unruly to turn a highlight of the social calendar into a near riot. It is no surprise that in the nineteenth century, when a more ordered way of life was stamped across the nation in the name of Victorian moral values, such games were banned wherever possible. This included other sports of the lower classes, such as cock fighting, bull baiting, cock throwing etc. It wasn't the cruelty of the sport which became the target, for fox and stag hunting survived. It was the ability of the upper class to enforce their will through the new police forces, established under the *Police Act, 1840*, which saw the downfall of mass football etc.

Only in Ashbourne did hug ball survive at Shrovetide. This was not the original intention of the magistrates (who were local gentry) but the town's people, including many tradesmen, were in favour of the game continuing. However, the game could be played without the streets in the commercial part of the town being used. Perhaps equally importantly, a ribbon of fields divided the town into two along the line of the River Henmore and so the game could be quickly away from the streets in any event. Nonetheless the magistrates fined the players on no less than eight times and there were attempts to bring prosecutions on two other occasions.

The original football games were often only played annually, and although it had purpose, it had neither organisation or structure. Individual characteristics developed such as whether you could carry the ball or only kick it and of course who the opponents were – married men against the unmarried; one side of town against the other; parish against parish etc. Rules were usually minimal, often consisting of the bare necessities such as starting time, the way you scored a goal and how play terminated. Some social characteristics have been identified such as the honour bestowed on the winner by being able to keep the ball, being carried shoulder height in a victor's procession (both of which still occur at Ashbourne and elsewhere). Indeed personal esteem must have something to do with the will to stand for ages, sometimes for hours, in freezing cold water. Yet on the other hand, some games devolved into a custom where there is little contest, such as at Corfe in Dorset. There were even games between women, such as at Inveresk and Kirkwall. Even when they were not a noticeable constituent part (the absence of male dignity and deference in the hug being one obvious factor), women seem to have played a major vocal role in support. Many of the slogans shouted at Ashbourne have now past from use and have little meaning today, such as "Ginger Dan 'em" and "Rollick it". They were also noted, at least on occasions in Ashbourne, for the extreme coarseness of language and their fighting.

Once the game began to be played regularly, such as in the schools, it was usually as an internal game only, developing unique characteristics. It was the desire to play the game competitively on a more regular basis which created the demand for a more structured game with uniform rules. In this way the current games of soccer and rugby became established, paving the way for the national games which developed. In *Village Community* by Gomme (1), the arguement is advanced that in the 19th Century, mass football epitomised the development of what is described as "the local struggle". Magoun, writing later, doesn't agree. It seems hard to swallow that the notion of teams pitting themselves against each other developed in the 19th Century. It is certainly true that regulated games became established – one has to think no further than the F.A. and the Football League, but the evidence shows that Shrovetide Football was played between opposing sides several centuries earlier. Importantly, Gomme suggests that there was some sort of permanent rivalry that lasted all the year round. This is far from convincing. Allegiance to one's side is one thing but there is little evidence advanced to suggest that this was elevated to opposition throughout the year.

As Magoun states:

"A number of Shrove Tuesday football games were played between rival local groups: parish against parish, one part of a town against another, bachelors against married men, and married women against the unmarried, school team against school team, and town against country. But do these particular rivalries, when expressed in a football game, whether on Shrove Tuesday or any other day, point to anything more than a natural sense of solidarity? Perhaps all human rivalries and the corresponding loyalties can be pursued to ulterior origins, but need we in any given case follow the hunt without good and sufficient reasons? When all is said and done, the existence of rival groups is a prerequisite to a football game of any sort.... For an apparently irrational custom we may be forced or otherwise inclined to seek a remote explanation, but for a familiar game played on a great holiday the natural human desire for sport and a good time may well suffice." (2)

He has a point.

Camp Ball

Ball playing encompassed several variations, including Camp ball, hug ball, and hurling. They were all variations on a similar theme. With hug ball, you could pick it up and run with it if you chose to. Hurling, still played in Cornwall, is a game of handball.

Camp ball seems to have been similar to what we now know as football and was played in East Anglia, although Strutt (3) states that the goals were 80-100 yards apart and the goals comprised of sticks, about two or three feet apart. E. Porter quoting a different edition of Strutt (4) gives a different description of Camp Ball as given by a Major More in 1823:

"Goals were pitched 150 to 200 yards apart, formed of the thrown-off clothes of the competitors. Each party has two goals, 10 to 15 yards apart. The parties, 10 to 15 a side, stand in a line facing their own goals and each other, at 10 yards distance, midway between the goals and nearest that of their adversaries. An indifferent spectator throws up the ball — the size of a cricket ball — midway between the confronted players, whose object is to seize and convey it between their own goals. The shock of the first onset to catch the ball is very great; if the player who seizes it speeds home pursued by his opponents, through whom he has to make his way, aided by the jostlings of his own side.

If caught and held, he throws the ball . . . to a comrade who, if it be not arrested in its course, or bejostled away by his eager foes, catches it and hurries home, winning the notch or snotch if he continues to carry —not throw— it between the goals. A holder of the ball caught with it in his possession loses a snotch. At the loss of each of these the game recommences, after a breathing time. Seven or nine snotches are the game, and these it will sometimes take two or three hours to win. At times it will sometimes take two or three hours to win. At times a large football was used, and the game was then called 'kicking camp', and if played with shoes on was termed 'savage camp'." (5)

Jennifer Macrory writing as the Archivist of Rugby School, mentions a link between "snotches" and and the Roman name for football, which she states is derived from a Greek word meaning "to snatch". (6)

Porter records that in many Cambridgeshire villages – e.g. Sawston, Abington, Whittlesford, Thetford – the name *Camping Close* recalls the contests of Camp Ball or Camping which used to be held there. She states that it is significant that these Closes were for long the scene of children's games, as, for example, the Whittlesford Shrove Tuesday game of *Pig in the Gutter*. This was a dance using long brambles (minus the thorns) as an arch. In Wilburton there is a Champion's Field, while a Camping Close House in Ely adjoins a football field. (7) For more extensive detail on Camp ball and where it was played, see (8).

Hug Ball

Hug ball seems to have involved play over a much larger distance. Derby's game was known as hug ball and the Ashbourne game was the same although only one record exists of it being referred to locally as this. Hug ball was mass football, where the ball was kicked, thrown, clutched tightly etc. The body of players is still referred to as "the hug". It was played between two teams of varying character. In the case of Ashbourne and Derby, it was played by different local parishes. Cotton, see below, refers to the play between two towns, which confused Magoun. What he (Cotton) relates to are the ancient townships of Ashbourne and Compton & Clifton, situated either side of the River Henmore.

In a culture which views football as a regulated game, controlled since 1863 by the Football Association, together with its sister sport rugby, what was/is Shrovetide Football, hug ball style? It certainly was not regulated, it had few rules and no fixed number of players. Today, it only survives in England in its true sense in Ashbourne. Shrovetide hugball is mass football. It enjoys cult status beyond the imagination of those who have never experienced it. Outsiders can find the game bewildering. For what may seem like an age, the ball can be out of sight, surrounded by the "hug", or group of players.

The object is to score a goal of course, but in some cases such as at Ashbourne, it is an own goal. The two goals at Ashbourne are three miles apart and this long distance was not unique. Even the river is part of the play. Consequently, the ball may not only be stationary, it may also be under water. At other times, the play is fast and furious. It isn't for those unprepared to sustain a few knocks or more punitive measures for trying to direct the play. Surrounded by maybe a thousand spectators, it is only the locals who recognise players beyond the hug and the crowd, patiently waiting for the ball to be released. These are the runners, who can change static play into a mad dash before you have noticed, taking the ball away, hopefully in the direction of one of the goals and leaving you confused as to which direction you should go in an attempt to find play again.

The game at Derby, stopped in 1846 by the Mayor, reinforced with the Riot Act in hand, a large contingent of special constables and two companies of the County Militia, gave Association Football the expression "a local Derby" meaning when two local teams play each other. There can be no other game which, simultaneously, stimulates such allegiance to one's own team and an over-riding self-interest in scoring the goal than Ashbourne's football game. It is a town where neighbours may be friends for 363 days a year, but do not to speak to each other on Shrove Tuesday and Ash Wednesday; where friends would not dream of not thumping each other during play (if the other had the ball), only to be out drinking together that night. The consequences when one member of a family scored at the "wrong goal" are still talked about decades later. Here, you are an "Up'ard" or a "Down'ard" first and last, if you have any honour. In 2001, both sides came together to discuss whether to play or not as a result of Foot and Mouth Disease. It was a structured and ordered meeting; the ultimate future of the game being uppermost in peoples' minds. As Carol Frost wrote in an editorial in the local paper in January 2002: let no one dispute whether the players act in a responsible manner. In deciding not to play for the first time in recorded history, they had clearly shown this. (9) Gomme's 'local struggle' certainly did/does not exist here.

The game has more than some measure of responsibility on the part of its players. It has structure too: the runners stategically placed; the desire to reach the advantage of the river (to the Down'ards); the holding tactics seen today by Down'ards against superior Up'ard opposition. These are all elements of a game that enjoys an element of maturity about it. Understandably, the very nature of the game leaves some spectators doubting the validity of this arguement. A dozen years ago, this author would have felt the same. However, those who express the opinion that this is a game played by hooligans show more of their lack of understanding about it than they are often prepared to admit.

Although the game is rough, injuries are rarely serious but fatalities have occurred. A man died in

1709 from playing Shrove Tuesday football at Ness in Shropshire. Although the account does not mention that the game was on Shrove Tuesday, he died on February 28th and Shrove Tuesday fell on February 18th or thereabouts that year. (10) The Ashbourne game has suffered two fatalities since the game has been reported in the press. The first of these was when James Barker drowned in the mill pond at Clifton in 1878. Another player had brought the ball all the way from the town – a distance of 1 mile – and was in the mill pond, about to score the goal by hitting the water wheel three times, when exhaustion took over and he had to be rescued from drowning. His rescuer received the Bronze Medal of the Royal Humane Society for this act. However, while this was happening, the ball had come loose, and Barker, who worked at the corn mill, jumped into the water and drowned. In a second incident in 1906, a player was found dead in a field near to the Clifton Mill. He seems to have died during the night, probably from the cold and maybe after a bout of drinking, although this cannot be confirmed. It is understood that a John Snape also drowned at Derby after being thrown into the River Derwent in 1796.

It is perhaps fitting that the earliest reference to the game concerns the desire to abolish it. In this case it was the municipal authorities who brought about its demise in Chester (see page 18). Elsewhere, the history of the game is littered with efforts by other similar authorities or the gentry to follow suit. In 1797, the magistrates at Kingston-on-Thames tried unsuccessfully to suppress the game. However, they needed the support of the middle classes and the tradesmen of the community and so long as these followed the game, both playing and bringing some influence on the behaviour of the crowd, the magistrates experienced difficulties in preventing it.

Despite repeated attempts at Ashbourne to ban the game including the arrest of over 100 people on at least one occasion and successful prosecutions in several other years, the game continued without interruption. Here tradesmen and several professional people played the game annually. In fact in 1860, a solicitor and a draper appealed against conviction to the High Court and a glance at the list of defendants reveals that they included two solicitors, two gentlemen, plus a vet, various shop keepers and a builder, to repeat the point made above.

Unfortunately for the game, imposition of the 'common good' prevailed and Alexander states that 'it was this combination of middle-class withdrawal and middle-class fear of the mob which led to the downfall of Shrove Tuesday football in Surrey'. (11) He could have said 'across the country' instead of 'Surrey'. The fact that the game had been played 'since the memory of man runneth not to the contrary' seemed to be enough for the players in their attempts to justify the continuance of the game. Alexander states that there was no attempt to legitimise the game by the involvement of the church (12), despite the fact that it was played on a religious festival day. In fact this is not strictly true (see below) but it seems to miss the point that the game was played with a sense of legitimacy purely because of its great antiquity.

During the nineteenth century there was a revival of interest in old civic customs to some extent and the establishment of new Shrovetide games should be seen in that context. Alexander (pers. comm.) believes that this happened in Surrey as the large conurbation of London pushed the game away from the old centres into the new ones. However, this resurgence in interest in old customs met up against the perception that mass football was little short of a riot. In Derbyshire there were no nineteenth century introductions of the game, despite Glover's remarks that the game in Ashbourne was of recent date. (13)

This has to be seen against a renewed interest in the ancient custom of well-dressing. This had died out with the sole exception of Tissington village, but was reintroduced or introduced as a new custom in many other villages during the century. The arrival of the London and North Western Railway in Buxton in 1863 brought 20-30,000 people a few days later to see the well dressing, established in the town in 1840. One may be cynical, but the financial injection this must have brought to the town just to see the flowers decorating the town well must have contrasted strongly with football down the road in Ashbourne.

From time to time, various sports were banned in favour of archery. This was not because of any particular objection with sport but because it was seen to interfere with the perceived necessity to practice archery. Football was banned in this manner in 1349. (14)

Ball playing at Shrovetide was first recorded by Fitzstephen in the 12th century. (15) He states that after dinner, schoolboys went into the fields and played at the celebrated game of ball, each party of boys carrying their own ball. Over the centuries since, historians have argued whether this was a reference to football or handball – partly from the fact that schoolboys were involved. (16) Those in the latter school of thought seem to have overlooked that in several places where the adults played mass football, there was a boys' game as well, the latter being played at Ashbourne until 1918 at least and at Kirkwall for much longer.

A great deal of research was undertaken in the 1920s on the history of the game in this country by Francis Magoun. (17) Much of the following early detail is from his work although most of his references have been checked at source. Most of the early references to the Shrovetide game are given in full. They constitute an important record in the understanding of its history and how it faired over the centuries.

Chester

The first reference to mass football at Shrovetide was at Chester in 1533 in an attempt to stop the game. However, it does not appear to have been successful and it was finally achieved in 1540 as the reference indicates:

"It is orderyd, assentyd, and agreed by Henry Gee, Mayre of the Citie of Chester, the aldermen, sheriffs, and common counsell of the same citie, and at an assemble houlden within the said citie in the Pentyce, ther the tent daye of January in the xxxi. yeare of the reign of our most dere sovereng Lorde, now being Kynge Henry th' Eyght, [i.e. 1540] wyth ther full assent and consent, and allso of the hole occupaycons of drapers, sadlers, and shoumaykers of and wythin the said citie, that the said occupacions of shoumacres which always tyme out of mann's remembrance have geven and delyvered yerleye upon Teuesday commonly cauld Shroft Teuesday, othewyse Goteddesday, at afternoune of the same unto the drapars afore the mayre of the citie at the Cros upon the Rood Dee one ball of lether, cauled a *fout baule*, of the value of iii *s. iiii* d. or about to pley at from thens to the Common Haule of said citie and further at pleasure of evill disposed persons, wherfore hath ryssen grete inconvenynce.

Ffrom hensforth shall yerlie upon the said Teuesday geve and deliver unto the said drapars afore the Mayre of the said citie for the tyme being at this said playce and tyme syx gleaves of silver to the value of every of them vi d. or above to the order at the discresion of the drapars and the Mayre of the said citie the said citie for the tyme being to whom shall run best and farthest upon foute before them upon the said Rode Hee that day or any other daye after at the drapers' pleasure with the oversight of the Mayre for the tyme being." (18)

The Roodhee became the site of an annual Shrovetide race and is the current site of Chester Races. Magoun believed that the stopping of the football game was partly due to the public nuisance caused. It appears to have also been influenced by contemporary legislation to encourage archery. Clearly in Chester it was the custom for the shoemakers to deliver a ball worth 3/4d (17p) to the drapers and this was replaced from 1540 by a foot-race with a prize of equivalent value. There is an interesting analogy between the Chester shoemakers (cordwainers) and the value of the footballs in Scotland at Glasgow (see below). Marples states that the Mayor also inaugurated a horse race, traditionally the origin of the current Chester Races, for which there was a prize of a silver bell. He also altered an old custom by which all men married within the year had to offer a silk ball as homage to the Company of Drapers, substituting silver arrows instead. Marples continued: "It is to be hoped that the king appreciated this imaginative and intelligent way of dealing with the situation; for it got rid of the public nuisance of street football in Chester, but, as is pointed out by the account of these proceedings quoted by Lysons, it stimulated 'three of the most commendable exercises and practices of war-like feates, namely running on foot, riding and shooting." (19)

Perhaps the suppression of the game at Chester should be seen in the light of not only archery but also changing civic perceptions in the growing town, for the Common Hall was also replaced in 1545. (20) The town's other main pageant, first recorded in 1564, continued until 1599 when the mayor, 'a godly and zealous man', stopped it. It was held on the eve of the festival of St John the Baptist 'according to ancient custom' even in 1564. It consisted of four giants, one unicorn, one dromedary, one luce, one camel, one ass, one dragon, six hobby-horses and sixteen naked boys. It was resurrected in 1661 following the Restoration and all the models such as the dragon were remade as similar as possible to the original designs. Just for the record, six naked boys were used to beat the dragon and arsenic was put into the paste used to make the giants to prevent them being eaten by rats. (21) The mayor replaced the pageant with another presumably less inoccuous one and also had the bull ring taken up, but clearly the town's people didn't share his Puritanical sentiments. This was mirrored at Bristol (see page 22) where there was a protest at the removal of ancient customs at Shrovetide during the Commonwealth.

Carlisle

Cumbria seems to have been a stronghold of mass football and the game is still played at Workington, but at Easter, not Shrovetide. Mr Jeremy Godwin has researched mass football games in the area and two or three copies of his work have been deposited for public viewing. (22)

The records of Shrove Tuesday football in Carlisle are amongst the oldest in the country. They are to be found in the Carlisle Chamberlain's accounts and in the orders of the City's Shoemakers' Guild who made the balls. The first minute book of 1607 contains entries of earlier orders, indicating that the game was being played c.1600 and probably earlier. At this time, journeymen or apprentices were prohibited from making footballs 'to sell or play withall without consent and knowledge of his or their masters and that they shall not play at football within the liberties of this cittie…' The fine was 7d, the cost of the ball. Clearly the shoemakers wanted the business for themselves.

The Chamberlain paid 8d for a football in January 1610 (1611 by the modern calendar) 'for the games upon Shrovetewesdaie' at 'Mr Maior Commande' (ie the Mayor). The game was played upon the sands, rather than through the streets. In 1613(14) is recorded 'For A foote Ball upon the sandes' (6d) and 'To a Boy that wonn the foote Ball 12d'.

Football was not the only game played on Shrove Tuesday, for the accounts record payment 'for a Cocke' and for making a cockpit (presumably in the sands), plus for 'the silver games' and 'for a doore and paisboard pro the gunners that day'.

Shrove Tuesday was abandoned in favour of Easter Tuesday in 1676(77) and by and large retained that day. Whether the Workington Easter game originated at Shrovetide is not recorded. The Carlisle game was still being played at the end of the 19th century, but has since been abandoned.

Corfe, Dorset

The concept of abandoning customs such as Shrovetide football in favour of civic dignity and the 'greater good' had yet to catch on, as will be seen below. However, within fifty years it was gaining pace. One place which was recorded at a very early date and continues to play the game is Corfe Castle in Dorset. Here the Company of Freeman Marblers or Quarriers of Corfe Castle in the Royal Warren of the Isle of Purbeck still carry on the custom as laid down over 450 years ago:

"The Quarriers or workers of stone, otherwise called 'Marblers', form a Company…. On Shrove Tuesday which is the great day of the company, the officers are nominated by the out-going ones … on Candlemas Day … all persons who wish to take out their Freedom of the Company assemble, and with a band … used to parade the streets of Corfe and Swanage … the Neophytes [novices] go by the name of 'free boys' … the qualification of the 'free boy' is, that he must be the son of a 'free man…. The admittance takes place on Shrove Tuesday, when the Roll of Apprentices is made up.' … On the occasion of the marriage of any member, he pays a marriage shilling. This is received in acknowledgement of the right, in case of his death, of his widow to have an apprentice to work for her.

At the same meeting on Shrove Tuesday, a foot-ball is to be provided by the last married man, who thereupon is freed from the payment of the marriage shilling. In the event of no free man having been married during the year the old football is used, but not much so by the quarriers, being generally seized by others than the quarriers. It is, however, carried on Ash Wednesday, together with a pound of pepper, the acknowledgement to the Lord of the Manor in respect of the right of way to Owre, by the Steward of each body down to that place. The cottager at Owre generally provides pancakes for the stewards who have brought the pepper and the foot-ball."

At what time the Company of Marblers was first formed is not apparently known but articles of agreement are extant, drawn from their ancient records, and renewed and confirmed in the year 1551.

These articles run as follows: "Articles which are to be performed, used, and kept by the whole Company of Marblers inhabiting within the towne of Corfe Castle in the Island of Purbeck in the Countie of Dorset for the good and well ordering of the company, ... as they are drawn out of the auntient records and the same renewed and confirmed by them at their accustomed day of meeting on Shrovtewsday yearly. This Shrovtewsday it was done, being the third day of March in the year of our Lord one thousand fifve hundred fifty one as their hands and seales doe witnes....

Seaventhly: that any man in our Company the Shrovtewsday after his marriage shall paie unto the Wardings for the use and benefit of the Company twelve pence and the last married man to bring a football according to the Custome of our Company. . ."

The custom is still maintained in connection with keeping open a right of way between Corfe Castle and Ower Farm on the shore of Poole Harbour – the old route for transporting Purbeck stone before the use of lorries. Today, each free boy must provide 34 pence, a penny loaf and a quart of beer. In accordance with ancient custom, the last one to be married must also provide the football. Note that there was a Wednesday game here.

The traditional meeting is held at noon and after two hours, the free boys emerge to cross the road to the Fox Inn to obtain the beer and the "marblers' rolls". Other marblers appear and attempt to jostle the free boys to make them spill the beer. This latter custom has been extant since at least the end of the Great War. (23) The kicking of the football by about a dozen marblers down West Street, across The Halves (a large field), back up East Street and round to the Town Hall (24) is a large cry from the combative games played elsewhere, although there is a suggestion that in the 19th century, the ball was also played in a field. Nonetheless, Robson states that it is difficult to avoid the conclusion that the custom evolved from an earlier mass football game, of the usual Shrovetide type.

Although of a much later date, a similar custom existed among the colliers of the North of England: "It is customary for a party to watch the bridegroom's coming out of the church after the ceremony, in order to demand Money for a Foot-ball, a claim that admits of no refusal." (25)

Peebles

Whether it was with Yuletide or Shrovetide festivities in mind, (or both), the authorities in Peebles decreed on 20th December, 1570, that "the bailies counsel and the community orders that there be no football played on the High Gate in the future, on pain of each person found playing [being fined] 8s (40p) and the ball being cut". (26)

Glasgow

A further 16th century reference survives from Scotland from the Glasgow burgh records and indicates that the game at least received the support of the authorities there:

In February 23, 1573/4, (the old calendar year did not end in December but in early Spring) we read, " Gevin to Johne Andro for futt ballis ... xii s."; on Fastens-een of the next year, " Item, to Tobn An dro for sax futballis ... xii s." John Andro, cordiner, then furnished footballs annually at 2/- a ball until February 20, 1578/9; later, John Neill assumed this duty: January 31, 1589/90 "In presens of the baillies and counsall, Johnne Neill, cordiner, is maid burges and frieman ... qhwais fienes ar remittit to him for furneissing yeirli during his lyftyme upon Fastreinis Ewin of sex guid and sufficient fut ballis, or ellis tuentie schillingis as the price thairof, conforme to ane supplicatioun gevin in be the said Johnne befoir the saidis baillies and counsall to that effect".

Nearly twenty years afterwards a John Neill, presumably the son of the above, is maintaining the cordiners' connection with the game. The Glasgow Treasurer's account for February 28, 1609, states: "Gifin ... John Neill, cordoner, younger, for fute ballis to the town, at Fasterins Evin, conforme to the ald use . . . 26s. 8d." (27)

Despite this encouraging sign, south of the border the local authorities in various places were still banning football because it was a nuisance and led to disorder: in fact the wording of the prohibition in several cases suggests that it was more of a nuisance than before, and that peaceful and law-abiding citizens objected to it strongly. This proclamation was made in London on November 27th, 1572, and November 7th, 1581 that 'No foteballe play be used or suffered within the City of London and the liberties thereof upon pain of imprisonment' and in 1615 an 'order touching Foot-ball', was issued, to the effect that "whereas greate disorders and tumults doe often arise and happen within the streetes and lanes neere adjoyninge to ye Cittye of London by playing at the foote-ball: It is now ordered that henceforthe all constables doe from tyme to tyme represse and restrayne all manner of Foot-ball-playe in the lanes and streets adjoyninge to the Cittye of London." (28)

Ruislip

A case brought against a group of men on 20th March, 1576 would seem to be following Shrovetide play in the above Middlesex town. The Court record states "that on the said day at Ruyslippe Co Midd., Arthur Reynoldes, husbandman (with five others), all of Ruyslippe aforesaid, Thomas Darcye, of Woxbridge, yeoman (with seven others, four of whom were husbandmen, one a tailor, one a harness-maker, one a yeoman), all seven of Woxbridge aforesaid, with unknown malefactors to the number of a hundred, assembled themselves unlawfully and played an unlawful game called foote-ball, by reason of which unlawfull game there was among them a great affray, likely to result in homicides and serious accident." (29) It is likely that the harness-maker had made the ball. In Ashbourne, the harness-makers always made the best balls and made them well into the 20th Century. Moreover it would appear that the play was between Ruislip and Woxbridge (?Uxbridge). It has all the hallmarks of Shrovetide play!

Shrewsbury

In 1594, the Council at Shrewsbury placed a ban upon football, bear- and bull-baiting within the city walls. (30) However, the ban is known to have been tested. On May 31st, 1601, the justices at Shrewsbury received a petition from John Gyttyns the younger, for his discharge from imprisonment, having been committed "for playing at the foot balle upon Shroftusdaie, and for throwinge the balle from hime whene the serigent Hardinge demaunded the same." (31)

Manchester

Here the authorities beame fed up with the damage, specifically the breakage of windows, that in 1608 they imposed a fine of 12d for anyone playing at football: "That whereas there hath beene heretofore great disorder in our towne of Manchester, and the inhabitants thereof greatelye wronged and charged with makings and the amendinge of their glasse windows broken yearlye and spoyled by a companye of lewd and disordered p'sns usinge that unlawfull exercise of playinge with the fote-ball in ye streets of the said toune, breaking many men's windowes and glasse at theire pleasures and other great inormytes. Therefore, wee of this jurye doe order that no maner of p'sns hereafter shall playe or use the footeball in any street within the said toune of Manchester, subpoend to evye one that shall so use the same for evye time xij d." (32)

Oxford

If play in the towns was starting to be suppressed, it was possible to play it beyond the town boundary where civic jurisdiction did not hold sway. Marples quotes a manuscript note of 26th February, 1608, which describes how Oxford students 'during a match at football burned the fursesses'. He doesn't add whether the reference relates to Shrovetide but the timing looks telling. (33)

Guisborough, Yorkshire

Marples quotes a curious case before the Special Sessions in 1616 which he wonders whether it was as a result of Shrovetide play: A man appeared before the court charged with making a 'banquett for football players on the Sabaoth.' (34) The Puritans were very much against football play on a Sunday and the case is a useful reminder of that, but whether there was any connection with Shrove Tuesday seems somewhat tenuous. Would it take so long to bring a case before a Special Session of the magistrates?

Camp Ball near Ely

Although it is not clear that the reference is to Shrovetide, in June, 1638, an Edward Powell was prosecuted for instigating riots in the Fens which resulted from the playing of mass football (there called Camp Ball). This is a clear example of the game being used as a cover for an illegal act, something which was not that unusual. Over a century later, in 1765, a mass protest against the Enclosure Acts at Northampton was made under the guise of a football game. In this instance in the Fens, the banks raised by the Commissioners of the Bedford Level were destroyed as a consequence. The game was played between Littleport and Ely. It was recorded that Powell, using the alias Anderson, would have the first blow at the ball and would bring with him 100 men from Ely. Informants advised that there was to be a footballe playe or campe in Whelpmore and that "I did see John Bryse with a camping ball and he did campe the same two furlongs into a greate parte of the towne [Ely] and so camped backe againe and so carried it into Whelpmore." (35)

Finsbury Fields, London

Four years later in 1642, a poem called *Satyre against Seperatists* was published which indicates that the London prentices in the mid-seventeenth century played football in Finsbury Fields:
.... "if upon Shrove-tuesday or May-day
Beat an old Baud, or fright poor whores they cou'd
Thought themselves greater than their founder Lud,
Have now vast thoughts, and scorne to set upon
And, whore lesse then her of Babilon.
Thei 'r mounted high, contemne the humble play
Of trap, or fooleball on an holyday
In Finesbury Fields. No 'tis their brave intent
Wisely, t'advise the King, and Parliament...."

Magoun adds that the realism of this passage is supported by several contemporary letters from the Lords of the Council of London to the Lord Mayor instructing the latter to keep police in readiness to suppress the rioting of the local apprentices on Shrove Tuesday and May Day. (36)

Although the banning of the Chester game may have been in part due to civic pride, it may well have also have been due to Puritanical beliefs influencing the civic authorities, as discussed in the Introduction. A document survives which indicates that the Puritan doctrine imposed during the Commonwealth did not always meet with acceptance (see Bristol, below).

Bristol

Many customs were banned during the Commonwealth and in 1660, the people of Bristol expressed their indignation at the imposition. Their success gave them encouragement and it was reported "The authority of the magistrates had been greatly shaken by the youthful mutiny, and by the impotence of their efforts for its suppression; and the lower classes were soon ripe for further disturbance. On March 5th, the day before Shrove Tuesday, the justices made their customary proclamation by the bellman, prohibiting the ancient sports of the season – cock-throwing, dog-tossing, and football-playing in the streets. But the bellman was knocked about by a mob, and had his livery destroyed, and next day the apprentices threw at geese and hens instead of cocks, and tossed bitches and cats instead of dogs, committing some of these pranks before the Mayor's windows, and breaking the head of one of the Sheriffs into the bargain. The turmoil, which is reported by Royalist chroniclers with great glee, had no serious consequences. The Corporation, soon afterwards, were so satisfied with the aspect of affairs that on March 25th the Chamberlain paid £20 to two troops of horse that were in town, to send them going." (37)

Reference was made in the Introduction to the acquiescence of Shrovetide exuberance on the basis that the status quo was restored the following day. The above would seem to support that view, however, it should also be noted that the event also fell in the interregnum between the resignation of Richard Cromwell and the Restoration.

Ashbourne, Derbyshire

In 1683, Charles Cotton, the friend and companion of Izaak Walton wrote a poem called 'A Burlesque on the Great Frost". Apparently the weather was so bad that the players were eventually forced to give up the game until the thaw set in. Unfortunately, Cotton is not too clear about where the game was being played. He owned Fenny Bentley Old Hall, four miles north of Ashbourne and clearly there is a presumption that his poem relates to that town. Cotton states that there were at least a dozen players who were frozen:

"like Rolle-rich stones, if you've seen 'em,
And could no more run, kick or trype,
Than I can quaff of Aganippe;
Til ale, which crowns all such pretences,
Mull'd them again into their senses." (38)

Clearly the players were tough as well as rough. Cotton's poem also alludes to the Civil War which also lends credence that his reference is to Ashbourne. The town had initially been a Royalist stronghold, but the troops were routed by Commonwealth forces. Later the King came north from Tutbury but the Parliamentarians were not far behind and over a hundred Royalists were killed or taken prisoner by them after a skirmish at Tissington, just north of the town. Cotton wrote:

'Two towns that long that war had raged, Being at football now engaged'. The fact that the players were frozen would suggest Shrovetide, but it doesn't actually say so, and it could have equally referred to play at Christmas or New Year.

In 'The Arkwrights, Spinners of Fortune', it is recorded that the sons of Sir Richard Arkwright, the cotton spinner of Cromford, Derbyshire, attended Queen Elizabeth's Grammar School (QEGS) in Ashbourne. His son John wrote to his father in 1797. It is the familiar story of a child requesting more money! He then goes on to say that:

"Mr William Walker was so good as to give us a football on Shrove Tuesday and as we were playing the town boys came to take it from us they said that they would only we were too many for them so we said we would let no more of our boys hinder them from taking it than they had on their side nor no bigger so we put the football before their feet and no one dare touch it." (39)

This is the only evidence of the game being played in the 18th Century. Was the QEGS game the origin of the boys' game? Is this how the Wednesday game was started? Ashbourne is the only town to play an adult game on both days. Some towns had a boys' game on the Wednesday. Did someone prevail on the school boys to have a Wednesday game against the town boys? Was it possible that the town had two games on the same day in its streets? John Arkwright's letter raises more questions than it answers! See also a reference to the Grammar School game on page 53.

Jedburgh, Scotland

If the 17th Century Derbyshire winters couldn't stop the game, the Town Council at Jedburgh in Scotland were prepared to try to do so in 1704: "considering that the continuance of the annual game of football at Fastern's E'en tended to the great prejudice of the old inhabitants" and that "sometimes both old and young near lost their lives thereby 'unanimously' discharge the game now and all time coming, as also the ringing, of the watch-bell at that time...". The trades also lent their aid to suppress the game, for on 6th February, 1706, all the 'breithrene' of the Fleshers' Corporation found 'guiltie at the rastling at the football' are fined. As late as 1849 a fruitless effort was made to suppress the game. Ultimately at an unknown date handball was substituted as less dangerous. Jedburgh handball was played much in the style of football, with water-play, and so forth.' (40)

The old Town Council would no doubt be bemused to know that the game is still going strong in their town.

Duns, Scotland

In 1724 by John Gray, bailie of the burgh of Duns in Berwickshire brought a complaint against William Home, shoemaker, and others:

"Mr John Gray having laid down proper expedients to prevent riots and tumults within the burgh of barronie of Dunse, and particularly on the anniversary of Fasting's Even, when all the idle people in that brugh were usually, conveened by touck of drum to play at the football. which did always end and determine in the effusion of blood among the inhabitants, and did in following out that just purpose order the drummer to bring the drum of that town to his house on the 18th of February last, being Fasting's Even, and yet notwithstanding of the said precaution, the persons above complained upon and manie others did gather themselves together upon pretence of placing at the football on the said day above mentioned, and came up to the said Mr John Gray, complainer, his house and insolently demanded of him that he should deliver up the drum to them, threatning and swearing revenge and mischief against him in case of his non-compliance: and the said Mr John Gray having in the maintenance of his authoritie not only refused to deliver up the drum, but likeways commanded the said persons to retire to their respective homes in a peaceable manner, then still persisted in their outrage, and went away together in a body to a place called the Cloack miln, where they played at the football.

And when the game was over they did return to the Tolbooth stair, and that the winners were then to shew the ball and proclaim the victory, certain particular persons, loosers in the game, opposed them therein and would not suffer the winners to gett up to the Tolbooth stair to shew the ball unless they brought the drum alongst with them. Whereupon they fell a fighting and beating and blooding of one another, but att length went into one common concert to goe in a body and seize by force the drum in the said Mr John Gray." (41)

Rioting ensued, both that day and the next, and a jury-trial was finally demanded. The Duns game continued to be played until 1835 and was between the married and unmarried men.

Derby

At Derby there were several unsuccessful attempts to suppress the Shrovetide match in the eighteenth century. In 1731, the Mayor (Isaac Borrow) had tried to achieve this, but was unsuccessful. In 1746, the Mayor was equally unsuccessful. He had a notice placed in the Derby Mercury which stated:

"It having been represented to the magistrates of this Borough that on Shrove Tuesday which will be Tuesday the third of March next there will be a public foot-ball playing in the said Borough and such hatrh been lately Notyfied and proclaimed in Towns and counties adjacent to the borough aforesaid by some person or persons disposed to be at the Head of Tumults and Disorders – These are to give notice that Mr Mayor and others of His Majesty's Justices of the Peace for the said Borough do direct and order that there be no Riotous and Tumultuous meeting of any persons (and more particularly of Foreigners at this unhappy time of Contagion amond horned cattle) ... do appear at the time and for the purpose aforesaid in the said Borough on Pain of being Rigourously Prosecuted by the same as well as forthe consequences of breaking Windows, and doing other mischief to the Person and Properties of the Inhabitants of this Borough.

Humphery Booth, Mayor, Feb. 26, 1746." (42)

One of the earliest accounts of play in the town was published in 1791: "There is also one amusement of the amphibious kind, which, if not peculiar to Derby, is pursued with an avidity I have not observed elsewhere, football. I have seen this coarse sport carried to the barbarous height of an election-contest; nay, I have known a foot-ball hero chaired through the streets like a successful member, although his utmost elevation of character was no more than that of a butcher's apprentice. Black eyes, bruised arms, and broken shins, are equally the marks of victory and defeat. I need not say that this is the delight of the lower ranks, and is attained at an early period; the very infant learns to kick, and then to walk. The professors of this athletic art think themselves bound to follow the ball wherever it flies; as Derby is fenced in with rivers, it seldom flies far without flying into the water; and I have seen these amphibious practitioners of football-kicking jump into the river upon a Shrove-Tuesday when the ground was covered with snow. Whether the benefits arising from exercise pay for the bloody nose is doubtful; whether this rough pastime improves the mind, I leave to the decision of its votaries; and whether the wounds in youth produce the pains in age, I leave to threescore." (43)

In 1796, a player was drowned in the River Derwent, but an appeal by the Borough for the game to be abandoned fell on deaf ears.

Hawick, Scotland

Magoun recorded that "in the border town of Hawick (Roxburghshire) a species of handball was at least until very recently, if not still current [i.e. about 1930], the Fastens-een game, but that this has not always been the case, and that football between the residents of the east and west parts of the town was still played c. 1760 appears from the following account, published in 1825:

'About fifty six years ago, a foot-ball was played annually on Fastern's-eve within the town, the inhabitants who lived on the West Side of the water of Slitrig being matched against those who resided on the East Side of it. This amusement had a bad tendency, in keeping up, and promoting, a species of war or fighting that had been carried on, time out of mind between the people (principally boys) of the East and West divisions of the town. This feud, in which the boys below sixteen years of age were the chief combatants, was fostered by their seniors: and even parents and masters have been known to encourage their apprentices and children in the scene of contention.' (44)

Watson prints a traditional rhyme in which one side taunts the other:
"Wassla waiter wuns the day;
Eassla waiter canna play,
For eatin' sodden dumplin's." (45)

Bromfield, Cumbria

A similar situation existed south of the Border in Bromfield in Cumia. Here the game was also fought by school boys. It had become obsolete by 1794, but the reason for its demise isn't known:

"Till within the last twenty or thirty years, it had been a custom, time out of mind, for the scholars of the free-school of Bromfield, about the beginning of Lent ... at Fasting's Even, to bar out the Master; i.e. to depose and exclude him from his school and keep him out for three days. During the period of this expulsion the doors of the school were strongly barricaded within and the boys were armed with elder pop-guns." The master endeavoured to recover his authority, which often was not successful. After three days, negotiations opened and the event concluded with a festivity, with cakes and ale provided by the scholars. "One of the articles always stipulated for, and granted, was the privilege of immediately celebrating certain games of long standing; viz. a foot-ball match, and a cock-fight. Captains, as they were called, were then chosen to manage and preside over these games; one from the part of the parish which lay to the westward of the school, and the other from the east. Cocks, and foot-ball players, were sought for with great diligence." The prize for the victor at the cock fight was a small silver bell, suspended to the button of the victor's hat and worn for three successive Sundays.

"After the cock-fight was ended, the foot-ball was thrown down in the church-yard; and the point then to be contested, was, which party could carry it to the house of his respective captain; – to Dundraw, perhaps, or to West-Newton, a distance of two or three miles; every inch of which ground was keenly disputed. All the honour accruing to the conqueror at foot-ball, was that of possessing the ball. Details of these matches were the general topics of conversation among the villagers; and were dwelt on, with hardly less satisfaction than their ancestors enjoyed in relating their feats in the border wars." (46)

Kirkmichael, Scotland

A further game between schoolboys was played at Kirkmichael in Perthshire prior to 1795. It is said to have been "a common amusement with the schoolboys who also preserve the custom of cock fighting on Shrove Tuesday." (47)

Scone, Perthshire

The inhabitants of Scone in Perthshire were not so lucky for a report of 1796 stated that the game had been abolished a few years previously.

Fortunately, quite a good description of the game survives:

"Every year on Shrove-Tuesday, the bachelors and married men drew themselves up at the cross of Scone on opposite sides. The ball was then thrown up, and they played from 2 o'clock till sunset. The game was this. He who, at any time got the ball into his hands, run with it till overtaken by one of the opposite party, and then, if be could shake himself loose from those on the opposite side, who seized him, he run on: if not, he threw the ball from him, unless it was wrested from him by the other part; but no person was allowed to kick it.

The object of the married men was to hang it, i.e. to put it three times into a small hole in the moor, the door or limit on the one hand; that of the bachelors was to drown it, i.e. to dip it three times into a deep place in the river, the limit of the other. The part who could effect either of these objects, won the game. But, if neither party won, the ball was cut into two equal parts at sunset. In the course of the play one might always see some scene of violence between the parties: but, as the proverb of this part of the country, expresses it, all was fair at the ball of Scone.

The custom is supposed to have had its origin in the days of chivalry. An Italian, it is said came into this part of the country, challenging all the parishes, under a certain penalty in case of declining his challenge. All the parishes declined the challenge excepting Scone, which beat the foreigner; and in commemoration of this gallant action the game was instituted. Whilst the custom continued, every man in the parish, the gentry not excepted, was obliged to turn out and support the side to which he belonged; and the person who neglected to do his part on that occasion was fined." (48)

This account is interesting for it shows quite a few similarities with the Ashbourne game, although it will be noted that at Scone, you were not allowed to kick the ball. Similarities include running with the ball, play starting at 2pm, goaling by repeating the goaling process three times and one side only involving river play (at Ashbourne the Up'ards did not use the river to goal a ball prior to 1877).

Alnwick, Northumberland

A similar game between married and unmarried men was played at Alnwick in Northumberland. This game continues today, but is now played between the parishes of St Michael's and St Paul's. It was described by John Brand who watched the Shrove Tuesday game on February 5, 1788, when:

" the waits belonging to the town, come playing to the castle every year ... at two o'clock p.m. when a foot-ball was thrown over the castle-walls to the populace." (49)

It was originally played in the streets but in 1818 an act was obtained prohibiting this. However, this was apparently not implemented until 1828, when arrangements were made by the Duke of Northumberland for the game to be played on the Demesne north of the Aln, where it is still played.

The goaling is called a hale and the play ends after the third hale is scored. The football is received at the castle barbican at 2pm and play starts at 2.15pm. After being received by the game's committee, it is taken to the North Demesne preceded by the Duke's piper. There it is given to the victor of the former year who have the honour of kicking it up the centre of the goals. The ball, in contrast to Scone, can only be kicked; it cannot be carried or thrown. After the third hale, the ball is thrown up and kept by whoever can carry it away. The goals are 400 yards apart and when the ball has been haled, it is announced by trumpet.

Inveresk, Midlothian

More unusual was a match between married and unmarried women! It was played by the fishwives of Inveresk in Midlothian, Scotland. The report dates from 1795: "From the kind of life these women lead, it may naturally be concluded, that their manners are peculiar, as they certainly are.... As they do the work of men, their manners are masculine ... On holidays they frequently play at golf; and on Shrove Tuesday there is a standing match at foot-ball between the married and unmarried women in which the former are always victors." (50)

Devon

Prior to 1785, football had also been banned in Devon. However, it is unclear if the reference relates to Shrovetide: "Not only on the principal Holidays, but sometimes (tho' seldom) Two Parishes have engaged with each other, on a Day fix'd on by mutual Appointment, at a Football-Match; in which Game (if I mistake not) there is usually somewhat like the Cornish Hurling introduced, whenever any of the Players can catch up the Ball, and hurl it towards the Gole aim'd at by those of his own Party. But the poorer Sort cannot now afford to keep such Holidays, and the Gentry of the present Age have substituted other Species of Gaming." (51)

Kingston, Surrey

At Kingston-upon-Thames the several efforts during the 1790s to put down the sport were successfully resisted. On 24 February 1799 three Kingston magistrates wrote to the Home Secretary concerning their difficulties in dealing with the annual custom:

"It having been a practice for the populace to kick foot ball in the Market Place and Streets of this Town on Shrove Tuesday to the great nuisance of the Inhabitants and of persons travelling through the Town and complaints having been made by several Gentlemen of the County to the Magistrates of the Town they previous to Shrove Tuesday 1797 gave public Notice by the distribution of hand bills of their determination to suppress the Practice...

... which not having the desired effect several of the offenders were Indicted and at the last Assizes convicted but sentence was respited and has not yet been declared the judge thinking that after having warn'd them of their situation that they would not attempt to kick again but we the present Magistrates of the Town having been previously informed it was their intention with others to kick again as on last Shrove Tuesday some days before issued hand bills giving Notice of our intention to prosecute any persons who should on that day kick foot ball in the said Town and apprehending that we should find great opposition two days previous thereto addressed a Letter to the officer commanding the Cavalry at Hampton Court informing him of the Circumstance and stating that if we found it necessary we should call on him for the assistance of the Military.

On the Shrove Tuesday a great number of persons having assembled and begun to kick a ball in the market place we caused three that seemed the most active to be taken into Custody hoping that would induce the others to disperse but not having that effect we then caused the Riot Act to be read and the Mob not then dispersing but increasing in Number and threatening to Use violence in liberating those in Custody we addressed another Letter to the Officer on Command at Hampton Court requiring him to send part of the Cavalry to our assistance but not receiving an answer in a reasonable time one of Us went to Hampton Court in search for the Officer when it was said that Major Hawker was the Officer on Duty there but was gone from home and not to be seen nor could any other be found who could Act and the Men at the same time kicking foot ball on Hampton Court Green.

Nor being able to obtain the assistance required the persons in Custody were rescued by the mob as the Constables were conveying them to Prison and the Keeper was violently assaulted and much hurt. If the Military had attended we should have succeeded in abolishing the nuisance without much difficulty but not having met with such support the Game will be carried on to a greater height than it ever has been the mob conceiving they have got the better of Us and that the Military would not attend." (52)

Although a set back that in this case was to last for several decades, an observer of the game at the end of the 18th Century must have been perturbed about the prospects of the survival of the game as a national institution. He/she could not have foreseen that it would be replaced by the league football we have today.

References

1. Gomme, GL., *The Village Community*, 1890, pp241/2
2. Magoun, F.P., *Shrove Tuesday Football*, 1931, p44
3. Strutt, *Sports and Pastimes*, 1834 edition, p100, ed. Wm. Hone)
4. (see *Notes and Queries*, Series VIII, ii p214)
5. Porter E., *Cambridgeshire Customs and Folklore*, 1969)
6. Macrory J., *Running With The Ball: The Birth of Rugby Football*, 1991) p5
7. E Porter, op cit., p230
8. Malcomson, RW., *Popular Recreations in English Society, 1700-1850*, 1973, p113 et al)
9. Ashbourne New Telegraph
10. Bygones NS Vol V1, 1900, p514
11. Alexander, M., *Shrove Tuesday Football in Surrey*, p204
12. ibid, p197
13. Glover, S., *The History etc of the County of Derby*, 1829, p311
14. Strutt, op. cit., p100
15. *Descritio Nobilissimae Civitatis*, 1175, quoted in Stow, *Survey of London*, 1596).
16. Strutt, op. cit., p100
17. Magoun, op. cit., pp11-39
18. ibid, p13
19. Marples, M., *A History of Football*, 1954, p46
20. Magoun, op. cit., p13
21. *Sports and Pastimes*, op cit., pp xliii/xlv
22. Godwin J. *Mass Football in Cumberland and Elsewhere*, 1986 typescript available at Cumbria Record Office, Carlisle and at Ashbourne Library
23. Robson, *Calendar Customs in 19th and 20th Century Dorset*, 1988, thesis, Univ. Of Sheffield, Dept., of English Language, p37
24. ibid, p38

25 Brand, ed. W.C. Hazlitt, *Observations on Popular Antiquities,* 1870, Vol II, p101
26 Marples, op. cit., p46
27 Magoun, op. cit., pp15/16
28 Marples, op. cit., p44
29 ibid, pp47/48
30 Owen and Blakeway, *History of Shrewsbury*, 1825, Vol1, p391
31 HMC 15th Report, App X
32 Marples, op. cit., p45
33 ibid, p45
34 ibid, p55
35 Porter, E., *Cambridgeshire Customs and Folklore,* 1969
36 Magoun, op cit, p17
37 Latimer, *Annals of Bristol*, Vol1, 1900, p292
38 Beresford, J., ed., *Poems of Charles Cotton,* 1630-1687,
39 I am grateful to George and Trilby Shaw for this reference
40 Magoun, op. cit., pp17/18
41 HMC Report of Manuscripts in Various Collections, 1909, No. V, pp43/4
42 Marples, op. cit., pp98-99. Marples also suggests that the cattle desease was foot and mouth, but this is unlikely. It is more likely to be Cattle Plague, or Rinderpest. See Moore-Colyer, R., *Welsh Cattle Drovers,* p90
43 Hutton, *The History of Derby etc*, 1791, pp218/19
44 Magoun, op. cit., p19
45 Watson, "Annual Border Ball-Games," *Hawick Archology. Soc., Trans* Session 1922, p7
46 Hutchinson, W., *The History of the County of Cumberland*, 1794, Vol II, pp322-23
47 Statistical Account of Scotland, 1795, Vol XV, p521
48 Statistical Account of Scotland, 1796, Vol XVIII, pp88/89
49 Ellis, *Observations on Popular Antiquities,* 1841 Vol1, 52, no. 28
50 Statistical Account of Scotland, 1795, Vol XVI, pp18/19
51 Chapple, *Review of Part of Risdon's Survey of Devon,* 1785, p38
52 Malcolmson, op. cit., pp139/40

Shrovetide Football in the Nineteenth Century

During the 19th Century, the desire to be rid of what was seen as a troublesome custom grew, despite the popular belief that antiquity was sufficient reason to continue and that the public streets were the legitimate place for it. Whatever merit there might have been for this arguement, it became increasingly untenable in the face of additional powers to the local authorities to not only ban the game but also to enforce it. Malcolmson (1), illustrates this particular point with the following example of an incident of 1818 in **Hull**: elaborating on a report concerning a man who had recently been fined 40s. for playing football in the streets, a local newspaper pointed out that:

"the police of Sculcoates have strict orders to prevent any person from playing at any games in the streets troublesome to the inhabitants of the said parish, which have of late been so prevalent, to the great annoyance and personal danger of the public."

In 1829 and 1836 the vestry of **Barnes**, Surrey, complained of the nuisance of street football and recommended its suppression to the officers of the peace and this must have become an increasing common occurrence, whether at Shrovetide or not.

A letter of February 1815 tells of the games being played in nearby towns:

"Upon entering **Teddington**, I was not a little amused to see all the inhabitants securing the glass of all their front windows ... some by placing hurdles before them, and some by nailing laths across the frames.

At **Twickenham, Bushy**, and **Hampton-Wick** they were all engaged in the same way: having to stop a few hours at Hampton-Wick and Kingston, I had an opportunity of seeing the whole of the custom, which is, to carry a football from door to door and beg money: at about 12 o'clock the ball is turned loose, and those who can, kick it. In the town of Kingston, all the shops are purposely kept shut upon that day; there were several balls in the town, and of course several parties." (2)

And a history (1885) of **Hampton-on-Thames** likewise informs the reader:

"Until some twelve years ago (i.e. c. 1873) the advent of Shrove Tuesday used to be eagerly anticipated by the rougher portion of Hampton's residents, as, on that day, the ceremony of kicking the football round the parish, and flooding the Lion Square, took place. There does not seem to have been much sense in this custom, which was apparently imitated from Kingston, and not of very ancient date." (3)

Derby

Despite the desire of the Borough Council to suppress the game, play continued. This account of the game dates from 1829, only 17 years before it was banned:

"Football continues to be played at in many parts of England on Shrove Tuesday and Ash Wednesday, but the mode of playing this game at Ashbourn and Derby differs very much from the usual practice of this sport. In the town of Derby the contest lies between the parishes of St Peter and All Saints, and the goals to which the ball is to be taken are Nun's mill for the latter, and Gallow's bank on the Normanton road for the former. None of the other parishes of the borough take any direct part in the contest, but the inhabitants of all join in the sport, together with persons from all parts of the adjacent country. The players are young men from eighteen to thirty or upwards, married as well as single, and many veterans who retain a relish for the sport are occasionally seen in the very heat of the conflict.

The game commences in the market-place, where the partisans of each parish are drawn up on each side; and, about noon, a large ball is tossed up in the midst of them. This is seized upon by some of the strongest and most active men of each party. The rest of the players immediately close in upon them, and a solid mass is formed. It then becomes the object of each party to impel the course of the crowd towards their particular goal. The struggle to obtain the ball, which is carried in the arms of those who have possessed themselves of it, is then violent, and the motion of the human tide heaving to and fro, without the least regard to consequences is tremendous.

Broken shins, broken heads, torn coats and lost hats are among the minor accidents of this fearful contest, and it frequently happens that persons fall in consequence of the intensity of the pressure, fainting and bleeding beneath the feet of the surrounding mob. But it would be difficult to give an adequate idea of this ruthless sport: a Frenchman passing through Derby remarked, that if Englishmen called this playing, it would be impossible to say what they call fighting. Still the crowd is encouraged by respectable persons attached to each party, and who take a surprising interest in the result of the day's sport; urging on the players with shouts, and even handing to those who are exhausted, oranges and other refreshment.

The object of the St Peters' party is to get the ball into the water, down the Morledge brook into the Derwent as soon as they can, while the All Saints party endeavour to prevent this, and to urge the ball westward. The St Peter players are considered to be equal to the best water-spaniels, and it is certainly curious to see two or three hundred men up to their chins in the Derwent continually ducking each other. The numbers engaged on both sides exceed a thousand, and the streets are crowded with lookers on. The shops are closed, and the town presents the aspect of a place suddenly taken by storm." (4)

An Ashbourne supporter would recognise all the aspects of play described here 170 years ago. Only the geography is different. A description of the ball used in those days at Derby survives too. 'The ball is made of very strong leather, about a foot in diameter, and stuffed hard with cork shavings'. (5) Today an Ashbourne ball is the same except for the size being $10^1/_2$ inches in diameter.

The Penny Magazine also stated that:

"when the game lasts late, stratagems are resorted to goal the ball, eg. the cork shavings are removed and the cover is smuggled in under a countryman's smock or in a woman's gown. The following day, Ash Wednesday, is called the 'Boys' day', when a juvenile performance of the same kind takes place... Attempts have been made to put down the game as tending to foment quarrels and to endanger life; the fact is, however, that life is hardly ever lost..."

A reporter in the *Derby and Chesterfield Reporter*, of 23 February, 1832 said:

"It is not so much with a wish to deprive the lovers of this sport of their enjoyment, that I advocate its abolition but more particularly to condemn the fitness of the place of its competition for such a purpose; instead of emanating from the centre of the town, let them assemble in the Siddals, or some such place, so as not to interfere with the avocation of the industrious part of the community; it is not a trifling consideration that a suspension of business for nearly two days should be created to the inhabitants for the mere gratification of a sport at once so useless and barbarous."

Two short poems commemorate the game. The first refers to the different parishes:

"Pancakes and fritters,'
Say All Saints' and St Peter's;
When will the ball come?'
Say the bells of St Alkmun;
'At two they will throw,'
Says Saint Werabo';
'O! very well!'
Says little Michael" (6)

The second poem clearly refers to the Ash Wednesday Boys' game:

"The Derby Ram
The little boys of Darby, Sir,
They came to beg his eyes,
To kick about the streets, Sir,
For they were football size.
Daddle-i-day, daddle-i-day,
Fal-de-ral, fal-de-r al, daddle-i-day."

In 1845 the Mayor stated that:
"In former times, when the town contained but few inhabitants, the game was not attended with its present evils, but it was now a well ascertained fact that many of the inhabitants suffered considerable injury, in person as well as property, from this annual exhibition; and he himself knew of instances where persons having an interest in houses, especially the larger ones, had experienced losses from want of occupiers, at adequate rents; parties who would otherwise have expended many thousands a year on the trade of the town, having left it, or declined to reside in it, because they did not like to bring up their families here, under the idea that Derby was one of the lowest and wickedest places in the kingdoms."(7)

The prosecution of players in 1846 gives a succinct description of the attitude of the magistrates which must have been followed by those in Ashbourne in 1860 and thereafter:
"in a town consisting of 40,000 inhabitants, one-third of whom were labouring population, persons must not assemble for such low and improper amusements at the present day in the public streets, whatever they might have done when football was originally practised, Derby being at that time a very small place; but at the present time the town had become very large. Persons from a distance occasionally residing in it, whose characters were unknown, availed themselves of this opportunity of injuring persons by destroying property, alarming the timid and well-disposed inhabitants, and putting a stop to all business for the greater part of two days." (8)

Malcolmson goes on to describe how the game in Derby came to an end, drawing on the local papers of the time:
"Shrovetide football in Derby was only put down after considerable controversy. During the early decades of the nineteenth century its practice had been periodically deplored, but no direct action was taken until 1845. In January a petition to end the match was presented to the Mayor; and at the same time a subscription was taken up to promote alternative sports on the customary holiday on the condition that football in the streets was abandoned, a bargain which was alleged to have the support of 'a large number of those who have heretofore been the leading players on both sides'."

There was a general concern among men of property to avoid giving the impression that they were callously crushing a favourite amusement without offering some sort of compensation. Surprisingly energetic efforts were made to win the support of the working people for the new arrangements: the Mayor met with many of the footballers and (it was said) found that his proposals were well received; notices were posted to publicise the new sports and the prizes they carried; and on Tuesday 'bands of music were engaged to perambulate the streets, preceded by banners' with 'suitable mottoes', and several thousand people collected to test the innovations.

However, when it was learned a little later that a football was being kicked through the streets by a few dissidents (apparently only a fraction of the usual numbers), the new amusements were called off and the large crowd was left in the lurch, unoccupied and discontented. Later that month the Town Council voted to re-establish the Derby races, and thereafter it was common to regard the races as a recreational substitute for the Shrovetide sports and a further justification for eliminating the older holiday.

The next year, at a Town Council meeting of February 4th, the football question was again introduced. The mayor and others agreed that there ought to be no pudding exhibitions, no swarming greased poles, nor grinning through collars, as were proposed last year. (These remarks elicited much laughter.) For his own part he delighted to see the working classes enjoy a rational amusement; and he thought if they were denied one amusement, they ought to have some others provided. The Races having been established, he thought that the irrational and disgraceful pastime ought now to be put down; and he should be happy to use what influence he possessed, in conjunction with his fellow magistrates, to effect its abolition.

An order prohibiting football was issued, several hundred 'respectable inhabitants' were sworn in as special constables, and (with the approval of the Home Secretary) two troops of dragoons were summoned from Nottingham. Some of the footballers acquiesced and on the evening before Shrove Tuesday formally surrendered the ball to the Mayor and promised to try to persuade their fellows to obey the ban.

Others were less obliging. A report at the time gave the details: "Precautions were taken to block off the market place, and one ball which appeared on Tuesday was quickly captured by the police and cut up, but in mid-afternoon another ball was thrown up and taken down the river as rapidly as possible, and a detachment of police and specials ... proceeded to the Railway Bridge to intercept it, but were overpowered.

The Mayor and other Magistrates came up. Some ruffian threw a brick bat and bludgeon – one or both of which hit the Mayor upon the shoulder. The ruffian was seized ... and [soon] rescued by considerable violence being offered to his capturer; other unmistakeable manifestations of the temper of the mob were given, and the civil power being found insufficient, the Riot Act was read and the military called out; but before they could reach the Railway Bridge the players had made all speed with the ball down the river out of the bounds of the borough'.

Under the direction of a County magistrate, the dragoons, specials, and regular police were soon in hot pursuit, and a later confrontation occurred around Normanton where the players and police skirmished for the ball. This, however, was the last time of resistance: during the next three years precautions were taken before each Shrove Tuesday and dragoons were posted nearby, but there was no further attempt to perpetuate a tradition which the magistrates had determined to suppress." (9)

Today, the memory of the ancient game lives on through out the world where Association Football is played. Mostly without knowing the reason, supporters refer to a local match as a 'Derby Game.'

Ashford-in-the-Water, Derbyshire

Thomas Brushfield recorded that on Shrove Tuesday, the Pancake bell was rung at 11am. The children, no doubt waiting for the first ring of the bell, took the rest of the day off and 'a game of football was generally played during the after part of the day.' (10) Given that Derby and Ashbourne embraced the game so enthusiastically, it is perhaps surprising that this is the only known other record of play in the county.

Beverley

Magoun states that at Beverley, the game was abolished in 1825. On that occasion, when the constables tried to stop the game, they were roughly handled, and the match continued; but the aggressors were arrested later, tried and condemned to hard labour, which effectively put an end to the game. (11) Regrettably, attempts to substantiate this through the library at Beverley met with no success.

Stonyhurst College, near Blackburn

At Stonyhurst College, Lancashire, the Shrovetide Grand (Football). Matches survived until nearly the end of the century. They were one of the red-letter events of the year. These matches were played on the Thursday preceding Quinquagesima Sunday, and on the Monday and Tuesday following. Technically, the game was known as 'Stonyhurst football', "a species of football that allowed some sixty or seventy to play in one match. The opposing sides were known as 'English' and 'French'; during the match great enthusiasm always prevailed – flags were flying and cannons firing. At the 'Lemonade' on Shrove Monday or Tuesday, extra pancakes were provided for such of the players as had especially distinguished themselves." (12) Eventually the game was replaced by Association Football.

Surrey

This section is drawn from the splendid article written by Mathew Alexander: (13)

"In Surrey, Shrove Tuesday football was widespread in the north of the county, centred on **Kingston-upon-Thames** where the game attracted visitors from the London suburbs. Throughout Surrey the game usually began with a procession on the morning of Shrove Tuesday collecting money, ostensibly to defray any damage done to buildings during the game but in practice for refreshments for the players. Shops in the main streets were then shuttered and barricaded and a ball thrown in or kicked off at a central point. Usually half the town played the other half, the player's allegiance being determined by which side of the central point he lived. Two or three balls might be thrown in during the afternoon: it became the practice for the first to be the boys' ball, and the last to be the most important. The ball had to be carried either to a set goal on either side or simply retained in the team's own half of the town at the hour fixed to finish the game. Afterwards the players would disperse to celebrate in the local pubs. It seems to have been the general custom for the boys game to preceed the main game and this occured at Ashbourne and at Kirkwall where the game was the same as Shrovetide football but played on New Years Day.

It has been suggested that such rough and disorderly customs were opportunities for the mob to protest against the authorities, but there is little evidence for this in Surrey save the burning of the effigy of a tradesman at **Thames Ditton** in 1862, and the snowballing of respectably dressed passersby in Dorking in 1873. (Incidentally, the excuse offered for the effigy burning that it formed part of the Shrove Tuesday football was accepted by the magistrates)." One of the objections to the Derby game was that soot was being thrown at passersby. The throwing of snowballs at Ashbourne is par for the course these days and is likely to have occcured in times gone by, but the throwing of soot is not recorded.

Alexander goes on to say that there was more evidence of deference rather than defiance shown towards the social superiors of the players: "Gentlemen were offered free kicks of the ball in Kingston and loyal toasts and patriotic sentiments were common at the feasts afterwards. He states that while the open opposition of two halves of the town may seem to be divisive rather than encouraging communal solidarity, the rivalry seems in most cases to have been purely temporary. The violent disagreements inevitable in such a game were either restrained by nearby players or - as at Kingston - settled by an organised boxing fight afterwards.' Both sides ate and drank together afterwards, and there seems usually to have been one pub as a headquarters rather than two. The game was mainly played by youths but their elders treated the game as a time of reunion and reminiscing. The presence of respectable tradesmen is emphasised in early reports but later their absence is increasingly mentioned: in this lay the decline and fall of Shrove Tuesday football in Surrey."

The comparison with Ashbourne is close. There, both sides use the Green Man Hotel (more strictly, the Green Man and Black's Head Royal Hotel) as the headquarters of the game. It is to this inn that the goal scorer brings his ball after scoring and the rivalries of the two days are quickly forgotten for another year. Disputes or old scores were settled on the day as various magistrates hearings shortly afterwards have testified over the years.

"In Surrey, the sources are mostly newspaper reports, or undatable memories. They are rarely written by a player, and clearly many details of the game are imperfectly understood. For example, the most important aspect of a modern football report is the result, but this was only ever noted in Dorking. Significant variations in the kick-off times, the names of the two sides, and the methods of winning the game may simply be uninformed reporting – or may be evidence of quite radical changes in the 'tradition' as time went by, as is known to be the case at Kirkwall. Alexander states that the reports cannot be considered entirely reliable, and they often manifest conflicting attitudes between antiquarian sentimentality and disgust at lower-class disorder.

There are scattered references to Shrove Tuesday football being played in a number of Surrey towns in Victorian times: **Cheam, Epsom, Ewell, Molesey, Mortlake, Richmond, Ripley, Thames Ditton, Walton-on-Thames,** and **Weybridge.** There are only two towns, however, where newspaper reports are consistent enough to chart the development of the game – Kingston and Dorking.

In 1815 it was noted that 'several persons of respectability' participated. This is a common feature of

Shrovetide Football in Kingston-upon-Thames, *Illustrated London News*, 28 February 1846

early reports of the game in which the presence of gentlemen and leading tradesmen was seen as making Shrove Tuesday football socially acceptable. The 1830s saw the repression of Shrove Tuesday football at **Barnes**, Mortlake and Richmond as being a manifestation of 'mob law', but it may have been at this time that it was first played at Dorking. See also Chapter 4 for a further reference to Barnes.

The new *Police Act* which came into effect in 1840 gave the magistrates of Kingston the means to extinguish the game; indeed, a senior police officer came to the mayor asking for his authority to suppress it, as several gentlemen had jointly complained. In Ashbourne, the prosecution case rested upon obstruction to passengers on the highway under The Highways Act, 1835, s 72 and as at Kingston, the magistrates relied upon the police to take the names of the participants, bring the prosecution and endeavor to stop the play. They never succeeded in the last endeavour.

A meeting of the Kingston Borough Council on 6 May 1840 passed a motion which condemned the football as 'an obstruction to the Passengers, a great annoyance to the peaceable Inhabitants, subversive of good order and prejudicial to the Morality of the Town'. The mayor refused to act, however, and the game continued. In 1846 it was reported that 'the annual game is supported by some of the wealthiest inhabitants in and around Kingston: the majority of the Corporation are understood to be favourable to the maintenance of this old English Custom.'

This appeal to antiquity and tradition is characteristic of the more conservative and paternal amongst the gentry. The game drew larger and larger crowds – spectators from the suburbs of London, and players from nearby towns where the game had been banned – the police merely looking on and keeping order. As the crowds grew, actually kicking the ball became rarer and 'hugging' it in a huge scrum became the rule. The loss of the afternoon's business, however, was increasingly resented but many of those who would like to have seen an end of the game feared rioting and resulting ill-feeling if an attempt was made to suppress it. In 1857 the mayor denounced the game as a drunken riot and suggested its removal to a park away from the main streets of the town." A year later saw the first recorded suggestion that the Ashbourne game be moved to Ashbourne Green, on the outskirts of the town.

"However, the influential John Williams, a member of the Kingston Council and landlord of the Griffin Inn, where the annual Shrove Tuesday supper was held, opposed the move and reminded the Council that this was 'free England'. In East Molesey, however, arrests and fines saw the removal of that town's game to a field on the outskirts. In Kingston the controversy continued the following year. The abolitionists were described as 'revolutionaries' and the point was made by one councillor that it was inequitable that 'the rich can have their sports while they would curtail the enjoyment of the poor – did not hunting injure very frequently the farmer's crops?' However, it was noted that fewer tradesmen were playing the game and so it had become vulgar and coarse. The council voted for the game to continue and even paid for the footballs for that year, which were paraded in triumph in the procession before the game.

The 1860s saw a definite change in mood by the gentry who had previously supported Shrove Tuesday football in Kingston. Comparisons with states of siege, revolution, and civil disturbances were more frequent in newspaper accounts, together with observations that respectable inhabitants were no longer prominent in the game. By this date it had become the practice for the mayor to kick the first ball, although this may only have been initiated by John Williams himself in 1858. Previously the landlord of the Castle public house in the Market Square had kicked off – the Castle being the point which divided the two halves of the town.

In 1866, the mayor refused to take the kick and a council meeting afterwards decided to abolish the game. Many outsiders had joined in, it was claimed, and many of these were merely young boys or unemployed labourers. In the same year the game was suppressed at Walton-on-Thames. Shrove Tuesday 1867 saw large numbers of police drafted into Kingston to stop the game. The crowd were described as the 'great unwashed' with only twenty 'respectable artisans' amongst them. Arrests were followed by riotous scenes where councillors who had opposed the game were roughly handled and their houses stoned: a hay rick belonging to one of them was burned. An old inhabitant, Frederick Pyle, who had p!ayed since boyhood was carried shoulder high in a disorderly procession singing 'Work, boys, work, and be contented'.

The following years saw attempts to 'keep up the old charter' by playing in the Fairfield, a park outside the town centre. After a while the ball was kicked into the streets, however, and Pyle was again carried in processions. Nevertheless, arrests and fines discouraged subsequent attempts. Played on the Fairfield, the game had little appeal and it petered out. The more liberal of the councillors had seen this removal to a 'Peoples' Park' as an acceptable remodelling of the custom. In the event, the game did not survive transplantation.

Dorking

In Dorking, however, Shrove Tuesday football was still going strong. Lying in the very centre of Surrey, Dorking preserved the custom longest, perhaps because it retained the conservatism of an old country town long after the suburbs had been 'colonised' by incomers.The day's festivities were heralded by a bizarre group that paraded the town in the morning, led by a man carrying a pole with a cross-bar from the ends of which hung two - and later three – painted footballs. On the cross-bar was painted the slogan 'wind and water's Dorking's glory' supposedly a reference to the bad weather that often accompanied the game. Later this was prefixed with'Kick away both Whig and Tory' though the political significance of this is lost.

The half dozen or so characters in the procession were in fancy dress, with their faces daubed with soot and red ochre. A drummer accompanied whistle players, and sometimes a fiddler, who attempted to render the traditional 'football tune'. All witnesses agree, however, that the noise they made could scarcely be called music. There was always a man dressed as a woman, who exchanged banter with the onlookers. Most important of all, though, at least one of the group carried a collecting box for contributions. In theory the money went to pay for any damage to the windows and paintwork of the town centre shops that might result from the game: in practice, though, most was spent on drink in the pubs afterwards.

Soon after midday the shops were closed and shuttered, and the fragile street lamps covered with sacking. After barricading their premises, the shop assistants had the rest of the day as a holiday, and many would join the crowd that began to assemble to see the fun. As the clock struck two, the first ball was kicked off from the top of the church passage: a privilege claimed by the Town Crier, John Sandford, from the 1860s until his death in 1895. The first ball was the Boys' Ball, and comparatively few youngsters joined in at first. They observed the tradition that the Eastenders played the Westenders, the church passage marking the boundary, and each side tried to keep the ball in their own territory.

After an hour, a second ball was sent off, but the really important one was the large, gilded ball that started at 5 o'clock. By this time the crowd of players had usually grown to several hundred men, young and not so young. The play was very rough but generally good humoured. If the ball was carried into a pub, it was the tradition to take a break for a quick drink before the ball was thrown back into play from an upper window. An early feature of the game used to be splashing through the blood and other filth that had flowed out from the slaughterhouse in West Street, and also violent duckings in the Brook: these, wisely, had been given up by the 1870s. The play grew more and more aggressive and tense as 6 o'clock approached, for whichever side held the ball in their territory when the church clock struck was the winner for the year.

The West usually triumphed, simply because there were more people living in the western part of the town. The Eastenders are only recorded as having won seven times, and in 1866 this was only because they were reinforced by navvies building the London & Brighton Railway nearby. After 6 o'clock the town rapidly returned to normal. Many of the footballers held a dinner at the Sun, their headquarters, and that part of the collection not claimed for damages was convivially spent. As a rival attraction to the demon drink, the Church of England Temperance Society gave a free tea party after the game in the years around 1890." This also happened at Ashbourne.

"A move to end the game in the 1850s was foiled when a local JP refused to read the Riot Act because the son of a principal tradesman was seen to be playing. In 1873, however, there occurred an incident which marked a change of attitude, at least by the local newspaper. Snow lay on the ground and in the hour or two before the game started snowballs were thrown at respectably dressed passersby, including a Roman Catholic priest.' Suggestions began to be made that the game should be moved to a field outside the town and the game was increasingly compared with Socialistic riots and trade union strikes as examples of civil disorder.

Increasingly it was noted that respectable tradesmen no longer played the game, and in the mid-1890s street shopkeepers made an official complaint about the obstruction of the highway and their loss of business. The Dorking Urban District Council was, perhaps surprisingly, in favour of the game continuing – and indeed one of the councillors, J T Maybank, was an active player. The Surrey County Council over-ruled them, however, and in 1897 large numbers of police broke up the game. Some 2,000 people watched the game in this year. (14) In the court proceedings that followed, both prosecution and defence accepted that the Shrove Tuesday game was hundreds of years old, despite the evidence of an old inhabitant who seemed to suggest that it began in Dorking only in the 1830s. Attempts to find documentary proof of the legality of the game among old manorial records were unsuccessful. Furthermore, the objectors, who preferred to remain anonymous, were derided as newcomers bringing alien attitudes to Dorking's ancient traditions.

Nevertheless, the prosecution maintained that no tradition, no matter how ancient, could override the provisions of the Highway Act of 1835, which specifically prohibited street football. Convictions followed, with much heavier fines than expected. The old custom died hard, and attempts were made to keep it alive for nearly ten years after. Arrests and fines, though, took their toll and it degenerated into a token scuffle with schoolboys kicking balls made of newspaper. Police confiscation made these paper balls necessary: leather footballs would have been too valuable to lose. Until 1899, it had been the practice to give schoolboys a half holiday on the afternoon of Shrove Tuesday in order to play the game. This holiday was then discontinued, but nevertheless there was considerable truancy on the day until 1904.

Extra police were drafted into the town on every Shrove Tuesday until 1909, by which date the custom had been thoroughly exterminated. A dinner was held on Shrove Tuesday 1928 at the White Horse when H J Chaldecote, who had been chairman of the Dorking UDC at the time of the suppression, expressed his regret at the passing of the game and a token football was kicked in the streets. All that remains of Shrove Tuesday football in Surrey is the cross-frame that carried the balls in procession, now on display in Dorking Museum."

It is interesting to note that the balls were painted as at Ashbourne. The first ball was painted red and green, the second red, white and blue, like 19th Century Ashbourne balls, and the third was covered with gold leaf. Mathew Alexander's study of the game in Surrey is most welcome. It enables us to see how the game fared prior to its supression. Given that Dorking persisted into the 20th Century – play and prosecutions there being reported in the Ashbourne paper – it's a pity that it did not manage to hang on.

References

1. Malcomson, R.W., *Popular Recreations in English Society*, 1700-1850, 1973, p140
2. Hone, W., *Every-day Book*, 1, 1835, p245
3. Ripley, H, *The History and Topography of Hampton-on-Thames*, 1885, p108
4. Glover S., *The History etc of the County of Derby*, 1829, pp310/11
5. *The Penny Magazine*, 1839, VIII, pp131/32
6. Jewitt, L., *On Ancient Customs and Sports of the County of Derby*, Journ. British Archaeolog. Ass'n, 1852, VII, p203). Magoun, F.P., *Shrove Tuesday Football*, 1931, p28 states that there is a similarity in the first two verses of this poem in the pancake songs of Daventry and Northampton
7. Derby and Chesterfield Reporter, 7 February, 1745
8. Derby Mercury, 25 March 1846
9. Malcomson, op. cit., p142
10. Brushfield, *A second Notice of Customs, Notices and Practices at Ashford in the Water, Sixty Years Ago*, The Relquary, 1864/65, Vol V, pp152/155
11. Magoun op. cit.,
12. Gerard, J., *Stonyhurst College*, 1894, p. 25. See also Percy Fitzgerald, *Stonyhurst Memories; or, Six Years at School*, 1895, pp. 144-151. Charles Waterton in *Essays on Natural History, chiefly Ornithology*, 1844), p. xxvii, describes one of his occupations while at Stonyhurst (c. 1800) as 'foot-ball-maker'!
13. Alexander M., *Shrove Tuesday Football in Surrey*, Surrey Arch. Coll. 1986, Vol 77 pp197/206
14. *Dorking: a Surrey Market Town through Twenty Centuries*

Gazetter of Shrovetide Football games & Ball Customs

3

Alnwick, Northumberland
Details survive of play in 1788 and the game survives to this day. See page 27.

Ashbourne, Derbyshire
The last place in England where mass football, hug ball style, is still practiced with a full size ball at Shrovetide. Although football is played elsewhere on that day, it is with smaller balls (Atherstone, St Columb, Sedgefield) or may only be kicked (Alnwick).

Ashford-in-the-Water, Derbyshire
Play recorded here in the 1860s.

Barnes, Surrey
In March 1829 and February 1836, the vestry meeting complained of the nuisance of street football and recommended its suppression to the officers of the peace. (1)

Bedworth
Football was played here.

Beverley, Yorkshire
In Beverley an annual Shrove Tuesday game, begun on the race-course, was common until 1825, when it was suppressed after much difficulty and some violence. At **Kirby Grindalyte** also in the former East Riding of Yorkshire, Shrove Tuesday was called 'Ball Day,' and the school children expected a half-holiday on purpose to play at ball.

Blackburn
Play at Stonyhurst College, see p33

Bletchley
In the diary of William Cole of Bletchley for Shrove Tuesday, 1767, he mentions 'football playing on the green.' (2)

Bristol
See page 23 for details of an attempt to suppress the game in 1660.

Bromfield, Cumberland
The school boys played football, possibly by bringing in outside assistance, as players were 'sought for with great diligence' See Chapter 2.

Bury, Lancs
On 2nd February, 1742, Richard Kay of Baldingstone, Lancs, wrote in his diary that 'in the afternoon, took a walk to Bury with great numbers beside to see a football match between town and country' (3)

Bushy, near London
Shrovetide football was played here according to Alexander, see Chapter 3.

Carlisle
See page 19.

Chester
See page 18 for details of attempts to suppress the game between 1533 and 1540.

Chester-le-Street
Shrovetide football took the form of a contest between the Up-streeters and the Down-streeters who tried respectively to get the ball to the top or the bottom of the town. It was still being played here in 1896 when the Down-streeters won. In 1887 the players broke down a lamp-post by their violence. A game lasting nearly four hours, was played a year later. The game was being played as late as 1930. (4)

Corfe, Dorset
Football is still played here, but it is not now a mass football game. See pp19/20 for more details.

Cornwall
The story of Cornish hurling during the nineteenth century mirrors that of football. To judge from the comments of writers at the beginning of the century, it was then almost extinct. Wesley, writing in 1781, stated that it was 'now hardly heard of' while Gilbert in 1817 stated that it was seldom practised as a result of the numerous accidents which attend it'. It survived at Helston until about 1880 and is still played at Bodmin, St. Columb Major, and St. Ives. Marples states that Newquay has even thought it worth while to introduce hurling in recent years as an attraction to visitors. (5) Hurling is a handball, rather than a football, game.

Derby
The game ended here in 1846 and gave it's name to the expression 'a local Derby match'. See Chapters 2 and 3 for more details.

Dorking
See pages 36/37 particularly

Duns, Scotland
A riot accompanied play here in 1724, after an attempt to stop the game. See p24.

East Mousley and Hampton-Wick, Surrey
The football game was forcibly stopped here in 1857. (6) See also see Chapter 3.

Finsbury Fields, London
Played here in 1642, see p22 for more details.

Glasgow
See pages 20/21 for details from 1573/74.

Guisborough, Yorkshire
Case of 1616 against football players.

Hampton, Surrey
The game was also stopped here in 1864. (7) See also Alexander, Chapter 3.

Hawick, Scotland
See page 25 for details of play in 1760.

Haxey, Dorset
A game was played here, called the Hood Game and is said to have been a variant of mass football.

Hornsea, Yorkshire
Football at Hornsea: The eating of eggs and collops was practised on Shrove Monday, with pancakes on Shrove Tuesday. On Wednesday tut-ball was played (elsewhere it was known as hand-ball or stool-ball). 'At present, this is only practised by children, but, within the memory of persons yet living, old as well as young turned out into the closes or on the Common for this play, and it was a saying that they who did not play at Tut-ball on Ash Wednesday would be sick in harvest-time.' (9)

Ickleton, Cambridgeshire
In 1935, Women's Institute menbers recalled that on Shrove Tuesday, stalls of home made sweets were formerly set up in the meadow near the Duke of Wellington Inn and football was played in the streets. (10)

Inveresk, Midlothian
See page 27.

Jedburgh, Scotland
Mass football is still played here. See Chapter 2 for a reference in 1704 and Chapter 3 for more recent details. There was an attempt to stop the game here in 1849, but an appeal was made to the Scottish High Court, which ruled that the game had the right to continue as it was a tradition custom. Unfortunately, Scottish law had no writ in England.

Kingston, Surrey
The game lasted here until 1867 (see pp27/28 and Chapter 5).

Kirkmichael, Perthshire
Played prior to 1795, see p26.

Landbeach, Cambridgeshire
Football was played here until the end of the eighteenth century at Camping Close. The churchwarden's accounts contain records of payments of 2/6d (12$\frac{1}{2}$p) made by the Rector to the 'football men' on Shrove Tuesday (11). The payments by the clergy to the poor was a common practice but the custom varied as to the time of year and the reason for making the donation. (12)

Manchester
See page 21 regarding play in 1608.

Melrose, Roxburghshire
In Melrose, the Fastens-een game was played until 1866 between the married men and bachelors or the East and West parts of the town. After the foundation of the Football Club in 1879, the match was between the members of the Club and all others until 1900 when the game was discontinued after considerable opposition. (13)

Messingham, Lincolnshire
On the morning of Shrove Tuesday, it was customary to have a cock fight at the public house. In the afternoon, football was played and the day was concluded with dancing and cards. (14)

Ness, Shropshire
A man died from playing Shrove Tuesday football in 1709. (15) He died on February 28th and Shrove Tuesday fell on February 18th or thereabouts.

Northumberland
In addition to Alnwick (see Chapter 2) there are three other Northumberland parishes where Shrovetide football was once played: **Rothbury, Wooler,** and **Ilderton**. Magoun states (16) that the Rothbury game was discontinued in 1867, though preserved in name in the 'Foot Ball Cairn ' on West Hills, and in 1913 a gift was made to the museum of a 'football, stuffed with hay, such as was used at the old fashioned football plays at Rothbury on Shrove Tuesdays'. The Wooler game used, it is said, to last three days and is reported in 1889. In connection with Percy's Cross, erected in the parish of Ilderton to the memory of Sir Ralph Percy, who fell April 25, 1464, it is said that 'here they were accustomed to assemble annually to play at football'. Shrove Tuesday is not specified, but it seems the likely occasion.

Nuneaton, Warwickshire
A Shrovetide football game was played here in 1881.

Oxford
See page 21 for details of play in 1608.

Richmond, Surrey
The game here was stopped in 1840. (17) See also Alexander in Chapter 3.

Ruislip
See page 21 for details of play in 1576.

Scarborough
There are no known references to mass football being held in Scarborough, but one wonders whether the custom of ball tossing there was introduced as a replacement. Shrove Tuesday was known as Ball Day. Apprentices, servants and children had an afternoon's holiday on the South Sands, playing ball tossing and other ball games. The balls were made out of cloth filled with sawdust. Booths were set up on the sands selling refreshments and various children's toys. By 1905, the cloth balls had been replaced by 'dainty woollen balls'. Charity football matches became popular. They were played between two local breweries, Nesfield's (later Moors and Robson's) and Scarborough & Whitby and in 1915, a huge crowd gathered on the South Sands to watch the match. Money raised were donated to the Workpeople's Hospital Fund. The game was played again in 1916 but then it lapsed until 1920. Thereafter it was played until the Second World War. In 1935, the game was watched by some 4,000 people. (18) It would be nice to know if the breweries provided liquid refreshment to the winners! Nowadays skipping is the popular Shrovetide pastime.

Scone, Perthshire
Here the game had been abolished by 1796, but a good description of it survives, see p26.

Sedgefield
The earliest record dates from 1827 when it was stated that "an ancient custom prevails at Sedgefield on Sbrove Tuesday, on which dav the parish clerk is obliged to find a ball for the use of the townsmen and the country people, who assemble for thc purposc of playing a game at football, after which the victorious and the vanquished resort to the public houses where they generally 'drink deep e'er they depart'." (19)

Seventy years later, the following description records: "The usual old-time game of football was played at Sedgefield yesterday between the tradesmen and the countrymen of the district. Two or three thousand spectators and players assembled on the village green, and at one o'clock Mr. Webb, the parish clerk, made his appearance, and amidst loud cheering proceeded to the bull-ring. Passing the ball three times through this ring, it was thrown high in the air, and on its descent it became public property. The play was of shorter duration than usual, lasting only forty minutes. The countrymen had the game well in hand throughout, being decidedly stronger numerically than their opponents, and succeeded in landing the ball into their alley - the North End Pond. The ball was secured by B. Hart, who was carried shoulder high in his dripping clothes up the North End to the bull-ring, where the ball was again passed through the ring and handed back to Hart. There was less rough play than usual." (20)

The game is still played today.

Shrewsbury

Football played in Shrewsbury in 1601 when a petition was issued for discharge from prison for playing Shrovetide football (21) see Chapter 2.

Surrey

Played here at Cheam, Epsom, Ewell, Molesey, Mortlake, Ripley, Thames Dritton, Walton-on-Thames and Weybridge. See page 34. Also at Kingston on Thames and Dorking.

Twickenham

At Twickenham in 1840 the magistrates prevented the Shrovetide football from "taking place in the town, but it was most spiritedly carried on in a meadow belonging to Mr Cole, the brewer of that parish, under the superintendence of a man named Kirby, who has been 'master of the sports' for the last 50 years"; "formerly ... the sport had been extended throughout every avenue of the place; but of late years, and more particularly since the passing of the new Highway Act, by which it has altogether been prohibited in any public thoroughfare ... it has been confined to the meadow of Mr. Cole, who kindly offered it for the purpose". (22)

Whitby, Yorkshire

In 1817, the festivities in Whitby were reported as being pancakes and bellringing and a general jubilee for the children, apprentices and servants. (23) He makes no reference to Shrovetide Football, but it was common in books at that time. By the middle of the century, matters were much clearer: "The general custom of a pancake dinner is here observed; and after the ringing of the pancake bell at eleven o'clock in the forenoon, children and apprentices enter upon a holiday for the rest of the day." (24)

The same title but in the edition of 1876 (p170) adds: 'The pancake dinner is here observed with 'Collop Monday', or fare of bacon rashers, along with the Tuesday afternoon's holiday for the youngsters, who go into the fields to play at ball'. This must relate to football for the author goes on to say "Easter (is) 'ball time', when it is said, if the balls are not 'well played' by our country youths, more particularly on the preceding Shrove Tuesday, when the time commences, they will be sure to fall sick at harvest." (25)

In the East and West Ridings, school-children called Shrove Tuesday 'Ball Day'. On this day every child had a halfpenny and a new ball, which was made of four pieces of coloured leather sewn together and filled with sawdust. Everybody caught one of these balls when it was thrown up, and it was said that if you did not 'kep' or catch a ball before noon on this day you would be ill all through the harvest. (26) The Holderness Glossary, p82, states that In the North and West Ridings, Shrove Tuesday was known as 'Keppen-day', so called because part of the amusement of girls on that day consists of keppin or catching balls. (27)

Yetholm, Roxburghshire

Athletic sports, followed by football, have been held on the town haugh. They were dropped during the Great War, but the game was revived in 1920.

The late Jack Smith of Ashbourne kept a book of details of Shrovetide and other mass football games, which has recently been located again. It includes details of where the game had been played and when it ceased. The source of the information is generally not given and further research is clearly needed. The book was made available immediately prior to this book going into production. Details from the list are included with the proviso that confirmation of its accuracy still needs to be determined:

South Mimms 1583
Leicester
Bothall, Northumberland; played Easter Tuesday 1680
Llanwennog, Celland and Pencarreg, Formerly in Cardiganshire. Played on Christmas Day
Hardington, Lanarkshire
Tenby, South Wales
Barnett, Herts, abandoned 1775
Narberth, Laugharne, Dolgellau and Maentwrog, Wales
Lanton and Camptown, Westruther, Coldingham, Foulden, all in Scotland

References

1. Malcomson, R.W., *Popular Recreations in English Society*, 1700-1850, 1973, p140
2. Stokes, ed., *Bletcheley Diary of Rev Wm Cole*, 1765-1767, 1931, p186
3. Brockbank & Kenworthy, The Diary of R Kay, 1716-1751, of Baldingstone, near Bury: A Lancashire Doctor, Chetham Soc, 1968, 3rd Series, XVI, p47
4. Magoun, F.P., *Shrove Tuesday Football*, 1931, p33
5. Marples, ibid, p105
6. Malcolmson op. cit., p141, quoting the Surrey Comet, 28/2/1857
7. ibid, p141,
8. Robson, *Calendar Customs in 19th and 20th Century Dorset*, 1988, thesis, Univ. Of Sheffield, Dept., of English Language, p39
9. Bedell, p89, quoted in Gutch 1912
10. Porter E., *Cambridgeshire Customs and Folklore*, 1969
11. ibid
12. see Bushaway, ibid, pp39/41
13. Magoun, ibid, p36
14. ed Peacock, *MacKinnon's Account of Messingham in the County of Lincoln*, 1881, p10
15. *Everyday Life in Tudor Shrewsbury*, Bygones NS Vol VI, 1900, p514
16. ibid., p24
17. Malcolmson ibid, p141 and also quoting the Surrey Standard, 6/3/1840
18. Scarborough Evening News 18/2/1985
19. Parson and White, History, Directory, and Gazetteer of the Counties of Durham and Northumberland, Vol I, 1827, p276
20. The Yorkshire Post, 19/2/1896, quoted in Magoun, ibid, p33
21. Hist MSS Com 15th App X, p62
22. Malcomson, ibid, p143, quoting The Times, 2 and 6/3/1840
23. Young, History of Whitby, 1817
24. Glossary of Words and Phrases collected in Whitby and the neighbourhood, 1855
25. Robinson, Glossary of Words used in the Neighbourhood of Whitby, Pt. ii (English Dialect Soc., Series C, Vol. IV, 1876, p.170
26. Gutch 1912, quoting Addy, pp116/7
27. Gutch, 1912, p92

Ashbourne Royal Shrovetide Football: Early Days

Since the publication of the first edition of this Official History, all further attempts to prove that the adult game existed before 1821 have largely proved fruitless. I have felt some unease that Charles Cotton's poem of 1683 was taken as the earliest reference to the game without any justification that it referred to Ashbourne rather than Derby. Cotton wrote 'Two towns where once war had waged now at football are engaged'. Clearly the 'towns' could have been Ashbourne and Compton, but did they see any action during the Civil War? The answer would appear to be 'yes'. King Charles I came to the town in 1645 and attended divine service at the church. There had been a skirmish to the south as he came north from Tutbury and some men were killed. However, perhaps Cotton had in mind the events of February 1644 when Royalists from Derbyshire gathered in Ashbourne. The men gathered daily in such numbers as to obstruct all communication between the town and neighbouring villages.

They were dispersed by Parliamentarian troops under Major Sanders who remained in the town for some time. The Royalists regrouped but Major Sanders learnt of their intentions, withdrawing his troops to the surrounding lanes etc. He routed the Royalists, pursuing them to Tissington where 170 were taken prisoner and others killed or wounded. (*Ashbourn and the Valley of the Dove* pp19-20).

It is reasonable to argue that Cotton could have had these events in mind. Given that most festivals were apparently banned by the Commonwealth, Cotton would have been recording the start, or restart of the game. If this is correct, the date could well have been the first Shrovetide after the Restoration, i.e. 1667. It also needs mentioning that Cotton does not refer to Shrovetide. The game could have been at Christmas or New Year.

Glover's reference to the game in 1844 stated that in Ashbourne the institution, i.e. the game, was of recent date and indeed he could have meant that the game had started not too many years earlier. It is of course perfectly feasible that the game ceased between the 17th and 19th centuries. However, this was a time when efforts were being made to end Shrovetide football in towns because of the havoc it created even then.

Additionally, inertia seemed to have threatened customs in general, at least in Derbyshire. The well dressing in Bakewell ended in 1752 and by the end of that century, it only survived at Tissington. It made a comeback in the 19th century with the establishment of better supplies of drinking water and the realisation that the new railways offered the opportunity to make money from tourism. This arose from the experience of Buxton where 30,000 visitors came to the well dressing in 1863 on the recently opened railway.

If the game had started some years before Glover wrote about it when could have this been? Clearly it was well established in 1821 when it was referred to at the local Theatre in Dig Street. This therefore precludes 1820 and a celebration of the new king, George IV. It could have been in 1760, when his father succeeded to the throne but this conflicts with the experience of the local well dressing custom. The suggestion in the Official History that Glover was referring to the change of goals to Clifton and Sturston still has a ring of truth about it, and maybe we may never know. However the following theory is offered as a plausible explanation.

In January 1858, a ball was turned up in the Market Place to celebrate the marriage of the Princess Royal, the oldest daughter of Queen Victoria, to the future Frederick III of Prussia. It is stated on p196, that almost at the end of the 18th Century, a trial game was held between the two mills which

ASHBOURNE About 1890

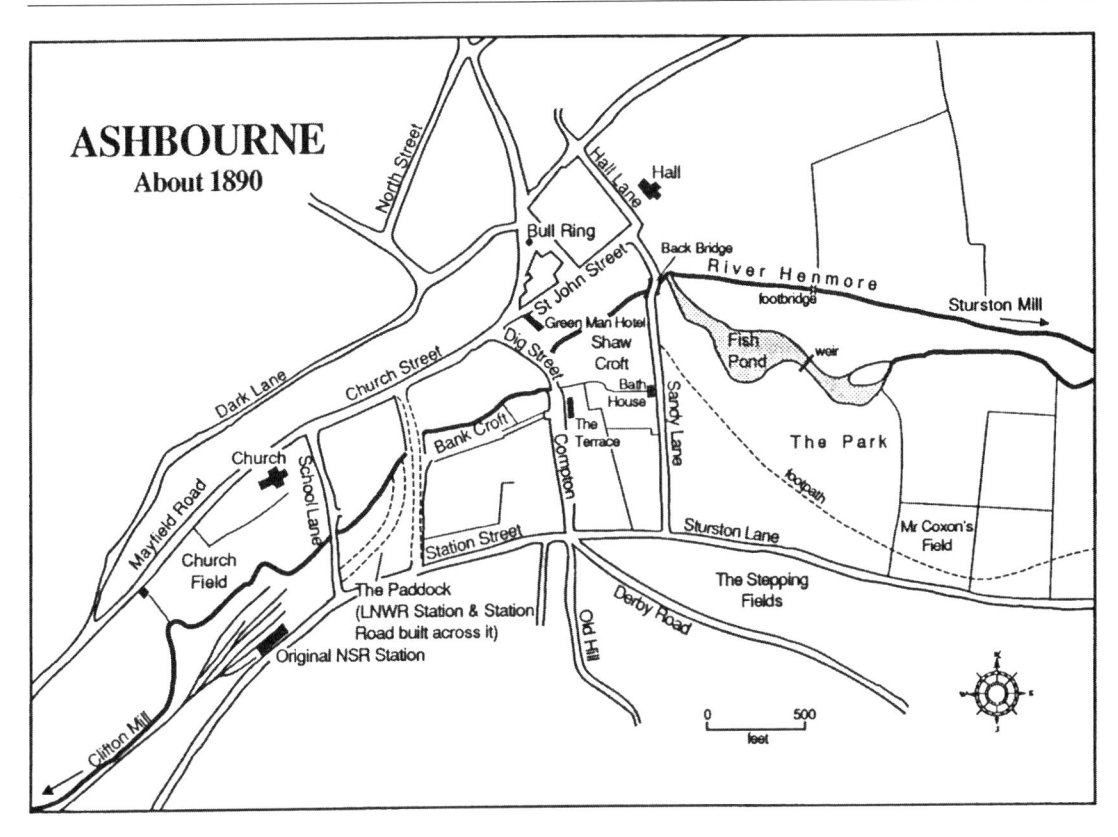

was so successful, it was adopted for the Shrovetide game thereafter. This was based upon information given by Mr Thomas Tomlinson, who died in 1879 aged 90 years, to his grandson, the Revd. F Tomlinson. The former could remember the game. What could that event have been? If the game in January 1858 was following in the way of tradition, there would have been a precedent for it and there is one, at least in all probability.

The previous marriage of a Princess Royal was George III's oldest daughter. She married the Prince of Wurtemberg in 1797. This fits in well with what Thomas Tomlinson recalled. It is most persuasive to suggest that in 1797, a ball was turned up in the Market Place and played to the two mills as an experiment on the occasion of the marriage of the Princess Royal. This was so well received that the Shrovetide game in 1798 adopted this revised plan of goaling and has played this way ever since. This would also offer an explanation for Glover's comment in 1829 that the game was of a recent date. It is also not unreasonable to suggest that Thomas Tomlinson was old enough to remember the event.

There is no documentary proof of this, but if this is wrong, what on earth was the event to which Mr Tomlinson related? The Prince of Wales was married in April 1794, but he was unpopular and of course, Mr Tomlinson would have been either four or five at the time and less able to rely on his memory. Crucially, the dawn of the new century may also be ruled out; Mr Tomlinson expressly said it was prior to 1800.

Ashbourne is the last place in England to play hug football at Shrovetide. The Kirkwall Ba'game, played on Christmas Day and New Year's Day in the Orkneys, is similar to Ashbourne's. Instead of Up'ards and Down'ards, Kirkwall has Uppies and Doonies, but the similarity is striking. It is a street game like Ashbourne's and the Uppies take the ba' upstreet to their goal, the same as the Up'ards would have played up the hill from the Henmore to their goal. In both cases, the idea is to score an own goal. At Kirkwall you played according to how you entered the town from the sea, but nowadays families retain allegiance to the side they have historically played for.

Continued on page 48.

Clifton Mill

The mill was originally three stories in height with a lower two-storey extension towards the road which included the mill house on the end and farm buildings between the house and the mill. A photo survives of the railway station which clearly shows that there was a break in the roof line. A photo of the mill appeared in *The Field* in March 1963, which indicates that the roof of the Mill had been lowered for there is a continuous roof line. The wheel was contained in a two-storey extension on the west side and the railway ran past the east side. Until the end of the nineteenth century at least, the outflow from the wheel, having reached the end of the mill house then flowed along the roadside. The road from Clifton first forded the millrace water and then the river. This ford was replaced by two small bridges (see below).

There was no millpond separate from the river as at Sturston. The river was dammed at the side of the wheel. River players with the ball bound for Clifton wheel had to swim across the impounded water to reach their objective. It was here that James Barker, the brother of the ball painter John Barker, lost his life when he drowned in 1878. By coincidence this year was the first time John painted a ball.

Players approaching along Watery Lane had a problem crossing the Henmore when it was in flood if Up'ards blocked the footbridge by the mill. From November 1899, the new road bridges solved the problem. The one nearest the mill was built to clear the mill race water and the other one spans the Henmore. A new river bed was cut for this purpose. The original course of the river can be seen north of the mill race bridge. The mill race came down the side of the road and then turned sharply under the bridge. The steel work for the bridges is second hand and was provided by the North Staffordshire Railway Company. The one on the downstream side of the mill race bridge bears the date 1848. It would be very interesting to know where it came from as a lot of the NSR bridges in the area were originally built of wood. That at Oakamoor in the Churnet Valley was not replaced with steel until 1888, for instance. The two bridges, built by subscription, cost £700.

James Brindley came to Ashbourne around 1755 to a cornmill, so Clifton was possibly the mill he came to see. In 1835, the miller was Francis Tabberer (*Pigots Directory*). In September 1858, The Green Hall was offered for sale together with various parcels of land including Clifton Mill. It was described as a:

'messuage, water cornmill, stable, garden and outbuildings. The above Mill is in good repair and full work, the waterwheel is lately new'.

The tenant was Samuel Redfern. The Green Hall estate had been owned by the Hayne family at least since 1807 when John Hayne's will was made.

In 1876, the miller was Samuel Taylor and he was still there in 1881. He was also the Registrar of Births, Marriages and Deaths for Mayfield District. An article in the local paper records that the miller goaled the ball in 1880. (AN 9/10/1934) It was Samuel Taylor's employee who drowned in the millpond in 1878. Mr Taylor died in July 1892 and was still resident at the mill. He was 61 years old. In addition to being the Mayfield Registrar, he was also Collector of Income Tax for the parishes of Ashbourne and Clifton and Overseer for the parish of Clifton. He was not the miller at this time as adverts were appearing prior to his death for J O Jones, miller, Clifton Cornmill. He was advertising corn, oilcake, seed, manure and coal from Swanwick Colliery.

At a meeting of the Ashbourne UDC in September 1895, it was reported by the surveyor, Mr D Roberts, that the Clifton milldam had been cleansed in compliance with the orders of the Sanitary Committee. This arrangement had been made in 1891 when the terms had been reached with Mr J O Jones (the mill tenant) and Mr S Taylor for the periodic flushing of the milldam. (AN 16/05/1891). According to the Inland Revenue land survey of 1911, the mill was then owned by W R Holland.

The mill wheel was housed in a two-storey building. A door in the orchard (the area of land between the river and the millrace) gave access to the wheel pit. A set of stone steps went down to the water level on the right hand side, once inside the building. In 1967, the mill had been partly demolished prior to Shrovetide, but the wheel house wall was still standing and Alec Smith goaled his ball by hitting it three times. Afterwards, the rest of the building was demolished. The site of the wheel pit was marked by the stone plinth, donated by Herbert Plumbly. At sometime after the removal of the wheel, the wheel pit was filled in, a floor made and access made to the mill building by knocking through the connecting wall.

Sturston Mill

In September 1905, George Dethick, the Sturston miller, and his son John brought assault charges against a neighbour, William Gadsby. It gave a little insight into the scant information which is known about the mill. Gadsby had land adjacent to the millpond and claimed that he had access to it. The miller removed sedges from the silted areas of the pond and used them for thatching. This year, Gadsby had cut them. He came back for more of them and was confronted by the Dethicks. Gadsby attacked George Dethick with a hay rake, breaking it over his head. Gadsby's sons then protected their father with pitchforks. The latter was fined a total of £3 and costs. At the hearing it was stated that the millpond provided water for a waterwheel (ie not two wheels in use at that time) and Mr Dethick had been living at Sturston Mill for 23 years.

In July, 1914, the Sturston Estate was offered for sale. It included Sturston Hall (let to C. Allen) and the Mill (let to George Dethick). The mill was described as being a three-storey water corn mill, used for "milling and stowage and fitted with two pairs of greystones, two pairs of French stones, a wire dressing machine, also an oat drying kiln, office, millwright's shop etc." There were two waterwheels, presumably for each set of stones. The grey stones would be used for grinding animal feed and were probably Peak stones from the Hathersage area. The French Burr stones were used for domestic purposes, grinding for human consumption. They were composite grindstones made from several pieces of stone cemented with Plaster of Paris and held together with iron bands. The stone came from near to Paris, hence the name. The mill and the four bedroom house was let at £110 per annum.

In 1981, the mill tenancy was surrendered and the owners, Nestlé, demolished the mill ahead of the Shrovetide game. They had demolished the Clifton Mill in 1967.

Ashbourne Station

Shrovetide was lucky to enjoy the tolerance of the North Staffordshire Railway Company, for the game was frequently played through the station and the goods yard, especially around the waggons which sometimes helped a quick getaway. There is even a story of the ball going to Clifton in the guard's van (see below). Occasionally trains were delayed by the game or the game was temporarily suspended as a train went through. Perhaps the last time this happened was in 1963 when Bill Bennett scored after play in the tunnel had delayed the train from Buxton for quite a while.

The Railway Company was not always so tolerant about trespass. In 1894, a chap called Harris was fined ten shillings (50p) and 14/6d (72.5p) costs or 14 days imprisonment at Derby Gaol. Also, Edwin Shaw was fined 5/- (25p) and the same costs or seven days gaol. Both elected to go to gaol. Neither of these incidents were associated with Shrovetide, however, when half the town could pass through. (AN 02/02/1894)

The station master at the time was David Dean. He had been appointed in 1882. At his retirement in 1909, many comments were made about his considerate nature. Clearly Shrovetide saw the benefits of this. He had served over fifty years with the N S R. The year before, ie 1908, a local engine driver (William Davies, of Station Street) had retired also having done fifty years service. He was the oldest engine driver employed by the Company and was aged seventy. At that time (1908) George Goodall was an N S R guard with over 46 years spent the Company. He lived in Clifton Road and one wonders if he was the guard who allowed the ball to travel to Clifton in his van? Living in Clifton Road, if he had any allegiance at all, it may have been Down'ards! (see AN 13/11/1908, 04/12/1908, 22/10/1909)

George Goodall had often travelled as guard on William Davies's trains as he had been the Ashbourne to Uttoxeter guard since before 1881. He retired in 1911 and became the attendant at the Green Lane, Clifton, level-crossing. It certainly explains why a guard would risk disciplinary action for allowing an unauthorised passenger to travel in his van; both the engine driver and the station master being relied upon to turn a blind eye. Following the turn up of the ball, there were trains to Clifton at 4.20pm, 5.25pm and 7.05pm. It took four minutes to get there!

At Ashbourne the Up'ards were those born in Ashbourne i.e. north of the Henmore. The Down'ards were those from Compton, which used to be a separate hamlet. It was probable that in early times the game was played not in Ashbourne but by teams based upriver or downriver of a dividing line running along Compton. Even then, the expression Up'ards and Down'ards would have been appropriate once the mills had been fixed as goals. The opening of the maternity hospital meant that most Ashbourne children entered the world as Up'ards, but maintained the family allegiance as at Kirkwall. It is only in recent years that the notion that if you were born in the maternity hospital, you were an Up'ard. The idea was that in a time when social mobility was unheard of, you continued in the family tradition.

Kirkwall balls are hand-stitched in leather and filled with ground cork similar to Ashbourne, which uses cork shavings. The cork enables the ball to be particularly robust and conveniently ensures that the ball floats in water. Water play being a feature at Ashbourne – (the River Henmore or the Fish Pond) – and in the sea at Kirkwall. One area of difference would appear to be the manner of play. John Robertson, writing on the Kirkwall game states that: "up to 1850 or so, the game was basically one of street football and consisted of fast open play ... the ball was kicked or dribbled but never held."

This would seem not to have been the case at Ashbourne. Glover, writing in 1829 states '[the ball] is carried in the arms of those who have possessed themselves of it.'

There is unfortunately very little early-recorded data on the Shrovetide game in Derbyshire, despite it being played both in Derby, Ashford and Ashbourne. The first reference was in 1683 by Charles Cotton who lived at Beresford Hall near Hartington. He also owned Fenny Bentley Old Hall just north of Ashbourne having aquired it through marriage. In his *Burlesque on the Great Frost* are the words: 'Two towns, that long that war had waged, being at football now engaged'. What a pity Cotton was not more explicit. The two towns are probably Ashbourne and Compton and Clifton townships, which would date the use of the Henmore as the boundary earlier than most people think. It would be interesting to know if the game had been stopped during Cromwell's Commonwealth. The Restoration was a recent occurrence and the 'war' would relate to events during the Civil War. However did Cotton use the word 'now' to refer to a re-commencement of play? If a celebration of Lent was frowned upon then it is conceivable that the game had been abandoned during the Commonwealth, as elsewhere. We shall never know.

There is a perplexing reference in *Ashbourne and the Valley of the Dove* which was published in 1839. After quoting Glover (see below) it goes on to say: "The game is supposed to have been played in Derby at a very early period. It was general in England in the reign of Henry II but its introduction into Ashbourn [sic] is of more recent date."

However, what is clear is that this author was relying heavily on Glover who clearly states: "This game is played in a similar manner at Ashbourn (sic), but the institution of it there is of a modern date." It would be easy to assume that the commencement of the Ashbourne game was only a short time before Glover's reference. However, we know the game was going strong in 1821. Llewellyn Jewitt's 'Derbyshire Ballads' (which quotes the 1821 song) was published in *The Reliquary* in 1867 and states (p254):

"The game has been played from time immemorial until 'put down' by the strong arm of the law – not without much unpleasantness and strenuous opposition – a few years ago."

However, it is clear that he is getting confused with Derby. The game was played throughout the 1850s – Supt Corbishley's evidence at the magistrates court in 1860 proves this.

The Rev Tomlinson's article (Chapter 8) mentions play 'about the year 1840'. His article, which recalls the memories of his predecessors back to the close of the eighteenth century, would surely have mentioned any cessation of play. It is clear that Glover's reference relates to the change of the goals to the two mills, thirty or so years previous. In this sense, the game was newly established. Glover also notes that 'a desperate game at football, in which the ball is struck by the feet of the players, is also played at Ashover and at other wakes'. His reference is worth quoting in full:

"Football continues to be played at in many parts of England on Shrove Tuesday and Ash Wednesday, but the mode of playing this game at Ashbourn and Derby, differs very much from the usual practice of this sport. In the town of Derby the contest lies between the parishes of St Peter and All Saints, and the goals to which the ball is to be taken are, Nun's mill for the latter, and the Gallow's balk on the

> **Goal Scoring Achievements**
>
> Mathew Cleaver, goaled his eight balls in the days when they were turned up at the bull ring. He was a runner and was noted for being very difficult to catch once he was away. He stated at Shrovetide in 1907 that he had goaled more balls than anyone else. However Alec Smith recalls that one of his family was a Samuel Smith of Clifton who lies buried between the church and Cock Hill. He is reputed to have goaled nine balls. He was a huge man and had a fourteen-inch span between his thumb and his little finger when his hand was outstretched. Apparently he became disenchanted with the game and burnt all nine of his trophies.
>
> The goal scoring achievements of Joe Burton are well recorded and stretched over the 19th and the 20th centuries. However at least one of his goals was in the boys' game. Don Lowndes scored two goals in his own name. He scored a third and then allowed Stan Cope to hit the wheel after him and take the honour. To his cost, Cope then tried to sell the ball at Sturston and Don took it from him. The ball is down in the Roll Of Honour in joint names, but the honour clearly belonged to Don. The latter scored another three goals and then allowed someone else to repeat the scoring and take the honour. This means he scored a total of six goals. Sam Sowter Snr is also understood to have done something similar.

Normanton road for the former. None of the other parishes of the borough take any direct part in the contest, but the inhabitants of all join in the sport, together with persons from all parts of the adjacent country. The players are young men from eighteen to thirty or upwards, married as well as single, and many veterans who retain a relish for the sport are occasionally seen in the very heat of the conflict.

The game commences in the market place, where the partisans of each parish are drawn up on each side; and, about noon, a large ball is tossed up in the midst of them. This is seized upon by some of the strongest and most active men of each party. The rest of the players immediately close in upon them, and a solid mass is formed. It then becomes the object of each party to impel the course of the crowd towards their particular goal. The struggle to obtain the ball, which is carried in the arms of those who have possessed themselves of it, is then violent, and the motion of this human tide heaving to and fro, without the least regard to consequences, is tremendous. Broken shins, broken heads, torn coats and lost hats, are among the minor accidents of this fearful contest, and it frequently happens that persons fall in consequence of the intensity of the pressure, fainting and bleeding beneath the feet of the surrounding mob.

But it would be difficult to give an adequate idea of this ruthless sport: a Frenchman passing through Derby remarked, that if Englishmen called this playing, it would be impossible to say what they would call fighting. Still the crowd is encouraged by respectable persons attached to each party, and who take a surprising interest in the result of the day's sport; urging on the players with shouts, and even handing to those who are exhausted, oranges and other refreshment. The object of the St Peters' party is to get the ball into the water, down the Morledge brook into the Derwent as soon as they can, while the All Saints party endeavour to prevent this, and to urge the ball westward. The St Peter players are considered to be equal to the best water-spaniels, and it is certainly curious to see two or three hundred men up to their chins in the Derwent continually ducking each other.

The numbers engaged on both sides exceed a thousand, and the streets are crowded with lookers-on. The shops are closed, and the town presents the aspect of a place suddenly taken by storm. – The origin of this violent game is lost in its antiquity, but there exists a tradition, that a cohort of Roman soldiers, marching through the town to Derventio, or Little Chester, were thrust out by the unarmed populace, and this mode of celebrating the occurrence has been continued to the present day. It is even added that this conflict occurred in the year 217, and that the Roman troops at Little Chester were slain by the Britons. – This game is played in a similar manner at Ashbourn, but the institution of it there is of a modern date. In Scotland, [referring to Scone near Perth] it appears that there is an ancient game at football which resembles the Derby football very closely."

> ## Knives in the hug
>
> In 1942, a knife was produced in the hug. The match report states that this is the only documentary evidence of this. However, it is known that Mr G Marple had his hand cut in the hug. It was after the ball had been hugged for nearly three hours in front of the Bell Inn, now Barclays Bank. Mr Marple had a permanent injury to his hand. (AN14/02/1891)
>
> In 1951, Col Ridout turned up the ball and it was not goaled. He gave it to Jack Smith who had probably saved his life rendering first aid after a car crash at the Jug and Glass Inn, near Hartington. This ball had been slashed during play. One wonders, given the proximity of the dates, whether the same person was responsible. During that year's play, an open razor was produced in the hug while it was outside the Westminster Bank at the top of Dig Street. The offender was hauled out of the hug and harm's way according to Alec Smith. Slashing the ball to prevent further play was quite prevalent in the 19th century. It is referred to in the poem of 1821 as well as in the earliest match report of 1848.

The earliest specific reference to the Ashbourne game is February 1821 when a song was sung at the theatre in Dig Street about the game. The theatre is believed to have been at the rear of the Cock Inn, now replaced by the modern shops at the top of Dig Street. It was composed by an actor named Fawcett and ran to six verses. It is quoted in Appendix A, page 205.

Glover's reference to the ball being picked up and carried has a further significance. The game of rugby football is credited as being first played at Rugby School, when William Webb Ellis picked up the ball and ran with it, probably in 1823. Ellis was at Rugby School between 1816 and 1825 and R T Rivington has found that there were three Ashbourne boys at the school at this time (*The International Journal of the History of Sport*, May 1991). Barnard Dewes, aged 14 and Granville Dewes, aged 13 entered in 1818. Edward Webster, aged 14 entered in 1820.

Clearly the seeds of rugby football may have grown from conversations between the Ashbourne boys and the younger Webb Ellis (who entered in 1816 aged nine) although street football was also played at Rugby prior to 1750. However, it is not known whether this was mass football. ('*Running with the ball*', J Macrory, 1991, pp16-17). It is interesting to speculate whether the boys had watched the Ashbourne town game, or whether the boys' game dates from this time and the Ashbourne lads had actually been participants. Even if they had not attended The Grammar School as minors, they would have been aware of the school's game in any event. The boys were probably the sons of Court Dewes who rented Vine House in Church Street between 1811 and 1819. This was only a few doors away from the Grammar School.

Court Dewes was the nephew of Rev John Dewes Granville of Calwich Abbey (*A Georgian Country Town, Ashbourne 1725-1825*, Vol 1). The latter was the nephew of Bernard Granville, from whom he had inherited the Calwich estate. Granville was a friend of Handel and was left a folio of music manuscripts in Handel's will. The boys were clearly named after Bernard Granville. It is fascinating to think that rugby football has this link with Ashbourne's football game.

In 1859, the vicar of Ashbourne, the Rev J Errington made an unsuccessful effort to have the game played on the Monday and Tuesday and the ball thrown up on Ashbourne Green. Presumably his intention was to bow to mounting pressure to stop the game being played in the town's streets. A poster was issued on 3 March 1859 stating that the football would be thrown up on Ashbourne Green in order to move the game from the town. A reward of £5 would be made to the man who goaled it. However, another poster dated 13 March 1859 stated that the old game would be played in the old way and the ball would be thrown up in the old place. (AT 07/3/1930)

Early match reports

The forced abandonment of the Shrovetide game in Derby in 1846 clearly would have been received favourably by those wanting the end of street play in Ashbourne. The essential difference was that Ashbourne was favoured with agricultural land which effectively divided the town into two. The Park and Shaw Croft extending down to Compton Bridge and The Paddock covering the bulk of the area from what is now the bus station to School Lane. The anti-lobby continually stressed the desire to see play restricted to the fields. Eventually Mr Frank turned against this, seeking the end of the game entirely but he could not motivate enough people to his point of view. The absurdity of the situation was that the desire to see the game removed from the streets was confined to north of the Henmore. Play in Dig Street was not acceptable although play in Compton was tolerated.

The oldest reference to play centres around a small group of cuttings of 1848 which were not ascribed to any specific paper, but were quoted in our local paper almost a century later. (AT 27/7/1934) The crux of one of the articles came down to a letter to the paper complaining about the game. The writer had been caught in the crowd between his house and the Ashbourne Post Office and did not like it, especially the 'rude, boisterous and unseemly sight in the Market Place. He suggested that the game should be played from the commencement to termination in the open fields.

In the same set of cuttings was a note about an assault at Shrovetide 1848 by William Frost on the Constable, James Hard, which was subsequently brought before the Bench. The evidence stated that the incident had happened after three men – Shaw, Pearson, and Cundy, who played Up'ards, had taken the ball onto the Fishpond and cut it. This incidentally, is further proof that the Park was open to the players in the mid-years of the 19th century. Clearly the desire to see the game moved from the Market Place persisted. Just what caused the desire to bring the prosecutions in 1860 isn't known but probably was precipitated by the nature of play and/or accompanying rowdiness in 1859.

If play in Derby had been denied to Shrovetide enthusiasts, the opening of the Railway Station in 1852 meant that they could now travel by train from Derby to Ashbourne via Uttoxeter. According to a letter written to Jack Hawksworth, the Committee Secretary in 1934 and relating to the game in 1880, a carriage from the Green Man Hotel used to meet the trains to convey customers to the hotel prior to the game starting. In those days, the trains stopped short of the Paddock and the station was at the side of School Lane, which formerly extended to Clifton Road. It did not move to the new site in Station Road until 1890.

An interesting event took place in 1858 for in this year, a ball was turned up on the occasion of the marriage of the Princess Royal. (AN 4/3/1927) The record of it came from Mr GT Marple, a former member of the Board of Guardians, who was writing a historical sketch on the game. The Princess, the oldest child of Queen Victoria, was married in January to the future Frederick III of Prussia. This was the last time that an incumbent Princess Royal was married (except for the second marriage of Princess Anne). The ball was turned up in the Market Place but no record of any goals being scored is known. Nor is it known if it was usual at that time (and in times previous) to celebrate coronations and special royal events with the playing of mass football in Ashbourne. See further consideration of this above on page 44.

Mr George Shaw has discovered that the diary of the headmaster of the National School in Ashbourne, Mr Francis, contains an entry for the game on Ash Wednesday 1859. It records that the ball was goaled at Clifton. This is the earliest documentary evidence of the goaling of a ball. There is no reference of a ball being goaled on the Tuesday. Mr Francis was also choirmaster at St Oswald's Church.

1860

The year 1860 saw a turning point in the history of the Shrovetide game with deliberate attempts being made to prevent play in the streets of the town. This really meant the Market Place, St John Street, Church Street and Dig Street, or at least play elsewhere was tolerated more or less, so long as the highway was not impeded. Play along Sandy Lane, now Park Road, was usually tolerated although some constables even prevented this in 1898. Once The Park became closed, the Up'ards had no option but to use Sandy Lane.

In 1860, the magistrates issued a notice stating that, in their view, the playing of the game in the streets was illegal. A similar notice had been issued in 1859, but had been ignored. Perhaps this was why the Rev Errington had suggested the move to Ashbourne Green. There was much discontent in the town about the posting of the notice. The first of several press articles gives an idea of what happened. (DM 22/02/1860)

The discontent had increased once it became known that the police were preparing active measures to enforce the orders of the Bench. The Market Place was full of men and boys on Shrove Tuesday as 2.00pm approached and then the mill hands from Mayfield began to pour in. The threat of taking down the names of those who kicked the ball delayed the throwing up for a few minutes but at the stroke of two a cheer announced that the ball had appeared from a local inn.

The police attempted to seize it but the passage from hand to hand prevented this and at last, amidst a deafening 'hurrah', the ball flew into the air. It was gradually rolled by the crowd down the hill. The police appeared (according to the report) to be 'perfectly intimidated by the crowd'. Five or six hundred persons were assembled. No violent measures were resorted to and by 2.15pm the Market Place was empty.

The following week there was detail on the Wednesday's game. (DM 29/02/1860) The play was not so good-natured or peaceful in character. Much exasperation was felt against the order to stop the play. Many, 'knowing that their names were taken down became careless of further consequences and urged on to desperate courses'. Females joined in the feeling of love for the game and on Wednesday the ball was turned up 'by a fair one', and fights occurred in several places.

Supt James Corbishley wrote to the paper (DM 29/02/1860) about the Tuesday game and what in his view was inaccurate reporting of events. He stated: "no seizure of the ball was ever attempted nor was such an act ever even contemplated. Upon two persons appearing in the Market Place with the ball, I informed them that if the game were played in the streets to the annoyance of passengers, proceedings would be taken against those who joined in it; that I should not attempt to interfere with the play, but simply take the names of those who took active part in it. I also informed them that Capt Holland had authorized me to say that the ball might be thrown up in his park. The ball was thrown up in the Market Place since which summons have been taken out."

The Court Hearing

Things did not rest here however, for the following week, the reporter responded to Supt Corbishley's letter. (DM 07/03/1860) He reasserted that a policeman did attempt to seize the ball at 2.00pm as reported. He stated that he was in a position to 'command an uninterrupted view of all the proceedings'. Moreover, he had not trusted to memory, but had taken notes on the spot. The same paper carries a note of the Magistrates Court hearing that followed. The hearing was before: Francis Wright of Osmaston Manor; his son John; Capt Frederick Holland RN of Ashbourne Hall; Capt Goodwin Johnson RN; Peter Bainbrigg-le-Hunt and a Mr Cox of Brailsford. A collection was made which raised £60, enough for the defendants to brief counsel. A list of those prosecuted is given under Appendix C. Mr O'Brien and Mr Chambers (of Sheffield) appeared on behalf of the defendants. The hearing was in St John's Hall, Ashbourne. Mr Brittlebank was charged with playing football to the annoyance of the passengers and not for causing an obstruction. It appears two balls were turned up during the course of play.

The second defendant heard was George Tomlinson, against a complaint brought by Supt Corbishley, who had been requested by the magistrates to make the complaint if the game was played subsequent to the notices being issued. The request had been made to him by Mr F Wright, Mr Goodwin Johnson and Capt Holland. It appears that Corbishley was entitled to half of any penalties laid down and had made complaints previously, under the Highways Act, but not at Ashbourne, although he had been in the town for ten years. The game had been played in each of those ten years.

Mr O'Brien for the defence claimed that the magistrates could not issue a summons until a complaint had been made. He complained that it was a breach of natural justice for the magistrates to direct a man to complain of footballers and then for the same magistrates to issue the summons. The case against Mr George Woolley was then brought by Sgt Jolliffe, but the defence argued that Jolliffe hadn't been annoyed by his own admission.

The Highways Act 1835, s.72 clearly stated that any person who shall do certain things 'or shall play at foot-ball or any other game on any part of the said highway, to the annoyance of any passenger or passengers shall be liable ...'. Woolley had been seen playing the game when it had turned into St John Street having left the Market Place. Despite the oration of Mr O'Brien, the bench retired to make their decision and upon returning fined Mr Brittlebank, Mr Tomlinson and Mr Woolley forty shillings each and costs and in default with three months imprisonment.

Four further defendants were then called, despite a request that the rest of the hearings be held pending an appeal on the first case to the Queen's Bench. The magistrates declined this. During the next case, against Robert Dawson, PC Walker stated that the second ball had been thrown up by Mrs Woolley. It also transpired that, prior to the game being started, it was usual to remove the public lamps to prevent damage. This had not happened in 1860 and not one had been cracked or damaged. George Woolley does not appear to have been part of Mrs Woolley's immediate family. The latter, as Elizabeth Barnes, married William Woolley, a draper, in 1841, but she was widowed in 1851. She had a son, Frederick Charles Woolley who was born in 1842. He married Elizabeth Lamb and died in 1874. Maybe George (who was also a draper) was one of William's family. Perhaps Frederick was in the crowd as his mother started the game.

Mr Chambers, acting on behalf of Dawson made the interesting point that despite the *Highways Act* being passed twenty five years previously, no case had been brought before in the town. The chairman then made the point that their 'notice' had in fact been issued a year earlier as well. During a heated exchange with the bench, it was repeatedly stated that the latter did not wish to stop the game – only prevent it from being played in the streets.

Dawson was fined forty shillings and he advised the Court that 'I'll have forty shillings worth of skilly galee in Derby goal'. The magistrates were mindful to dismiss the other cases, but Mr Brittlebank asked for the costs, whereupon, it was decided to hear the case against Charles Hudson Hall, one of the surveyors, for whom Mr Brittlebank as a town solicitor appeared.

Sgt Jolliffe said he saw Hall in the hug after Mrs Woolley's ball had been thrown up. He had not been seen to kick the ball. There then followed an interesting exchange between Brittlebank and Supt Corbishley. Apparently, he had previously taken a ball from the Grammar School boys and was summoned to appear before Derby County Court to give the ball back. This must be a reference to the boy's game and the ball was filled with 'shavings', which would distinguish it from any other football game. Perhaps this matter was settled out of court for no report of it has been located. Finally Mr Brinsley, also a town surveyor, was called and he claimed that he and Mr Hall were not playing, only trying to push the hug out of the way. However, Hall was also fined forty shillings, the maximum penalty, plus costs. The remaining summonses were then withdrawn. The case had taken nearly five hours.

The case before the Ashbourne Bench was well reported, with a lot of the dialogue transcribed. However, it did not include another element of the case which was reported by the *Derbyshire Advertiser*, quoted in *Lloyd's Newspaper* of 08/03/1860 and recalled in the *Ashbourne News* of 23/02/1928.

Part of the case was reported as follows:

"Mr Brittlebank appealed to the Chairman (F Wright) whether the witness was not bound to answer the question.

The Chairman (to witness): Oh answer the question if you like but I really did not hear what it was.

Mr Brittlebank said the Chairman was bound to attend to the cross-examination of the witnesses and indignantly protested against the cavalier treatment which the Chairman's answer to his appeal implied.

The Chairman: We cannot waste our time in this way. Our services are given to the public. You are paid for yours."

Francis Wright must have regretted that astonishing outburst. *Lloyds Newspaper* reported "The above is about as fine a specimen of the country unpaid magistrate as we have met with for a long time. First of all the chairman (who certainly by his own confession does 'waste his time' by sitting on the Bench) does not attend to the case, and upon having his ears very properly pulled for his neglect of duty by the solicitor engaged for the defence, he attempts to justify it by saying 'that his services are GIVEN to the public' – things given for nothing are generally said to be worth nothing and we should say Mr Wright's 'services' took a very prominent lead amongst the worthless instances. He begins by showing that he is incompetent and ends by providing that he can be insulting."

Lloyd's continued "It was an innocent and healthy amusement that had lasted for upwards of twelve centuries, surely there was no harm in allowing the ball to roll merrily on for a few more years."

The ball thrown up by Mrs Woolley remains an enigma. Traditionally, she is reputed to have smuggled the ball into the Market Place hidden under her skirt and thrown it out of an upstairs window into the crowd. The report of the Court case makes it clear that she actually did turn up the ball – in this case – 'throw' being a more appropriate expression than 'turn'! Mr Tom Webster wrote to the paper (ANT 12/03/1981) to state that the lady who turned up the ball in the Market Place was his Great Aunt. She had done so out of an upstairs window of a grocer's shop called Mellor's (now the Haig Bar of Ashbourne Ex-Servicemen's Club). He also stated however, that the year was 1878, which is not accurate unless she did it twice. Some local people are of the belief that the ball was thrown out of a window at Spencer's Café.

An interesting aside was reported later (DM 23/03/1860) when an action was brought against Mr Brittlebank by Mr C J Welch, also a solicitor, who was clerk to the Ashbourne magistrates. Welch was claiming assault and his case was proved, with Brittlebank being fined £20. Unfortunately, the name of the clerk during the football hearing was not stated. Was Brittlebank bearing a grudge after the hearing?

It was later agreed that Mr Tomlinson and Mr Woolley would appeal to the Court of Queen's Bench. The appeals were heard on 16/11/1860 and reported (DM 21/11/1860) under the hearing of *Woolley v Corbishley*. The case turned on whether PC Jolliffe was a passenger and that annoyance had not been proved. The magistrates had additionally felt that the drivers of two carts, which tried to pass the hug, had also been obstructed (although the drivers do not appear to have been called to the Ashbourne Court). The Judges decided that as the carts had been obstructed and the drivers had had difficulty controlling the horses, the magistrates were right in assuming that the drivers were annoyed. The appeal was therefore dismissed. A further appeal, *Tomlinson v Corbishley* was covered by the same judgement.

A short report of the Court's decision survives in a hand written volume of cases deposited at the Public Records Office (Papers KB 21/72). It is dated 14/11/1860 and is quoted in full below. The decision was repeated for the judgement in the second case of *George Withnall Tomlinson v James Corbishley*.

George Woolley Appellent and James Corbishley Respondent
"By the Court, Upon hearing Counsel on both sides, It is ordered that the Judgement or determination of Francis Wright, P Bainbrigge Le Hunt, J Godwin Johnson and Frederick Holland, four of Her Majesty's Justices of the Peace in and for the County of Derby Convicting the Appellant of playing at a certain Game called Football on a certain Highway to the annoyance of passengers thereon, contary to the Statute of the 5th and 6th William 4th Cap 50 sec 72, in respect of which this case has been stated, be affirmed with costs to be paid by the Appellant to the Respondent or his Attorney, such costs if necessary to be taxed by the Coroner and Attorney of this Court. Mr O'Brien for the Appellants. The Honourable George Denman for the Respondent."

Research by George Shaw reveals that G W Tomlinson had a law firm in St John Street. His father was an Attorney in Church Street. This is particularly interesting as it shows that the first three cases heard by the magistrates in 1860 were against solicitors (Mr Brittlebank and Mr Tomlinson) and a draper (George Woolley). A glance at the list of defendants (see p211) clearly indicates that the game was not just being played by working class players. Two were described as 'gentlemen' and there was a vet, various shopkeepers and a builder.

1861

James Corbishley had been appointed a paid constable (possibly the first one in Ashbourne) by the local Bench in 1850. The reason apparently was that Ashbourne had 14 fairs a year and this created the need for someone permanent. There was already a resident keeper of the lock-up whose name was Field. (AT 31/8/1934)

The issue of the 1860 summonses made the townspeople more determined than ever and the following year fresh summonses were issued. It was reported extensively (DM 06/03/1861). The summonses against players of the 1861 game produced a less excited atmosphere than the previous year. The first hearing was against George Yeomans 'on the information and complaint of James Corbishley'. Again, the charge was one of annoyance to passengers on the highway. Yeomans pleaded not guilty, whereupon Francis Wright (Chairman of the Bench) observed that even if it was not the desire of the Bench to be unmerciful, it had to uphold the law. He hoped that the defendants would pledge to stop playing the game in the streets. He had clearly hoped for 'guilty' pleas.

It was Yeomans who had entered the Market Place with the ball. Supt Corbishley advised him that his name would be taken if he threw it up in the Market Place. Yeomans replied, pointing at the Town Hall clock, that he intended to do so at 2.00pm. He did just that from the Bull Ring and play progressed down to St John Street. Yeomans apparently was drunk when he appeared in the Court. He said, 'I did not play'. His attorney, Mr Brittlebank retorted 'If you open your mouth again I shall retire from the case'. 'I shall throw it up next year', Yeomans responded, beligerently. Mr Corbishley said that the case against Yeomans was that a horse was coming up the Market Place with a pair of head panniers and the rider had to turn off the road and gallop across the Market Place 'out of the way of the mob'. Yeomans was fined forty shillings and costs (9/6d) which Brittlebank paid on his behalf. All the remaining cases were heard and the cases wound up with Mr Wright commenting upon the many anonymous letters he had received, which several people in Court deplored. It does appear that Mr Wright tried to be lenient with those pleading guilty. He had his job to do and the law was clear.

The players had their job to do too: the game had to be preserved and they were clearly determined to ensure it did. The essential difference between Ashbourne and Derby is that the game could be played outside the main streets and the authorities could reach an accommodation with the town given goodwill. That goodwill (and common sense, under the circumstances) was not found until after summonses had been served for a third year running in 1862. George Yeomans would be pleased to know that his surname is still carried in the hug today.

Details of the fines in 1861 are also given in Appendix C. In addition to detail of the court case, the 1861 game was also reported. (DM 20/02/1861) The Tuesday ball was thrown up at 2.00pm in the Market Place, with the shops closed as usual. A large blue flag was flown from an adjacent property bearing the words (in gold letters) 'Britons never shall be slaves'. There was 'an extra posse of policemen' present. The ball was quickly kicked out of the Market Place into St John Street, heading for Sandy Lane. The police took down the names of those playing en route. There was much hard play in The Park but eventually, despite thin ice on the Fish Pond, a player waded across and gave the ball to an Up'ards player waiting on the other side. He ran off with it, but was stopped by a Down'ard man before he had run many hundred yards. The ball was eventually goaled at Sturston Mill a little before dusk. In the evening, the Ashbourne Brass Band played in the Market Place and later still, a dance was held, the scene being illuminated with numerous candles – presumably because the town lamps had not been replaced.

On the Wednesday an even larger crowd was present. There are two reports in the *Derby Mercury*. The more detailed account states that the ball left the Market Place at a rapid rate and was goaled at Clifton in about half an hour. (The other report says it was kept longer in the town and was eventually goaled at Clifton). The first report seems more accurate, being more detailed. This then states that a second ball was turned up at 3.00pm in the Market Place and was quickly heading for Clifton again. The play towards Clifton ended when the ball was intercepted by an Up'ards man who ran off with it. Making a circuitous route to Sturston, it was goaled at about 8.00pm. The band of the Rifle Corp afterwards assembled in the Market Place and dancing kept up until a late hour. The report considered less reliable mentions dancing on the Tuesday and says the Wednesday evening was quiet. The Brass Band/Rifle Corp was the Volunteer Corp band, which was reorganised (practically restarted) in May 1892. This band still exists today as the Ashbourne Town Band.

On 6 March 1861, Ashbourne Hall was sold following the death of Capt. Holland. Together with 92 acres of land, it fetched £17,850. It appears that this was when it was sold to Mr Frank. After his death, his wife continued to live there until 1898. In 1862, a Mr Day painted the Shrovetide painting of players in the Market Place. When finished, it was offered for sale but failed to find a buyer. It was later raffled off after photographs had been reproduced of it and those sold.

1862

The 1928 *Ashbourne News* article (*ibid*) states that in 1862 the police were present when the ball was thrown up in the Market Place. This was confirmed (DM 12/03/1862), although the latter reported that there was little disposition shown to play the game in the streets. Many, however, joined in as the ball cleared the town. It is clear that over 60 people had their names taken for playing the game from the Market Place and summonses were issued for a hearing on 15 March 1862, with Mr Brittlebank acting for the defendants.

Five principal members of the community offered to pay the fines and use their influence to prevent a breach of the law in future. They were Messrs Bradley, Lister, Whittam, Woolley and Hall. The Bench Chairman (Mr Wright) accepted the proposal and said that the magistrates did not wish to suppress the game. 'Anywhere on the outskirts of the town they might play the game', he said. The Bench hoped that all present would not offend again and ordered that only the expenses would be asked for, ie no fines would be handed down. The five defendants signed an undertaking not to play the game other than in the outskirts of the town. It read as follows:

"Magistrates Room Ashbourne March 15th 1862. We, the undersigned, having been summoned for a breach of the law by playing the game of football in the streets of Ashbourne, do hereby engage and bind ourselves, severally, not to offend in like manner for the future, and promise that we will not join in playing any game of football that may or shall be turned up in any other place than the outskirts of this or any other town, and also that we will severally use our best endeavours to discourage others from again offending in like manner as we have done." It was quoted in the paper. (AN 14/02/1891)

Eaton's *History of the Beresford Family, part 3* includes this sketch by Mr Beresford Wright: "It had been the custom out of mind for Compton and Ashbourne to play an annual match of football, the goals being the church gates at one end and I think Ashbourne Hall gates at the other. The game was played in very rough fashion and many injuries were the result, besides the public being driven out of the main streets and windows having to be shuttered up. Frequently the ball was passed along the meadows, crossing and recrossing the dividing stream but no amount of ducking was sufficient to damp the ardour of the combatants. The magistrates at last decided to stop the game in the town and permission was obtained to play it in Ashbourne Park. Going down from Osmaston however, on the day of the match, my father found a furious conflict going on along the forbidden street. Riding at once into their midst with 'throw me up the ball, lads' the ball was at once pitched to him in half surprise. 'Follow me boys' and away he rode to the border of The Park, where he threw it over the wall."

This must relate to 1862. In 1861 the ball was played all the way to The Park and in 1863 it wasn't played in the streets. Presumably his father was Francis Wright who chaired the Bench and was criticised for his comments during the 1860 hearing. Playing in the streets was only forbidden after the 1860 games had been played, so it had to be after then. The reference to playing the game between the gates of the hall and church is interesting. Prior to the mills being chosen as goals, the latter changed (possibly annually). It is therefore quite possible for the two sets of gates to have been used. However, the Rev Tomlinson stated that his grandfather had told him that the change to the two mills was close to the end of the eighteenth century.

It would seem likely that the writer was referring to how the game used to be played or was simply in error rather than trying to infer that that was the practice in the 1860s.

1863-64

The following year, a hand bill was widely circulated by the five men, listed above, reminding the public of the pledge they had signed in Court the previous year. They urged the townspeople not to throw up a ball in the streets on the following two days. They need not have worried. On Shrove Tuesday, 1863, the ball was turned up on Shaw Croft for the first time. No attempt was made to start it from the Bull Ring or to play the game through the streets on either day. (DM 25/02/1863) Mr R H Frank, of Ashbourne Hall gave a pledge that he would give permission to the players to use The Park and that the gate in Sandy Lane would be left open and every facility given to the players. (AN 28/02/1891) This facility survived until 1879 when The Park was closed against the players. Shaw Croft was made available to the players by Mr Wallis, of the Green Man Hotel. He had been the landlord of the Green Man since at least 1840.

However, there does appear to have been a backlash against the change. In 1864 it was reported (DM 17/02/1864) that the game was 'played in a more friendly spirit than it had been for several years'. In terms of Ashbourne's game, this signals more passive play, although the report says the game was 'ably contested'. By 1867 (DM 13/03/1867) there 'was a very small sprinkling of those tradesmen who were seen to take part in the play on former occasions'. None the less, play had continued, and this is confirmed in the 1872 Court hearing (see below). It survived therefore, the cattle plague that was widespread across the nation in 1866. The first reported case in the area was at Mr George Gough's farm at Mappleton. (DM 14/02/1866) This was quickly followed by other cases in the district, with several at Hartington, where it started at the Charles Cotton Hotel. Incidentally, the keenness displayed by Supt Corbishley in the 1861 court case had lost none of its edge. In 1867 (DM 27/02/1867) Mr C T F Simpson, a photographer, was summonsed for taking a likeness in his travelling van at Clifton on the Lord's Day. He was fined five shillings, plus costs!

In 1868, parts of the townships of Clifton and Compton plus parts of Sturston, Offcote and Underwood were merged within the district of Ashbourne. (DM 03/06/1868)

Play in the 1870s

In 1870 the inhabitants of Ashbourne turned out in greater strength than usual. On Tuesday the ball was turned up on Shaw Croft at 2.00pm. It was slowly fought up through The Park to the meadows beyond, where a severe struggle took place. The Down'ards at length succeeded in turning the ball and after a hard fought game the ball was goaled at Clifton Mill at about 4.30pm. On Wednesday, the play was more exciting than the previous day, but was soon played into the town. The shops were all closed, and the inhabitants turned out *en masse* to witness the game. Both sides were equally matched and for a long time it was doubtful which would be successful. At length, after slow but fierce play, the ball was kicked up the Market Place, along Ashbourne Green and finally goaled at Sturston Mill thus reversing the victory of the previous day (DM 09/03/1870). It does not appear that a second ball was thrown up on the Tuesday, so perhaps the time reported was a little inaccurate.

In 1871 it was stated (DM 01/03/1871) 'until the last year or two, the game had become almost a thing of the past'. The report confirmed that the balls had been turned up on Shaw Croft since the court case before the Queen's Bench. This year however, 'the old custom has been kept up with more vigour than has been the case for many years'. On the Tuesday, the game was fiercely contested, especially in the Fish Pond, through which it was kicked several times. The Up'ards succeeded in getting the ball three-quarters of the way to Sturston, when the ball came to pieces. It was after 5.00pm and no further ball was thrown up – the game being declared drawn. On the Wednesday, there were 300 to 400 on each side and the ball was kicked for four hours, backwards and forwards within a space of four or five acres. About 6.00pm it was kicked over a wall and a man named Whieldon ran away with it, goaling the ball at Sturston Mill.

The following year, 1872, saw the Tuesday ball goaled at Sturston Mill. However, the Wednesday game showed that Ashbourne tenacity was exerting itself once more. The first ball went to Clifton with a second ball being turned up at about 4.00pm. (DM 28/02/1872) There was subsequently a lot of water play and when the ball was thrown out, it was caught by an Up'ard – Mr H Holyoak. He went up one of the yards, evading the police who were stationed to prevent the play going up the yards and into the streets. The runner was stopped in the centre of the town by a Down'ard. A hug seems to have formed, with police 'interference' to seize the ball delaying movement out of the town. Down Church Street the game progressed, the ball eventually being goaled at Clifton. The police had been taking down the names of the players, with some sixty in all being noted, including some of the most respected inhabitants of the town.

The magistrates summoned ten of the offenders – Mr J S Whitham, and Messrs Wise, G Marple, H Holyoak, John Miers, Fred Miers, Alfred Hall, S Bridden, G Wildsmith and Mr James Sellers. The magistrates were Sir William Fitzherbert and John Wright. Mr Brittlebank appeared for the defendents; Supt Whieldon appearing for the prosecution. The game reached the town streets at about 4.30pm. The ball was cut and another thrown up. Supt Whieldon had ten policemen with him. He said he tried to seize the ball to take it out of the town, but was unsuccessful. Brittlebank said that the game had been kept successfully out of the streets for twelve years. In reality, it was only eleven. He contended that there was no intention to play the game in the streets and that the summonses should be withdrawn. In view of this, Mr Whitham was fined £1 and costs of ten shillings. Although it was Mr Holyoak who ran the ball into the town, it could not be proved and therefore the case against him was dismissed. In the remaining eight cases, the defendants were fined ten shillings with ten shillings costs.

On 26 February 1873, Francis Wright died of kidney failure. A memorial was erected to him in the Market Place. It states that it was 'erected as a record of the valuable services rendered by him to this town and neighbourhood'. This is rather strange. It was only just over a decade since he was fining the cream of Ashbourne for doing what it liked best. Moreover he had caused a schism with the Church of England which resulted in him building St John's Church. This was because the vicar refused to give him a pew for his exclusive use. Even to this day, no one knows who owns this monument. It is ironic that it was built next to the site of the bull ring. He was the ancestor of the Duchess of York. In 1999, the monument was restored by the Derbyshire Dales District Council at a cost reportedly above £2,600.

The *Derby Mercury* did not report the game during 1873 to 1875 (and again in 1877). In 1876, however, the ball was turned up on Shaw Croft, with the Up'ards having the initial advantage, with a keen contest in the Fish Pond. The Down'ards recovered lost ground, bringing the ball back to the Vicar's Close, where play lasted for two hours. The ball eventually went upriver, contested the whole way, to be goaled at Sturston. On the Wednesday, it took the Down'ards three hours to bring the ball to the Vicar's Close via the Paddock. However, by the goods station, the ball was cut and came to pieces. Play continued with another ball and resulted in a goal at Clifton. The Rev Tomlinson's reminiscences, see below, include a note that in 1877, the Up'ards waded all the way upriver to goal for the first time.

Little was reported on the game in the 1870s although the incidents of 1878 received more than enough coverage. The reports that appeared in the press for that year are recorded in the next chapter. However, some anecdotal evidence does survive. Ironically it was for one of two years which were not reported at the time. Mr J Millington wrote to the local paper (AN 27/3/1914) from West Wickham in Kent. He stated that:

"the game has not altered a bit since 1873 and 1874; those were the years we used to watch it and I see there are still some familiar names, the descendants, I suppose, of those we used to watch — Wibberley, Sowter and Burton. The weather is more kind to them than it used to be. There was plenty of snow and ice at the time I refer to and I remember a man called Bratby or Joe Bradley running with the ball across the Park pond on the ice. He was a light man, others tried to follow him and were let in. Another year there were three (a butcher in his smock being one) who broke the thin ice and swam across. We were much more hardy then."

The butcher sounds like William Coxon who turned up at the 1891 Court hearing in his smock. This letter also confirms that the Park was still open to the players at this date.

Local Shrovetide enthusiast Mr Tom Webster has a long-held assertion that his great grandmother turned up the ball by throwing it out of a window in the Market Place in 1878. However, see comments under the Reports for 1993.

Difficult Times   5

In 1878 it was reported that 'the rough element has predominated' in recent years. On the Tuesday, the ball was played into the Paddock where it was fought for until dark, when it was cut up 'and the case was in some manner conveyed to the upward goal'. By this time a large number of players were worse for drink and fighting 'became the order of the night'.

On the Wednesday, the ball was turned up but barely six players were near it and it was rapidly passed from hand to hand 'by men evidently posted upon purpose' and it was soon taken without opposition to Sturston. More fighting then broke out. 'Men and women vied with each other in fighting in a brutal manner. As soon as the police stopped one fight another was commenced'. A second ball was turned up at 3.00pm and the Down'ards gradually worked it to Clifton – or rather those of them not helplessly drunk. It was also reported that in the evening 'disgraceful fighting was continued in the town and it was all the police could do to prevent a further loss of life. We are heartily glad to know that some steps are likely to be taken to put a stop for the future to such scenes'. (DM 13/03/1878)

The *Staffordshire Advertiser* carried a graphic account of the game with all its drunkenness and fighting portrayed to the full – perhaps even a little over the top. However, there can be no doubt that this was the games lowest moment. There were even scenes (i.e. more than one instance) of women fighting each other in the streets. The article concluded that 'Shrove Tuesday and Ash Wednesday in Ashbourne will be a bye-word and a disgrace to the whole surrounding country.'

Two days later, Frank Pentland, T Hodgkinson, Joseph Chell, Arthur Chell and others were charged before the magistrates of being drunk and assaulting the police during the game. On the bench was R H Frank. Supt Whieldon said he never saw such disgraceful scenes of riot and fighting. The police had to call in some of the tradesmen to assist in quelling the riotous proceedings. In each case heavy fines were inflicted.

The editorial column of the *Derby Mercury* stated ' it is gratifying to us to receive the assurance that this unmannerly custom which has so long been perversely persisted in by some and indulgently tolerated by others – in spite of the better judgement of all – has been observed for the last time, and by common consent will in future be forever abandoned.' The editor, incidentally, had also been asked to make it clear that Barker (who was drowned) was sober and jumped into the mill pool knowing its depth (being an employee there). There are further comments on the drowning which confirm the report quoted below by the Revd. Tomlinson, who witnessed it. The editorial finally ends with an intriguing reference to the French officers held prisoners in the town finding the game astonishing!

The following week it was reported that there was a general wish that the game be discontinued. In actual, fact a notice calling for the discontinuance of the game had been signed by 232 people. More importantly, a form of public notice was also signed by most of the owners and occupiers of the land upon which the game was usually played. It signified that if necesssary, the law of trespass will be put into force 'in order to carry out the almost universal desire that this peculiar and objectionable custom should be abolished'. (DM 20/03/1878)

During the Ash Wednesday game, on 6th March a nineteen year old youth was drowned at Clifton Mill. He was James William Barker, a carter employed by Samuel Taylor, the Clifton miller. It was late in the afternoon and the ball had been brought all the way to Clifton down the river. Two men wading downstream approached the mill, one with the ball under his arm, the other helping his companion along. The men found themselves in deep water and had to swim. Jimmy Harrison who had the ball got within a few yards of the goal, when he was met by a strong gust of wind. He fought against it a few moments, without making any headway. Getting exhausted, the ball slipped from him and his head went underwater. If he had not been promptly rescued there would have been two drowned that day. (DM 20/03/1878) It was at this point that Barker jumped into the mill pond to obtain the ball which was floating free. The inquest, at the Cock Inn in Clifton, (DM 13/03/1878) heard that Barker had been advised to keep out of the water 'as the mud would be too much for him'. 'I know all about it', was his reply. There was some seven feet of mud and water in the mill pond and after it was realised he was missing, he was found lying face down in eighteen inches of mud. A verdict of accidental death was returned. Barker was lifted out within fifteen or so minutes, so the pool must have been emptied straight away.

In 1909, the *Ashbourne News* carried reminiscences of the game by the Rev J F Tomlinson. He was present when the tragedy occurred and his experiences still makes a graphic record of the event (AN 26/02/1909):

"On the 'Down'ards' side the players' names were not quite so familiar to me. No one, however, could mistake or help noticing Jimmy Harrison. He was always hard at it in the thick of the fight. He played a particularly powerful game in the water, and very seldom got the worst of it there. I consider he was at that period the finest water player (within his depth) on either side. He was a very fair and good-tempered player too, always playing the ball in preference to the man. Hence you seldom saw Jimmy quarrelling. It was he, if memory serves me rightly, who took the ball all the way down the river to Clifton Mill dam, in 1878, on the occasion when a young fellow was unfortunately drowned close to the mill. Jimmy's own football career came very near to being closed at that time, for when within a dozen yards of the mill wheel and while still carrying the ball, he collapsed, fell over helplessly out of his depth in the dam, and would certainly have found a watery grave had not Mr Joseph Osborne, who was a very fine swimmer, instantly and without waiting to divest himself of any clothing, dived in from the bank, and with great difficulty and no little danger brought his bulky and senseless frame to land. For this meritorious action Mr Osborne was afterwards awarded the Bronze Medal of the Royal Humane Society.

Meanwhile the one dark tragedy associated with the ancient game had been taking place. The writer at the moment was standing on the sloping north bank within a few feet of the tragic spot. A young man (whose name it afterwards transpired was Barker) was seen to take a running jump feet first into the water from the south bank, but unfortunately he missed his grab at the ball. The latter being sent by the splash nearer to the north side, five others of different sides were the very next instant struggling and fighting for possession. In the confusion of this kaleidoscopic tussle it was almost impossible to be certain, but I, along with several others near me, had a horrible suspicion that the number visible in the water was one less than had entered it. Moreover, I have a distinct recollection (it is like a nightmare to me still) of a momentary vision of hands held up, as in distress, wistfully towards the surface of the water. But, at the time, the splashing and confusion were such that it was impossible to judge whether those hands did not belong to one of those struggling on the surface. Mr Osborne went in again and dived several times, also a grocer's assistant named Jackson, but neither could find any trace of the missing man. Afterwards, however, when the water had been let off, and Barker's body was found with feet and hands stuck fast deep in the mud, it was impossible for me to dissociate those hands, so wistfully held up, and groping as it were for help, from the corpse which was found beneath the very spot where I had seen them."

It is most likely that this same Mr Osborne founded the local paper in 1891. His description – 'a good swimmer' – fits with the fact that Joseph Osborne, the paper's founder, was shipwrecked on board the *Underlay* bound for Australia, off the Isle of Wight. He made the shore 'being a good swimmer' (*London Illustrated News*).

Shrovetide Festivities

Shrovetide was traditionally a period of enjoyment before the austerity of Lent. The playing of football was an example of this but it was not the only way Ashbourne marked the festivity.

Bulls were baited in the Market Place on Shrove Tuesday (AN 10/12/1920) and the 1862 painting of the players shows them standing by the bull ring, the traditional place for turning up the ball. Additionally, the Pancake Bell was rung at Midday at St Oswald's Church. The little bell used for this purpose may still be seen below the steeple. Sir W FitzHerbert referred to Ashbourne bull baiting while sitting on the Bench to hear prosecutions of Shrovetide footballers in 1880. He said that the practice was carried on 'in Ashbourne longer than in any other town'. Luke Faulkner (seen holding the ball in the 1862 painting) allegedly used to take bulls to Bakewell for baiting and presumably elsewhere as well.

After the 1861 game, which ended just before dusk, the Ashbourne Brass Band played in the Market Place and a dance was held, illuminated with many candles. The usual illumination was by gas light but the mantles had been removed before the game. What a splendid sight this must have presented, despite the cold weather which must have attended it. During the temperance era, a Shrovetide temperance meeting was held annually but it is not likely to have worried the town's landlords. The meeting took the form of a free concert given by the Misses Clough of Rochdale for the Womens' Total Abstinence Union. Meetings were held in 1900 and for several years later. An unusual custom was the selling of oranges and lemons at Shrovetide. Betty Blore a vendor of nuts and oranges appears in the 1862 painting. As late as 1909, someone was following the hug selling oranges.

1879

Despite the apparent determination to terminate the custom, it was clear that players were intending to play the game in 1879. Mr R H Frank hired Shaw Croft for the week to prevent the ball being turned up there. The Park was also closed to the players and it is clear that other landowners were of a similar mind. Frank had notices posted along the boundary of the Park. They made it clear that a consequence of trespass could be imprisonment without the option of a fine. On Shrove Tuesday, there were some fifty to sixty policemen in the town, and Shaw Croft was being patrolled by 'a strong body of police'. At 2.00pm over a dozen men jumped across the brook (from one of the yards) with the ball and attempted to throw it up. The person with the ball was a licensed victualler. The men were surrounded by the police who took the ball, which was then cut to pieces by one of them. The players were ordered out of the Croft but would not go and were therefore ejected by the policemen after having their names taken.

A short time later, another ball was turned up at the top of Compton and played in the direction of Clifton. Some good play took place near the railway station and eventually the ball was goaled at Clifton. The police seemed hesitant as to what to do. About 4.00pm a third ball was thrown up on Compton Bridge. It was played into the Market Place, along St John Street and up Hall Lane, down Church Street and reached the top of Compton again. The police during all this time were in another part of the town. After a ball had been played in a field on the Old Hill for a considerable time, the police rejoined the crowd and on some slight provocation, drew their staves and 'knocked people about a good deal'. One man named Atterbury, received a 'fearful gash on the head', and Dr Mclean had to be sent for. The large force of police were billeted in several pubs for the night ready for the next day. The police version of events is given below.

On the Wednesday, as the ball could not be turned up on Shaw Croft, a large body of the police were present in the Market Place. A ball was thrown up at 2.00pm and the police immediately rushed out of the Market Hall (now the Town Hall) with their staves drawn and in use pretty freely once more. At this juncture Capt Parry, who had arrived in the town during the morning rode onto the scene and gave some advice which was received with loud cheers. Two bystanders were then seized by the police and marched to the hall. The ball was also seized by the police. However, this was a dummy ball. In fact, much later, it was reported that the ball was cut up and found to be full of horse dung! (AN 03/03/1938)

The Market Hall contained the Literary Institute and Library, Assembly rooms, armoury of the Dove Valley Rifle Corp and Masonic Lodge (*Black's Guide to Derbyshire, 1872*).

In the meantime, another ball had gone down the Butchery and was played down Mayfield Road and into some fields. Capt Parry (the Chief Constable) rode to the players who picked up the ball and surrounded him. He told them not to play on the highway or trespass on the land of those who had signed the requisition the year before. Play then resumed and the ball was eventually goaled at Clifton. It was reported that it was the intervention of Capt Parry, who held the respect of the crowd, which prevented a serious breach of the peace. The above report was carried against a letter which independently claimed that the police had been stoned. The letter also claimed that some of the signatures to the notice of 1878 had clearly had second thoughts. (DM 05/03/1879) The drunks, the street players and the trespassers on Shaw Croft all had a moment of reckoning a few days later before Ashbourne Petty Sessions, which included R H Frank – hardly an example of the execution of natural justice. Eleven men were prosecuted for cases involving drunkenness. The first case was against Luke Faulkner. He was charged with an assault on Inspector Aaron Hollingworth (who retired as Superintendent in 1902). The bench heard that on the Tuesday some 300 – 400 people were playing football at the top of Compton. The ball was seized by the police and the crowd surrounded them, throwing large stones at them, some of which were produced in evidence.

Several policemen were struck and one was knocked down and kicked. Mr Hollingworth went to his assistance, when the defendant came up to him in a drunken state, using very bad language. He struck Mr Hollingworth in the chest twice, before being arrested. The crowd closed in and laid hold of the prisoner, and the officer was kicked and struck, with stones flying about. He called to the police to draw their staves and keep the crowd back. They did so as the defendant was taken off to the lock-up. The bench sent him down for two months with hard labour. By the time Mr Hollingworth retired in 1902 the game's future had been assured. He would no doubt have been pleased that his great grandson goaled the ball on Ash Wednesday 1983.

Samuel Bridden was charged with being drunk in the street and fined ten shillings with costs. James Harrison was charged with being drunk and disorderly in the Market Place. Harrison had struck PC Hawkins several times saying 'You stopped us yesterday, we won't let you stop us today'. He was fined £2 and costs or two months imprisonment. He was lucky to be alive, following the incident the year before at Clifton Mill pool. George Faulkner of the Roebuck beer-house was convicted of being drunk and assaulting the police on Shrove Tuesday in Compton. He had been taken home by a woman but rushed out when his son, Luke, (see above) was being taken into custody, and seized Pc Knowles by the throat. The latter drew his staff and hit Faulkner on the head. He appeared in court with a plaster on it! He was fined £1 and costs. Others fined were: James Atterbury, Edward Tunnicliffe, James Wibberley, Charles Sowter, Charles Woolley, John Gallimore and Joseph Chell (all for being drunk). Sam Wibberley's charge was dismissed. Some refused to pay and went to gaol in default.

A total of twenty-one people were prosecuted for playing football in the streets. Details are given in Appendix A. The third matter concerned the nineteen people whose names were taken for trespassing on Shaw Croft. The Clerk to the Court laid before the bench the list of names. Mr Bridden (one of the players and possibly S Bridden who was fined for drunkenness) appeared before the bench at the suggestion of Mr Frank. The men were let off with a warning, Bridden agreeing to advise the others that the bench viewed the trespass as a serious offence.

Public opinion seemed to be slowly turning in favour of the game. The more that effort was made to suppress it, the effect was to strengthen the resolve to ensure its survival. The game seemed to find supporters in unexpected places too. Capt Parry's efforts mentioned above were to carry the day in 1881 as well. Clearly there were people about whose efforts went unrecorded but helped perhaps inadvertently, to protect the game during this difficult time.

There was an interesting letter in the *Derby Mercury* (18/02/1880). It referred to the determination of people to stamp out the game and the many signatures to the requisition signed in 1878. Mr Alfred Hall – whose case at Court is noted below – had signed the requisition and in 1879 was present at a meeting which unanimously passed a resolution calling for the suppression of the game. It was the closure of Shaw Croft, which seemed to have caused many people to change camps. The letter referred to comment in the *Derbyshire Advertiser* which 'pandered to the passion of the hour'. Signatures of the 1878 requisition (or petition) were now 'encouraging and inciting the lowest elements of the population openly to break the law and defy the authorities'. It was in this kind of atmosphere that the 1880 game was played.

1880

It was reported (DM 18/02/1880) that a good deal of obstruction was caused in some of the streets, but there was not much playing in the town as the police kept the Shaw Croft clear. No attempt was made to play in The Park, where a notice was posted warning trespassers that they were liable to imprisonment without the option of a fine. A considerable number of policemen were present. At about 2.00pm, the ball was carried through the streets to the end of Compton Bridge. Several men entered the water and walked up the river to about level with the centre of the Shaw Croft, where the ball was thrown up in the water. It was played down the stream and into The Paddock. The ball was soon carried off and taken quickly to Clifton Mill where it was goaled.

Another ball was thrown up in the same manner, but instead of going down stream, it was carried upriver to Sandy Lane Bridge (later called Back Bridge). Several Up'ards carried the ball across the road and into The Park, accompanied by a great crowd of spectators, but none of them left the public footpath. Upon arriving at Mr Coxon's fields, where the men had permission to play, the game began in earnest. The language used by some of the spectators, especially by 'certain women, was vile in the extreme'.

On Ash Wednesday at 2.00pm, the attempt to walk upriver from Compton Bridge was blocked by the police and a struggle ensued. Brick ends and stones were thrown at the police, who then drew their staves and struck many people severely on the head, causing blood to flow. The bridge was then cleared of people by the police but the ball was taken downwards under the bridge. It appears to have been turned up under the bridge. Some very energetic play took place in the fields outside the town, below the church.

The following Saturday, ten people were brought before the magistrates on charges of either being drunk or assaulting the police. These included Charles Sowter 'who had received a smart crack on the head in the conflict', as was noted above. He was charged with hitting a county policeman with a 'three-quarter brick'. He was fined £1 and costs. The same hearing heard the football cases 'for playing football on the highway on Shrove Tuesday and Ash Wednesday'.

The bench was Sir W FitzHerbert Bart, Sir T P Heywood Bart, R H Goodwin, G B Kingdon, G M Dixon, A C Duncombe, S W Clowes and H C Okeover. R H Frank was present but did not sit on the bench. Mr Joseph Simpson of Mayfield stated that he wished to make a statement. A meeting, attended by seventy to eighty people had been held on 13 February 1880, the Friday after the games and day before the Court hearing. He was offering a possible solution to this type of hearing being held again. He and his brother owned some fields in the valley below Ashbourne. These would be offered to the public on the distinct understanding that the ball should not go into the town and played in the streets. He had mentioned this to Mr Frank and the latter had responded that a similar undertaking had been given in previous years and that had been broken. Mr Simpson was prepared to enter into a £100 bond to back the undertaking. A large number of summonses had been issued, but the number was not stated. It appears the number may have been ninety seven. (ANT 23/02/1928)

Sir W FitzHerbert commented on the fact that this type of case had been brought before (no news to anybody) and then interestingly, he said 'Ashbourne was a noted place for keeping up everything as long as they possibly could. Bull-baiting was carried on in Ashbourne longer than in any other town'. Before deciding upon the suggestion of Mr Simpson, it was decided to hear the case of Mr A Hall, who was represented by Mr Brittlebank. During the hearing of this, it was stated by Supt Whieldon that he was on duty and assisted on Shrove Tuesday by Supt Cruitt of Egginton district, with forty-eight men. These men had been brought to Ashbourne for the purpose of preventing the game from being played in the town and for protection of the Croft. Hall was asked by Whieldon to desist playing, while he was in the brook. Hall responded that 'I am the Local Board and this brook belongs to the Local Board'. Prior to the second ball being turned up, it had been carried about in the town by James Harrison.

Despite a comment from the Clerk to decide on Mr Simpson's suggestion, a case was then heard against Charles Coxon. Supt Whieldon commented that some 3,000 (sic) people were around Compton Bridge. Eventually, the Bench decided to dismiss the cases that related to the playing of football and take their guarantee for the future. However, costs would have to be paid. The cases would be supposed not guilty.

Mr Frank asked what guarantee would be given and Mr Simpson said he was willing to pay the £100 down, 'but he could not bind half the people present'. The Clerk then said that this should be done. The cases of trespass still remained before the Bench and Mr Simpson stated that his guarantee extended to The Park as well as the town. Mr Frank was willing to overlook the cases for trespass 'this time' (he had done it before in 1879) on the same terms as the other cases, but expecting the costs to be paid. Mr Simpson gave an undertaking to pay the expenses and so these cases were also dismissed. This was a remarkable intervention by a local mill owner. Mr Simpson owned the Mayfield cotton mill and lived at Sunnyside, Mayfield. After the game, a handbill was circulated in the town which is quoted in full:

"ASHBOURN FOOTBALL

1880

Men of Ashbourn, what are you going to do in this matter. It is quite time you put a stop to these disturbances that took place in this Town Tuesday and Wednesday. Why are the police brought into the Town? For the clear reason to irritate and compel a row. We know the police how they like to exceed their duty. Mr Weildon, after the Ball passed under the bridge, was heard to say, charge the people on the bridge, which they did, using their staffs pretty freely; this man it is known far and wide is quite unfit for the Office he holds. It is also known he is not quite sound in his head. But if the crowd had known how they would have been served they would have come armed, and then woe to any policeman who dared to have drawn his staff on property the police had no right on, (ie 4 feet from wall). Now Men of Ashbourn about the real disturber of the Peace. Who is he? A Gentleman. No. A Liverpool Tradesman, who has a share in the business still, having 200 acres of land, thinks he will rule Ashbourn with a rod of iron. Will you stand this? By whose right does he bring the police here to protect private property? Is it Law? the people do not want to play in the Street, but they will play over the Old Ground. Mr Fraks (sic) can leave Ashbourn, it will be no loss, but the old Game will & shall be played. You people of Ashbourn, if you let a man like Fraks ride you down you are not fit to bear the proud name of Englishmen.

AN ASHBOURN TRADESMAN"

One of the 1880 players wrote to Mr Hawksworth in 1934 and his letter was printed in the paper (AT 09/03/1934). It was from Mr R Yates of Meir. He was in his twentieth year in 1880 and came from Uttoxeter by train and then by bus to The Green Man Hotel. After lunch, he was:

"on Compton Bridge when the players came marching down, singing 'Rule Britannia'. I think the man who threw up the ball was Mr Hall – he had a green baize apron on.

The police from Derby stood in the Shaw Croft and anyone getting out of the water was soon collared by them. One policeman was pushed into the water and I can remember his helmet went sailing down the brook and several policemen had to get into the water to pull him out.

The Chief of the Police made a speech and told them that he was there to suppress the game, but someone let fly with a nice rounded clod and hit him straight in the mouth. It stopped him talking and the game went on. One big fat sergeant told me I was trespassing and he ran after me down the road until I hopped over some railings into the field. The players got back into the brook and under Compton Bridge they went.

I ran round to the front of the railway station. The ball was here some time until at last it went into the goods yard and me after it. I got it under some trucks and then I saw I had a clear run down to Clifton with it. The miller stood there if my memory serves me right and he hit the mill wheel three times and declared it a goal. He then came out and gave the ball up to be played again. I always understood that those who goaled the ball claimed it.

The ball was thrown up again on the bridge and I had not been playing long before I got a beautiful kick behind my thigh. It took me some time to walk to the station.

I used to know some of the old athletes, Harry Gettliffe, Sowters, Burtons, Charlie Purdy and the Browns, one of whom was a very good walker. I saw the name J Barker, who painted the ball, and if it is the same one I remember he once beat me in a mile handicap. The first mile race I won was on the Shaw Croft (1879). I won two mile races and was second in another at Ashbourne and was first in a two mile steeple chase at Clifton."

This sheds a little more light on the conflict with the police. Presumably it was Supt Whieldon who was struck in the mouth by the clod. This experience was no doubt behind the decision on the Wednesday for the police to draw their 'staves' when the brick ends and stones were thrown. Mr Yates confirms the report in the Derby Mercury that the police were from 'Derby' (ie Eggington district).

The Clifton steeplechases were run from Long Doles Farm and the course was to Mappleton.

1881

On 8 February 1881 there was a lot of flooding in the Peak District following a heavy fall of snow. In Dig Street, the river reached the Cock Inn. Compton was flooded and The Park, Shaw Croft and Paddock were sheets of water. A great deal of damage was done at Mr Simpson's cotton mills, where some 'fine machinery and valuable stock' was saturated. The railway bridge between Clifton Station and Mayfield Mill across the River Dove was carried away. The loss to Mr Simpson was several thousand pounds. At the old toll gate in Green Lane, Clifton, the water lay three to four feet deep in the road. At Woodeaves Mills, the top dam burst. Three days later there was another flood and terrific wind. The high breast wall adjoining Clifton Cottage (home of T H Smith) was brought down and there were many land-slips in the area. A man was drowned at Thorpe, near Coldwall Bridge.

A letter to the Derby Mercury (23/02/1881) states that the river in Ashbourne used to be some three feet deeper. It was suggested that the river be deepened under Compton Bridge, a comment which would no doubt have interested the Down'ards. It might have helped to prevent the flooding, but would not have done them much good. The Local Board decided to deepen the river bed from 'the bend below the School-house Bridge to the bottom end of the Bank Meadow', (Bank Croft). There was further flooding before the action was undertaken and at the beginning of March, Mr Simpson's temporary bridge was washed away. (DM 09/03/1881) The state of the river during the game is not recorded.

Despite Mr Hall having given his undertaking, associated with Mr Simpson's bond the previous year, he wrote to the Derbyshire Advertiser ignoring the settlement made in the court. He stated that 'it is intended to play the ancient game as usual, but that on no account will it be played on the northwardly side of the Henmore from Compton Bridge till it has reached the bounds of the Ashbourne Hall domain'. It was alleged (DM 23/02/1881) that although the letter bore Hall's signature, it had come from Mr Brittlebank.

This prompted an open letter from Mr Simpson dated 21/02/1881. (DM 02/03/1881) He stated that the promise made to the court was that there would be no play in the town, on the highway or on land on which leave to play had not been given. He called on Mr Hall to honour the promise. As permission had been obtained to play on the fields between the church and Clifton Mill, he suggested that the game should be played there. In this way, Mr Hall avoided 'placing me in a position which I should feel to be exceedingly humiliating.'

A meeting was held the next day at the Green Man and Blacks Head Royal Hotel (hereafter called the Green Man Hotel) to consider the position. It was chaired by a Mr Howell. A resolution was passed at the meeting:

"That the usual game of football be played on Shrove Tuesday and Ash Wednesday to the ancient goals of Sturston and Clifton, and that it be clearly understood that no playing take place in the town or the highway, or upon any land where permission to play has not been obtained." (AN 04/03/1927) Mr Wallis had agreed to be neutral so far as playing in Shaw Croft was concerned. A notice stating the resolution of the meeting was printed and circulated in the town. Mr Simpson was content with this and play was kept out of the streets until 1887 when summonses were again issued but no prosecutions handed down.

On Shrove Tuesday, at 2.00pm, the game began in Shaw Croft. It was emphasised that there must be no playing in the streets or The Park. Play in Sandy Lane was allowed and Capt Parry, the Chief Constable of Derbyshire, rode about on a white horse, ordering play to be suspended when necessary. This was greeted with cheers of approval. Play on the second day followed that of Tuesday. The ball would probably have been forced into The Park under Sandy Lane Bridge but for Capt Parry whose call of 'pick it up' was obeyed by the players. The ball was given to him and he rode off with it to a field near the Derby Road where the game continued. There was no breach of the peace and very little drunkenness. There was a small force of policemen in the town but they were not needed.

On the Tuesday, the ball was thrown up by Alfred Hall. It never went below the Paddock and eventually it was taken upwards, avoiding The Park, to be goaled at Sturston. On the Wednesday, the ball went downstream and was played for a long time in the fields below the church. The ball was eventually played into The Paddock, back to Shaw Croft and then to Sandy Lane Bridge, where Capt Parry took it. Eventually it was goaled at Sturston. Capt Parry's good-humoured firmness clearly won the day.

With hindsight it is arguable that the action of Mr Hall – whether prompted by Mr Brittlebank or not – did more to protect the game's future than was realised at the time. The whole momentum would have changed if the decision to play the game near Clifton had been implemented. This nearly happened after the move from the Market Place to Shaw Croft, although in that instance the two ancient goals remained unchanged.

Mr Hall and Mr Brittlebank must have realised the impact this would have made. The effect was really to blatantly ignore the undertaking given to the magistrates. Mr FitzHerbert was correct; the undertaking had been given on a previous occasion and then ignored. Here it was being overturned within twelve months! The action of Capt Parry turned the decision to play virtually as normal (but outside The Park) in the town's favour. The magistrates did not have the police on their side to force further prosecutions. The action of Capt Parry and the players' willingness to follow his orders resulted in the game being played and no breach of the peace or Highways Act being committed. It very much tied the hands of Mr Frank, the game's chief protagonist.

It must have been a tough decision to fly in the face of Mr Simpson's generosity. It risked turning people against the game so soon after the 1878 petition. It would be nice to know what collusion, if any, had gone on behind the scenes between Mr Brittlebank and Mr Parry. The game could easily have died but for the timely intervention of such people as these.

Mr Simpson was a native of Manchester and moved to Mayfield in 1866 when Mayfield Mill was purchased by Simpson Brothers. He became an Ashbourne magistrate in 1884 and at all times acted at least fairly with the Shrovetiders, often doing his best to avoid conflict with the Bench. He became Chairman of Mayfield Parish Council and Vice President of the West Derbyshire Liberal-Unionist Association. He died on 02/10/1901 of a heart attack at his home, 'Sunnyside' in Mayfield, aged 66 years.

1882

In February 1882 The Paddock was sold by Mr John Osmaston. Extending to eight acres, it was purchased by 14 gentlemen at the instigation of the vicar, for the benefit of the town. It was sold (at auction) to Mr Bradley on behalf of the others at a price of £2,600 plus £80 for the timber. It was hoped that the Cricket Club would be able to play again on the land. Play there the previous year had not proved possible as a new lease could not be agreed. Mr Osmaston (a member of the Wright family who had taken the name Omaston) also sold the manorial rights and cattle market at this time to the Local Board for £3,000. (DM 8/2/1882)

On Shrove Tuesday 1882, the ball quickly went down the river to The Paddock and was there taken down the river to Clifton Mill and goaled. There was very little play in the fields but a great deal of ducking and fighting occurred. On the Wednesday, the same routine took place, but the ball was very strongly contested and then a goal was scored at Sturston. Another ball was turned up at about 4.30pm and after a hard fought game in both Shaw Croft and The Paddock, it was 'landed at Clifton'. Presumably it was goaled after going down the river to the goal. There was very little fighting.

'There is no doubt that the game has lost much of its interest, owing to the fact that the play is nearly all one way', (DA 24/02/1882). Capt Parry was present and 'kept the players within the pale of the law, his good temper and advice acting better than a large force of policemen. Many of the fair sex were present, some actually taking part in the game. We think it would not be amiss to turn up a football for their special benefit, as they take such a great interest in the game'. A girls' game is not unknown at Kirkwall, but no such game was introduced at Ashbourne. However, did this indicate that there was no boys' game either at this time?

1883

In 1883, the game was played 'but not with so much zeal and spirit as it used to be.' (DA 09/02/1883) The paper again reported that much interest had been lost through the closure of The Park. The ball was thrown up at 2.00pm after a speech by Mr A Hall. It was soon in the river and carried downstream and into The Paddock, where some good kicking was enjoyed. Play returned to the water and the ball was carried down as far as the Gasworks. It then went across the road into Booth's Pasture and was eventually run away and goaled at Clifton Mill. The play was very good all afternoon and no fighting took place.

On Wednesday the ball was taken down the Henmore to The Paddock again and then went back into the river. The man with the ball had a rope tied around his waist to prevent him getting drowned and in this manner the ball was taken to Clifton Mill and goaled. Another ball was turned up at 4.30pm and was carried along the road into a field above The Park and finally goaled at Sturston. The police were not required and very few drunken men were about. The paper considered that in a few more years the game would be a thing of the past.

1884

In 1884, the game was played as usual 'with indications that it is in a moribund state' (DM 05/03/1884). 'No incident worth recording took place, except that several gardens were invaded and seriously damaged. A newspaper which not very long ago strongly supported the game now describes it as worn out and adds that 'the sooner it is abolished the better!' This other paper is probably the *Derbyshire Advertiser*, but the relevant section of the Derby Library copy is missing.

1885

By 1885, the paper (DM 25/02/1885) describes the game as 'ancient but now almost worn out'. The ball was turned up in Shaw Croft at 10.00am (sic) on Tuesday by Alfred Hall who was the captain of the Down'ards. Mr Harry Gallimore being captain of the Up'ards. As Alfred Hall usually turned up the ball on a Tuesday, it would seem that Down'ards turned up the ball on the Tuesday and the Up'ards on the Wednesday.

The Down'ards soon took it into the brook. It was thrown out when near The Paddock, and some good play took place here. It was thrown over the wall into the road and was carried through the station yard. Then it went into the brook again and was taken down river below the Gasworks, where the Up'ards made a start and endeavoured to get away with it, but it was to no avail. The Down'ards had all of the best play. Eventually reaching the River Dove, above the weir at Hanging Bridge, it was taken down the river as far as the point where the Henmore runs in, below the Clifton Mill dam. Here the Up'ards made another determined stand.

A hand to hand scuffle took place in the bed of the brook and indiscriminate ducking seemed to be the order of the day. The ball was at last goaled at about 5.00pm. As usual, a considerable number of women followed the ball. There were a few fights and some drunkenness but nothing in comparison to previous years.

On Wednesday the ball was thrown up at the usual time but was quickly played downwards and goaled at Clifton. The next ball was thrown up about 4.00pm when some old fashioned play took place in the Croft and on Sandy Lane. The Up'ards succeeded in getting this and a subsequent ball to their goal at Sturston Mill. It was reported that the interest in the game was 'in a great measure gone'.

At the Petty Sessions Court held the Saturday after the games, William Burton, innkeeper, Oliver Eley, innkeeper, and Arthur Jones, butcher, all of Ashbourne were summoned by Mrs Frank of Ashbourne Hall, for trespassing in The Park on Ash Wednesday. The bench heard that after an undertaking given in the Court in 1880 that the game would be kept out of The Park, it had been adhered to until this year. There had been a determined effort to play the second ball in The Park. It had been thrown over from Sandy Lane several times, but thrown back by Mrs Frank's men. The defendants went into The Park and were off the footpath, endeavouring to gain possession and doing notional damage to the grass to the amount of one penny.

Despite raising several technical and legal objections and after a lengthy hearing the defendants were convicted and ordered to pay a penny damage, a shilling fine and costs.

Mrs Harriet Elizabeth Frank of the Hall, was then summoned by Arthur Jones, one of the defendants in the above case, for assaulting him. It was alleged that she had struck him several blows with her umbrella. Mrs Frank denied it, but admitted striking him once. The case was dismissed. The courtroom was crowded and the cases took four hours to hear.

1886

In 1886 the ball was thrown up by Mr A Hall and in a few minutes it was in the Henmore. The ball then got into Compton and went up the street into Clifton Lane, arriving at The Paddock where some good play took place. It then moved very quickly down the fields below the church and got down to the Gasworks. Here it was played across the road into the Long Doles and down to the River Dove. Eventually it arrived back at Clifton Mill where it was goaled by Atterbury and Hurst. There was an immense company of spectators, amongst whom were noticed a large sprinkling of strangers. It was estimated that 'there would not be less than 1,200 people present, including a large number of respectable females'. There was a small body of the county police present under the command of Supt Lytle. Capt Parry was also amongst the onlookers. On Wednesday the ball went quickly to Compton Bridge and was played into The Paddock. The game was very similar to the previous day. Ashbourne Park was strictly guarded as usual and the customary notices to trespassers were posted up, but the ball never went near (DA 12/03/1886).

1887

A year later, in 1887 and on the Tuesday, play was described (DM 2/3/1887) as being good humoured and with little or no drunkenness. The Down'ards scored two goals and the Up'ards one goal. The ball had been kept out of the streets. On the Wednesday, the ball was rushed into the river and from there it was thrown into Dig Street where the Up'ards made a determined rush and got the ball into St John Street. At the bottom of the Market Place, the police, under Capt Parry and Supt Lytle 'made a determined effort to obtain possession of the ball'. One constable obtained the ball but was made to drop it. There was a scene of 'indescribable confusion' for some twenty minutes, with the police trying to force the game out of the town and the Up'ards endeavouring to force it up.

The police remained cool and good tempered, but the Captain was reported to have got a bit too excited in the hug. The ball eventually was played back down Dig Street, into the Henmore, through

The Paddock and down Mayfield Road. It continued across Booth's Pastures and into the River Dove where it was taken down river before being goaled at about 5.00pm at Clifton.

At the following sitting of the Petty Sessions, Supt Lytle stated that he had been instructed by Capt Parry, the Chief Constable, to make an application for summonses against a number of persons for playing football on the highway on Ash Wednesday. However, the Justices declined to do so as it did not appear that the ball had been wilfully played into the streets with the direct intention of obstructing the highway. The ball had only been in the streets for about twenty minutes and no complaints had been received. It was made clear that football could not be allowed to be played in the streets to four people who had been playing and who were present in Court. Mr Lytle was instructed to have handbills printed the following year calling on the players to co-operate in keeping the ball in the fields, and threatening proceedings against offenders.

One of the 1887 balls survives, although the owner was hoping to take it to New Zealand in 1994. It is supposed to be a Clifton ball and goaled by John Wibberley, who was a butcher in the town. However, Wibberleys were Up'ards.

It has fragments of paint on its central panel and traditionally it is held that it had a painting of Queen Victoria (it was her golden jubilee year). There are references to this ball in the local paper in 1955 and 1993.

1888

The following year, 1888, duly arrived and the first ball was goaled at Clifton on a bitter cold day at about 4.00pm. The second ball was goaled at Sturston and by 5.30pm the game was over for the day. There was no play in the streets. On the Wednesday, after some twenty minutes play, the Up'ards adopted the tactics of the previous day and rushed the ball into the brook and up one of the yards. Two Up'ards got away followed by three Down'ards who pursued the two as far as Dove Holes in Dovedale, where the pursuit was abandoned!

A second ball was thrown up at 3.00pm and until 4.50pm it was played in the Croft. Then it was thrown into the brook and taken into St John Street and played in the Market Place and the Butchery. The police made no effort to obtain the ball but took down the names of players. The game proceeded above Ashbourne Green. The Up'ards eased off as they approached Sturston and Heywood, a member of the Burton Harriers did a runner with the ball. He went to the top of the Derby Road, across by the Tinker's Inn and goaled the ball at Clifton. It was reported that 'the bulk of the players cannot be made to understand that this is against the law, but doggedly hold to their opinion that it is a suppression of an ancient right peculiar to their own'.

The following Thursday, the Local Board passed a resolution that in the case of summonses being issued, the Local Board would wait upon the magistrates and request them not to grant the police the summonses. The resolution was proposed by J T Marple and seconded by Alfred Hall. Two days later Supt Lytle applied for ninety-four summonses (under instructions, presumably from Capt Parry). Mr Lytle said that the ball had not been kept in the streets for very long and no complaints had been received. The Local Board deputation made its request (present were Mr Farmer, the chairman of the Local Board, and Messrs Marple and Marsden).

The Justices asked Supt Lytle to withdraw the application 'on condition that the Local Board would use what influence they had to prevent the ball from being played in the streets in future years'. Mr Simpson suggested that a meeting of ratepayers should be held prior to the next game and some arrangement reached between the two sides not to play in the streets. Mr Marple enquired what would happen if the ball was played across Sandy Lane, Bradley Road or Clifton Road. The Bench Chairman replied that 'so long as the ball was got out of the road or highway as quickly as possible, no action would be taken.' (DM 22/02/1888)

1889

In 1889 the Tuesday ball was quickly taken under Compton Bridge and down into The Paddock. There was determined play here for ninety minutes. The ball was, on more than one occasion, taken into Col Wilkie's garden at the Mansion and also into General MacBean's. Eventually, it went under Station Bridge and into the station yard where it was played amongst the wagons, coal heaps and other goods before being worked back into The Paddock. The ball was then run to Sturston Lane where there was some hard play in some of the back yards. However, the Up'ards prevailed and goaled it at about 6.00pm.

The Wednesday ball was, as usual, turned up before a larger crowd. It was played into Compton and round by the bank into The Paddock. It eventually moved on via the chapel-yard and ran away with, being goaled at Clifton after being taken on a very circuitous route.

A second ball was turned up and kept in the vicinity of the Croft until 6.00pm. The ball occasionally got into Sandy Lane and up to the St John Street corner as well as being hugged for a considerable time on Compton Bridge. It was eventually worked downwards and was goaled at about 7.30pm at Clifton. Mr Alfred Hall was as usual, captain of the Down'ards and Mr Charles Coxon of the Up'ards. The latter were exceptionally strong on the first day and it was many years since the first ball that was thrown up went upwards. No summonses were applied for. It was not reported whether the meeting requested by Mr Simpson was held but the players had obvious regard to his words.

It is mentioned above that the ball was played on more than one occasion in Col Wilkie's garden at the Mansion. This was risky business. Col Wilkie was a local JP and the entrance hall of the Mansion was registered as a court of justice. Trials frequently were held there. Col Wilkie was born in Cupar in Fifeshire. He fought in India and retired from the Army in 1861, settling in 1862 at Bradbourne Hall until 1885, when he moved to the Mansion. He died in December 1894, aged 85 years.

1890

In 1890 despite fine and dry weather, there was a cutting east wind which affected attendance on the Tuesday. Two balls were turned up, both being goaled at Clifton, the second long after dark. On the Wednesday, only one ball was turned up. It was played for nearly an hour in the Croft before it was taken under Compton Bridge and into The Paddock. Eventually, the station was reached and the ball was played hard all through the station yard and along the platform amongst the milk cans for a considerable time.

Up'ards pressure began to tell and the game worked back through The Paddock, into Compton and Sturston Lane. It continued on to Sturston where it was goaled by Charles Coxon, the Up'ards captain. At one point, Mr Joseph Simpson JP endeavoured to persuade players to give him the ball and for him to take it to the nearest field, but this could not be agreed and play went on. No prosecutions were brought.

1891

Police Take Names of Players

The first edition of the *Official History* states that in 1891, Mr Alfred Hall turned up the painted ball from the knoll on Shaw Croft on February 10. However a further perusal of the 1891 *Ashbourne News* reveals that there is a possibility that Alfred Hall did not turn up the 1891 ball after all. The known facts are these: Just before 2pm, Alfred Hall and a group of players wended their way down Dig Street with the painted ball held by Mr E Burton. From the knoll in Shaw Croft, Mr Hall delivered a few words of exhortation, Rule Britannia was sung and after a round of cheers, the ball rose into the air.

Was the ball turned up by Mr Burton? Mr Hall gave a speech in 1892 but crucially, the ball was turned up by Mr Wallis. It seems likely that Mr Burton did in fact turn up the 1891 ball and the Roll of Honour has been changed accordingly. Why else did he carry the ball to the plinth? As there was no record of a guest turning up the ball previously, it is probable that this exception was because the year was the first one of the new century.

This was the first time that the practice of inviting someone to turn up the ball started. Before 1892, the records often did not state who had turned up the ball. There are comments However, about each side having a captain of the team and Alfred Hall is known to have been the Down'ards captain. On the few occasions that the person turning up the ball was named, it was consistently Alfred Hall back as far as 1880. He always turned up the ball on a Tuesday too, so it would appear that the Up'ards turned up the ball on the Wednesday. It is probably significant that in 1880, when Joseph Simpson offered a £100 bond to the Court, the undertaking was not considered until the cases against Alfred Hall and Charles Coxon had been heard. Was this because they had turned up the balls and/or because they were the captains? It seems probable.

Incidentally, this is the earliest written reference to the ball being painted although we know that John Barker had been painting them for some time. The ball was soon in Sandy Lane and the game reached the Hall but was returned down the lane and eventually reached the Croft again. Around 2.30pm, the ball was taken up the Black's Head yard and into the Market Place. It did not remain long here but was forced steadily down the Butchery, along St John Street and into Church Street.

Here police began noting the names of the players. The ball was pushed by the Up'ards back into Dig Street where it proceeded along Compton into Station Street and then was thrown into The Paddock. The ball was keenly contested here for some two hours and was repeatedly thrown over into Mr Cooper's field, only to be thrown back again. At last it was transferred to the river near to the brewery, before returning to land.

Eventually the game reached Compton via the brewery gate. After play in the street, the ball was returned to Shaw Croft around 5.30pm. As darkness fell, the ball was taken up Hall Lane, along Ashbourne Green Road towards Sturston Mill where it was goaled a little after 7.30pm by Mr William Lytle. He was the son of police superintendent Lytle who had applied for the ninety-four summonses against the players in 1888 and who lived at the Ashbourne lockup on Derby Road.

Incidentally, the brewery had been started in 1874 by Thomas Cooper with Frank Wilson. Cooper bought out his partner in 1875 and invested £8,300 in the concern. However, he was insolvent in 1886. Had someone else continued the brewing business or was the reporter recalling former days?

Mr Lombard Gets His Own Back

On the Wednesday there was a considerable police presence (some fifty men) in the Market Place, but they were not required. Immediately after the turn up, the ball was played into the river. Within five minutes it was away under Compton Bridge. The Down'ards took it to the fields beyond the station before the Up'ards began to assert themselves. The game was then played across Mr Tomlinson's field before it returned to The Paddock and eventually into Compton and the corner of Sturston Lane. The Up'ards continued the pressure and the game went past The Park to Mr Lombard's field into which the ball was thrown. The police who had been accompanying the game tried to gain entry to the field through the gate. However, Mr Lombard was leaning on it and refused to allow them through. He also 'treated the police to a bit of his mind, which was by no means favourable to them.' The ball soon reached Sturston and was goaled by Mr Avery, of the Post Office, at 4.30pm.

Another ball was turned up at 5.20pm despite Black Harry's (Henry Hawksworth's) objection that a ball turned up after 5.00pm was a no-ball. There were fewer players now and the Down'ards took the ball down the river to the station. It was played on the railway for a long time before being goaled at Clifton at 9.00pm by J Barker. The paper (AN 14/02/1891) noted that several prominent tradesmen played in the games this year, including Dr Boswell.

The Roll of Honour records the Avery goal at Sturston Mill. It is not known if this was the decision of the Committee but there is a *prima facie* case for the goal being accorded to John Derbyshire. Letters to the local paper take up the story. The ball was carried from Coxon's field to Sturston by F Brown of Belle Vue, where he was stopped by the Down'ards who took possession of the ball. A hard struggle then took place and Brown entered the mill door and stood on the axle waiting to goal the ball. Derbyshire followed him in saying: 'if you will go down under the wheel I will stand here and throw the ball to you.' Brown agreed to do this, Derbyshire promising faithfully that he would keep his word. It was alleged that Derbyshire was a Down'ard and that he did not keep his word. (AN 28/

02/1891). The latter responded the following week, stating that he had told Brown that he would pass the ball to him if he could, but when the ball did arrive (passed to Derbyshire, who was on the wheel axle, by Joseph Handley), there were too many people about and he decided to goal the ball himself. He had always played as an Up'ard. Whether he was or not, the ball had been goaled in the proper manner and it is difficult to see why he was not accorded the ball.

Of more concern at the time perhaps was the threat of more prosecutions. The paper (AN 21/02/1891) quoted a letter of 1861 from Sir Edward Webster, a local man and a barrister at Lincoln's Inn. He had sent in 1861 £2 to help defray the cost of the summonses in that year's prosecutions. He defended the players at the time against 'a very unfortunate exercise of magisterial authority'. Unfortunately Ashbourne was about to experience another example of it. The paper's editorial comment made a sound point (AN 21/02/1891). It was alleged that the police were at fault in allowing a player to bring the ball up the yard and into the town. This was contrary to an agreement made with the police in 1888. It was noted that there was no police action the last time Lord Cavendish and Mr Arkwright addressed the electors. Then, for two or three hours in the middle of market day, the streets were almost impassable and there was far more disturbance than that which took place during the previous week's play. 'Perhaps it requires a well balanced mind and the legal acumen of a police official to draw the distinction between such cases but to ordinary mortals who call a spade a spade, the difference is not perceptible.' The paper had summed it up rather well.

There was no further comment until the decision to prosecute had been made. On 07/03/1891 the editorial comment continued and lambasted the magistrate's decision. It drew a comparison with other recent events in the previous few weeks – there had been a meet of the Meynell Hunt when seventy horses and a pack of hounds obstructed traffic for some time. On the previous Friday night, a drunken woman was howling and screaming for 35 minutes in the very centre of town, causing a gathering of hundreds of people before a policeman could be found. Lastly, on the following night 'we had a hooting mob escorting the superintendent of police [it was Supt Borratt] about the streets, until he took refuge in the lockup'. It made the point that the law should be both respected as well as obeyed. It was clear that there was little respect for the magistrates decision and for the first time, the townspeople had their own significant vehicle for comment: the local paper.

The drunken woman, incidentally, was Mary Lynch, a traveller, who was well known to the Court and had forty-seven previous convictions (and forty-seven detentions in Derby gaol). She was sent down for another month.

The Public Meeting

A 'public indignation meeting' was called and the report was quoted at length:

"The meeting was called by crier on Wednesday for the purpose of protesting against the action of the police with regard to Shrovetide football. Though at short notice, the lower Town Hall was crowded by a thoroughly representative gathering of townsmen with a slight sprinkling of ladies, at which 700 or 800 people were present. At eight o'clock Mr J T Marple was unanimously voted to the chair. On rising to speak, the chairman was greeted with loud and continued cheers. Speaking for his personal liking for the game, he stated the object of the meeting to be a protest against the unnecessary interference on the part of the police with the liberties of the people of the town, and contended that the police ought to consult to some extent the wishes of the inhabitants, especially in such a case as the present. Mr Marple spoke of Mr Mathews having offered to undertake the defence, an observation which elicited hearty applause. Characterising the playing in the streets as accidental and not wilful, he referred to the previous agreement not to play in the streets. This, he contended, was faithfully carried out until The Park was closed in 1879.

Whilst admitting a technical breach of the Highways Act, Mr Marple thought a breach had been just as much committed at the Meynell Hunt in front of the station. Amidst applause he claimed that the same treatment should be accorded football as was accorded the meet. After referring to varied positions of people summoned, he expressed the hope that the magistrates would dismiss the summonses, and concluded by calling upon Mr Henstock to move a resolution. Mr Henstock moved 'That this meeting of the inhabitants of Ashbourne desires to press its emphatic condemnation of the action of the police in summoning a large number of persons for playing football in the streets, such action being entirely opposed to the wishes of the large majority of ratepayers, and trusts that the magistrates will see their way to dismiss the summonses.' Mr W H Smedley seconded. Mr Mathews in a speech, pointed out that similar games at Nuneaton and Atherstone were not interfered with."

The *Ashbourne News* of 07/03/1891 reported on the Court hearing, which was heard on 28th February before Capt Goodwin Gladwyn (in the chair), C B Kingdom, W B Badnall, T O Farmer, H C Okeover and Joseph Simpson. Mr Mathews of Messrs Bamford, Son and Mathews, solicitors, appeared for the majority of the defendants. Mr Mathews proposed that the cases be heard under four heads: (1) those admitting guilt; (2) those not playing in the place charged; (3) those who really played on the outskirts of the town and who objected to being charged with the playing in the town proper; and (4) those who did not play at all. In fact he hoped to prove that one defendant was not even in the town.

Thirty men were heard in the first category. The witness for the prosecution was Inspector B T Talbot who accepted that behaviour was very good and he did not see anyone annoyed. He asserted that the defendants did not take the ball out of the street when requested to do so. There were some 300 to 500 people blocking the street, so it was hardly surprising. In further cross examination he admitted taking the name of one man who was not even in Ashbourne 'but policemen were liable to make mistakes as other people.' He was not aware that a coal cart had passed through the crowd during the game and this was central to the case of proving annoyance. Some fifteen policemen were on duty. All the witnesses were policemen. Supt Borrett said that two Woodeaves coal carts were held up for about twenty minutes.

Mr Mathews raised the comparison of the obstruction caused by the Meynell Hunt which prevented free passage to the railway station for a considerable time. There had been no evidence that anyone was annoyed or that any damage had been caused. A fine of 2s 6d and 7s 6d (12½p and 37½p) costs was imposed in each case, with a suggestion that the position of the goals be moved so that the law would not be broken. Fourteen days was allowed for payment, with £50 security in the case of an appeal.

Henry Smith was possibly the Town Crier in 1891. See also p95

After an adjournment, the case against Frank Swindell was heard next. The Court was uncomfortably crowded. Swindell pleaded not guilty to playing in Church Street, as he was a carter, employed by Mr Wright and could account for his whereabouts. It appeared to be a case of mistaken identity but the case was adjourned, for the attendance of Wright's booking clerk. At that hearing, it was confirmed that there were three carts, Swindell's and the two Woodeaves carts. However, he was found guilty and fined liked the others. Full details of the convictions are given in Appendix C.

In order to pay for the fines, a concert was held and the money required was over subscribed. A letter to the local paper makes it clear that someone on the Local Board tried to obstruct the success of the concert. This was possibly Board Chairman T O Farmer, one of the magistrates, who said he was 'sick of hearing about football' at the 9th March meeting (see below) and who did not seek re-election to the Board a little later). The football song which is sung at the dinner annually was composed by George Porter for this concert, although the original music does not survive. The entertainment had to be repeated as hundreds could not gain admission on the first night. Each evening the entertainment was preceded by a march round of the Top-hat Band, accompanied by an immense number of people, and a placard of the concert and a football on a pole were carried conspicuously at the front (AN 19/02/1926). George Porter lived at the Durham Ox Inn in Compton. He lost an arm playing the game in School Lane, sometime prior to 1891 and had a wooden arm. He had played cricket for the county and died in 1895, while in his thirties. His granddaughter is Mary Winstone of Clifton.

At a meeting of the Ashbourne Local Board on 9 March, Mr J T Marple proposed: "That this Board expresses its regret that it was thought necessary to incur the expense of bringing over a large number of additional police on two recent occasions, and that a copy of this resolution be sent to Captain Parry and the Police Committee of the County Council." It was seconded by Mr James Osborne.

During the debate which followed, the essence of the issue arose. It was not the magistrates who were at fault for bringing the prosecutions, as had been the case thirty years before. The report didn't say whether it was the police or the police committee, but the resolution was passed *nem con*. Capt Parry replied stating that he had sent thirty extra men for the Wednesday's game at the request of the police superintendent. This was as a result of the 'rough ending of the football playing' on the Tuesday. The superintendent felt that there might be damage to property as a result on the Wednesday. He further commented that on the Tuesday evening the police had been stoned. (AN 18/04/1891) No further action was taken by the Board, but it was really all the town could do. Unlike some larger towns, Ashbourne did not have its own police force or police committee. This was however, the last time that prosecutions were applied for. Since that time, close liaison between the police and the committee has proved satisfactory and play in the streets is not only tolerated but often the norm.

There was, perhaps understandably, some animosity directed towards the police in the following weeks including a serious assault case. The latter was not linked to the game, but one wonders if there was an indirect link.

An interesting letter was published anonymously. (AN 21/03/1891) It was probably written by the Rev Tomlinson (one of those summonsed) as it refers to stories heard from the writer's grandfather and the Rev Tomlinson repeated this link some years later. There had been further talk of playing the game in the field down river from the town (as Mr Simpson had suggested a decade previously – and he was on the 1891 bench). The writer felt this would destroy the game and encourage play on the railway line. The magistrates had given the impression that they had no sympathy with the game and were determined to stop it. The new railway was going to be built across part of The Paddock, including a new station. This would block in play like the closed Park was doing. He then went on to state that prior to the game switching to Clifton and Sturston Mills (perhaps about 1795) the goals were Paper Houses Farm for the Up'ards and 'the farm till recently occupied by Mr Phillips of Nether Sturston' for the Down'ards.

The writer suggested that the game should go back to this as play would be directed away from the streets quickly. However, it was not to be. The game carried on 'in the old way'.

The high profile of the game resulting from the summonses resulted in several press items and one gave anecdotal comments on the game which are worth recording (AN 14/02/1891):

"On one occasion it is recorded that the ball was hugged for nearly three hours in front of the Bell Inn – now the Birmingham and Dudley Bank [the Bluebell Inn, now Barclay's Bank] – and was eventually cut, the late Mr G Marple receiving a permanent injury to his hand. On more than one occasion it (the ball) has been taken on horseback and once, we believe, it went down to Clifton by rail, in the guard's van.

Not many years since it was taken through Mappleton, Blore, Dovedale, Wetton, Hanson Grange and back by Tissington before being goaled at Sturston Mill very late at night [this must relate to 1888].

It has always been considered an honour to be summoned in connection with the game and not many years since, several tradesmen signalised the event of being fined by a supper at the Green Man Hotel. [Within days of receiving the 1891 summonses some were framed and hanging proudly on the wall].

In one year a large number of navvies were employed in constructing the mill dam at Woodeaves, and on Ash Wednesday they came down in a body and succeeded in getting hold of the ball. They carried it up the Buxton Road and back to Woodeaves."

Woodeaves was a cotton spinning mill built by John Cooper in 1784, but this must relate to the rebuilding of the top dam in 1881 after it had burst in the February floods. The newspaper report does not mention the navvies.

It can now be confirmed that the number of summonses sought by Supt Borratt on behalf of Capt Parry was against 95 and not 84 as quoted in the first edition. (AN 14/02/1891)

Difficult Times

This drawing of play in 1907 probably shows part of the Bath House in Sandy Lane

The drunken woman (Mary Lynch) cited as an example of obstruction on the streets (see above) was sent down twice more during the year, bringing her total to 49 convictions. She received three weeks in July and within a month of her release went down again for a month with hard labour. Both offences concerned the smashing of windows at the Coach and Horses Inn. A 'shower of filthy language' was directed at James Gadsby, the landlord, as she was led away for the third time since Shrovetide. She had accused Mr Gadsby of having thrown a poker at her. Life in the town streets seems to have been very colourful in those days! She had caused quite a commotion in Compton in July before being led away to the lock up and subsequent remand in gaol. She was still in the news in 1908 when she made her 120th court appearance. (AT 11/09/1908)

Supt Borratt was based at the County Police HQ in Chesterfield after being in Ashbourne from 1888-1890. Unfortunately he died in September 1891, aged 52 years.

Game Reports 1892-1949 — 6

1892
Away From the Highway

After the street play of the previous year, the Tuesday crowd was addressed and warned that greater fines could be imposed if the magistrates saw fit, to a maximum of £2.00 per person. There was a punctual start, with the ball being turned up by Mr R Wallis for the start of what turned out to be a vigorously contested game, with a cold easterly wind and flurries of snow.

It was 2½ hours before the ball left the Croft with the leather being played end to end repeatedly and some water play with up to twenty players in the river. Eventually it reached Compton after passing under the bridge. As it proceeded up the street, it was noted that there were 'efforts to keep the ball off the highway as much as possible and so prevent magisterial proceedings'. After a desperate hug adjacent to The Plough, the ball moved into Sturston Lane (now Road) before being played through a field back to Compton. It was soon played down a yard and on to The Paddock where a couple of runners – J Barker and T Burns – made off with it to Clifton Mill, the ball being goaled at 7.15pm.

May We Have Our Ball Back, Please?

If the game on the Tuesday was hard fought, the Wednesday game was more so. Mr C Purdy turned up the ball which was played hard around the Croft 'at an express rate'. Eventually it was swiftly on its way down river to Bank Croft and was then played in The Paddock. Eventually it left here and the best part of the day appears to have begun with considerable movement, long throws and no quarter spared. It went across the station, into Tomlinson's field by the church and then on from one field to another, both sides of the river, hotly contested all the while. Near to the engine shed, the leather was in an evident state of collapse, but play continued until only the case remained, being hugged by some 200 players.

The ball was thrown over into the garden of Mr Langford, who, armed with a substantial cudgel, refused to return it, before being summarily relieved of his trophy. Mr John Winterton then arrived with a new ball in any event, which he threw up. It was quickly played into another garden by the Down'ards 'where last year's bean sticks offered but slight impediment'. The reporter was obviously enjoying himself – "with thoughtful cries of 'Mind the brussell sprouts', the imposing body of rate payers passed on to inspect the Local Board tip field, (now Nestlé), where the game was strongly contested."

The Up'ards rallied and forced the ball into the station just as the 4.20pm train was starting out! Play moved into Clifton Road by the Goods Warehouse before returning to the station platform and eventually reaching the safety of The Paddock. The crowd was deafening – it was chiefly the fair sex – with shouts of 'Go it, Up'ards', and 'Stick to the leather, mi byes'! After considerable movement in and around the area of Station Street and the Paddock, a break was made along Sturston Lane, past The Park and into the fields. After being played across the river, a Down'ards runner lying in ambush got the ball and broke away.

Proceeding via Ashbourne Green brickyard, the top of the Green, Sandybrook and Okeover weir, he goaled it at Clifton Mill at about 9.00pm. Captain Matthews was reported as being in the thick of play in the afternoon. The police 'behaved with good judgement... and never was there less disorder.' It was a good omen for the future.

Although it is unknown when the Committee was formed, it is known that Jack Hawksworth became its secretary in 1897. Its objects were 'systemising the game, freeing it from objectionable features and ensuring its continuance by a compliance with the conditions laid down by the authorities. (AN 08/03/1912) It is suggested that the Committee was formed after the Public Indignation Meeting of 1891 and that John Winterton (of the Cock Inn) was the first chairman. The decision to have formal guests to turn up the ball would have come from the Committee and introduced in 1892. Perhaps the lunch dates from this time too. It would be rather nice to think that their first guest was Mr Robert Wallis of the Green Man Hotel.

The traditional link between the game and the Hotel stemmed from the fact that in 1863, Mr R Wallis had allowed the Shaw Croft to be used for the turning up of the ball. This had allowed the game to be started in the town but out of the streets north of the river. It was not the same Mr Wallis, however. Mr Wallis senior had died in 1870 and the ball was probably turned up his son in recognition of the annual availablity of Shaw Croft for nearly three decades. Incidentally, as late as 1903, Mr Ernest Porter who turned up the ball was described as 'the captain of the day'. (AT 27/02/1903)

Capt Parry, the Chief Constable, took up his position in 1873 and kept it until 1892. However, it is possible that his post was vacant at Shrovetide, for the post was advertised in March and was already vacant then owing to Capt Parry's promotion. Most of the prosecutions occurred while he was Chief Constable. Although he seems to have been content to allow the tradition to continue, he was determined to uphold the law.

None the less it is clear that the prosecutions were becoming increasingly untenable. A successful prosecution depended upon the premise that an obstruction had taken place, yet the Shrovetide obstruction was no worse than that at an election meeting. There was no moral justification for turning a blind eye to some events and bringing the full force of the law to bear at Shrovetide.

Capt Parry's successor, Major Godfrey (previously Chief Constable of Montgomeryshire) must have realised this in 1894 when play went from Station Road down Church Street to The Green Man Hotel. Moreover, an obstruction had always been permitted south of the river in Compton, but not in Dig Street. What possible justification was there for this? Presumably Major Godfrey bowed to the inevitable which is why there were no further prosecutions after 1891. The following year although the crowd was warned about higher fines if they played in the streets, play did keep away and there was little or no disorder. It was 1894 before street play was seen again before a crowd of 5,000 people and Major Godfrey let sleeping dogs lie, his chances of securing a successful prosecution weighing against him.

Thereafter, the police were used as a buffer to stop progress down a particular street if possible or to push the hug out of a street. Nonetheless, players were still being urged to keep the play out of the streets as late as 1910. In 1900, on the Wednesday, the players were warned that their names would be taken by the police if a repetition of Tuesday's street play occurred. The word 'prosecution' was not used and in any event, there was no problem that day.

The roughness of the game was no doubt a major factor in the desire to stop mass football in the streets. The suggestion of the vicar in 1859 that the game be played on Ashbourne Green must have been because of this. The Derby paper (DM 28/02/1844) carried a letter complaining of soot being thrown in Wardwick, Derby during the game. There was a call to get rid of 'the annual nuisance'. A further letter in the same vein was published the following week. Following the stopping of the game in 1846 in Derby, it is easy to see how attention became focussed on Ashbourne. It is a pity that details of any pressure after 1846 have not survived except for the brief report of 1859.

Crowd behaviour after 1891 did improve, that is clear. Mr W H Mathews and Mr J T Marple appealed to the players to keep the ball out of the street in 1893 in a letter to the local paper, noting that 'everything passed off very pleasantly' in 1892. (AN 10/02/1893) The 1893 game caused no problems and Supt Wheeldon and only a small force of men were needed to keep order. By 1895, The Clerk reported at the Magistrates Court that there had been no trouble at Shrovetide football. There were no related cases of any kind before the Bench. Mr Simpson said that he had never seen the game played in a more orderly manner. He had taken his daughters to see the play and would do so again. (AN 08/03/1895) Clearly the work of the Committee was having a positive effect. The same issue of the paper reported the death of Capt R H Goodwin - Gladwin who had chaired the Bench at the prosecutions of 1891. He lived at Hinckley Wood, Mappleton.

1893

Half A Ball Is Better Than None

The ball was thrown up in brilliant sunshine by Mr John Marple, chairman of the Local Board (predecessor of the Urban District Council).The crowd was reminded to keep out of the streets, but if it got 'thrown over into Sandy Lane, to play it up there to the end of The Park and then throw it into the fields'. No police action was promised if this happened. The 4lb painted leather was played around the Croft before being thrown over into Sandy Lane and returning to make its way into Compton. Clearly some street play was being tolerated. The ball was played into the Henmore by the Down'ards but was thrown out at Bank Croft. It was then played into The Paddock where it remained for a long time. Eventually it was hugged back to Bank Croft in the early evening. It was hugged and run into Clifton Lane (Road) with some spirited resistance from the Up'ards. However, the leather was unexpectedly cut at the pointsman's box on the railway line. The ball was then cut in two, one half for each side and a 'no ball' declared. The *Ashbourne News* noted that some visitors had travelled long distance and included Judge Kenelm Digby. He presided over the Derbyshire County Court and was the brother-in-law of Lord Belper. The park was closed and placarded with 'keepout' bills. Barbed wire had also been added to the railings.

Wednesday's ball was thrown up by Mr William Hall, on behalf of his brother (Mr A Hall 'a veteran player'), who was ill. It appears that Mr Hall then took part in the game. The ball was played for a long time between Shaw Croft and St John Street in Sandy Lane, with an estimated crowd of 1,500 to 2,000 people. It was reported that The Hall was well protected by estate labourers, but they made no attempt 'to get the ball onto forbidden ground'. Eventually, the runners broke up the play with the Up'ards the strongest and getting to within two fields of Sturston Mill before the Down'ards forced a hug. Eventually T Cundy carried it up the mill race to the wheel at 4.10pm.

Mr Henry Taylor of Hopton turned up the second ball. This time, the ball was soon heading downstream and then over to The Paddock. It was quickly moved on to Clifton Road and into the fields 'where the best play took place'. Eventually as darkness fell, it was thrown over the railway and an Up'ards man 'made off with it', being stopped by the Gasworks. After a little more river and field play, a Down'ards runner took possession and it was goaled at Clifton Mill at 6.05pm by W Mellor and C Bratby. The report concluded by adding that there was very little drunkenness on either day. The 'celebrated Ashbourne Football Picture, from the oil painting by Day' was still being offered at 6d each, postage 2d!

Mr Frank Oaten, reminisced about his time as an Ashbourne News reporter between 1892–97. He said that before John Marple had thrown up the ball, he (i.e. Oaten) had gone home to lunch at the bidding of the Pancake Bell (the little sanctus bell in St Oswald's church tower) at 12 o'clock, and had hurried over his pancakes to join the huge crowd waiting at the Croft. (AN 03/03/1938)

This year is the earliest on record where the tradition of carrying the turner-up shoulder high is mentioned. Initially, the person concerned walked to the knoll on Shaw Croft and was then lifted shoulder high, presumably to make it easier to get the ball well into the surrounding players. As we all know, the current practice is to carry the guest of honour from Dig Street to the Shaw Croft plinth. For the record, in 1893, Mr Marple was lifted up and presumably Mr Hall on the Wednesday.

1894

The Double For Sturston

In favourable weather, the ball was thrown up by Captain Mathews after urging players to keep away from the streets. After much play on the Croft, the ball was played by the Down'ards over Sandy Lane

Bridge and up to the end of St John Street. Captain Mathews prevailed upon the players not to enter the streets. However, the ball in any event, returned towards the bridge and entered the Henmore. There was much water play involving some twenty men 'till one poor fellow, named Wibberley, was literally stripped to the waist, and had to go home with what show of decency he could'. This was 'Bumper' Wibberley and he was back within twenty minutes with fresh clothing. He reckoned he could not feel the cold when he was in the hug. (AN 03/03/1938)

Back in Sandy Lane, the ball was played and hugged to Belper Road, the men becoming besmeared in mud en route. The path of the ball was then along what is now Sturston Road and then down Compton to the bridge. After water play down to Bank Croft, there was rapid (and illegal) play along Church Street to the Green Man Yard and onto Shaw Croft again. It was now 5.00pm. With a good throw, the ball reached the Wellington pub yard where Joseph Millington again entered the town, running with it, up the Market Place and on to Sandybrook where he hid in a shed. It was eventually goaled at Sturston at 6.30pm by a Mr Chell after an afternoon of good weather.

Wednesday's ball was turned up by Mr Harrison of Macclesfield. The ball was quickly played towards the Bath Gardens and then into the Terrace Gardens (between Sandy Lane and Compton) 'whose tenants we should advise to use their Brussel sprouts and curled greens in future before Shrovetide'. After some water play, the play found itself back in Sandy Lane where there was some very stiff play in the lane, adjacent fields and two gardens.

Eventually the break came as darkness fell. The park was skirted and the ball thrown into Mr Coxon's field. It was then played through the fields by a succession of Up'ards despite Down'ards opposition. Mr G Everatt (sic) touching the Sturston wheel at 7.50pm. After the game was over, the ball was weighed and turned the scale at 5lb.

Other News

Capt Mathews ran the local Volunteer Corps. He was a well respected figure in the town until he moved to London at the end of 1895.

Although no mention was made of it at the time, it is likely that the number of visitors to the game in the year would have been lower than usual. In fact the number of visitors to Ashbourne was less than usual throughout the year. This was because of an outbreak of cholera in Autumn 1893 at the Coach and Horses Yard and the adverse publicity it created. There were a total of 39 inhabitants in the yard and in a seven-day period, fifteen cases of the disease were diagnosed, resulting in nine deaths. The yard had been inspected in1888 by Dr Bruce Low on account of the prevalence of diptheria there. As a result, the water supply had been condemned but the Local Board refused to comply with a request for a new supply, considering the town to be well supplied with water. At the time, the death of the late Capt Holland was lamented as he had been 'zealous in advocating a pure supply of water'. In fact the pump on the corner of Union Street and Belle Vue had been erected in his memory and presumably accounts for the fact that the pump survived the removals which were inevitable as a fresh source of water was eventually provided. It is the only public pump left in Ashbourne.

The local paper stated that the town needed a good water supply, a good sewage scheme 'and a thorough overhauling of some of the most thickly populated yards in the town'. (AN 03/05/1895) It was of course to get all of these, but the water supply was the first to be sorted out, in 1896. An effect of this was the closure of many of the wells. In April 1898, a proposal was made to close the public pumps at Compton,The Market Place and Dove House Green (the pump refered to above) plus private pumps at Compton, Clevedon Terrace, Wheel Inn Yard, Smiths Yard, Lumbards Yard, Bank Yard and Church Street.

Durind the year, the Ashbourne Local Board was replaced by the Urban District Council. The Board had been very sympathetic to the game with some of its members being players or ardent supporters. Alfred Hall did not seek election to the Council, retiring through ill health. The honour of turning up the balls in 1893 had gone to two members of the Board – John Marple the Board's chairman on the Tuesday and Alfred Hall on the Wednesday. The latter was to ill to do it and his brother deputised for him in the event. On one previous occasion when the police tried to stop Mr Hall making progress up the river by saying the river was the property of the Local Board, he had replied 'I am the Local Board' ! And so he had been.

Mr Hall died on 02/04/1896 aged only 54 years. He had been suffering from a liver complaint for four years. He was a partner in Thomas Hall and Sons, coach builders on the site of the bus station. The firm was describes as being one of the oldest businesses in the town. (AN 10/04/1896) He had turned the ball up on countless occasions, being the 'captain' of the Down'ards. For a photograph of the works see *Victorian Times in and Around Ashbourne* p75.

1894 saw the inauguration of Sturston welldressing. (AN 04/01/1895) The custom of dressing the wells was more prevalent in those days than it is now. Wells were of course dressed at Tissington and also at Kniveton, Roston and Wyaston (where it had been started in 1860, dressing the Edlaston well and Wyaston pump). In 1896, three wells were dressed at Mayfield for the first time but the ceremony only lasted two years. The Sturston well dressing concerned wells and pumps in the Ashbourne parts of Sturston parish. 1894 had been a very hot summer and water had to be pumped from these wells to supply the neighbourhood.

1895

Now We Have It, Now We Don't

A short speech by Mr Edward Ball started the Tuesday proceedings. There was the usual vigorous play in the Croft before the ball was thrown over into Sandy Lane. After 20 minutes play it was thrown back into the Croft where play was 'majestic in its earnestness'. Each side being urged on 'by the fair sex, who almost screamed themselves frantic'. The ball, after some river play despite the cold weather, left the Croft via a gateway and into Compton. It eventually went someway up The Old Hill, into and out of both Sturston Lane and Station Street, before a runner took it back down Compton, over the bridge and into the river. Here a man named Everett went off with it into the back of one of the Church Street premises. He remained hidden for some hours despite a careful search. Eventually at about 9.00pm, he surfaced and made his way to Sturston, goaling the ball and getting back again at about 10.30pm. There was no report on his fellow players feelings about the loss of play, especially after the marvellous play of the previous year.

Sturston's Year

Wednesday was cold but bright with a chilly easterly wind. Mr Frank Tomlinson – hoisted shoulder high – turned up the ball. It was unpainted this time, but bore the lettering 'C T 1894 (sic) and A B T'.

The leather quickly headed for the river at a start of a day which saw some of the best play for years. The ball was quickly landed back in the Croft before being carried under Compton Bridge to the Fox Holes by Charles Burns and James Sowter. Play eventually reached the Paddock which was covered with iced-over flood water. Down'ards pressure saw play proceeding under Station Bridge, and eventually over the railway into Clifton Road. Here was the best of the play with the Up'ards turning the Down'ards tide. The ball was forced back to The Paddock, with more players than previously. Down a yard and Compton was reached. Up another, and the fields to Sturston (blocked by The Park of course) lay ahead. Into Sandy Lane, around The Park, the Down'ards contested every inch until Mr C Etches goaled at Sturston Mill at 5.20pm.

The initials on the ball are perplexing. Had Frank got married the year before, and was it 'F' not 'C'?

Other News

In April, William ' Frenchman' Etches was found dead. He had been living in very poor circumstances and clearly had not been able to look after himself. It raised editorial comment in the local paper (AN 12/04/1895) that people like Mr Etches ought to be sharing alms houses so that someone could keep an eye on them. He lived in the Coopers alms houses at the bottom of Derby Road. ' Frenchman' Etches features on the 1862 Shrovetide painting as the left one of the three central figures around the bull ring. One of his forebears, Richard Cadman Etches left Ashbourne as a young man and later secured the release of some 12,000 British prisoners of war in France during 1795. Is this where the 'Frenchman' nickname came from? It seems likely. For more detail on R C Etches see *Ashbourne and the Valley of the Dove* pp41-54.

Eleven days after the death of Mr Etches, George Porter died at the Durham Ox Inn. He was the landlord and had written the Shrovetide song in 1891 for the Public Indignation Meeting. Regrettably his wife died seven months later on November 11th, leaving five young children. His granddaughter, Mary Winstone, is still living. There is a photograph of him in *Spirit of Ashbourne* p172.

1896

A Diversion And A Dispute

Frank Tomlinson at shoulder height, turned up the Tuesday ball which had been made three years previously and was painted the customary red, white and blue. Players on both days were less than in previous years, but after the usual solicitation about street play, the ball was off in a rush to the river at Compton Bridge. Up'ards play stopped the surge and by 2.10pm the ball was over the hedge and into Sandy Lane.

It was promptly thrown back and there were successive waves of play across the Croft to the brook and back again. Twice it entered someone's garden to be thrown back out rather quickly. There was some spirited water play despite one of the coldest days of the winter. After repeated successes at reaching Sandy Lane (only to find the leather thrown back) the ball left the Croft after an hour's play. Played along Sandy Lane and in Mr Potter's field (between what is now Peter Street and Shaw Croft flats), the ball progressed around the side of The Park. There was some diversionary play with a dead cat en-route. With darkness falling and mist rising in the fields, some 300 to 400 people watched a hard fought game that edged towards Sturston Mill.

Around the top side of the mill, the ball was rolled into a culvert leading to the wheel where James Handley and Joseph Wibberley were waiting. The two men goaled the ball together. This was disputed initially by the Down'ards, but after a cheer, followed by 'Rule Britannia', play ended. There had been from one to two thousand spectators and players. Play had been keen, but it had turned away from the Down'ards at the strategic point of the corner of Sandy Lane and Sturston Road.

Two Games At Once

Wednesday started with the singing of Auld Lang Syne, Rule Britannia and God Save the Queen, the latter finished as a solo by a 'lady in blue'. Mr Edward Ball threw up his namesake on a beautiful, calm day.

Within minutes it was away, down Sandy Lane and up Sturston Road, but progress was blocked in the field beyond The Park – 'Mr Coxon's'. The ball was quickly freed, ran to the river and thrown across to Joe Burton. It then passed amongst various runners heading for Ashbourne Green brickyard. The ball was lost for a while until seven Up'ards were seen with Joe Burton and the ball, plus a man on horse back. The party set off towards Kniveton, returning via Atlow and Hognaston Winn and goaling at 4.30pm amidst much criticism.

Because the ball had been missing for so long, it was decided to turn up a second ball and this was done at 3.45pm, at Shaw Croft by Mr R Wallis. Consequently there were two balls in play at one time. Play was largely confined to Shaw Croft for a while, when Down'ards pressure saw the ball moving on to Bank Croft and The Paddock area. Eventually the runners got it and Walter Allsop goaled it at Clifton. In an effort to keep up with play, hundreds proceeded both down the road and the railway line. The 4.20pm train was due to leave and many people boarded it, arriving in Clifton a few minutes later!

A third ball was thrown up by Frank Tomlinson and was immediately taken up Sandy Lane where it was handed to Joseph Holbrook who ran off with it up Hall Lane. There was confusion as to whether he was an Up'ard or a Down'ard and while people tried to decide which way the ball was likely to be going, Joe Burton appeared with the first ball, diverting attention for precious minutes. Holbrook and Frank Howard headed for Ashbourne Green and then, via Sandybrook Hall, Ketchem's Inn (now The Ketch) and the Fox Holes to Sturston where Howard goaled it at 6.50pm. It was estimated that a crowd of 2,000 had watched the play. With three goals, they had had a real treat.

1897

Playing Amongst The Trains

A new year saw the ball being brought down the Green Man Yard to the knoll on Shaw Croft. The ball was turned up by Frank Tomlinson, hoisted onto the shoulders of two men. The newspaper report carries several quotations of the female onlookers which seem quite strange today: 'Go it ye little Down'ards'; 'Rollicks it on'em'; 'Go it ye little beef-steak men'; 'Go it ye little bread and treacle men'; 'Bone 'em rough, boys'; 'Ginger Dan'em'!

After much evenness of play, the Down'ards broke under Compton Bridge. The reporter noted that once the Down'ards had the advantage of the water, they were 'as safe as a thief in a mill'! The ball proceeded down the river to the church where the ball was thrown out and hugged for some time in The Church Field before being pushed into the station yard. The 3.30pm train had just steamed into the station. A hug formed on the rails in the station yard amidst the shunting operations, which carried on as though the hug wasn't there! More than once play had to be suspended while the engine went by to move wagons around!

After a prolonged hug by the Railway Tavern, the ball headed for The Paddock and via Shaw Croft to Sandy Lane. It was now just after 5.00pm. Gradually it reached the fields above the park as rain fell. In the dark the hug eventually realised the ball was not beneath them as the female spectators kept shouting 'Knife it, ye little Down'ards, knife it'! The ball had been got away by Chas Etches who carried it closer to Sturston before another hug formed. However, the ball again disappeared and at about 10.00pm was goaled at Clifton by Chas Hill.

Sturston's Day

The morning of Ash Wednesday saw driving rain mixed with thick sleet and snow, but it lifted and the afternoon was bright and sunny. Mr Carter of Long Eaton 'by virtue of a subscription' i.e. he paid for the honour, threw up the leather. There was a larger crowd of players than on the previous day. The Up'ards clearly were the stronger and it was to be their day. They denied the Down'ards the water, the ball quickly heading up Sandy Lane and Hall Lane, where it was hugged by the side entrance to the Hall. There was a vain attempt to get it into the Rev Neele's garden where several players were waiting for the ball. Eventually, it reached the Wirksworth Road, the crowd stringing along to the Boothby Arms. Once into the fields beyond the Hall there was a break intercepted by Joe Burton but eventually play reached Sturston Mill. Tom Waterfall made for the culvert and goaled the ball at 3.15pm.

At 4.10pm Mr L C Coxon of Clifton turned up the second ball at Shaw Croft and there was a repeat performance with the ball proceeding to Sturston via Hall Lane and Wirksworth Road. Albert Lymm goaled it after breaking free in the fields. It was however, now after 5.00pm and the goal brought play to an end for another year.

1898

A Trial Game

Once again, Frank Tomlinson did the honours and up went the Tuesday ball on a lovely, but frosty day. Play seemed to be evenly matched and there was two hours play on Shaw Croft, before the break downstream. The Up'ards were hindered not only by Down'ards, but by the police who refused to allow the ball onto Sandy Lane. This year there was a lot of play in the new railway cutting near the tunnel, before the ball moved to the Railway Tavern. See *Spirit of Ashbourne* Vol 2 for a photograph of this building. Sometime after 6.00pm the ball was thrown into the garden adjacent to the station master's house and Charlie Howard, a Down'ard runner carried it down the old station platform, but was stopped adjacent to the goods warehouse, where the ball was hugged for a considerable time. Eventually, Sam Sowter and John Faulkner ran down the river to goal at Clifton. The Ashbourne News reported that one visitor had gone away with a desire to see the Wednesday game, having been told that Tuesday was 'only a trial game'!

Two More Wednesday Goals For Up'ards

The visitor at the previous day's 'trial' would have believed that Wednesday's game was indeed the main one. The police did not hinder play either and the day was a repeat of the previous year. George Gather turned up the ball after the usual ceremonies. Into Sandy Lane and up Hall Lane the ball was moved. Hug after hug, the game progressed towards the Boothby Arms in Wirksworth Road. After some running in the fields, Joe Burton headed up the Sturston Mill culvert at 4.30pm.

On the stroke of 5.00pm, up went the second ball, released by Mr Tomlinson. The Down'ards were soon away with it but were denied a break having reached the edge of town. Some hard work and good throwing reversed the play and the ball was returned to the Croft. Travelling rapidly along Sandy Lane towards Sturston Lane, two milk carts were met. Fortunately the ball was picked up and carried past them. With darkness falling, the Up'ards relied on the runners who got it to the river. F Bradley of the Engine Inn waded upstream for nearly half a mile with the leather before W Prince of the Izaak Walton Hotel, took the ball and goaled it at 6.30pm. He turned up the ball in 1905 and 1907.

Other News
The Sale of The Green Man

The local paper (AN 11/03/1898) reported that the cost of the balls, including one shilling for painting, was £2.11.0d. A total of £4.16.6d had been collected and the difference was remitted to Derby Childrens' Hospital by Messrs E B Ball and F Tomlinson. The same issue reported on prosecutions following Shrovetide games at Dorking.

Just after Shrovetide a proposal was made (AN 18/03/1898) for the erection of a road bridge over the brook near Clifton Mill. The work started in October and was nearing completion in March 1899. Prior to the bridge, a ford existed here (see detail on Clifton Mill, p46).

The year saw another milestone. On 31/03/1898, the Green Man & Blacks Head Hotel (the 'Royal' was not in use at this time) was offered for sale by auction with 200 people present. There were two lots. Lot 1 consisted of 16 bedrooms, dining and billiard rooms, commercial, coffee, drawing and two sitting rooms, two bars, stillroom, travellers luggage room etc. There was also a suite of rooms used as the boardroom by the Guardians of the Ashbourne Union and more recently by the Rural District Council. Down the yard was stabling for about 60 horses, a cottage for the head ostler or stable man etc.

Lot 2 consisted of Shaw Croft extending to 4 ac, 1 rood and 4 perches. Bids started at £6,000 and the hotel was withdrawn at £9,750. Lot 2 was not offered.

A buyer was found at the beginning of July when it was sold to Messrs Stretton of Derby for a reported £11,500. (AN 08/07/1898) In 1919, J C Prince purchased it (see detail under 1919). At that time the 1898 purchase price was quoted as £11,250. Four days after the sale to Strettons, Mrs Fanny Wallis (the hotel's licensee) died, on 06/07/1898. She was 64 years old and the daughter of John Wheeldon of Wyaston and the widow of Robert Wallis who died in 1870. She was connected with the Green Man for over forty years and the Wallis's had been landlords there since at least 1840. The hotel had been on the market for some years.

It was Robert Wallis who had thrown the game a lifeline in 1863 offering the Shaw Croft as an alternative venue for turning up the balls. The tradition has continued to this day except in 1879 and 1880 (when R H Frank rented the field to prevent the balls being turned up) plus 1968 and 2001 when there was no official game.

Notable guests at the Hotel included Dr Johnson but perhaps the most unusual was Madamoiselle d'Jeck who stayed for two nights – 22 and 23 September 1830. She was on her way to Birmingham and was an elephant! Her attendant rode on a pony and it followed like a spaniel behind her master. She had given a bow to the tollgate keeper near the town (? Green Lane). On reaching the town, one observer (who had clearly never seen an illustration of an elephant) was so terrified he froze to the spot exclaiming 'Will nobody tell me what it is? Will nobody stop it?'

She was exhibited to the public on the Thursday (23 September) and early the next day left with a following of curious bystanders. She weighed $7^1/_2$ tons and had killed a man in Newcastle a short time previously. (DC 25/09/1830)

The 1898 sale particulars of the hotel (above) refer to the Board Room. This was the Committee Room of the Board of Guardians and had been used as such for 50 years. The *Parish Councils Act* of 1894 forbid meetings on licensed premises but Ashbourne ignored this. In 1895 a Local Government Board Inspector told the Guardians to find alternative premises. This too was ignored until the Guardians were surcharged for the rent of the room. Meetings then moved to the Town Hall before buying the premises adjacent to Lloyds Bank on Compton. (AN 26/04/1901) Prior to the meetings at the Hotel of the Board of Guardians, the Hotel was used by the Magistrates of the Wirksworth Hundred to hear cases. (DC 26/12/1829) This room later became the hotel dining room.

1899

Celery and Cabbages On The Road To Clifton

The Shaw Croft had changed hands since the last game and was now owned by Mr F Stretton who placed the field at the disposal of the town. Shrove Tuesday was sunny and warm as the shutters went up. The ball came down Dig Street and after the singing, Mr W Coxon hoisted up the ball. The leather was a present from a London well wisher (Mr W Wibberley) but only survived 20 minutes play before it was kicked to pieces. A new ball was thrown up at 2.33pm by J Gallimore and nearly an hour later Sam and Jim Sowter got it away down river through the Fox Holes and on towards the Station Bridge where one of the hug reportedly lost the back of his trousers. Someone lost a bowler hat too, for it was to be seen sailing along ahead of the players! The ball was landed however, and carried into Mayfield Road where 'a lady asserted herself, and with a bean stick she defended her celery and cabbages from the onslaught of sundry youths'. Play moved on down the road to the relief of both lady and players who gradually worked down to the town football field, which was described as being a swamp. Here play wallowed before reaching the railway as the 4.20pm train ran through.

The ball crossed the Clifton Road and unusually proceeded up the fields to The Hollow before James Bradley, of Mayfield, goaled at Clifton at 5.20pm.

Play In the Park

Mr F Tomlinson turned up the Wednesday ball once more. It immediately went to the river, but within three minutes Joe Burton had thrown it first into Sandy Lane, and then into The Park. The crowd followed, jubilant at treading ground denied them for over 20 years. Burton tried to run it but was stopped and a Down'ard, Collins, threw the ball into Sturston Lane (now Belper Road). The fence consisted of iron railings which were topped with barbed wire.

After some play in the road, the ball went back into The Park for some of the day's best play. Eventually it was thrown into Coxon's field 'after a terrific struggle'. Having reached the river, the runners picked it up and it disappeared for a long time. Off to the Ketcham's Inn and Agnes Meadow it went, with the crowd at Sturston slowly dwindling. At 5.52pm John Hawksworth carefully brought it into the wheel. It had been raining since mid-afternoon, but play in The Park made up for that!

Messrs Frank Tomlinson, W Coxon and G Furber made the collection for the balls and collected £3.18.6d. Three balls were procured at a cost of £2.5.0d and the balance given to the Cottage Hospital. Comment was made in the paper (AN 17/02/1899) that the relations with the police were good. When the ball had got into Mayfield Road and Sturston Lane, the police superintendent only had to wave his hand and the crowd cleared to allow Joe Burton to pilot vehicles safely through. There was very little fighting and drunkeness. The same paper reported, however, that at Dorking four balls had been turned up and all four were seized by the police.

This was the first year that play had been allowed in The Park. There is an indication above that it had been allowed previously although the 1821 song makes it clear that it was out of bounds at that time and probably had been for a considerable time, as the house was the height of local society. The Hall had been purchased by R H Frank upon the death of Sir John Bent (? a tenant). Frank had been prominent in trying to suppress the game, both as a local landowner and as a magistrate. After his death, his wife forbid access, but the estate had been sold in 1898 on her death. It had opened as a hotel by 1901 with William Prince the landlord – he sought to extend the dining room in that year.

(AN 01/3/1901). Clearly the new occupiers took a more lenient view of football access. The *Ashbourne News* (27/02/1903) states that The Park was closed against the players in 1879 although Tom Cundy said it was in 1881 when he had goaled the ball. (AN 28/02/1908)

1900
Street Play For A Change

The Boer War was uppermost in many minds. Some of the previous year's players were now fighting for a different goal. The news of the capitulation of General Cronje (the Boer Commander) and 4,000 men had been received in the town on Shrove Tuesday morning. After the lunch, Mr W Coxon turned up the ball. Within five minutes Joe Burton tossed it into Sandy Lane and it was then thrown into The Park. The war was not too far away with cries of 'where's Mester Buller today?'

Eventually the ball was pitched into Sturston Lane and 'Tug' Bradley ran it to Station Street where it was hugged for a while before J Haycock threw the ball into The Paddock. Play continued via the Wesleyan Chapel Garden into Church Street and up St John Street. 'Just like old times' an old lady remarked. The police held back and at 3.30pm the ball turned the corner into Sandy Lane. For nearly 90 minutes it veered around Shaw Croft before Sam Sowter took it under Compton Bridge. It was played around The Paddock for a while and then the game lurched via the station into Church Street. It travelled the whole length of the two streets to Sandy Lane yet again, closely contested the whole way. In the dark the ball disappeared into Shaw Croft where Joe Burton picked it up and ran it up The Park. The ball at one stage went over the railings into the enclosed portion of The Park (really forbidden ground) but it was quickly retrieved. After more close play, the runners got it and Tom Taylor goaled it at Sturston after one of 'the most stubborn football days that Ashbourne has ever known'.

Up'ards Clean Sweep

The Wednesday's game saw Mr F Tomlinson turning up the ball with a warning that the police would not tolerate street play as seen the day before. Initial Shaw Croft play quickly saw the ball heading into The Park where it was played up and down before being picked up by Frank Smith of Tissington who ran with it and threw it into Coxon's field. Further running saw it goaled at Sturston at 3.30pm, after a final hug by the mill, by Jack Etches of Ballidon. Tom Waterfall threw up the second ball at 4.20pm. The leather was played through the Bath House Garden fronting Sandy Lane and Shaw Croft before reaching Sturston Lane. The ball worked its way to Sturston by road with Fred Ashton of Tissington goaling it just after 7.00pm.

Other News

For years the Up'ards had the barrier of The Park which now seems to have been lifted. It was replaced by the new railway. The railway line to Buxton had caused a realignment of the station and a line across The Paddock creating a potentially formidable barrier to the Down'ards. The balls had been made by Mr Charles Tarlton of Buxton Road. Out of the collection, a broken window was repaired at a cost of 2s 4d, the three new balls provided for, and over £4 given to the local War Fund.

During the evening of Shrove Tuesday and Ash Wednesday, a free concert was given by the Misses Clough of Rochdale for the Women's Total Abstinence Union. This was repeated for several years thereafter and probably had been held previously. However, in 1901 Supt Burford of the police advised the Petty Sessions justices that there was not a single case of drunkenness or any other misdemeanour arising out of the Shrovetide football.

Incidentally in 1900 W Edge of Dig Street advertised oranges and lemons 'for Shrovetide'. There is another report in 1909 of someone following the hug down Clifton Road, selling oranges and the 1862 Shrovetide painting includes Betty Blore with her basket. She was described as being a vendor of nuts and oranges. This must have been an old custom now lost.

In late August 1900 an application was received by the licensing justices for a new hotel on part of The Paddock in Station Road. Thus the Station Hotel was to be built on yet another part of this traditional area of play for the old game. It opened in November 1901.

Perhaps the most important thing in peoples' minds during the year was the Boer War, with a long list of local men seeing active service. They included for instance, Private Williamson of the Military Frontier Force who 'took a very active part in the Shrovetide football games last year'. (AN 02/02/1900)

The local paper refers to Tom Cundy's 1893 ball accompanying Dan Cockayne on the last train into Mafeking quoting a report. (ANT 04/03/1982) It is clear that this is not quite accurate. The incident is referred to in the *Natal Witness* of 10/10/1899 (partially quoted in AN 15/12/1899). On 2 November Dan Cockayne drove the last mail train out of Ladysmith (not Mafeking) under fire after volunteering to do so. He was 50 years old at the time and lived in Pietermaritzburg. He had formerly been an engine driver on the Midland Railway and his father had run the brickyard at Ashbourne Green.

Our local paper quotes a poem on the event. This was followed by a rather long and rambling letter from Mr Cockayne describing the war etc. (AN 23/03/1900)

"Two Heroes
There are heroes many in battle,
There are heroes by flood and field,
But I tell in simple story of heroes who would not yield
Of men who were like their engines,
Composed of iron and steel,
Who never stopped for shot or shell, or the cannon's thunder peal;
Of heroes brave on the railroad track,
Of men who would never quail
Just list to a simple story of two heroes of the rail.

The first is an engine driver;
He was driving the last mail train,
Well known among the drivers, was my hero, Dan Cockayne.
The bullets were flying o'er him,
From the foe on the nearest ridge,
And he said ' Thank God!' as round the curve at last he saw the bridge.
He thought of the lives behind him,
And he heard the wheels as they said –
' Make a rush, make a rush, make a rush,
Dan, steam ahead, steam ahead, steam ahead!'
But there on the bridge before him
Stood a man with natives two,
He knew 'twas the guardian of the bridge, staunch – to his task still true.
He thought of the lives behind him –
For the one, they might all fall dead;
But he heard the rumble of the wheels –
' Slow her down, slow her down,' they said.
He slowed her down, and he dragged them in;
Then full speed went the train,
Safe and sound to Estcourt across the Weenon plain.

My second hero, a volunteer,
He offered to drive the train
When others thought it as hopeless chance – his name was Joe Borain.
' I'll drive her if you'll let me –
It is either do or die;
We may as well smash in the armoured train as here like cowards lie'.
So he drove her, drove her safely
Through hurtling shot and shell,

Out to a very Heaven, after that shrieking hell.
So I've told in simple story
Of heroes brave and true,
Who dared for England's honour what all brave men will do.
They risked their lives – and our children
Will tell aye again and again,
Of the trains and the men who drove them – Dan Cockayne and Joe Borain."

In both cases there is no mention of Mr Cockayne having Tom Cundy's ball with him but it makes a nice story even if it cannot be confirmed!

Dan Cockayne's exploits were not confined to this one event however. On 07/02/1901 he was blown up while going to the assistance of another train wrecked nine miles from Standerton and he was in another train which the Boers tried to wreck but failed. (AN 06/03/1903) It is clear from the above that Dan Cockayne was quite a hero and his full recognition is long overdue.

1901

Down'ards At Atlow

The sun broke through as Frank Tomlinson turned up the first ball of the new century. The ball quickly left Shaw Croft for The Park where it was played from end to end with some fast and loose play for an hour before it ended up in Sturston Lane. The hug moved very slowly up the lane past The Park and into Coxon's field where the ball moved with greater freedom. Eventually after a lot of play the ball reached Sturston Mill. A turn of events occured and five Down'ards set off in possession of the ball towards Agnes Meadow, with Joe Burton and Tom Taylor in pursuit. At Atlow, two more Up'ards arrived and a hug was formed. The latter obtained possession and ran it back to Sturston – Joe Burton taking the honour at 6.30pm.

'Old Ninety's' Day

Mr Jack Hawksworth turned up the Wednesday ball, which was dedicated to the new King. 'Rule Britannia' was sung and the National Anthem, in keeping with the new monarch, was sung twice. Play centred around Shaw Croft and Sandy Lane until mid afternoon, with one lady exhorting the players with shouts of 'Play for the King, play for the Queen, my lads, give it em my little lads in blue'!

The ball eventually reached Compton after a tremendous hug. Play turned into Station Street after action between the Dog and Partridge Inn and the Roebuck Inn in Compton. After reaching the corset works, it returned to Compton. 'Down it my lads; don't let 'Ninety' have it!' was a cry against Joe Burton. 'Ninety' Burton is an expression still heard in Ashbourne to this day. The ball then returned down Compton to meet a line of policemen blocking the way to Dig Street, but with good humour this time. After a lot of play around Shaw Croft and The Park boundary, Up'ards took the ball along by Bradley Wood, across to Corley and into the mill. Only a score of people remained – it was now 8.15pm and George Hall took the ball to the wheel for another Up'ards victory.

1902

Refreshments Before Ritual At Sturston

It was a white Shrove Tuesday and Mr Stephen Bloomer, the International and Derby County forward was to have turned up the ball. But he was unable to come and W Storer, the Derbyshire cricketer had the honour, although the ball was not hurled from shoulder height. The ball had been painted by Mr John Bell of Buxton Road with portraits of the new King and Queen.

After initial play in the Croft, the ball reached Sandy Lane at 3.40pm, with 'the snow playing down'ards'. The vicar and his curates were 'keen followers' and in the hug were two men from the legal profession – Messrs Bamford and Wilson. Play skirted The Park and into Sturston Lane where a milk float, driven by a farmer received a barrage of snowballs. Diversions over, interest returned to the game progressing through the fields before Up'ards runners made off with the leather. Their journey took in the Ketcham's Inn and Pethills, stopping for bread, cheese and jugs of tea at one farm, and milk and ales at another before reaching Sturston Mill inwardly fortified. Only three Down'ards were waiting and Joe Burton slipped through to goal the ball at 6.30pm.

Hide And Seek

Wednesday was a sunny day and play livelier, longer and more keenly contested. Dennis Allsopp, the ex Nottingham Forest goalkeeper turned up the ball. The latter bore the words 'Coronation, 1902' and had been painted by Messrs E M Sellers & Son. Play initially concentrated around the Croft and Sandy Lane, with occasional diversions into The Park. Eventually The Park saw a lot of running play and some hugging. Some participants fell down a well, but no injuries were reported.

The game eventually worked along Sandy Lane, into Sturston Road and then Compton. Play was hard as it worked down towards the line of policemen drawn up across the bridge. However, play never reached them, heading down King Edward Street to The Paddock. George Wibberley broke away and also broke ice as he went under the Station Road bridge. After play near the station, Joe Burton ran off with the ball, disappearing into the garden at the back of Dr Sadler's (The Mansion). Everyone knew he had hidden it, but nobody knew where.

Eventually only a faithful few watched and waited and at 8.30pm Joe was spotted returning to his prize. He withdrew on realising he had been seen. A further search was made and Tom Slater found the ball in a closet behind the almshouses. Despite the apparent Down'ards advantage, Joe Burton again found himself with it and hid it yet again, in the railway tunnel. It was found at 10.00pm by George Ainsworth who made off to Clifton where the first goal in three years was scored – presumably by Ainsworth, although the report is not clear. The balls this year had been made by Mr C Tarlton.

1903

Play In The Yards

The previous year's snow was replaced by storm clouds and a 'wild wind from the west' that brought driving rain. The red, white and blue leather was turned up by Mr John Winterton, as usual hoisted onto the shoulders of stalwarts. For 40 minutes, play ebbed and flowed across Shaw Croft. Four times the ball landed in Sandy Lane, only to be thrown back. It even clattered on the tiles of rear buildings of The Bath House before it eventually emerged into Compton. A tide of humanity saw play progress into Station Street. The ball disappeared over a door at the Corset Works, returning to Station Street via Brown's Yard. The game then returned to Compton with a hug opposite the Durham Ox Inn.

Captain Holland (Chief Constable of Derbyshire) was present and the bridge was blocked by a strong police presence. The ball was pitched into the water and was thrown out again into the White Hart yard. There was then considerable play – and some damage to strawberry beds etc – in the adjacent gardens before the ball returned to the water. Play proceeded upriver and the ball left the water at Blacks Head Yard and into St John Street but the police forced play back down the yard and into the river yet again. Up'ards pressure persisted and Back Bridge was reached after diversions across Shaw Croft. Play reached Sandy Lane and then Hall Lane before reaching the Market Place via Town Hall Yard. Having reached Union Street, George Parkin, who was getting changed to join the play, saw the ball outside his Union Street shop. He grabbed it and ran it up Dove House Green, down Mappleton Lane to the Tanyard where he passed it on. Josiah Walker eventually got it and goaled it at Sturston, 'partaking of tea en-route' and also after being chased seven times around a hay rick by an opponent. He entered the wheel pit along the spindle of the wheel to goal his ball.

Even Honours

A better day saw a much bigger crowd as an old Ashburnian, Ernest Porter of Buxton, turned up the leather. The ball was soon in The Park and then across to Sturston Lane where it was hugged before it eventually landed in Coxon's field. Play made for Sturston, interrupting golfers en route. After continuing struggles, George Roome of Kniveton was escorted to the wheel for a goal just before 4.00pm. The ball was then taken to the knoll adjoining the Mill for the customary singing of 'Rule Britannia'.

Mr Guy Derbyshire turned up the second ball at Shaw Croft. The ball was hugged for a while before reaching Hall Lane and St John Street. Despite police pressure with almost a hug of their own, the ball got into the street, proceeding to the Blacks Head Yard and then Shaw Croft. Charlie Ainsworth secured it and reached Sandy Lane, only to be stopped by five men on a dray. The ball then proceeded up Sturston Road and into Compton as darkness fell. After a hug in the middle of the street, the ball moved to The Paddock via Malbon's Yard, where a player in a white smock was in the action.

From The Paddock, play reverted to Shaw Croft yet again before George Ainsworth and Bob Harding got away up the gardens at the back of Compton. They ran it via Derby Road and The Firs to Old Hill and then on to Clifton, losing their bearings en route. They eventually emerged by Clifton School and goaled the ball at 11.20pm.

Other News

Indirect evidence of the Committee's members is furnished from a note that the annual Shrovetide Collection had been made by Frank Tomlinson, Jack Hawksworth and Samuel Boden (of the Green Man Hotel, who turned up the ball in 1904). The following year (i.e. 1904), the same men did it together with John Winterton of the Cock Inn. It seems likely that these men composed the Committee, or at least part of it at that time. The donations, amounting to £7/10/5d (£7.52p) in 1903 and a little more the year after, was given to Derby Infirmary, Ashbourne Cottage Hospital and Ashbourne Nursing Home after deducting for the cost of new balls and damage caused during the two day's play.

The local paper reported continuing problems for the game in Dorking, where twenty people were summonsed and 10/- (50p) fines imposed on eighteen of them. (AN 13/03/1903) A report to the licensing justices indicated that at the end of 1902, there were 61 licensed victuallers in the town (three of whom had a six day license), 8 beer house keepers, 1 beer off licence holder, 3 people licensed for the sale of wines and spirits and two for wines and sweets (off the premises), making a total of 75. This meant one establishment for every 115 people in the parish of Ashbourne. The current figure, excluding restaurants and supermarkets is about 1:400. In 1902, 96 males and 5 females had been convicted for drink-related offences. (AN 20/02/1903) When Dan Dockayne returned to the town on holiday from South Africa after more than two decades of absence, he was pleased to find that the number of pubs was much lower than when he left.

As Shrovetide drew near, it was reported that the first ball would be turned up by S Boden on the Tuesday and Joseph Harrison of Buxton on the Wednesday, but this of course did not happen. (AT 20/02/1903)

1904

Police Play

There was a sunny start to Tuesday's play, despite considerable rain of late. The ball was turned up by Mr Morgan Roberts, secretary of the Derbyshire Football Association. After a short amount of play in the Croft, with some good throwing being seen, the ball quickly reached Hall Lane and then turned into St John Street. It was hugged outside the Wellington Inn before the police – who had been caught off guard – managed to push the play back up the street, where it went into The Park. Despite a lot of hugging, there was some good throwing and kicking this afternoon. From The Park the play worked upriver despite strenuous opposition, and Harry Buckley touched the millwheel at about 4.00pm. The usual ceremony occurred before the return to Shaw Croft.

Mr C Tarlton (the ball maker) turned up the second ball and after some loose play, the ball eventually made for Compton Bridge and down river. In the gardens behind the Wesleyan Chapel, Joe Burton transferred play to Church Street. Eventually the hug turned into Station Road, where the police started pushing play along to Station Street. After a hug on the railway line near to the tunnel, the ball returned to the water and a hug near to the Old Station. Joe Burton and George Parkin, in the dark, got it after play had reached Mayfield Road. They hid it, but George Leese, a Down'ard found it near Mr Key's barn at the top of Church Bank. He turned for home and goaled at Clifton at 7.35pm.

An Early End

Tuesday's sunshine was followed by snow the next day. Mr S Boden turned up the ball and some fast and loose play saw the ball moving all over the Croft, in and out of Sandy Lane and the river. At one point many caps were seen floating down river after a hard hug in the Henmore. Eventually play moved off down Sandy Lane, across Mr Potter's field to Compton and The Paddock as the Down'ards took advantage. Progress ended here and the ball returned up river to Shaw Croft and then into The Park. The game was tightly fought, the ball going in and out of The Park, and being quickly thrown back out of cottage gardens at Sturston Lane. Each Up'ards advance was quickly checked but eventually, play left The Park for Sturston. Dick Botham made up river, in and out of deep water with Up'ards support. Down'ards pressure melted away and Botham goaled it at 5.30pm.

Other News

Mr John Burton died on April 5th, aged 77 years. He had 168 descendants, some having predeceased him. The included 11 children, 85 grand children and 72 great grandchildren. He lived in Union Street next door to the house in which he had been born. At one time he had been the caretaker at the Workhouse. (AN 09/04/1920) He was the father of ' Ninety' Burton.

The ANT of 17/02/1977 carried an article comparing the goaling achievements of the Burtons and the Sowters. 'Ninety' Burton goaled seven balls, including a boy's game ball. His daughter Doris Mugglestone and son Norman scored in 1943 and 1931 respectively. Two cousins were Fred Hallam (1936) and Redvers Wibberley (1924 and 1927). Other family members who scored were Charles Mee (1930) and Charles Coxon (1964). The article carried a photo of Edward Burton. Trilby Shaw recalls that each Shrovetide, John Burton erected a table at the top of Tiger Yard with a barrel of beer on it, freely available for members of his family. Just before 2pm, he walked down to Shaw Croft carring the Union flag with his family behind him in procession. With 168 descendants, draining the barrel would presumably have been no problem! After his death, 'Ninety' carried the flag and was reported doing just that in 1915.

1905

Play In The Market Place

Mr W Prince landlord of Ashbourne Hall Hotel until 1910, turned up the last of the balls made by Mr Tarlton. The ball immediately went for the Bath House corner of Shaw Croft with feminine cries of 'lash it at 'em, Down'ards'. Rain fell as play moved around the Croft and in and out of the river, the ball having to be retrieved from the rear of R J Potter's premises at one point.

The ground was very soft from rain but play progressed to The Park for a while before returning to Sandy Lane, where new houses were being built. After inspection by players and crowd, play reached Sturston Road. Down'ards pressure saw much play mid-road to the consternation of a car driver honking his horn! After further loose play in The Park, Down'ards regained control, and the play reached Compton via Sturston Lane. King Edward Street at this time was a cul-de-sac with a wall across the road. Such was the pressure that the wall gave way and the ball crossed Bank Croft to reach the river. A good throw saw the ball in the gardens behind Church Street with the game continuing on Mr Cooke's lawn. Play then resumed in Church Street and Dig Street with a police line across St John Street. There used to be a footbridge from the Dig Street end of the Green Man Yard across the river to Shaw Croft and this saw action before the ball took to the river once more.

It left the water up Horse & Jockey Yard and reached the Market Place where there was a menagerie. Round and round the latter the game progressed to the accompaniment of growling from alarmed animals. To their relief, play returned to Horse & Jockey Yard, pushed on its way by the police. The ball reached the Croft with thunder and lightening overhead. In the dark, George Ainsworth got the ball away under Compton Bridge and it was played on Bank Croft through hail and rain. After being thrown into Dr Maclean's garden, the ball was lost to view for a while, probably being hidden. Found between 6.00pm and 7.00pm by a Mr Tunnicliffe and others they took it quietly down to Clifton, where Tunnicliffe goaled it at 7.20pm.

A Drenching In And Out Of The Water

The Wednesday ball was turned up by Frank Evershed, not Mr Ernest Evershed of Burton-on-Trent as reported in the paper. Vigorous play saw more action in and out of the river with attempts to get the ball onto Back Bridge. A parson ended up in the water and on the bridge, the ball smashed into a camera erected there and also knocked off a parlour maid's white cap, 'but it was quickly returned by Mr Rigby'. A stampede along Sandy Lane saw a hug outside Hilton's warehouse for 15 minutes and a bombardment of ownerless and muddy caps, with more than one person getting a swipe on the face. Round by the Roebuck and Compton play proceeded, reaching the water again at the bridge. The game turned up through the Croft to The Park with heavy rain falling. Play was grounded for an hour before the drenched outing reached Coxon's field where the game was 'very exciting'. Up'ards pressure won the day though, and Tom Botham goaled the ball at 6.30pm.

Other News

This was the last year that one of Charles Tarlton's balls were turned up (by William Prince of the Ashbourne Hall Hotel). He had made, or helped to make, balls for over forty years. This means that he could well have been involved with the making of the first ball thrown up on Shaw Croft, in 1863. Mrs Woolley's ball in 1860 was made by Joseph Brandreath, however. Mr Tarlton had been a postman for over thirty years but was not on the staff and therefore not eligible for a pension following a stroke. The Shrovetide Committee collected £33/10/0d (£33.50p) this year and after giving a guinea to the three usual charities, paying for the two balls (£1/15/0d or £1.75p) and 2/- (10p) postage, gave the rest to Mr Tarlton. It must be more than just a coincidence that John Wibberley who died in 1908 had also been a part time postman (he was a shoemaker by trade) and also made Shrovetide balls for many years (see page 96).

The 1905 game report states that the Wednesday ball was turned up by Ernest Evershed of Burton-on-Trent. However, it was reported later (AN 17/03/1905) that this was in error. The ball was turned up by Mr Frank Evershed, 'the noted international Rugby player, who on that occasion favoured the old game with his presence and assistance'.

The *Ashbourne Telegraph's* correspondent reported that during this year's play, the game was interrupted by a motor car for the first time. However, a week later, George Cantrell of Ripley wrote to say that his vehicle had been stopped at the top of Compton on Ash Wednesday, 1903 (AT 17/03/05). On 24/02/05, the same paper reported the death of Capt Parry at Stonehouse, Gloucestershire. He was 69 years old.

1906

A Storm of Snow And Sleet

With three inches of sleet on the ground, the ball was turned up by Mr Percy Morgan of London. The ball quickly entered the river and soon left the Croft under Back Bridge, taken by Jack Brown. The ball was trundled towards the Fish Pond where it was pushed and sniffed in the water by a dog. At last, as the ball bobbed about on its own, Jack Dyche braved the icy depths and was soon followed by others. After a lot of waterplay, including a long hug, the ball broke away while in Mr Coxon's field and play returned to The Park. Strenuous play saw the ball move upstream before returning to The Park for a third time. The game was seeing more water play than had been seen for a long time.

Eventually, the ball left the water and was hugged on land where 'steam from the saturated players rose as from a lime kiln'. C & G Ainsworth ran the ball towards The Green Road and a struggle took place behind Ashbourne Green Post Office. After some fast and furious play, the ball returned to the river and Up'ards pressure won the day. Tom Botham carried the ball upriver and Tom Waterfall touched the wheel at 4.30pm.

Mr Fred Ashton of Tissington turned up the second leather, urging play 'in the old style and out of the streets'. After some waterplay, Tom Waterfall threw the ball into Compton and play proceeded into Bank Croft. 'Don't let 'em get it in them gardens' cried one, obviously still rankled by the previous year's runaway ball. Play was described as terrific, with much catch and throw work as the loose ball made its way under Station Bridge and through the station. The Down'ards had the advantage and the ball was goaled without opposition at Clifton at about 7.00pm. The report (AN 02/03/1906) does not name the goaler but the inference is that it was Jim Sowter and this was confirmed by the *Ashbourne Telegraph*.

Honours Equal

After a hard frost, a thaw and drizzling rain set in. The ground was in a terrible state as Mr J C Prince of the George and Dragon turned up the Wednesday ball. Both he and his brother Bill, who turned up the year before, were Committee members. The ball quickly reached Sandy Lane where Joe Burton ran the ball through the gateway of The Hall Hotel and into The Park. The crowd followed as the police tried to shut them out! A rough game ensued on the Wednesday Football Club pitch before the hug tested the strength of The Hall stableyard doors. Play returned towards The Hall where Mr Prince awaited, intending to hoist the ball to the crowd for a second time if it entered The Hall garden. Sleet fell as play careered around the fields and river. Two players were knocked insensible and were carried away (there had been another carried away on the Tuesday). It was to be Up'ards ball however, and Charles 'Bossy' Goodwin goaled it around 3.30pm. Mr Goodwin lived until 5th January 1968, he was 83 years old.

Mr John Winterton of the Cock Inn turned up the second ball just after 4pm amid falling rain. After a little play, the ball reached the water at lightening speed. Play repeated the second ball game of the day before: at Compton Bridge, the leather was thrown out by Jack Prince into the street. Play proceeded to Station Street and back twice before the ball was pitched into the Henmore by Lloyds Bank. It came out at Bank Croft and returned down King Edward Street to Compton. Across the Croft next, the surge continued to Back Bridge where play entered the brook. Onwards into The Park, the ensemble progressed. The ball was thrown into the Fish Pond where Harry Buckley swam to recover it.

The Croft was revisited, the scene of the days best play only a little time before. On again it went, to the Station via King Edward Street. There the ball went missing before being found in some timber in one of the sidings. Charlie Ainsworth and others took it away to Bell's Pastures and later, on to Clifton where he goaled it at 11.28pm, not surprisingly, without any opposition per the *Ashbourne News*. The timing was 11.45pm according to the *Ashbourne Telegraph*!

A Tragedy

The 1906 Tuesday witnessed the second fatality during play. William Tunnicliffe, a 24-year-old labourer employed by Mr Chadfield of Yeaveley was found on Ash Wednesday. He was lying in a field at Clifton belonging to Mr Pegge by Mr J Leeson who had gone to measure some timber. Pegges were the tenants of Hollies Farm. The body was removed to the Cock Inn, Clifton, where an inquest was held the following day. It appears that Tunnicliffe had been drinking in town before taking a prominent part in the game, including the water play, as the game progressed from the Station down the river towards Clifton. He seems to have left the play which was near Peach's farm at Clifton. Possibly his intention had been to return home to Yeaveley. He had fallen down and for some reason, possibly exhaustion, had not got up again. The night had been very cold and frosty and he died from exposure. He was found lying on his back, his hands clenched. He had perhaps decided to rest for a while.

1907

Ball Kicked To Pieces Again

Snow and ice had been blanketing the town for sometime as Shrove Tuesday arrived. On the day, snow fell heavily until some four inches lay on the ground. The snow then turned to rain which then fell all day. Among the onlookers – rain or no rain – was Matthew Cleaver who (AN 15/02/1907) claimed to have goaled more balls than any other man, including the one thrown from the upper window in the Market Place. The quantity was not stated, but was given as eight goals years later. 'Black Harry' and 'Ninety' Burton were also in the crowd, so was Isaac Marsh who was heard to remark that he was the first player to be arrested forty years ago.

The ball carried the legend 'Shrovetide Football, Ye Olde Game 1907', and the Cockayne arms. It was turned up by Mr John C Prince, who had moved from The George & Dragon to the Green Man Hotel. Play moved off towards Sandy Lane with some fine throwing. As usual the female onlookers were giving their vocal support: 'Rollicks it Up'ards', etc. Now passed out of use, 'Rollicks' meant 'moving in a swaying manner, with a frolicsome air'; it was very apt! After a while, the ball went under Back Bridge and was thrown out towards Joe Burton. However, George Ainsworth, a Down'ards runner, intercepted it and made off towards The Green. He was stopped near the Green Hall and the hug moved the ball to the brickyard, where the ball was thrown into the claypit by George Brown. It was eventually retrieved and play continued on the football pitch. However, both players and spectators

Bill Prince at the knoll on Shaw Croft in 1907. In the right hand corner is Jack Hawksworth

were reduced in strength, as many had been left in town not knowing where the ball had gone to. Play continued in the fields for a while before the Up'ards came eventually in sight of the Mill and a one sided game was concluded, T Waterfall goaling the ball at 3.40pm. After a verse of 'Rule Britannia' on the adjacent knoll, everybody trudged back to town. Mr T L Demery turned up the second ball before many Up'ards players had returned, giving the Down'ards an advantage.

A bottle of whisky offered to the first player to touch the ball when it entered the water went to 'Trip' Connell. Down'ards pressure saw the ball heading down stream towards Bank Croft and the Fox Holes where a good throw reached Joe Burton. He crossed the gardens to Church Street, but was denied access up Henstock's Yard. Fierce play in Church Street ensued, with a police line blocking the street. Hug after hug continued to the tune of 'Rule Britannia'. The ball broke near the Wesleyan Chapel and open play up Church Street and into Dig Street followed. Police effort was rewarded as the ball returned to the Croft after a prolonged hug outside the Cock Inn in Dig Street.

There was much water play with some twenty people in the swollen waters which were nearly bank high. A fine throw cleared play from the Henmore, but a rent was noticed in the ball. As darkness approached, the ball was pulled to pieces and the game abandoned. This was a pity as the second game had been the better of the two with more kicking than hugging. Loss of the ball resulted from it 'being suspended near a gas jet which caused the stitches to give way', rather than bad workmanship.

Shoulder Deep in The River

Wednesday's weather was kinder as Mr William Prince, in the absence of Mr W Woodisse, turned up the ball. There was a lot of water lying in the Croft and water play was not confined to the river. Play made for Sturston through The Park with open play in Mr Coxon's field. Not many ventured into the shoulder high water to oppose Up'ards player George Roome who had the ball. He went a long way before the Down'ards tired of the scene and stopped him. A hug ensued on the bank before the whole lot fell into the water. Roome continued his progress upriver, the ball being thrown to the bank for 50 yards of difficult water. Others went in to aid him and the ball slowly made its way against the current. At the usually deep Cantrell's Hole – now exceptionally deep, the ball was landed again and the Down'ards made a last stand. Roome continued bravely on, nearing exhaustion, but the honour of goaling went to A Buckley at 3.10pm.

Mr R Cooke turned up the second ball and after some play in the Croft it reached Compton. Play pursued up the street and into Station Street with a hug outside the double doors of the Corset Works. Up'ards pressure saw play return to Compton where the Down'ards tried to force the ball into Malbon's Yard and onto The Paddock. This was denied, but they took the advantage down river from Compton Bridge. In the new street, ie the King Edward Street extension, 'which was made famous by the action in the High Court', another hug occurred by the Station Hotel, before reaching The Paddock. Up'ards pressure saw play return to the hotel and then across the road, with a hug on the railway lines, the crowd lining each platform.

Young girls following the hug, 1907

Play went down river, to Tomlinson's field adjacent to the churchyard where police were stationed in case the game came near. However, it re-crossed the river towards the Good's Station where hug after hug ensued, causing shunting operations to be suspended. The rails were completely blocked with spectators and an engine 'had to proceed with caution near the cleaning sheds'. A Down'ards break won the day and play made for Clifton down the river. Darkness had set in as 'Tummy' Chell reached the wheel. The balls had been made by Mr Fred Sellers, the saddler and Mr Trevor Yeomans, bootmaker.

Tom Cundy

The *Ashbourne News* of 28/02/1908 carried an article on Tom Cundy, who was born in 1848 and was 59 years old. He had been playing for 43 years, presumably starting with the boy's games. He recalled the Wednesday game 27 years previously (1881), when he had taken the last ball of the day's game up the hall pond when all other onlookers were afraid to venture in due to the depth of the bottom end. He said that this was the last occasion on which the late Mrs Frank allowed the ball to be played through The Park. He goaled at Sturston and afterwards presented the ball to Mr C Purdy of Dig Street.

He remembered when five balls had been goaled at Sturston in one year – two on the Tuesday and three on the Wednesday. He had avoided the prosecutions and reckoned that the play was not as hard as it had been. He cited as an example, times when the ball would have been thrown up in the Market Place at 2.00pm and by continuous hugging had got no further than The Butchery by 6.00pm. He complained that there was too much running off with the ball by the young fellows. An interesting

Game Reports 1892–1949

sequel was reported much later (ANT 04/03/1982). Mr Cundy had scored four goals himself and his last ball (Wednesday 1893) was given to his cousin, Dan Cockayne. The latter drove the last train into Mafeking (But see pages 85/87) before it was besieged during the Boer War. He also drove the first one out after the relief of the town. Apparently he had the ball with him on each occasion.

Other News

The community spirit of Shrovetide is today embodied in the two daily lunches and of course in the two games after 2pm. At the beginning of the century the annual collections were used to provide a donation to local charities as well as purchase new balls, pay for damages etc. In 1905, the bulk of the collection was raised as a subscription for Charles Tarlton who had suffered a stroke and who had no income. In 1907, the same approach was made with a guinea being donated to the three usual charities and the balance being paid to the widow of Sgt Joseph Holmes. He was a hero of the South African War but had been sent home with enteric fever. Over £100 had been collected in total since collections had started, incidentally.

This year was the first that the local paper specifically referred to the Committee. (AN 22/02/1907)

During the year, the town saw the compulsory closure of pubs which did not come up to standards laid down under *The Licensing Act, 1904*. These included The Tiger and Durham Ox which had a full license and two beer houses – the Three Horse Shoes and the Stag and Pheasant. An advert regarding their closure appeared the previous May (AN 25/05/1906) and compensation was paid in January 1907. They were followed in 1907 by the Queen's Vaults in the Market Place together with the Angel Inn, Kniveton; Crown Inn, Parwich and the Wheel, Hulland Ward.

The town crier, Henry Smith, died on July 6th. He hed been the town crier for some years, but their is no record of any connection with Shrovetide football other than the Public Indignation Meeting of 1891, which had been called by crier. This meeting was the one called to raise money for the defence of the players.

Shrovetide lost an important stalwart on August 6th with the death of Francis John Winterton. He was only 52 years old and kept the Cock Inn, Dig Street. For years he had collected money at Shrovetide for the Derby Infirmary. He had been in failing health for some time. He was on the Committee and had turned up the second Wednesday ball in 1906, plus balls in 1892 and 1903. The 1892 ball is probably significant as it is likely that he was the chairman of the newly formed Committee.

1908

Monotonous Hugging

The usual crowd of spectators were ready at 2.00pm, including noted players such as Ninety Burton, Trip Connell and Black Harry. The ball was turned up by Mr W C Tomlinson, manager of the local Lloyds Bank and an Ashburnian. It was quickly played into The Park and then Sturston Lane, where hug followed hug with one lasting nearly an hour. Eventually, after nearly two hours play, it was thrown back into The Park over a high fence, which gave the street players a big disadvantage. The ball travelled quickly towards the Fishpond, with many in the crowd heading for Sturston. Up'ards runners took the ball to Ashbourne Green brickyard before turning virtually unopposed towards Sturston. Amid deafening cheers C Phillips of Fenny Bentley goaled the ball at 4.30pm. There had been too much hugging for most people and no water play until after 4.00pm and possibly none after that either.

Mr T Finney of Thorpe turned up the second leather. There was some water play this time but the ball was played the length of the Croft for four times before it left under the arch of Back Bridge in the arms of G Roome. It was played in the area of the Fishpond for over an hour. The play then moved across the Henmore before the Rev Tomlinson ran the ball a considerable distance before it was brought back to the Fishpond. Play became suspended with the ball beyond reach in a part of the pond treacherous with mud. This only kept Joe Burton in check for a while, before he went in and took possession. At one point, as the Rev Tomlinson tried to draw the ball to the bank and out of the river, he was pushed in and drenched. Although not an unusual occurrence, the vicar (of Darley Dale in this case) was usually treated with more respect! His team kept the advantage however, and G Walker of Adin's Yard, goaled at Sturston at 7.55pm.

Joe Burton Wades A Mile To Goal

On a good day, with the crowd seemingly twice as big as the day before, Mr T W Birch (Chairman, Ashbourne Urban District Council) turned up the ball before joining the fray. The bank made by the Ashbourne Cycling and Athletic Club on the cycle track in Shaw Croft formed a miniature grandstand. The crowd was estimated at 4,000 people. Sturston pressure saw the ball going through the Back Bridge arch at 2.30pm. The ball seemed set for Sturston but Down'ards pressure pushed the ball back up Coxon's field and into The Park. J Gadsby checked a chance for Joe Burton to run off with it and the ball was eventually taken up Sandy Lane and into the Bradley Road, where the play met a cart drawn by two horses.

However, the struggle came back down the lane and into Shaw Croft; it looked as though Down'ards pressure was turning the tide. However, it was not to be and the struggle turned upriver yet again. Joe Burton took the ball up the river for a mile, pushing off Down'ards pressure most of the way. Joined by G Handley as he neared the mill, the latter took over the donkey-work and the honour of goaling. Mr Rowland Prince of the Station Hotel turned up the second ball at 4.58pm but the game was a poor affair, many players still returning to town. The ball travelled quickly down the river to the station, where a goods train towards Clifton had to proceed with caution, its whistle constantly sounding. At a little after 5.30pm, G Ainsworth touched the Clifton wheel. The day therefore ended with the honours even.

Other News

Mr John Wibberley died aged 77 years on 31/03/1908. He joined the Ashbourne Company of Volunteers when it started in 1859 and for many years he was the only postman delivering letters in Ashbourne. A shoemaker by trade, he had made the Shrovetide balls for many years. It is worth noting that he had been the postman from 1858 to 1897 and had been the town's first postman. Prior to him, letters had been delivered by a lady who went her rounds with a basket containing the letters! Mr Wibberley, prior to compulsory education, often had to read the contents of the letters he delivered to the recipients. (AN 10/04/1908)

A week before Shrovetide, the paper carried the names of the two guests invited to turn up the balls. In the event, neither of them did it! Mr R Vessey of Derby was down for Tuesday but had the flu and Mr John Hall of Alsop-en-le-Dale Hall was down for Wednesday. In their absence, WC Tomlinson turned up the first ball. He had been elected manager of Lloyds Bank the previous summer and was also the Treasurer of Mayfield RDC. On the Wednesday, TW Birch, the chairman of Ashbourne UDC stood in for Mr Hall. Mr Vessey was invited back the following year but Mr Hall never did do it.

The Committee met in March and present were Messrs W Prince, JC Prince, G Derbyshire, J Spencer, J Hawksworth, JT Colwell, R Prince and Supt Burford. Mr T Marsh was receiving contributions for the annual collection and was down as a Committee member in 1909, so he may also have been a member in 1908. He had succeeded John Winterton at the Cock Inn. At least two other members kept pubs: JC Prince was at The Green Man and Mr Colwell at the George and Dragon (where JC Prince had been previously) and of course, W Prince kept the Hall Hotel. This is the first recorded list of Committee members. There were joint secretaries: Jack Hawksworth and JF Spencer. In the 1908 match report, Roger Wibberley was described as being the Up'ards Captain.

A month later, the Ashbourne Volunteers (C Company, 2nd Vol. Batt. Notts and Derbys Regiment) under Capt Bond were wound up, to be replaced by the new Territorial Army. Coincidentally, the Volunteer Arms at Hartington was threatened with closure. It was also a shop and is the arched building in the Market Place. It closed early in 1909 along with the Cross Keys in Ashbourne. Both were compulsory closures. Parwich lost its second pub in two years when The Wheatsheaf closed voluntarily during 1908.

The opening of the Ashbourne Bathing Club in July 1908 would have perhaps have been of more interest to Shrovetiders. A weir had been erected across the Henmore creating a pool up to 5ft 8ins deep in places. It was situated in Mr Lombard's field near to Sturston. Over 90 members had enrolled and the secretary was Supt Burford. In fact the pool was his brainchild. Bathing was to be between April 1 and September 30. Fortunately this was after Shrovetide for it was stated that 'bathing drawers must in all cases be worn' and trespassers would be prosecuted. Membership cost 1/- (5p) for adults (half price if under 16 years) for the season. It was situated near what was called the 'Pancheon Hole' in the river and created another obstacle for river players. There were no facilities for females.

1909

Fine Sport With The Second Ball

After a sharp frost of 20 degrees, the sun produced a brilliant day for the game, started by Mr R H Vessey of Derby. Unfortunately he threw it a long way Down'ards towards Compton Bridge. However, before long the ball was heading under Back Bridge with rapid play towards Sturston via the grounds of Ashbourne Hall. It was so icy, the players passed ice-skaters en-route. A lot of spectators on the ice received a cold dip when the ice gave way. It even prevented a lot of water play – the players preferring the land to numbed limbs. However, as the ball neared Sturston, there was more water play, the ice having to be broken to make headway. Down'ards opposition weakened especially after the 'new bathing place' in the river. Field after field was crossed without opposition, much of the carrying being done by Jack Brown who goaled it at 3.10pm. The contest was described as 'tame in the extreme'.

At 3.55pm Mr Henry Prince of the White Hart, Uttoxeter threw up the second ball, as usual, while some Up'ards were still coming back to town. After a big struggle in the Croft, the ball reached Compton where there was an epic battle in the street, with the police assisting 'conveyances' held up on the Derby Road to proceed down the street. The huge crowd reached from one end of the street to the other. The hug continued past Cooper's offices where 'many good caps, having been tossed high into the air were irrecoverable'. Even a policeman lost his helmet in the fray, which lasted over an hour. Then there was a break and the huge railings skirting The Paddock were crossed. The ball returned to Station Street via the chapel yard, where it was in a monotonous hug for too long. A further break saw the ball quickly moving back down Compton and, eventually, back into the Croft where hundreds fell over the cycle track bank.

Play reached The Park with some good open kicking combined with several fine throws. After play beneath a gas lamp in Sturston Lane, the ball was thrown into The Park, at nearly 7.00pm. The ball was then picked up by Up'ards runners and after more hugging, C Eccles goaled it at Sturston about 7.30pm. Some 4,000 people had watched the game, and the ball, made by Mr Fred Sellers the saddler of Buxton Road, had withstood a severe testing.

The Keenest Struggle of Recent Years

Another beautiful day saw Mr F Granville of Derby throw up the Wednesday ball, with a reported 6,000 crowd. Play in Shaw Croft was excellent, before the Down'ards were off down the river, past the Station Hotel to Clifton Road. Progress was checked for an hour outside the Railway Inn. Play reached the station as the 4.20pm Clifton train was ready to leave and it passed slowly through the crowd without mishap. Despite a fierce struggle, Mayfield Road was reached with many people coming to grief crossing the river. Backwards and forwards between road and the railway the game was fought. There was an eventual break near the Gas Works, with a lady selling oranges being completely engulfed. Play reached the river and then the railway. As the 6.00pm train left Clifton, a long whistle signalling its approach, victory was in sight. At 6.35pm, Joe Harrison goaled it, with many people saying it was the best game in years.

Other News

At the January meeting of the Committee, Guy Derbyshire was in the chair. Present were W Coxon, T Marsh, JC Prince and J Hawksworth. Elected as new members were W Coxon, WC Tomlinson, AA Smith and WJ Williams. Mr Derbyshire had turned up the second Wednesday ball in 1903 and so he may have been on the Committee then. It's a pity that so little information survives of these early days of the Committee but all the early records were destroyed in a fire at a solicitor's office in the 1930s.

Rivalries between the Burtons and the Sowters surfaced at the game and in March, Edward Burton and Thomas Sowter were fined 2/6d (12.5p) and 8/6d (42.5p) costs. James Sowter and George Roome were fined similarly. All had been fighting on Shaw Croft but Supt Burford made the point that he did not want the cases to be dealt with severely, he just wanted it known that such behaviour would not be tolerated. He was not against the football game. There was little history of this kind of problem however. Compared to the disorders of thirty years previously, the game had matured to respectability.

During July, the Brickyard and 7½ acres of land had been offered for sale at The Green Man Hotel and failed to reach the reserve. On October 28, the buildings and plant were offered for sale. Amongst the items sold were a 20 hp horizontal engine, a Lancashire boiler, drying shed, brick oven, two chimney stacks and light tram lines. It was intended to offer the freehold for sale when the demolition had been completed. The following week, the paper carried a photo of the 90 feet tall chimney being felled by Joseph and Thomas Burton. Not all the site had been cleared by the following Shrovetide, when the game was described as being played over heaps of bricks in Brickyard Lane.

During September, Mr TW Birch who had turned up the 1908 Wednesday ball, fell 35 feet to his death while supervising the extension to Cooper's Corset Works, being built by his Company, P Birch and Sons. He lost his footing on the scaffolding. He was Chaiman of Ashbourne UDC and a son of P Birch.

The balls were made by Fred Sellers and Trevor Yeomans and were painted by Messrs EM Sellers and Son (by John Barker) and L Bell.

1910

Waterplay To Both Goals

A small band of organisers and supporters wended their way from the Green Man Hotel, down Dig Street, over the bridge and into the Croft, where on arrival at the historic mound a halt was made. The honour of turning up the ball was entrusted to Mr Sam Clarke, of Oldham, an old Ashburnian. Taking a turn towards Sandy Lane the ball was kicked close to Back Bridge. After being immediately returned from The Park into which it had been thrown the ball was safely landed back again, and played rapidly across The Park to the Fishpond. When in the vicinity of the bathing place a bolt with the ball across the fields towards Ashbourne Green was made by a player, F Ward, leaving the other players and the numerous spectators mostly on the other side of the river. The ball had travelled as far as the yard of the Boothby Farm, where its progress was checked by T Slater, and it was held until the main body of the players arrived.

Near the Paper House Farm it was loosened, kicked across a field, and then thrown over the hedge. Here, C Howard secured possession and made a good run downwards, some of the players were up to their calves in wet slush, and the ball was kicked in various directions to the accompaniment of a shower of mud. On being kicked into the stream possession was gained by two Up'ards men, Brown and Barton, and carried up stream. Some excellent water play was then witnessed, the Down'ards bent on resisting every inch of the ground. The Up'ards proved superior however, and a further attack was eluded by passing the ball to T Botham who, accompanied by a posse of supporters reached the mill stream safely with the trophy. Up the mill stream it was carried and was goaled at the mill wheel by S Grindey just before 4.00pm.

A second ball was turned up before 5.00pm by Mr W Prince. The Down'ards were stronger, for after the Croft had been crossed and re-crossed, they succeeded in forcing the play slowly towards Compton Bridge. In the stream the ball was trundled again, and some good water play was witnessed. The Down'ards were not to be denied, however, and by sheer strength forced the hug through the gates into Compton. It was played fairly quickly up the street to the top of Compton, at which point it was turned into Station Street. Near the police station it was temporarily checked, but after a short hug it was thrown over the wall into the railway station yard. It was carried rapidly across the metals into the railway gardens, where a prolonged hug took place, which had little regard for the garden produce. A band of Down'ards took possession, and after an attack by the Up'ards had forced it on to the north bank, it was again returned to the stream. The little band of Down'ards piloted the ball successfully down the stream, and, by this time it was rapidly becoming dark. There was not very much opposition and eventually, the ball was goaled at Clifton by Harold Massey at about 6.40pm.

Even Honours Yet Again

On Wednesday, there was a larger company present in the Croft and vicinity than had been seen for some years. Mr Guy Derbyshire was escorted by a band of enthusiasts to the mound.

For exactly an hour the ball was confined in the field, except for one or two visits to the Henmore river, and it struck 3.00pm as it was thrown over into Sandy Lane for the first time. A stern struggle then ensued, the ball being hugged tightly, and gradually forced up the lane towards Sturston. Slowly the solid mass of humanity proceeded till the gate leading into The Park was reached, when the struggle became fiercer than ever, the Down'ards resisting strongly an attempt to force the ball into The Park. The ball was soon dropped on reaching The Park, and was trundled merrily across the field to Sturston Road, into which it was thrown. Gradually the dense mass of humanity was forced by sheer weight of numbers up in the direction of Sturston. The Down'ards rallied and with 'a strong push, a long push and a push altogether' they forced the whole mass back to the top of Sandy Lane. Eventually, Fred Ward got away with it and goaled it at Sturston. This was one of the most strenuous games for many years.

Just before 5.00pm Mr W Coxon turned up a second ball. In a very few minutes the leather was in the water, and before the Up'ards could realise their position it had passed under Compton Bridge and was on its way down the stream. It was rapidly transferred to the Station Hotel. Suddenly it was thrown over into the station yard, and as it fell on the other side of the boarding it bounded off a plate-layer named Gould and rolled under the platform. After a brief hug the ball was thrown into the stream again. The leather was transferred once more to land, and played up School Lane to the church gates, and from here it was then eventually turned down to Mayfield Road. By the time the new cemetery ground was reached it was almost dark, and suddenly the ball disappeared and no one seemed to know where it had gone. Possession had been taken by a few Down'ards who carried it off, and it was ultimately goaled at Clifton by N Etherington.

The balls were made by Messrs F Sellers and Trevor Yeomans, and the decorated one was painted by Mr C Brown. It was painted red, white and blue and carried the legend: 'Ashbourne Shrovetide Football, 1910'.

An unusual event occurred on the Wednesday when two balls were in play at the same time. Fred Ward goaled the first ball at Sturston at 6.55pm after it had been missing for a long time. He and H Holbrook had run with the leather to Offcote where they were joined by others before proceeding to Agnes Meadows, Hall Fields and New House Farms before taking refreshments at Ox Close. Meanwhile, the Committee decided to turn up another ball for the satisfaction of visitors who could not arrive before the afternoon train reached Ashbourne from Derby at 3pm. This second ball was in turn goaled at Clifton by N Etherington a little while before the first ball was goaled.

It was not the first time that this had happened. The Committee had clearly elevated the game into a social occasion with important visitors turning up to view it. The release of a new ball was done to ensure the 'spectacle' element was not lost by over enthusiastic players. It had the right effect. The continuance of such an anachronism could only be contemplated if the actual game was seen as part of something bigger. In this case, as a provider of entertainment. This approach reached its ultimate height with the addition of the word 'Royal', followed by The Marquis of Hartington, The Duke of Devonshire and then the Prince of Wales coming to turn up the ball in 1928. The game was gaining status at last!

It is worth bearing in mind that the success of the game as a long standing custom lies as much with its acceptance with the townspeople as a whole as it does with the enthusiasts, let alone the players. This is why the lunches are such an integral feature of the custom today and so important for the maintenance of civic approval.

Other News

The Committee this year consisted of JC Prince, W Coxon, WC Tomlinson, AA Smith, G Derbyshire and J Hawksworth, the secretary. It is likely that Mr Derbyshire was still chairman when he unfortunately shot himself in the W/C of his shop in Church Street on 1st July 1910 at the age of 35 years. He had been an assistant with Barnes, Son and Callow and upon the dissolution of that Company, he took over its Church Street shop. He shot himself twice in the head. It was reported that he had business worries.

The 25th April that same year saw the death of Fred Sellars. He died young too, for he was 43 years old and had made the Tuesday balls since 1906 when he had opened his shop in the Market Place as a Saddler and Harness Maker. He had been apprenticed to the saddlery business with Mr Hall of St John Street. He enlisted in the Royal Artillery in 1885 and the same year he was drafted with his battery to India as Regimental Collar maker. He served in India for nearly nine years before returning to Ashbourne. He died of pneumonia. Apparently collar or harness makers often made the best balls, presumably because of the skill involved.

His business was taken over by Johnson Brothers, who made the balls the following year. Fred was the originator of the Ashbourne May Day Parade.

On a better note, Committee member W Coxon JP, the new Chairman of Ashbourne UDC read the Proclamation of the new King, George V, during May from the Town Hall balcony. In the same month, the local paper carried an advert giving details about the new Ashbourne Zoo in North Leys!

William Coxon is known to have been the Committee Chairman in 1912, so it seems likely that he had succeeded Mr Derbyshire. He had turned up the first ball of 1900 and the replacement ball of this year (1910). He was a butcher in Victoria Square and was the one who played in his smock. He even turned up at the 1891 Court hearing with it on, causing a lot of hilarity from fellow defendants.

1911

The New King's Portrait Gets To Sturston Wheel

The 1911 Tuesday ball bore a portrait of George V and was thrown up by Mr C G Busby JP, after 'apologies for Rule Britannia and God Save the King'. The ball quickly left the Croft for Park Road – the new name for Sandy Lane. Play was pursued in The Park with mud and water everywhere. Although the Down'ards gave their all, they were out numbered and as the ball neared Sturston Mill, it was remarked that it had lost none of its paint. Shortly after 4.00pm W Spencer reached the wheel and goal.

Mr William Coxon J.P. turned up the second ball, with Shaw Croft looking like a quagmire. The Down'ards were strongest now – Up'ards still on their way back – and play entered Dig Street. A break came when the ball was freed and thrown into the river. It was quickly taken through the station and on into Mayfield Road. Up'ards pressure prevailed and play was pushed back to the tunnel in Church Street. The ball was thrown out of the hug and made off towards Mappleton Road, being goaled later at Sturston by 'Sugar' Walker.

Pitched Battle On Dr Sadler's Lawn

There was a drying wind and sunshine as Ernest Wood of Derby launched the Wednesday ball upwards. Sides were evenly matched but at last a good throw saw the ball land in Compton. Play went down King Edward Street and not for the first time, the wall across the street gave way under the pressure. The ball entered the town football ground, but different rules were the order of the day. Although the ball was put through the goal at the Corset Works end, it did not count and at last play emerged to reach the river.

Several times the ball was thrown into Dr Sadler's garden near the railway (i.e. The Mansion House) and it was thrown out by Up'ards players until a good throw took it beyond their reach and a pitched battle took place on the lawn. Spectators were crowded on the railway line as the 3.30pm arrival from Buxton slowed down and sounded its whistle. Play reached Church Street at 4.00pm and Up'ards pressure repeated the play of Tuesday evening. The ball being pushed up the street and along past the Green Man Hotel. Pressure on Osborne's (now W H Smith) and Callow's shutters was relieved as the ball turned down Mr Harrison's yard to return to Shaw Croft at 4.40pm. Play seemed to be going Up'ards way, but it was not to be. The pressure pushed the game into Dig Street, Compton and Station Street. Proceeding to the church gates, the players made for the brook, but as the Gas Works was passed, the Up'ards yielded. James Bradley and Massey continued on downstream to goal the ball shortly before 7.00pm.

1912

Mud And Manure On The Way To Sturston

On a dry but dull Tuesday Capt W Jelf turned up the ball in place of his father Col R H Jelf. Lord Kerry the local MP had been invited but parliamentary duties prevented his attendance. The ball bore a portrait of the King and the Prince of Wales' feathers, the work of Mr J Barker. After a visit to the Bath House corner and then to the water, a tremendous throw relieved the pressure and the ball was quickly in The Park. The game ranged between the Hall field railings (where the lake was) and Sturston Road. Eventually the ball entered the Fishpond with Fred Wibberley behind it, experiencing a lot of difficulty with the deep mud. Play headed up stream through a field with many heaps of manure which the farmer found was spread for him. The game moved onwards towards Sturston Mill and J Dethick goaled it at 4.45pm.

Mr S H Bagshaw turned up the next ball, hoping it would go to the Down'ards. After ten minutes the ball reached Compton Street and was soon in King Edward Street. After play near the boy's school and in Mayfield Road, the ball was run to Clifton via Green Lane and goaled at 8.00pm by G Taylor of South Street.

Rumblings of Dispute

With a larger crowd and better day, Mr T H B Bamford (Chairman of the Urban District Council) turned up the Wednesday ball. It took an hour of strenuous effort for the ball to leave Shaw Croft and there was then another fifteen minutes hug in Park Road, before the ball was gone and quickly seen bobbing along in the Fishpond. W Spencer waded in and threw it out. Back it went with Spencer swimming after it. Play then transferred to the Hall Barn near the upper pond. After a lot of spirited play in the fields, a break left the crowd behind and W Shakespeare goaled the ball at Sturston just after 4.30pm.

Mr J Hawksworth turned up the second ball. He had been secretary for fifteen years and commented on dissent the day before when a second ball had been turned up. With unwritten rules some players believed the players had to return by 5.00pm and the second ball was illegal. It was wrong of course. A second ball was introduced to enable tradesmen to participate at the end of the day. Down'ards took early control and the ball went down river to Bank Croft and then into Station Road. Progress was checked at the junction with Church Street for a while, but it was then on to the church and fields adjacent to the Henmore. George Ainsworth goaling at Clifton for the Down'ards and play ending for the year at two goals each.

The dispute however, rumbled on and an interesting letter (AN 08/03/1912) from Mr Hawksworth revealed that the committee had been formed by the late John Winterton. Its objects were: "systemitising (sic) the game, freeing it from objectionable features and ensuring its continuance by a compliance with the conditions laid down by the authorities." Since formation, the committee had collected and distributed over £150 to charity. Mr W Coxon was the committee chairman.

The Committee had hoped that the local MP, Lord Kerry, would have turned up the Tuesday ball but other business prevented that, although he was keen to do it. Col Jelf was asked to stand in and he agreed. In the event, business precluded him from doing so, but his son, Capt Jelf did it. He was accompanied to the knoll in Shaw Croft by Jack Hawksworth and Mr E Willcocks and addressed the crowd on the shoulders of William Prince and Fred Ashton. Lord Kerry, incidentally, was the brother-in-law of the Duke of Devonshire.

The second ball was turned up by S H Bagshaw, of the auctioneers who was to be seen later playing in the river. Among the spectators were Capt Holland, the Chief Constable, and his son plus Canon Morris, Capt Bond and many other well known residents. The usual request: 'Don't play in the streets' was made by Capt Jelf.

Other News

The following May, the Empire Cinema opened on Whit Monday, the 27th, with seating for 650 people. It was also licensed for dancing. It had been built by Eades, the brewers who owned the adjacent Station Hotel and leased by them to Edgar Stebbings of Manchester. The only previous 'cinema' was a room at the Town Hall. Unfortunately, there was an electrical problem which prevented films being shown on the opening night. The following Monday, Ashbourne's first true cinema opened with two films: 'The Adventures of Lieut. Rose' and 'Strike at Johnnie Mines'.

The programme changed on Thursdays, so that week Ashbourne was also entertained with 'Robert Bruce' (described as a historical drama) and 'Stage Driver's Daughter' – whatever that was one can only surmise! There were two sittings, at 7pm and 9pm and prices were 3d, 6d, and 1/- with a 3pm Saturday matinee with childrens' prices of 1d, 2d and 3d. The following year on Ash Wednesday, Mr Stebbings was asked to turn up the ball and Shrovetide could be seen in his cinema later that week.

Also during May, W Shakespeare who scored the Ash Wednesday first ball, emigrated to the U.S.A. He took his ball with him and was interviewed about the game in the New York Police Gazette, which was described as a 'sporty journal'.

The *Ashbourne Telegraph* on 01/03/1912 sheds more light on the fact that two balls were turned up after 5.00pm. On each day the balls had been goaled at 4.45pm and 4.40pm respectively. Several old players interviewed by the paper – all with at least fifty years playing experience and two (including Matthew Cleaver) with over seventy years experience – were unanimous that a second ball had to be turned up before 5.00pm. The paper stated that it was possible for someone to turn up a ball after 5.00pm by himself and then walk off to one of the goals. This seems somewhat tenuous these days.

'The second balls had been turned up on the authority of the committee,' said the paper, '– we will forget for the moment who appointed them, –' it said pointedly. It ended by saying that ' the old game has been played for hundreds of years without this modern appendage and the old players are somewhat astonished at the modern trend of events.' The game moved on to encompass what is now one of it's few cherished features – the right to claim a ball after 5.00pm to replace one goaled before that time.

The same paper reported more detail on the boys' game that year. After Karl Blank had turned it up, it went across the Henmore and up the Black's Head Yard along St John Street and up the Butchery. It said however, that it was goaled by H Sowter.

1913

Seventh Goal For Joe Burton

Tuesday opened with bright weather and a strong wind and shortly after 2.00pm the procession to Shaw Croft set off from the Green Man Hotel. Mr T H B Bamford again turned up the ball which had a short stay in Shaw Croft. Play then proceeded towards Sturston Road down Park Road but Up'ards pressure turned the play from the road and into The Park. It was to be Sturston's goal and play wend its way up the fields despite spirited play by the Down'ards to prevent it. Play was pursued on land and in the water, which was chest deep in places. A dispute as to who should goal it looked like taking play past 5.00pm, but at 4.50pm Joe Burton gained possession and ended discussion at the wheel to goal for the seventh time.

The committee had decided that as the game was so early this year – 4th February – no ball would be thrown up after 5.00pm. However, the players clamoured for another ball and Mr Bamford did the honours at 5.20pm despite it being nearly dark. After some river play, the ball was carried along Compton to Station Street and on to the station. Despite a keen contest, 'young' Sowter took the honours at Clifton.

Tables Turned On Down'ards

Mr Edgar Stebbings, proprietor of the Ashbourne Empire turned up the Wednesday ball after reminding the crowd that his cinema was open twice nightly! After initial play in the Croft, the ball reached the station (via King Edward Street and the Empire cinema) at 2.35pm. There followed a terrific contest in front of the police house in Clifton Road. With progress reaching the Railway Hotel, it looked Clifton bound, but the Up'ards turned the tables and play returned to Station Road and eventually reached Church Street. The ball was rapidly trundled along to Dig Street and it reached the water and then Shaw Croft via Compton Bridge. Despite terrific play, the ball progressed to Sturston and was goaled about 6.30pm by Roger Hall.

In the 23 years since records had been kept in the local newspaper, the goal tally was Up'ards 44, Down'ards 22, exactly double the other score.

Other News

It must have been quite novel for Ashbourne people to see ' cinema photographers' recording the game this year. Presumably they had been commissioned by Edgar Stebbings, for a film of the game was shown later in the week at the Empire Cinema. Joe Burton scored his final goal, which was, according to the local paper, his seventh. He gave the ball to Jim Burton. William Coxon, the Committee Chairman was also re-elected Vice Chairman of the Ashbourne UDC. Other members of the Shrovetide Committee were J C Prince, E Willcocks and J Hawksworth.

Shortly after the game, the town was saddened to learn of the death of Supt Burford on 25/03/1913. He had joined the police in 1875 and served in the Ashbourne area for a long time before going to Ashford-in-the-Water and then Totley (where he was shot at but escaped injury). He became the Police Superintendent for Ashbourne in 1898 and founded both the Ashbourne Swimming Club (which used the River Henmore, near Sturston) and The Emergency and Relief Association. He was also a member of the bowling club and also served on the Shrovetide Committee for a while.

Col Jelf who had hoped to turn up the Tuesday ball the previous year died in May. He lived at Offcote Hurst and was, with his wife, a popular friend of the town. Yet another death in June robbed the game of one of its heroes. Mr Joseph Osbourne died on June 22. He was 62 years old and his obituary confirmed that it was he who had saved Jimmy Harrison from drowning in Clifton Millpool in 1878, when James Barker had drowned. He had founded the *Ashbourne News* in 1891 and held the bronze medal of the Royal Humane Society for his bravery.

The year ended with another death associated with the game. This time it was of William Roome of Kniveton. He was described as a doughty champion of Shrovetide. The fame of the Roomes in this respect deservedly descending to his sons, George and Arthur. George had scored the first Wednesday ball in 1903.

In April 1905, Supt Burford had been clearly shocked to find the desperate circumstances of the Moon family in White Horse Yard. The mother had been taken to the workhouse because of physical infirmity, although her husband was clearly trying to cope. Supt Burford found the children sleeping in bedding, which was oiled, dirty and unfit for use. He appealed for donations to buy fresh bedding and a week later reported that he had received £2.4s.0d. Adding more to it from his own pocket, he had the house cleansed and white washed and all beds and bedding replaced. Four fresh mattresses and an iron bedstead had been provided by two local retailers. He clearly was a man with a social conscience.

1914

A Lot Of Action For Spectators To See

Contrary to an old saying: as the days lengthen the cold strengthens, it had been a very mild winter. Mr C G Huntriss, Master of the Dove Valley Harriers turned up the ball. The sides were evenly matched and after two hours strenuous play the ball had left the Croft, proceeded down Park Road, into Compton and back to the Croft. The ball was pushed all around the field before Down'ards pressure saw it heading downstream to Station Road. Here, there was a break with G Walker (accompanied by V Wallis) running the ball towards the Red House (near the Buxton railway line). At 8.30pm, after resistance at Sturston, T Brown touched the wheel. It was reported (AN 27/02/1914) that the spectators saw a lot of play, the ball being close to the Croft for over 3½ hours.

Round And Round, Up And Down

Wednesday saw even better weather. Mr T H B Bamford turned up the ball, for the third year running (he did it again in 1915). After river play and some good throwing, Up'ards managed to get the ball into Park Road and then The Park. Unfortunately, railings between The Park and the Fishpond prevented further movement up river. However, Down'ards pressure saw play transferred to the Sturston Road side. Eventually it went on towards Compton passed new houses being built (probably in Peter Street) where play was ankle deep in mud. Compton was eventually reached via Chapel Yard.

Play continued via King Edward Street and Station Road into Church Street. It was reported (AN 27/02/1914) that from the Station Hotel and down Church Street to Dig Street was one mass of people. The ball progressed down Dig Street and then back down King Edward Street, where it reached the river at Bank Croft, having done a circuit. A throw into a garden saw the Up'ards get the advantage and the ball went via Church Street into Shaw Croft again. It looked like an Up'ards goal in the making with play reaching the Fishpond where swimmers had to retreive the ball. However, the Down'ards found fresh strength and hugged the ball back to Bank Croft. Eventually, the ball was goaled at Clifton by S Taylor at about 7.00pm.

Other News

This was the last game before the Great War. So many men were to die in France from the town and its surrounding villages. It was to have a pronounced effect on the town and its game. So many stalwarts would play no more, or at least for several years. Private James Lee wrote home to his mother in Compton at the end of the year. He was with the 2nd Battalion, Notts/Derbys Regt and his letter was written under fire. He expressed the hope that he would be home to see the first ball turned up on Shrove Tuesday; however, this war would not be over by Christmas.

Unfortunately for Mr Lee, he did not survive the war and his name is on the war memorial. It's the top name on the right hand panel. In the town the Century Hall on Derby Road was turned into a Red Cross Hospital and Belgian refugees were quartered at the Green Hall.

The Ashbourne Territorials were encamped at Hunmanby near Filey when war broke out, being there for their annual training exercise. They returned to Ashbourne and then proceeded to march to Chesterfield via Matlock under the colours of the 6th Battalion of the Notts and Derbys Regiment, being the Ashbourne section of C Company. Captain H E Okeover was the Commanding Officer at the end of 1914 and in charge of the local recruiting office was Dr H Hollick and Sergt W Davenport. Early casualties were Pte Charles Chell of Clifton who died at the Battle of Aisne and Pte George Skellen (both Sherwood Foresters) together with Pte Owen Slater of the Grenadier Guards, Pte Harry Walton (N Staffs Regt) and Cpl Reg Salt of the Royal Engineers. (AN 1/1/1915)

An interesting letter was published in the local paper (AN 27/03/1914). It was written by Mr J Millington of West Wickham in Kent. He stated that 'the game has not altered a bit since 1873 and 1874; those were the years we used to watch it and I see there are still some familiar names, the descendants, I suppose, of those we used to watch – Wibberly, Sowter and Burton. The weather is more kind to them than it used to be. There was plenty of snow and ice at the time I refer to and I remember a man called Bratby or Joe Bradley running with the ball across the park pond on the ice. He was a light man, others tried to follow him and were let in. Another year there were three (a butcher in his smock being one) who broke the thin ice and swam across. We were more hardy then.'

The butcher sounds like William Coxon who turned up at the 1891 court hearing in his smock. This letter also confirms that the park was open to the players in 1873/4.

1915

The Trains Wanting To Leave

This year saw stalwarts of the game fighting a sterner battle, although some, home on leave, were to be seen in the game and dressed in khaki. The report (AN 19/02/1915) recalled that during one charge in the Boer War, an Ashbourne man was heard to shout 'Now for the Up'ards' and to his great surprise a voice somewhere behind responded 'Go it Down'ards'. So despite the war and missing faces, the decision was made that the game must go on. 'The sport of our fathers and grandfathers will be maintained'.

Mr Bamford turned up the ball again. The boys in the trenches would be thinking of them, he said. The ball was painted with the portraits of Admiral Jellicoe and Lord Kitchener. At 2.25pm play passed under Compton Bridge Arches. However, it left the river and transferred to Church Street via a garden, with George Burton carrying the ball along the street. Play was soon back in Shaw Croft before it reached Lloyds Bank in Compton. After a diversion to the Machine Inn in Sturston Road, play returned via Compton and King Edward Street to reach the station just after 4.00pm. The L &

NWR and North Stafford trains were waiting to leave but the game passed quickly through. Pressure was continued down past the Gas Works where Up'ards bowed to the inevitable. George Smith took the ball into Clifton to the mill for a goal at 5.30pm.

A Near Fatality

A lot of overnight rain saw the Henmore almost at the top of its banks on the Wednesday. Mr B M Sims of Borrowash turned up the ball after the procession. Joe Burton head the procession with a Union flag. There was an appeal to keep the ball out of the water as well as the streets. By 2.05pm it had been in both, as it was run down Compton. The break continued to Clifton Road, where a move to reach the river was made near Nestlé. Play crossed the river and there was play in the field facing the cemetery. Several times play entered the river and the police had ropes in case they were needed. Play was pursued on the railway when shouts were heard that the express due at Ashbourne just before 3.00pm had left Clifton.

Without releasing their hold on the ball, an armistice was declared until the train had passed. In the subsequent hug was a lady – Miss E Morton. Play moved down towards Doles Farm, where C Gettliffe had a narrow escape from drowning. He was rescued by PC Taylor of Hatton and R Butcher with the aid of a long rope. At 3.30pm T Sowter placed the leather on the wheel before many people piled onto the 3.40pm train for Ashbourne.

Mr S H Beresford of Macclesfield turned up the second ball. Play was soon around the Fishpond and river with F Harrison and Fred Wibberley recovering it respectively. Down'ards pressure saw play return across The Park, up to the Machine Inn and into Compton. A series of hugs saw play then transfer to King Edward Street. J Faulkner waded from the flood arches (by the side of the Station Hotel) down to School Lane where, feeling exhausted, he threw the ball into the road. Although fiercely contested all the way to Clifton via Mayfield Road and Green Lane, Down'ards goaled it through J Bowler at about 7.30pm. After paying for new balls etc, the committee dispensed £8 5s 0d to local institutions. The balls were painted by Mr C E Brown and Mr J Barker.

Other News

It was quite common for men from a particular area to join forces during the Great War in one particular group. They were often known as the 'Pals Battalions'. It was supposed to be good for morale, but in the bloodshed of that war it also meant whole generations from families or even all the men from a particular street being wiped out.

Ashbourne was no exception and seventy-five men sailed for France in February 1915. They were the No 9 Platoon of the 1/6th Sherwood Foresters and included Joe Burton, Joe Wibberley and W Sowter amongst the Shrovetiders. It was the ninth Platoon, which played Shrovetide at the village of Sous St Ledger. The latter is situated just to the north of the Arras-Amiens main road.

Reference is made on p106 that in the game at Sous St Ledger, the ball was goaled by J Robinson. He appears on a reunion photograph when twenty-three of the twenty-seven soldiers still alive met at the Green Man. (ANT 22/02/1951) Mr Robinson returned to England with the ball and his daughter, Mrs Creswall, brought it to Ashbourne for the game in 1995. It was displayed at the Tuesday lunch and at the British Legion Club. The ball, now rather soft, was painted after the war, perhaps rather badly by contemporary means, for the paint has badly cracked.

The ball, made by Trevor Yeomans, bears the inscription:

On the face – *By C Company at Lus (Sic) St Ledger*
– *Played in France, Shrove Tuesday, 1916*
Side – *Notts and Derbys*
 Goaled by
 [number, ineligible]
 Robinson J H

Several of the players were hurt during the game and had to go to hospital (see report for 1921). In April 1915, the local paper (AN 16/04/1915) carried a letter from Lance Corporal Sid Smith and

Pte Walter Blake, describing life at the front. A few days after the letter had been written, Blake was killed in action. He was the nephew of William Coxon, the Committee Chairman. He died when a shell hit him, also killing Albert Harrison and Fred G Bull of Ashbourne and wounding W Birch of Mayfield. There must have been quite a lot of Ashbourne men involved with the war as the year went by. The paper records another 'enthusiastic player in the Shrovetide contest' was killed in September – he was George Bailey. He frequently distinguished himself in the water. He was one of nine soldiers from the town and district who died when the trench they were about to leave turned out to have been mined by the Germans. (AN 08/10/1915)

By the end of 1915, C Company had lost sixteen local lads. The war was to claim the lives of 115 Ashbourne men. (AT 29/7/1921)

Edgar Stebbings died in June 1915, aged 56 years, so soon after establishing his cinema in the town with its films of the game each Shrovetide. Incidentally, just before the 1915 game, the paper announced that Wednesday ball was to be turned up by Mr H A Simpson, which in the event did not occur.

1916

Play at the Front

A letter from Mr J Hawksworth (AN 21/01/1916) advised the town that the game would be played as usual. Over £200 had been collected over the last twenty years, he said, and given to local charities and a collection would be made again that year. Only one ball would be turned up unless it was goaled before 4.00pm. The Committee had also decided to send a ball to C Company of the 6th Sherwood Foresters who were in France. Mr J Barker would decorate the ball in the national colours and with patriotic inscriptions and it would be provided at the personal expense of the Committee. The ball was received by Lt Col G D Goodman who replied saying he would try and arrange for No 9 Platoon to play on Shrove Tuesday. He felt that the French authorities would hardly approve of their local village being used as a playground, but he would see what could be done! (AN 10/03/1916) The ball was thrown up by Col Goodman at Sous St Leger and goaled for the Down'ards by J Robinson. Lines were drawn at opposite ends of the village and the last man to kick the ball over either line was declared the goaler of the ball. Two companies of the Battalion played Down'ards and two Up'ards. (AN 26/02/1970)

Amongst The Snow Storms

Mr W Fowell of the Coach and Horses turned up the Tuesday ball after a week of stormy and snowy weather. The game started in a snow storm, with several lads playing in khaki as in 1915. At 2.30pm play moved to Park Road with several females dominating play. However, it quickly transferred to Compton as more snow fell. The ball was carried to the Old Hill before returning down Compton and the river. Play reached Church Street and despite fewer players than normal the police were not strong enough to divert play. The ball was hugged into Dig Street before it was taken through the Green Man yard, along St John Street to the Market Place and on up to Dove House Green. From here it came back to St John Street and Park Road bridge where the ball re-entered the water. After play at the Fishpond, Up'ards runners took the ball to the mill via Ashbourne Green, George Walker goaling it some two hours after it left The Park.

More Play In The Snow

On the Wednesday while it was snowing Councillor Eggleston of Derby turned up the ball . He was the local Secretary of the Amateur Athletic Association. After play all over the Croft, it reached Park Road before returning. The ball eventually left under Compton Bridge. It was keenly contested down and into Clifton Road where there was some fierce hugging as Up'ards tried to get the ball into Station Street. Upon breaking free play transferred to the river and W Brunt waded down the stream to goal at Clifton Mill at about 6.00pm. Four years play was seen during the Great War (1915-1918). Up'ards dominance changed during this time with all the goals bar two going to Clifton. It was the beginning of a Golden Age for the Down'ards.

1917

Two Goals By Two Brothers

Players were fewer than normal, with many men still at the front in France. Younger men were playing plus the welcome sight of some soldiers home on leave. Mr Joseph Harrison, who goaled at Clifton in 1909, turned up the year's first ball. The river was at the top of its banks and Shaw Croft was covered with mud and fog. Rain fell for most of the afternoon. At 18st 4lb it was no easy task hoisting Mr Harrison shoulder high, but traditions were maintained. After a short speech, urging the lads to 'stick to the leather', the fun commenced.

This is Sam Sowter (with the ball) with H (Peter) Sowter on the right

At 2.10pm the ball had been in the river, retrieved by 'China' Wibberley, and reached Compton. Up'ards stopped a move towards King Edward Street but Down'ards broke away down Compton to Station Street in the form of the Sowter brothers. So clean was the break, that Herbert 'Peter' Sowter goaled at Clifton at 2.45pm. The Committee had ruled that only one ball per day would be played, but Mr Harrison and others agreed that another ball ought to be turned up. He therefore turned up another ball at 3.30pm.

This ball was played all over the Croft before leaving under Compton Bridge. The fog was now at its worst, hindering the view of play. The ball reached The Paddock, where the game was pursued fast and furious, but being a F.A. pitch, it was difficult to extract the game from its confines. After another hour of hugging in the church field, play reached the spinney in Mr Peach's field. From here, the ball was soon back in the river, where Down'ards allowed it to bob along in the direction of Clifton. It was goaled by Albert Sowter at about 6.00pm. He was Peter's brother.

The Hat-trick For Down'ards

Councillor J W Chapman of Derby turned up the Wednesday ball and he was even heavier than Mr Harrison! Initial play followed the previous day, with the game reaching The Paddock via the river. It left The Paddock for the station, with play lasting nearly an hour in the station gardens. Eventually the Up'ards showed their strength and forced the play to Church Street. No doubt the station master was relieved once again to see the back of the huge crowd that had occupied his platforms, bridge and every other conceivable vantage point.

Play was forced along to Dig Street, where police formed a hug of their own to force play down to Compton Bridge. Up'ards attempted to get the ball over the parapet, but the Down'ards pushed play down Compton and Station Street to the police station. Here, the station master saw the return of the game as it reached the gardens adjacent to the railway once more. The leather was played on the line up to the footbridge and emerged into Clifton Road near the Railway Tavern. From here, play was pushed to Clifton, arriving just after 6.00pm, when the ball was goaled by Frank Harrison. It was noted that Councillor Chapman was often observed in the fiercest of the hugs.

The *Ashbourne Telegraph* report (AT 23/02/1917) gives more detail of the game claiming that the first goal on the Tuesday was a record, being goaled in 35 minutes – a little earlier than the time quoted in the Ashbourne News. The ball was played up Compton and into Station Street. Herbert Sowter (known as Peter to his friends) got the ball and ran with it down the railway line to Clifton. The spectators were naturally disappointed that the ball had been goaled (only one ball was to be played for, out of respect for the soldiers away at the war). Mr Harrison ' appeased the crowd' by purchasing the ball and agreeing to turn it up again. The balls this year were painted by John Barker and C E Brown.

This ball has to be unique for not only was it is turned up again on the same day, it was also goaled at Clifton by Albert Sowter, Herbert's brother. There was therefore the additional distinction of the same ball being turned up twice in one day by the same person and being goaled twice at the same mill by members of the same family! The first goal was also the 50th this century.

1918

A Hard Fought Game Pays Off At Sturston

The Tuesday ball was turned up by Mr John Etches of Royston Grange who had goaled the ball in 1900. He read a telegram from Commander Jelf, son of the late Col Jelf of Offcote Hurst. The Up'ards quickly asserted their strength this year, and the ball was soon seen being fiercely kicked in Park Road. Strongly contested play continued in the road with several females in the hug. After nearly two hours of very hard play, the ball was thrown into The Park and quickly reached the upper Fishpond. The struggle proceeded up the valley, with a long hug near the old brickyard. It was now 5.00pm and rain had started to fall. The hugging continued for another hour, with the ball being held by Herbert and Charles Sowter for the Down'ards. Eventually it was freed and after having tossed up for it, Pte W Fearn of the Sherwood Foresters goaled it at Sturston Mill at 6.15pm.

Second Game Abandoned

Mr John Barker of St John Street turned up the Wednesday ball from the famous knoll, saying that like John Etches he had goaled several balls and didn't think he was too old to goal another, and he did in 1925! The ball was soon away under Compton Bridge in the arms of James Sowter, but it was landed at Bank Croft. However, play quickly returned to the river and although many people crowded on to the station platforms, play proceeded down stream so quickly that before 2.30pm it was in the Church Field. It soon returned to the river, which was chest deep in places. C, W & S Sowter and J Bowler were the principal river players heading for Clifton. Joseph Harrison fastened a rope around them and supported them through the many dangerous places en route. The last stage was accomplished by W Sowter who, having negotiated the mill pool, floated the ball across to C Sowter who banged the wheel shortly before 4.00pm.

At 4.30pm a second ball was turned up by Mr A Bentley of Derby. After stiff play near Back Bridge, the ball left the field into Park Road. It returned to the Croft, but Mr Hawksworth, the Committee secretary, threw it back again into the road. The ball had not gone far, having reached Sturston Road, when darkness set in. The struggle continued until about 8.00pm when it was decided to declare the game a draw. The last efforts were in Mr Coxon's field. The result of the first day's play was sent by telegram (by the secretary) to Cpl G Wain of the R.A.M.C. in France. Wain was in a position to pass on the information to a number of other Ashbourne men.

The Committee had sent another ball to the front and a Lt Wood of 1/6th Sherwood Foresters wrote to his wife – a teacher at the Wesleyan School – to say that Ashbourne men and many others were about twelve miles behind the front and resting. He had seen the ball thrown up and played with by 500 – 600 soldiers. The game created great alarm amongst local villagers who for sometime did not realise what was happening. (AN 22/02/1918)

1919

An Old Friend Throws Up The Ball

World War I had ended, and men were back to pursue the ball rather than the Hun. The paper alluded to stories of the game being pursued by Ashbourne men in French villages, but no specific places were mentioned. Brig-General Rudolf Jelf D.S.O. turned up the first peace-time ball after the war. The ball was painted with the word 'Victory'. Play was soon in Park Road and then Peter Street where a stationary traction engine with a truck attached proved to be a temporary obstacle, if a good vantage point for spectators. Play returned to Shaw Croft and after spirited play emerged into Compton. Peter Sowter made off with the ball up Derby Old Road at about 3.40pm. He reached Clifton at about 6.00pm and the ball was goaled by Fred Sowter, a son of James Sowter, and a returned prisoner of war. The game was watched by Billy Meredith, the well known Manchester City player.

Complaints of No Open Play

Mr W Ludlow of Derby turned up the Wednesday ball in excellent weather. He had come with Steve Bloomer, the Derby County player (who had been a prisoner of war for four years). He was asked to turn up the ball himself the following year. After some good water play, at 2.50pm the ball was carried into Dig Street. Play continued down Church Street as far as Foster's shop (now Hamilton House), before the Up'ards forced the game back to Dig Street, where they were assisted by several policemen and special constables. There was play both in the river and adjacent area of Shaw Croft. A break eventually came and the ball was played around the station where the 4.25pm train was ready to leave, with steam up.

The game was forced along Station Road and into Clifton Road before the Down'ards took to the river and waded down it to the mill. Thomas Chell, another p.o.w., goaled it just before 6.00pm. There had been virtually no open play during both days play in marked contrast to recent years. The balls were as usual, made by Trevor Yeomans, and decorated by John Barker and Mr A Roberts.

The Green Man Hotel was bought by Mr J C Prince in November (AN 14/11/1919) for £5,500. The previous owner was Mr Frank Stretton and he presumably bought it in 1898 along with Shaw Croft. He had paid £11,250 for it and had spent £4,000 on the hotel. Mr Prince had been the manager for a number of years since 1907 and was a Shrovetide Committee member.

Joe Burton, who played Association Football as well as Shrovetide Football, ended his career as a player for the town during the year.

1920

Removal of The Clifton Millwheel

To Mr John Barker, of St John Street, had been given the honour of throwing up the ball on Tuesday, which he had artistically decorated.

Before throwing up the ball Mr Barker mentioned that the Clifton Mill wheel had been removed since last year's play, and should the ball be taken to that goal it must be carried to the spot where the wheel originally was. After twenty minutes a movement was made by the Down'ards, and without having touched the brook the ball was hugged into Compton. There was a fierce struggle near the Plough Inn, the Down'ards trying to force their way through to Station Street, and the Up'ards making equally strenuous efforts to get into Sturston Road. Back along Compton the ball came and some fierce hugging resulted before Shaw Croft was re-visited. After a time another move into Compton was made. Arriving at the top of Compton the scenes of the former visit were repeated, with the addition of cries of encouragement from many females who were often in the thick of the hug. Play was again transferred to Compton, where the plate-glass window of Mr F Bates's shop was smashed.

At last the brook was reached, and some of the finest water play witnessed for many years took place between the bank and the old workhouse. The ball was carried under the arches in the direction of the Shaw Croft. Land and water play continued for some time, and although the Up'ards managed to get as far as the Back Bridge on two or three occasions that was the farthest point of the stream to which they progressed. After further hugging it was carried under Compton Bridge, but before the Bank Croft was reached, play was again transferred to Compton and then Station Street where there was a tremendous effort near the police station. At the Church Street end of Station Road another fierce struggle took place and the policemen lined up to push the crowd towards St Oswald's Church. In this they failed, but their attention to the crowd resulted in a portion of the hug breaking away, and while they were pushing the people westerly the ball was being played near the Wesleyan Church.

John Barker, with the trilby, playing below Dig Street in the river

Progress along Church Street in the direction of St John Street was as rapid as it had been in Station Road, and soon Dig Street was reached. Eventually the ball was passed into the Green Man Yard, by way of the back entrance, and after some fierce kicking, it found its way into St John Street. Play then went up to the Market Place, going as far as King Street corner, then back through the Market Place, St John Street, and along Church Street, as far as Mellor's shop. Here there was a check; and a return was made to the top of Dig Street, and eventually a move was made along Church Street, Station Road, and Clifton Road. Niether side relaxed its efforts, and it was a fight all the way along Clifton Road to Clifton Mill, where at about 7.15pm the ball was goaled by Charles and William Sowter. Two years previously Charles Sowter, home from the front, scored the goal for the Down'ards on Ash Wednesday.

A Goal For The Goalkeeper

Steve Bloomer, the international footballer, and ex-Derby County player, threw up the Wednesday ball. It was some time before Bloomer could get the ball away owing to the dense crowd that surged around him after the singing. Eventually the pressure was relieved, and he made a good throw, and the fun commenced. The ball was transferred to the Henmore, about midway between the Green Man Hotel and the Back Bridge, the Up'ards making some good throws, but with the help of the current the Down'ards forced matters downstream to Compton Bridge. The Down'ards continued their advantage, as far as the White Hart Hotel garden, where possession had been gained by Algy Morton and Harold Hoptroff, who quickly made their way to Church Street, which was practically deserted. The vigilant eye of John Hilton, of St John Street, detected that they were having matters too much their own way. Owing to his efforts their progress was checked, and other players coming on the scene, the ball was played into Victoria Square, and after much kicking, a return to St John Street was made.

Play was carried along Church Street, where on several occasions the policemen on duty were pressed into the surging mass. By a series of hugs the ball was taken as far as the corner of Station Road, where the reinforced Up'ards temporarily managed to turn the tide in their favour, so that by three o' clock play was taking place along Church Street in the direction of Dig Street. At the junction of the two thoroughfares there was a slight check, and this having been overcome the players returned to the brook, where the performance previously witnessed was repeated, with the result that the venue changed to Church Street, and then to Station Road. A brisk pace was maintained until Station Street was reached. After a terrific struggle the Down'ards showed their superior strength. After a spell of hugging, the object of which appeared to be to get the ball on to the railway and if possible into the Henmore, Hieron's Barn field was reached. A large pool near the railway was the scene of some of the best water play of this year's contest. The ball was frequently thrown out, but some time elapsed before the Down'ards succeeded in getting the ball away.

The crowd had by this time taken up a good position on the line, and the 4.25pm train from Ashbourne came along with warning whistle and waving passengers, glad to get another glimpse of the play. A good deal of hugging of the ball followed, and in this way it was carried towards Clifton, where at 5.30pm it was goaled by G Faulkner the Ashbourne Town goalkeeper. The highest scorer for Derby County is still Steve Bloomer. Between 1892-1914, he scored 331 goals. The balls this year were decorated by John Barker (who turned up the Tuesday ball) and C Brown. Both were painted free of charge.

Shrovetide Dance

A dance arranged by the Shrovetide Football Committee, (of which Mr W Coxon was chairman and Mr J Hawkesworth secretary) was held in the Town Hall on Tuesday evening in aid of the funds of the Derbyshire Royal Infirmary. There was a very large attendance, numbering about 600.

1921

The Fence Now Leaving the Station

Ex-Inspector John Burton of Chesterfield, and a native of Ashbourne, turned up the first ball of the new decade. The ball soon reached Compton and was fiercely hugged down Station Street. After each hug there was a shower of hats and caps intended to divert attention from the ball. The fence between the railway gardens and the street in Station Road yielded to pressure and play was carried across the railway line to the church field. Here it remained for a considerable time. Spectators noticed that the visit to the station gardens had had an effect on the vegetable produce, remains of which floated down the river along with portions of fencing and other debris of the play.

After the hugging, play continued both in and adjacent to the river. A lot of currant bushes planted near to Nestlé's factory received rather rough treatment en route. The ball still bore its paint work. Several members, as one had come to expect, of the Sowter family were in the thick of it as play progressed towards Clifton. The water players were waist deep at certain places. Shortly after 5.00pm, C Sowter goaled the ball to end play. Mr Burton received an injury to his face in a hug after turning up the ball and another player had to be taken off to the doctor to have his leg treated.

Game To Up'ards But The Goal To Down'ards

The Wednesday ball was turned up by Councillor E G Morley of Derby. After a lot of play in the Croft, the Down'ards got the ball away under Compton Bridge. The crowd rushed to Bank Croft, but the Up'ards ensured that play returned to the Croft. Down'ard pressure followed and play moved up and down Compton before the game returned to Shaw Croft at 3.45pm. It took 45 minutes and a great tussle in the river before play reached Park Road and The Park. The ball was kicked into the Fishpond 'which is now much deeper than it used to be'. Up'ards pressure was asserting itself and George Burton ran off with the ball across the fields on the Ashbourne Green side of the river. It looked like a Sturston goal, but Burton was dispossessed. The ball was taken across the Green, then to Woodeaves Road and Fenny Bentley. After a tussle with four Up'ards, the four Down'ards continued on via Ashes Farm and Mappleton Road to goal at Clifton at 6.45pm, the honour going to L Hill and G Sowter. The day had seen a very keen struggle, with the Up'ards exerting themselves for most of the day's play. The balls were made as usual by Trevor Yeomans and painted by J Barker and C Brown.

The poor goal scoring of the Up'ards was beginning to become apparent. They had only scored two Tuesday goals since 1914 and no Wednesday goals since 1913.

Other News

The Tuesday ball was turned up by ex Inspector John Burton, formerly of the Chesterfield Police. He was Joe (Ninety) Burton's brother and the son of John Burton. Inspector Burton later became a hotelier, buying the County and Prince of Wales Hotels in Chesterfield and another in Jersey, later moving to the Woodeaves Estate at Fenny Bentley and leasing out the mill for cheese making. His daughter, Mrs Joan Parker, returned to Ashbourne for the game in 1995 and photos of her father and grandfather were reproduced in the paper before the games. (ANT 02/02/1995) 'Ninety' Burton was also associated with the police – he was a Special Constable. Both Joe and his brother John died when they were 96 years old.

Before turning up the ball, Inspector Burton addressed the crowd on Shaw Croft. He recalled 'that the game had been played in France during the war. He had been talking to a Chesterfield Doctor who was an Army Doctor in France at the time, who had told of 'several cases in his hospital' as a result of the playing of Shrovetide Football by the Ashbourne boys.

The balls had been made by Trevor Yeomans and decorated by J Barker and C Brown. The committee consisted of W Coxon (Chairman), J C Prince, J Harrison, E Willcocks, W Mellor and J Hawksworth. The week following the games, the Empire Cinema was showing a film of the action. Given the disruption in the town during play on each day, it is incredible that in July 1921, John Sowter (aged 17 years) and William Warner (aged 14 years) were fined 2/6d each for playing football in St John Street on 20th June. Supt Davies asserted that many complaints of the 'nuisance' caused by such activity had been received.

1922

Princess Mary, the only daughter of King George V was marrying Lord Lascelles on Shrove Tuesday and it was decided to send the ball, which had been allocated for that game, to her. Mr John Barker had decorated the ball with the portraits of the bride and groom. Lord Lascelles later became the Earl of Harewood and Princess Mary was accorded the title of Princess Royal. First of all, however, it was necessary to determine if the Princess would accept the ball. One of her bridesmaids was Rachel Cavendish, fourth daughter of the Duke of Devonshire. Mr Hawksworth therefore wrote to her brother, Lord Hartington in the absence of the Duke who had recently returned from the post of Governor of Canada.

The Marquess of Hartington met several members of the Committee at The Mansion, the residence of Dr and Mrs Sadler, and promised to do all in his power to bring their wishes to the notice of the Princess. Mr J Hawksworth had previously received the following letter from Lord Hartington:

"Dear Sir

I have to thank you for your letter of February 6th. I think the plan of presenting this year's football to Princess Mary is a very good one, and I shall be glad to do what I can to bring your kind intention to Her Royal Highness's notice, and to secure her acceptance of the gift. I have no doubt that when the matter is explained to her she will be much interested and greatly gratified at such a unique offering. I do not think that I need trouble you to send the football over to Chatsworth, as I shall be passing through Ashbourne shortly before 11.00am on Saturday next, and shall be glad to stop and have a look at it then. Capt Brooke Taylor, who commanded the Ashbourne platoon of the Sherwood

Foresters, will be with me. He will be keenly interested in the proposal, as he and his men greatly enjoyed the game with the balls you used to send out to them in France."

The ball, made by Mr Trevor Yeomans, was handed to Her Royal Highness by Lord Hartington at Buckingham Palace. Writing from Chatsworth on 17 February, Lord Hartington said:

"Dear Mr Hawksworth,

I went up to London today and presented the football to H R H Princess Mary, who was graciously pleased to accept it as an expression of goodwill from the footballers of Ashbourne. Her Royal Highness took a keen interest in the game, and was much pleased with the kind thought which prompted the committee to send her the ball.

I enclose her letter of thanks. Her Royal Highness also asked me to express her personal thanks to the members of the committee and to Mr Barker, who painted the ball. Lord Lascelles, who was present, was also keenly interested in the details of the game. 'May I take this opportunity of thanking you and the members of the committee for the honour you have done me in making me the channel of your unique gift."

The letter of thanks from Princess Mary was as follows:

"Lord Hartington,

It is very good of you to come here today to present me with this historic football on behalf of the inhabitants of the town and district of Ashbourne. Will you tell the donors how very grateful I am for their kind thought, and that their gift is rendered additionally interesting by the fact that the great annual match, in which all the inhabitants join, will be played as usual on Shrove Tuesday – my wedding day.

Mary

Buckingham Palace

17th February, 1922"

In order to aid the collection for the Derbyshire Royal Infirmary, a ball was used in a guess-the-weight competition. It appears that it was hung from the Green Man Hotel sign across St John Street.

A Fierce Battle

There was much bunting in the streets to celebrate the wedding and the church bells were also rung in celebration. Mr Yeomans, prior to turning up the ball said that he had made four this year, one of which he had given for the old game and the competition. There was a lot of hugging next to the 'new motor shed' – the Green Man Garage – which had been built on the site of an old stone mason's yard. At 2.30pm, the ball reached Compton. There was a great deal of kicking and hugging at the bridge end of Compton. Eventually through more open play the Derby Road end of Compton was reached and play was taken past the Corset Factory. The ball was carried as far as the police station, then into Station Road, and over the hoarding into the gardens adjoining the railway siding.

At last after some good throwing the ball was worked towards the railway houses, and then on to the station platform, where it was received by Mr John Harrison, who lost his hat in transferring the leather to the other side of the station. The ball had its first baptism as a result, but the water play was of brief duration, and a movement along the gardens to the Church Lane bridge was made. The Down'ards players pressed, and very quickly reached the old station yard. In and out among the railway trucks they went, and many of the spectators mounted the stationary milk vans, under one of which the ball was kicked and a fierce struggle took place.

The railway was thronged with people when the 3.37pm North Stafford train approached the station, and again when the 4.10pm L&NW train for Buxton took up its position at the departure platform. Play was then transferred to Clifton Road by way of the opening near Messrs J O Jones & Sons' mill, and for well over an hour hugging and kicking took place between the point where the ball left the railway property and Station Villas. Two windows at the Railway Hotel were broken by the pressure of the players, and the collapse of a wall at the stable yard adjoining was due to the same cause.

There was much heavy kicking near the goods warehouse, and an attempt to force the ball over the cattle dock was unsuccessful. Some of the players emerged from the hug for repairs, and others were minus a portion of their clothing. Scores of lost caps were trampled on in the roadway, and one player had been deprived of a coat and half a waistcoat. Frequently players were knocked down and trampled on. The ball was at last thrown over the fence near the engine shed, and the gardens between that building and Nestlé's factory were traversed. An accurate throw was soon made to someone standing on a railway waggon, and he transferred the ball to the railway, along which it was kicked to the brook where Harry Chell had possession, and waded for some distance. Near the Gas Works an enthusiastic stranger jumped into the brook and tackled four players, being followed by Jim Burton, and after a fierce fight the ball was landed on the Mayfield Road side of the Henmore. It was then played across to Mayfield Road, emerging next to the cemetery.

For a time the scene of the battle was in the field at the corner of which was the new Derbyshire County Council depot, and in the fields below near the Doles. The venue then changed, and after Mayfield Road had again been visited, the brook was reached. Here Tom Harrison and Sid Taylor took to the water and waded down stream to within a short distance of Clifton Mill. When they came to land, and practically all opposition having been withdrawn the ball was goaled at 6.30pm by Sid Taylor.

Up'ards Outwit The Down'ards

There was a heavy downpour on Tuesday night, and with the Henmore swollen to the top of the banks some exciting water play was anticipated. Mr Alf Holmes of the Peacock Hotel, Chesterfield, turned up the ball, artistically decorated by Mr C Brown. He was not an Ashburnian, but he had seen the game played for the past 32 years. A hug at once took place and after much struggling play was transferred towards the Bath House gardens. A sudden opening out led to vigorous kicking, the ball being propelled at a rapid rate to the corner of the Croft nearest the Back Bridge, where it was put into the turbulent Henmore. Harold Massey was the first to follow it. On several occasions it was kicked into the water, and some good throws were made, followed by kicking and hugging in the Croft.

After about a quarter of an hour's play it was being played for in Compton, travelling along rapidly. It was almost a direct run to the end of Compton, and it appeared as if the Up'ards were to gain a considerable advantage by getting the ball into Sturston Road. Their success was only short-lived for the Down'ards forced a return to Compton and by 2.45pm the ball had arrived at the bridge. With remarkable speed the play changed, and before the spectators could realise what had happened the ball had been carried across the Bath House gardens into Sturston Road, and run away with in the direction of Derby Road. From a spectator's point of view the game was over by 3.00pm. For a time it was thought that the Down'ards were in possession, and that they were making for Clifton by way of the fields above North Leys, but it was ultimately found that two Up'ards men had outwitted their opponents. The ball was eventually goaled at 4.15pm by Oswald Hill, assisted by Leslie Hill.

Two Balls In Play At Once

Owing to the first ball having been run away with so soon after the game commenced, Mr J Hawksworth decided to bring a second ball into play for the benefit of the large number of spectators who had come from many Midland and northern towns to see the game. The report stated that: "the committee feel very strongly on the question of the ball being run away with, and it is likely that a rule will be enforced in future that in the event of a similar occurence before 5.00pm 'no ball' will be the order, so that no credit will attach to the player who is in possession." At 3.45pm a second ball was thrown up by Mr M E Bland, of Derby, and very soon play was taking place in the brook at the Green Man Garage end of the Croft. The strong current naturally assisted the Down'ards, who succeeded in negotiating the arches of Compton Bridge, and on reaching Bank Croft. G Sowter had possession. The ball was quickly carried under Station Road and there was some excellent water play near the passenger station just as the 4.10pm train to Buxton was about to depart.

The Down'ards made rapid progress, and for a considerable distance along the brook course Baden Faulkner and Brailsford had little opposition. Harry Dyche then took a hand unaccompanied in the water, but assisted at times by comrades on the bank who held him up by means of a strap. Sometimes he swam with the ball under him, and in this way The Doles was passed. Then he came to land, and opposition being encountered he returned to the brook, which was followed to within a short distance of Clifton Mill. The ball was then brought to the bank, and the Up'ards, who had done little challenging made a sudden attack, the result being that the victory of the Down'ards was snatched from them, at any rate for the time being. Play then took place in the fields, and after a severe struggle the ball reached Green Lane, where there was an exceedingly hot contest. The ball was eventually goaled at Clifton at 6.45pm by William Birch.

Lord Hartington promised to throw up the ball on Shrove Tuesday next year, and Captain F E F Wright, of Lady Hole, on the following day.

1923

Ashbourne Honours A Good Friend

Shortly before two o'clock the Marquis of Hartington who, with the Shrovetide Football Committee, had attended the public lunch at the Green Man Hotel, was photographed on a char-a-banc in front of the hostelry. Then his lordship, bearing the gaily painted ball inscribed 'Ashbourne Royal Shrovetide Football, 1923' ('Royal' from the fact that Princess Mary accepted a similar ball as a wedding gift), led the procession to the Shaw Croft. Lord Hartington threw up the ball, which was immediately kicked into the Henmore, but quickly returned to land where there was much hugging. The game had been in progress only fifteen minutes, and the ball was propelled along Compton Street at a rapid rate. By a series of hugs it was returned to the Poor Law Offices, where fierce tussle ensued, the Down'ards intention being to turn the play into King Edward Street. Lord Hartington was frequently seen where the battle was hottest, and no one appeared to be enjoying the fun better than he. The Up'ards triumphed at length, and at 3.40pm the contending forces were back again in the Shaw Croft.

A repetition of the earlier play took place for some time, the ball being carried from side to side of the Croft, until at 3.15pm Park Road was reached from the corner nearest the Bath House. No sooner had the players got on the highway than the ball was thrown into the manure pit of some stables in Park Road. The more ardent followers scrambled into the unpleasant vault by way of a door only about a yard square and some few feet above the road. A few minutes later they emerged again, and play restarted. When the corner of Sturston Road was reached there was a check, from which the Down'ards succeeded in turning in the direction of Compton. At the corner of Compton the fight was less severe, and swaying from side to side the crowd carried the ball as far as Lloyds Bank. This second attempt of the Down'ards to force their way into King Edward Street eventually proved successful, and by 4.30pm play was taking place on The Paddock.

The ball was then passed behind the Station Hotel into King Edward Street, and owing to the main body of players finding a difficulty in getting out of The Paddock there was some fairly free kicking before the ball was again transferred to The Paddock, where much hugging took place. At last the ball was taken into the Station Hotel yard, in which it remained for a considerable time. When at last it was released a move was made to the railway station, and a great struggle under the platforms took place. Then the stream was reached and J Clowes, Frank Wibberley and others were in the water. After a brief return to land Charles Sowter was wading down stream when he was challenged and overcome by Jim Burton, who threw the ball out. The ball was hugged down to the Gas Works, where it remained for some time, and by slow stages the Down'ards, although challenged all the way, succeeded in pushing their way along Mayfield Road and Green Lane to Clifton Mill, where the ball was goaled by Edward Chell about 9.00pm.

A Good Deal Of 'Sprottling'

On Wednesday morning there was a covering of snow, and a thick fog hung over Ashbourne the whole of the day. The duty of throwing up the ball had been entrusted to Captain F E F Wright of Lady Hole, Yeldersley. Captain Wright gave the ball a good throw high into the air, and the sport commenced. No sooner had the ball reached the ground than it was hurried to the brook, which Albert Botham was the first to enter. Owing to the slippery state of the ground there was, to use the colloquial expression, a good deal of 'sprottling', and the game had not been in progress many minutes when such keen players as John Barker were covered from head to foot with mud. The ball was worked across the Croft several times, and there were fierce struggles in the brook.

There was a return to land, and in a moment play was taking place in Park Road. The ball was then slowly hugged in the direction of Sturston Road. At the corner there was a very tough fight, and the

Down'ards succeeded in turning the tide in the direction of Compton. Since leaving the Shaw Croft very few glimpses of the ball had been obtained, but near the Machine Inn it was released, and a few throws were made in both directions, the Down'ards still gaining the advantage. In a short time the end of Compton was reached, and the play opening out, there was some strong and rapid kicking up Compton, over the bridge, up Dig Street and into Church Street, where Leslie Hall set the pace.

Just as the Parish Church clock struck 3.00pm a hug was taking place near Dr Hollick's residence, and from this there was a breakaway down Church Lane (now School House Lane) as far as the back entrance to the Mansion grounds. When the players got going again the ball was taken to the goods station yard, and was hugged along the front of the coal merchants' offices to the oil tanks, where it passed over the brook into the church field. There it remained, except for brief visits to the river, for an hour and a quarter, and the players floundered in large pools of water. Almost every time the ball passed into the Henmore, Frank Wibberley was one of the first to enter, and once he succeeded in carrying it some distance up stream, but the opposition proved too great for him. After one of these water episodes Amos Clowes threw the ball on to the bank close to the oil tanks adjoining the station yard, and play was taken to some stationary railway trucks and amongst a pile of oil barrels! Another return to the church field was made where further hugging carried it to Mayfield Road.

By slow stages the players made their way down Mayfield Road to the corner of the lane beyond the cemetery. T C Waterfall, who had possession of the ball, was forced through the hedge. From this point operations moved to the sewage works, and then returned to Mayfield Road where more hugging occurred. The Down'ards proved the stronger side, and G Peach goaled the ball at Clifton shortly after 6.00pm.

1924

Chairman's Goal

"If past generations of Ashburnians had been told that one day the historic game, for which the town is noted, would have received royal recognition, and that the leading peers of the realm would give his presence and support, the assertion would probably have been doubted, but times have changed, and the conditions under which Shrovetide football is now played have raised the standard to the level of the high interest referred to. The Committee responsible for the arrangements this year consisted of Messrs Joseph Harrison (chairman), J C Prince, W H Kirkland, J Barker, E Wilcocks, and J Hawksworth (secretary)."

As this quote from the local paper (AN 07/03/1924) indicates, the game had come a long way from the disgraceful affairs of 46 years before. The welcome given to the Duke of Devonshire was a very enthusiastic one, and the committee had arranged a luncheon at the Green Man Hotel attended by 130 people.

The Duke threw up the ball, which had been painted in the national colours, with the Duke's coat of arms, and bore the inscriptions – 'Ashbourne Ancient Royal Shrovetide Football, 1924,' and 'Thrown up by his Grace the Duke of Devonshire'. As soon as the sphere descended it was taken in the direction of the Bath House gardens, and when the crowd moved from the starting place the Duke followed the play with evident interest. It soon passed to the water with Redvers Wibberley making some good throws and eventually the ball reached land, where more hugging occurred. Further traversing of the field took place, and the Down'ards getting the upper hand took the ball to the motor sheds near the Terrace, and gradually pressed into Compton Street which was reached at 2.45pm. The Up'ards prevented their opponents from turning into Station Street, the Down'ards forced their way into King Edward Street, and the river, but at length the ball was hugged to the Station Road side of Bank Croft, where a fierce struggle took place. Prominent in the hug was Mr Joseph Harrison, the chairman of the Shrovetide Football Committee, and at 3.45pm the ball was taken by way of the brook course behind the railway station.

Joseph Burton gained possession, and returned with it to the water. Then play was taken in the direction of the old station, at times in the brook and at others on land, and a hot contest took place near the footbridge leading to Clifton Road. A return was made to the Henmore, and wading down the stream the Down'ards seemed to be almost assured of victory, although they were always challenged by Up'ards players. Near Nestlé's factory the ball returned to land, and in the fields beyond there was much hugging. It was now after 5.00pm, and by a series of hugs the ball was carried by the Down'ards for a considerable distance on land. Eventually, shortly after 6.00pm, it was goaled by Joseph Harrison.

Honours Divided

On Wednesday there was an indication of a thaw about to set in. It was a matter of disappointment that W Meredith, of Manchester City, the famous Welsh international footballer, was unable to attend, as had been arranged, to throw up the first ball. Meredith was in his 50th year, and attained the half century on 28th July. There was a thick covering of snow on the Shaw Croft, when shortly before two o'clock the procession arrived with Miss Winnie Meredith, daughter of the footballer, carrying the ball. She was accompanied by Mr H J Newbould, secretary of the Association Football Players' and Trainers' Union of Manchester, who deputised for Meredith. Mr Meredith had sent his daughter to turn up the ball, but did not realise that ancient tradition precluded this. Therefore, Mr Newbould sent the leather into the air. There was some strong kicking for a few minutes and then a quick movement was made to the brook. The pace was extremely hot, and by 2.00pm the ball was being carried under the Park Road bridge. A few players got a good lead, and were bounding across the fields on the Hall Farm side of the Fishpond, a player named Walker being in possession. The Down'ards rallied and a long hug ensued in the Henmore. Pressure resulted in the transfer of play over the stream that feeds the Fishpond, and in the direction of Sturston Road.

A breakaway across the field was checked by a further hug, and the river was again visited. The Up'ards were using all the strategy they were capable of, George Fogg in particular braving the river with the water well above his waist. Then Redvers Wibberley, who like Fogg had been playing a great game, took a hand at carrying the ball, being joined by George Etches and several others. The Down'ards appeared to be willing for the Up'ards to goal the ball so that a second one could be turned up. When the mill race was reached Redvers Wibberley had possession of the ball, and was well supported by G Etches and others. Exactly at 4.00pm, Wibberley goaled the ball. The second ball was turned up by Gunner C E Stone VC, formerly of Belper, but now residing at the Haywood Farm, Ashbourne. The ball went into the brook, where it was picked up several times and thrown up and down the stream. The Down'ards made off in the direction of Compton Bridge, under which the ball was carried. They soon took play through the Bank Croft, under the Station Road bridge, and behind the railway station as they did on the previous day. They pressed on to the old station bridge, where a fierce hug occurred in the water, and by 5.00pm the church field had been reached. The play was then transferred to Mayfield Road, and the Down'ards continued to make progress. By continual hugging the corner of Green Lane was reached. Rain now came on, but play continued vigorously along Green Lane to Clifton Mill, where, at about 7.00pm the ball was goaled by Hubert Connell. The footballs used for this year's play had been painted by Mr John Barker, who was frequently seen in the hug on the Tuesday and Wednesday and Mr T A Bassano.

1925

Spectators On, Not In, Railway Coaches

The clear frosty morning gave way to rain, which was falling heavily when at two o'clock Mr W Meredith threw up the ball in the Shaw Croft, which was inches deep in mud. The number of players and spectators was, therefore, very much smaller than usual. It is worthy of mention that this year's play included 'Paully' Woolley, who had not missed a game for over 50 years. In recognition of his long connection with the game, the Committee provided a ball specially painted by Horace Davenport, a pupil of Mr Bassano, painter and decorator, of Ashbourne – in the event of a second one being required on either day. Having been brought to Princess Mary's attention, it was hoped that this year one of the Princes would have started the play, but this was found to be impossible, notwithstanding the good offices of the Duke of Devonshire, who threw up the ball in 1924.

Mr Meredith was hoisted on to the shoulders of Captain Unwin VC, and Mr Joseph Harrison, with Mr John Edge, C C, in support. After the singing Mr Meredith threw up the ball. There was then a rush into Compton, the ball being carried from the field without having reached the river. Much hugging took place near the Wheel Inn. There was a brief check near the surveyor's office, but the Up'ards had to give way to their opponents, and it was not long before the corrugated iron hoarding between the Mission Room and the Empire collapsed under the pressure of the crowd, who swerved into The Paddock.

Well before 3.00pm the ball had been carried through the Station Hotel yard into Station Road and to the allotment gardens between the passenger station and the police station. The spectators had a good view of the proceedings at this point, many climbing to the top of the railway coaches in the siding. Among those who were prominent in the fray were Joseph Harrison, Joseph Burton, J Barker, J Edge and 'Paully' Woolley. Hug after hug took place for an hour and a half, by which time almost every part of the gardens had been traversed. When at length the ball was taken into Clifton Road near the footbridge there was a fierce struggle in the vicinity of the Railway Hotel. From this point the progress of the Down'ards was slow, but they eventually reached their goal at 8.00pm. Shortly afterwards the ball was goaled by F Moon and S Sowter.

Several Hours' Street Play

Mr Andrew Knowles of The Grove Hall, Ashbourne and master of the Dove Valley Hounds, had been invited to throw up the ball, and was present at the luncheon at the Green Man Hotel. Supt Davies, of the Ashbourne police, spoke and said he saw no objection to the game being played so long as damage to property was avoided, and they could be sure that while he occupied the position of superintendent he would not oppose it.

Mr Knowles threw the ball high into the air, and the fun commenced. Some good throws were made in the water by Redvers Wibberley and W Brown and George Sowter was also prominent. The Up'ards were asserting themselves in no unmistakable manner, and as a result of some good throws up stream they were able to carry play under the bridge at Park Road. Land was reached on the Recreation Ground side of the stream, then a return was made to the Henmore, and after a good deal of splashing the ball was thrown on to the opposite bank. Here a breakaway occurred, and the ball was soon pitched into the Fish Pond. Play swayed between the river and the pond, Captain Bond and Mr Joseph Harrison being prominent in the hug. The Down'ards at last pressed into Park Road and forcing their way through Messrs Birch and Sons' timber yard they reached Compton. It looked as if they would succeed in getting into King Edward Street, as they did the previous day. However, success was denied them, and the full length of Compton was traversed. Returning along Compton, Shaw Croft was reached at 4.00pm and some good water play followed. At this point E W Hurd called for the ball and he made off with it across the lawn to his house.

It was not many minutes before it was being played in the Blacks Head Yard. W Keeling, a Down'ard, had possession and was heading down St John Street when he was tackled by Mr W Coxon. The ball was then transferred to Victoria Square before returning to St John Square. There was a fierce hug at the top of Dig Street with the police trying to force play down the street. However, play went into Church Street with much hugging before the Down'ards forced play into Station Road. Clifton Road was reached and following the tactics of the previous day, they arrived at Clifton just after 8.00pm and the ball was goaled by J Barker, the Committee member and decorator of the balls.

1926

Little Street Play

The footballs were made by Mr Trevor Yeomans, the first ball on Tuesday was painted by Mr J Barker, and Wednesday's ball by Messrs C Brown & Sons. Mr J Farmer, of the Derby and County Athletic Club, threw up the first ball. A Mr Turner of Derby had given £20, the largest the Shrovetide Fund had ever received. He was invited to throw up the first ball of 1927. Mr Farmer threw up the ball, which remained in the Croft for some time before it reached the river. From there it was taken into The Park, and there was a general scramble before it arrived at the Fish Pond, from where it was rescued by A Birch, of Clifton, who swam out to recover it. The ball was bandied about in the water for long periods, Harry, Sam and Albert Sowter, W Clews, W Brown and Baden Burton taking a prominent part. Several swift dashes across The Park only resulted in a return to the same spot in the Henmore. Several players seemed to be permanently in the water. One of them was heard to remark that the money in his pocket had 'gone rusty'.

Play was eventually carried across The Park and into the field beyond, and once Charlie Mee and R Carter retreived the ball from the mud near the Fish Pond, sinking in to their waists. An open and exciting interlude followed, but the Up'ards were now slowly but surely forcing their way towards their goal. Taking to the river with the ball, T Brown and Frank Clews started to wade upstream through deep water, chanting 'Ukele Lady'. They were joined by W Brown, but the battle was by no means over, the Down'ards contesting the ground (and the water) stubbornly. In and out of the water Brown and others made their way up the river, William Brown goaling the ball at 4.30pm. He had been playing for 45 years. This ball was later acquired by a Mr Emery who had an antiques shop in Church Street. It hung in his window for about a year or so and then he gave it to his errand boy – Alec Smith – who had worked for free for about a year in order to pay for it. Alec went on to be one of the game's stalwarts.

The second ball was thrown up by Mr Joseph Harrison. The Down'ards forced the ball out into Compton. Hugging proceeded from 'The Wheel' and along in the direction of Station Street. Emerging into King Edward Street, the ball went loose into the field opposite the Empire Cinema, and finally was carried into the Henmore and under Station Road Bridge. A wild dash was made through the station entrance, players and spectators swarming over the rails, but the Down'ards got clear away. A large number followed along the railway line and arrived at Clifton soon after 6.00pm, to find that overcoming what opposition was offered, Frank Taylor had already goaled the ball. There had been very little street play.

Two goals at Clifton

Mr F Beardsley, of Wigan, an old Ashburnian, who had been collecting for the fund in Wigan, had been invited to throw up the ball. A strenuous and prolonged hug ensued immediately. A rush was made to the Henmore, and in went the ball and players with a terrific splash. Play then emerged from the Croft into Compton. It was packed from end to end with a dense crowd. The Down'ards forced the ball into Station Street, but the Up'ards were just as determined. At length the Up'ards slowly turned the tide, the scrum swaying from side to side of the road back towards the Bridge. Baulked in one direction the Down'ards, who were much stronger than on the previous day, concentrated on getting into King Edward Street, but the ball was flung back into Compton, and a fine dribble carried it right to Station Street. The Down'ards were held, however, at the corner of Station Road. Amid general uproar, in which the shrill voices of women were heard, exhorting the Up'ards to 'set 'em alight', the game was transferred to the strip of land by the river. Leonard Avery took the ball downstream with a bodyguard of Down'ards. An amazing sight was presented as the throng burst through the station entrance and streamed over the metals in their anxiety to keep up with the play. Others accompanied the players on their progress, and the ball was goaled by Charles Colclough at 4.40pm.

A second ball was thrown up by Mr Fred Ward shortly after 5.00pm, play being carried across Park Road into a field beyond. The players burst through into The Park and the ball was kicked backward and forward before it was thrown into the field. It was soon back again, and was being swept toward the Fish Pond, where it was diverted by H G Holbrook; more kicking followed, and the Down'ards went careering away into Sturston Road. They quickly reached the corner of Compton where the Up'ards pressed home their opposition. Hugging continued until the police station was reached, and here the Up'ards made another great effort, succeeding in turning the game into Station Road, as they did earlier in the afternoon. They seemed to be gaining the upper hand when King Edward Street was reached, but in a few minutes the ball was in the Henmore, and their success was short lived. The Down'ards were quick to take advantage of this turn, C Sowter taking the ball under the bridge. No opposition was encountered when in the darkness and rain they set out for the goal at Clifton, W Sowter goaling the ball soon after 7.00pm.

There was a comment in the paper (AN 26/02/1926) that a second ball had become a rarity. Since 1891, thirty additional balls had been turned up in 36 years (including the two this year). However, in the last dozen year's games – which included the four World War I games – only seven had been turned up, of which two had been in 1926. Mr Harrison, throwing up the second Tuesday ball remarked that this was unusual. It was the first Tuesday second ball since 1917 and only the second since 1913. Since 1891, nineteen of the thirty additional balls had been turned up on a Wednesday. Of the eleven Tuesday balls nine had been turned up in the period 1904 to1913. Second balls on a Tuesday were indeed a rarity and must indicate the different composition of players on the two days.

1926 was the first time four balls had been goaled since 1912. The Down'ards had last scored three goals in a year in 1917. However, it was 1900 in the case of the Up'ards. The last time three balls had been goaled in one day was 1890. The Up'ards seemed to have lost their supremacy with the Great War. In fact counting the goals of both days per year, they hadn't won a year since 1913. The *Ashbourne News* had given the goal tally annually since 1889. The Up'ards had held the lead until 1926 when the Down'ards equalled the Up'ards tally at 52 goals each. 1926 saw another record too, with over £61 being given to charity. This was over three times the previous year's amount and was also in the Depression.

1927

A Runaway Ball

This year saw Mr Hawksworth reach 30 years as secretary of the committee. Mr F Turner, threw up the first ball, and had contributed £30 to the funds. The Shaw Croft was inches deep in mud. The ball, was immediately dribbled across the Croft but within two minutes it was rushed back and into the Henmore. Passing under Compton Bridge, the Down'ards went rapidly downstream to the Station Road bridge. Another halt was called a little lower down, but the Up'ards were weak in numbers and the game was assuming the aspect of a fiasco. The Down'ards worked in relay in carrying the ball down to Clifton along the Henmore, which was heavily swollen by recent rains. Throngs of people who followed picked their way with varying success through the quagmire, while others, more fatalistic, took the direct method of walking down the railway to Clifton Mill, where Jack Sowter goaled the ball at 3.15pm, an hour after it had been turned up.

A second ball was thrown up in the Shaw Croft shortly after 4.00pm by Mr J Farmer, of Derby, who said he had the unique honour of throwing up the first ball last year and the second one that day. When the ball was thrown up it was evident that a determined effort would be made to keep it out of the water, as the hug swayed out into Park Road. When a few women took a hand it turned the scale in favour of the Up'ards, and the hug went through into The Park. Here the ball went loose and some good throws were made. A rush carried the proceedings to Sturston Road, where a woman nipped in the bud an attempt by a Down'ard to run away with the leather. John Barker and William Brown, two 'old stagers', were noticed in the thick of the scrum, and 'Paully' Woolley looked on. For 45 minutes the hug had not gone beyond a radius of a dozen yards and the ball had been hidden all this time.

The Up'ards eventually gave way a little, and after an hour's hugging the ball was dropped and an exciting scramble followed. The Down'ards made some good throws, but another hug was formed at the Park Road corner and proceeded spasmodically to the top of Compton. For an hour and a half the hugs swirled up and down the street. At 8.00pm, when the battle was being as stubbornly contested as ever, the ball went into the water for the first time, by the Compton hoarding. W Brown and R Wibberley got in some hefty throws to bring the leather to land, but each time it went back and was carried under the arch. Thrown on to the bridge in the darkness it was dribbled up Dig Street, most of the spectators being unaware of what had happened. It disappeared along Church Street as if it had vanished into thin air. The ball was hidden by S Burton among coal wagons at the railway station and recovered later. It was goaled at Sturston Mill by Frank Smith at 11.45pm.

A Ball In The Market Place

Mr C Holmes, of the White Hart Hotel, who threw up the ball, said they hoped to have some fun with the ball, not as on the previous day. Running away with it spoilt matters for the visitors and for the townspeople. After some aimless swerving about the Croft the Down'ards forced the ball out into Compton. It was hugged right up to the bottom of Derby Road, where the Up'ards sent it back again easily holding their own at King Edward Street. Soon afterwards the ball became loose, and an exciting dribble ensued, with the spectators in full cry. Several good throws were made, but the top of Compton was well guarded, and hugging began again. The Down'ards, for whom Mr Joseph Harrison was prominent at this stage, were forced back into Sturston Road, but recovered. For three-quarters of an hour the game flowed up and down Compton. A return was made to the Shaw Croft, where the ball was dropped, and a rush for the Henmore was frustrated. The leather was flying loose for a few thrilling moments, and then a swoop took it into the water. Baden Burton eventually flung the ball out on the St John Street side and L Hill made away with it up the Wellington Yard. He dashed into the Market Place accompanied by A Turner and turned through the Town Hall Yard with a few Down'ards in full cry behind. The 'hares' were overtaken in Green Road, Charlie Colclough, Stan Griffiths and several others saving the situation for the Down'ards. The Up'ards offered strong resistance, but they were swept down the Hall Lane and past the Park.

Eventually, the ball went through Shaw Croft and into Compton. The ball was hugged via King Edward Street into Station Road and round into Clifton Road. Every inch of ground was stubbornly contested and by 8.00pm the hug was as fierce as ever. It took two hours to reach Nestlé's from the police station with the ball continually out of sight. The Up'ards forced the hug back again and the Down'ards were baulked when everything pointed to the ball 'going down'. At 9.00pm the ball was still being hugged in the drenching rain and soon afterwards the Up'ards triumphed, Redvers Wibberley goaling the ball at Sturston Mill at about 9.30pm.

1928

Prince of Wales Starts The Game

The streets of the town were gaily decorated with flags. On the British Legion Club was displayed 'Hearty greetings to our Prince', similar banners meeting the eye in the main streets. On the Compton hoarding, the centre portion was occupied by 'Ashbourne welcomes the Prince of Wales. God bless him'. An archway of evergreens at the entrance to the Shaw Croft had at its summit 'Ashbourne Royal Shrovetide Football. Welcome to our Prince', embellished with symbols of footballs bearing the date '1928'.

After three fine days the morning broke cold and misty but cloudless. From an early hour there was a steady influx of visitors by road and rail, the town was thronged with sightseers and the special parking places soon began to fill up. Long before 11.00am there were thousands of people on the Shaw Croft and in the streets, there was a general air of excitement. The Royal party, who had motored from Chatsworth by way of Matlock and Wirksworth, with a halt at Hopton quarries at Middleton, entered Ashbourne by The Green Road. They then proceeded to the Shaw Croft through cheering crowds by way of King Street, Market Place, St John Street and Dig Street. A halt was made while the massed school children sang 'God bless the Prince of Wales'.

At about 11.30am, the party alighted at the gates of the Croft. People were densely packed and the Prince, after being met by Capt R H Bond JP, passed between the ranks of the ex-service men, numbering about 350, who formed a lane to the platform erected over the Henmore. On the way His Highness recognised amongst them Mr J Rudge, who served during the war in the Welsh Guards, the Prince's old regiment, and stopped to shake hands and have a word with him. This incident, typical of the Royal visitor, aroused warm enthusiasm among the crowd and he was heartily cheered as he mounted to the lofty platform. He was accompanied by the Duke and Duchess of Devonshire, the Duke and Duchess of Rutland, Capt the Hon Evan Baillie, Lady Maud Baillie, the Hon Bruce Ogilvy (the Prince's Equerry), Lord and Lady Hartington, Lady Ann Cavendish, Mr and Mrs U R Burke and the County Chief Constable (Major Anley).

The Prince was received by Mr G M Bond JP (president of the Shrovetide Football Committee), who then presented to His Royal Highness, the following members of the Committee: Mr Joseph Harrison (chairman), Mr J Hawksworth (secretary), Messrs J Barker, W H Kirkland, J Farmer, E Willcocks, F N Turner, F W Henstock, J C Prince and H A Franklin. Addressing the Prince and the assembled multitude, Mr G M Bond then said:

"Your Royal Highness, Your Grace, My Lord, Ladies and Gentlemen – This is indeed a red letter day for the inhabitants of Ashbourne and the neighbourhood, His Royal Highness having graciously consented to visit the town in an informal way, and to take part in the ancient game of football as played here for so many hundreds of years on Shrove Tuesday and Ash Wednesday. I cannot trace that the game has previously been thus honoured by Royalty; and, on behalf of the Football Committee and this large assembly, I tender our grateful thanks to His Royal Highness for the honour he has conferred upon us by coming here today. Ashbourne has always been noted for its loyalty to the Crown. If it were possible further to cement that feeling, it would be by this visit of His Royal Highness. The origin of the game is lost in antiquity. Prior to 1869 the ball was turned up in the Market Place. In that year the venue was changed – for various good reasons (not unconnected with broken windows, I believe) – to the Shaw Croft, where we now stand. It may interest His Royal Highness to hear that the goals in this game are some two and a half miles apart – Sturston Mill in the North, and Clifton Mill in the South – Ashbourne being about the centre. There were no rules excepting the division of the players into Up'ards and Down'ards. It is 'catch as catch can' or 'go as you please', and there is no limit to the number of players. To the players on both sides I would say, play hard with all your might. Play the game, and keep the ball as much as possible out of the town. Those who follow the ball I would ask to do as little damage as possible to the fences and gates on the lands they roam over, remembering that they are on sufferance. I will now ask you to give three hearty British cheers for His Royal Highness, taking your time from me."

Stepping forward to speak, the Prince was greeted with thunderous cheers, and he said:

"Mr Bond, ladies and gentlemen, – I can assure you that it is a very great pleasure to have the opportunity of visting Ashbourne today, and, apart from your historic football game, to see so many of you. Your President says that he is proud that I am taking part in the game myself, but I think if I take any more part than throwing up the ball I shall be unable to fulfil one or two engagements I have in Derby this afternoon. I have great pleasure in throwing up the ball, and starting what I consider to be a very sporting game. I wish everybody in Ashbourne and district every possible success."

The National Anthem was then sung in accordance with custom, and afterwards the singing of 'For he's a jolly good fellow' was taken up lustily if not tunefully, the Prince laughing heartily in acknowledgement.

Mr Joseph Harrison handed the ball to His Highness with the words:

"Your Royal Highness, as chairman of the Shrovetide Football Committee, I have pleasure in handing you this ball and asking you to do us the honour of turning it up for the ancient game."

The players began to thread their way through the throng to positions in front of the platform, and, stepping back, the Prince hurled the ball far out into the midst of the vast concourse of people, as a battery of cameras recorded the historic act.

Up'ards and Down'ards immediately closed round it, and the police and photographers, taken by surprise, were caught in the turmoil, the latter with much concern for the safety of their cameras, struggling out of the battle area with difficulty. Pandemonium reigned for a time, cries of 'Up with it', 'Down with it'. 'Stick to it, my lads', causing the Prince much amusement. The ball was soon in the water near the platform, but was hugged a little too much. His Highness was keenly interested in the play, and was highly amused when the first 'duckings' took place.

Once the ball was thrown up on to the platform, but dropped back again into the water, and one of the participants, who was wearing his war medals, addressing the Prince from the middle of the river, reminded His Highness of some incident in France, which was smilingly acknowledged. After watching the play for about twenty minutes, the Prince passed over the bridge on to the lawn at the rear of Messrs Burgon's shop, where a number of disabled ex-service men were seated. The Royal visitor shook hands with each man and chatted for some time to Mr Stephen Higgins. At 12.15pm the Prince emerged into St John Street, where his car was waiting, and left for Derby amid the rousing cheers of the thousands of people lining St John Street.

The Play

While the Prince was looking on there were about forty players in the water, where the ball was hugged fiercely and a cine-photographer wearing waders set up his camera in the middle of the Henmore and calmly 'shot' the proceedings. At last the leather went loose and was played under the temporary bridge towards Compton, but the Down'ards could make no headway.

After three-quarters of an hour intermittent immersion in the Henmore, the ball was finally flung out and the Up'ards slowly forced their way towards Park Road. Eventually the ball was thrown into Park Road after an hour and a half's play in the Croft. It was quickly seized upon and tightly hugged but a sudden heave by the Up'ards almost gained them entrance to The Park. The Down'ards had a strong guard posted at the gate and the movement was frustrated and a terrific struggle raged at this spot. Once the hug was safely steered past the entrance but the Up'ards were undaunted and a second mighty effort carried them into The Park. The leather was hugged backwards and forwards there, for about three-quarters of an hour. There were several minor casualties and Norman Burton and W Hand were carried from the scene on improvised stretchers. After an exciting scramble the ball was kicked into the Fish Pond, and Francis Gregory swam with it to the other side accompanied by Tom Buckley, of Fenny Bentley. The Down'ards immediately joined the play, the ball being deposited in the Henmore, where Redvers Wibberley and Charlie Colclough got in useful throws.

The Down'ards were gaining no advantage from the water play and in the thrilling dribbles on land the Up'ards could make little headway either. They were very determined, however, and appeared to hold the ground they had gained. The Up'ards made a great effort and went away in full cry with the crowd streaming over the fields in pursuit. The river was re-entered higher up and there was a struggle in waist deep water, the hug collapsing in a heap. Joe Bowler collared the leather and was escorted upstream by a bodyguard, but in the shallow water at a bend a strong force of Down'ards were lying in wait.

The leather went to land and the Down'ards went tearing away across a couple of fields with it at their feet. They were checked near Sturston Lane and there was another hug. The ball was in the open much more now and the Down'ards regained considerable ground by means of hefty throws. It was a surprise and disappointment when the leather was flung across the Henmore and one or two Up'ards made off with it across the fields. The few who went in pursuit were outpaced and thus ended a magnificent game. Scores of people set out for Sturston Mill only to be informed before that destination was reached that the ball was goaled by G Ratcliffe, of Waterfall, Staffs, at 4.50pm.

Second Ball

A return was made to the Shaw Croft where a second ball was turned up at 5.30pm. Addressing the small gathering in front of the platform, Mr Hawksworth said that the Prince of Wales having thrown up the first ball, the Committee were giving the privilege of turning up the second to one of the oldest players in Ashbourne – Mr Sam Dakin. Among the small assembly the Down'ards predominated, most of the Up'ards being elsewhere, celebrating their victory, and they quickly forced the ball into Compton and King Edward Street, little opposition being met. Turning into Station Road in the dusk the players proceeded along Church Street and down Church Lane, where they took to the water. Here some resistance was offered, but the Down'ards were too strong in numbers to be checked, and they made steady progress to Clifton Mill, where Herbert Sowter and Louis Bill goaled the ball at 7.10pm. The balls were made as usual by Mr Trevor Yeomans, and that thrown up by the Prince of Wales was painted by Mr John Barker, bearing on one side the Prince's feathers with his motto 'Ich Dien', and on the other a crown. The ball used on Wednesday was painted by Mr Charles Brown.

Down The River To Clifton Again

On Wednesday glorious spring weather again prevailed, the ball being turned up by Mr G T Riding, of Garston, Liverpool. After about ten minutes 'hugging' in the Croft the Down'ards forced their way to the water, the hug collapsing on the bank. Several Up'ards were waiting in the water and one of them lugged Louis Sowter bodily into the stream, where he loosed the ball. Down'ards fought their way by inches to Compton Bridge, where they were checked. Eventually play was carried under the arch, and the spectators made a dash for the Bank Croft, where in the melee Sam Sowter lost the ball after holding it for nearly forty minutes. There was another battle under the railway bridge, but the Down'ards progress continued. Hundreds of spectators dashed into the station and clambered down on to the metals in their eagerness to keep up with the play.

At last a sight of the leather was obtained, and Ernest Taylor threw it out into the railway sidings. The Down'ards veered toward the river again and the 'hug' shifted one of the huts in the siding by several feet. There were shouts of 'Keep it out of the water' and 'Throw it Up'ards', and the advice was accepted, the ball being flung across the brook to 'Chick' Harrison. There was some fine play in the church field; once when the leather went over the wall it was quickly sent back. Both sides were very strong, and the best play of the afternoon ensued in the field. Several people could be seen watching the play from the parapet of the church tower, and there were some exhilarating dribbles.

Soon after this the Up'ards got a move on and Arthur Hill ran with the ball into Church Lane, where he was stopped and there was another 'hug' up to the church gates. The Down'ards managed to turn the tide and by skilful manoeuvring steered the 'hug' into Mayfield Road. John Spencer, Joe Burton and Sam Parkin were unable to resist the temptation to lend a hand in the 'hug', which at length crashed through a fence by the bill posting station and through into the church field again. The leather came out into the town football ground and the Up'ards stubbornly contested the issue. The Down'ards, however, gradually gained the upper hand and took to the water near the Gas Works as dusk was falling, Arthur Birch of Clifton and Harry Chell wading downstream with the ball to Clifton Mill, where it was goaled by Arthur Birch about 7.30pm. After the games a replica ball was sent to the Prince of Wales as a memento. St James Palace advise that this ball can no longer be found.

The late Mr Keith Smith of Clifton (born in November 1923) remembered sitting on the Compton Bridge parapet to see the Prince of Wales arrive (in the company of his mother). He also remembered a lady in a long gabardine mac throw up a tennis ball in front of The Terrace. This was played in Shrovetide fashion by a group of ladies for a while. Keith died in October 1996. Trevor Yeomans, who had made the balls as usual, apparently did not believe in the Monarchy and did not attend the lunch or go to the game in the presence of his future King. He held strict views and clearly kept to them; he did not allow people to smoke in his presence for instance.

He trained in London as a saddler and harness maker and purchased his cork shavings from his contacts there. His main hobby was cycling and he never made a ball for himself. It was 'just a job' to him. He was born in 1878 and died in 1958. He made his last ball in 1954 but spare balls lasted until 1957 (pers. comm. his daughter, Mrs Moreton).

1929

Stiff Play in Icy Weather

After 24 hours of severe wintry weather, Tuesday dawned with promise of the most trying conditions for the old game of recent years. The Henmore was frozen over in places, and the Fish Pond had a good coating of ice, whilst with the thermometer registering several degrees of frost, snow began to fall during the morning. The National Anthem was sung, followed by 'Auld Lang Syne', and Mr Mallison of Cressbrook Hall and prospective Liberal candidate for West Derbyshire threw the ball high in the air. Within a few minutes the ball had reached the Henmore, Billy Sowter and Jack Clowes following it but the players were very reluctant to enter the chilly stream, down which masses of ice were floating. Billy Sowter set off to wade to Clifton, but was submerged, and Tom Harrison met with no better fate. George Cundy waded upstream, but the ice got in his way, and as no reinforcements arrived he flung the ball out.

There was more kicking and throwing, and backwards and forwards across the Croft went the leather. After an hour's play in the Croft, the Up'ards succeeded in forcing their way into Park Road with a shout of triumph. Following a brief check, the hug reached The Park, several minor casualties occurring, and the ball became visible once more. An exciting dash and it lay on the frozen surface of the Fish Pond. Francis Gregory, who swam these waters with it last year, stepping on to retrieve it. He was unaccompanied, and made for the opposite bank, but unfortunately disaster overtook him when he was within a yard of *terra firma*. The ice gave way, and in he went, Bill Brown hauling him ashore.

Strenuous play continued both in and out of the river, slowly heading upriver. There was a short check at the brook, and then the ball was picked up on the other side by Les Hill, who made off with it in the direction of Green Road, before he could be challenged. Play had been in progress for three hours. A number of players made for Sturston Mill, but the ball had not arrived, and during the evening its whereabouts were a mystery. There were rumours of its presence at Fenny Bentley, and it was not until about 9.00pm that it was goaled at Sturston Mill by Arthur Hill.

Stern Street Play All Day

There was a big crowd on the Shaw Croft when Mr Lilley turned up the Wednesday ball. The Down'ards made for Compton and after a slight check, broke through. The ball turned into King Edward Street, but the Up'ards had other ideas and it was ejected. A terrific struggle took place, the Up'ards once forcing a way into Chapel Yard, but they were unable to stay there. Sam Sowter clung to the leather, and there was another brief entrance into King Edward Street, the hug moving towards Derby Road. All the outlets had their sentinels, and the cross roads were strongly guarded, but the Dog and Partridge proved the limit of advance.

With a sudden heave the Down'ards again made for King Edward Street, but the ball was dropped and there was a few moments of really thrilling play. The ball was kicked and hugged to Station Road. It was the Down'ards turn next, for they pushed the hug into Dig Street. Compton Bridge was reached, play making a tour of the streets almost unique in recent annals of the game. Sam Sowter carried the ball under the arches, and the crowd stampeded for Bank Croft, arriving in time to see Sowter slithering over ice and floundering through water, sometimes lying full length.

There was a hug against the station signal box, and when it surged forward the combatants tripped over rails and signal wires before the ball was thrown into Clifton Road. The ball was hugged down to the petrol tanks, but the Up'ards forced play back into Station Road, and into the Bank Croft. The ball found a resting place on the ice, and there was no rush to follow, but Jim Harrison walked over and made tracks up the Wesleyan schoolyard. In Church Street, play opened out, the leather being kicked and thrown as far as the Wellington Inn. Hugging carried play down Park Road and into The Park. The Down'ards then pushed the hug every inch of the way back along Sturston Road and down Compton.

At 7.30pm they were in the Shaw Croft, the perspiring mass of humanity swayed backwards and forwards in Compton until the Down'ards gained the entrance to Malbon's Yard. They emerged in King Edward Street, and despite stubborn resistance reached Station Road, but the Up'ards once more turned into Church Street, where the struggle was very fierce. The proceedings took another turn when the Down'ards pushed their way into Church Lane (the alternative name for School Lane), taking the ball over the railway bridge into Clifton Road. This magnificent struggle entered on its last phase with the Down'ards seeming to be definitely on top, but still the Up'ards would not yield. The cold was intense, but there was still a good following at 9.30pm, when the Up'ards regained some ground by Nestlé's factory. The Up'ards numbers were dwindling and eventually Fred Atkin goaled the ball at Clifton Mill at 10.40pm. Wednesday's play was the finest witnessed for a great number of years, and the old hands could not remember a first ball being so keenly contested in the streets at such a late hour. The ball circuited the town, and the issue was in doubt right to the last.

1930

Lots of River Play

For the first time in its history the game was started by someone who was not English born. Frank E Powell Jnr Esq, son of F E Powell Esq, an American business magnate, threw up the ball on Shrove Tuesday.

At the lunch, Mr Harrison said he was delighted to announce that the collection up to that moment had been a record. One feature was the special wooden bridge, which had been built across the

Henmore from Messrs Burgon's garden, 'for the accommodation of cinematograph operators'. These included Mrs Stebbing's film of the game which was shown at the Empire on the Thursday evening.

The ball was kicked towards the Henmore and soon cries of 'She's in!', were to be heard. Four times the ball was thrown into Mr Rose's garden, but each time it was quickly retrieved. A hefty throw suddenly then followed with a rush across the field towards the Park Road gate. Here the first real lull came in the game. Slow progress was made in Park Road as the hug swayed from one ditch to the other. Reaching the wall near the Recreation Ground, the Up'ards used strategy and forcing the hug right up to the wall quietly passed the ball over to one of their own side. The sight of the cold looking waters of the Fish Pond did not deter the hardy players and T Buckley, who was in possession of the ball, leaped in and started to swim across, pushing the ball in front of him.

Aided and protected by some of his own side, Buckley reached the waterfall that feeds the Pond by keeping just in the water. On land once more the ball was hugged again, Down'ards making their last real attempt to check the course of the ball but slowly the Up'ards, who were a much stronger force, pushed the ball into the Henmore. As the brook widened, opposition was practically non-existent and four of the victorious Up'ards players linked arms and 'walked' the ball up the stream, Charlie Mee goaling it about 4.50pm.

A second ball was thrown up shortly after 5.00pm by Mr George Roome, of Kniveton, a veteran Shrovetider. Mr Roome said he had played for 35 years, and it was 27 years ago since he goaled his last ball. On being released it was quickly played into the river. It was kicked up the stream under the arches of the Back Bridge, and on past the Recreation Ground. Here a determined attack by the Down'ards forced the ball on to the northern bank of the stream, and it was very slowly hugged and played across the fields in the direction of the old brick field. It was now getting dark, and here the ball was lost for some time. Two Down'ards J Robinson and – Bagnall ultimately got possession of it, and took it to Clifton where it was goaled for the Down'ards between 7.00 and 8.00pm.

Another Goal for the Sowters

Mr Frank Boden of Derby, hoisted on the shoulders of two stalwart players, threw up the Wednesday ball. The ball was played quickly right out of the Croft. Passing through the gate leading on to Park Road it was played into The Park where there were some large hugs. Steering the hug towards the hedge, the Down'ards heaved the ball over into Park Road again. A short journey was made along Sturston Road towards the top of Compton but this was checked and there followed an exciting rush again down Park Road with the ball at the feet of the players. Turning down Peter Street the ball was kicked through Birch's Woodyard into Bath House gardens and finally into the Shaw Croft again.

Slowly the ball worked its way down the brook, where a good throw landed it again, and the struggling mass thumped heavily against the lorry-sheds belonging to the Green Man Garage and Harrison Transport Co. After frustrating an attempt to steer the ball through the Terrace near the Trent waiting room, Down'ards pushed hard and slowly the crowd moved up Compton. A strong party of Down'ards guarded the entrance to Sturston Road while Up'ards also pressed hard to keep the ball from Station Street with the result that it came rather hurriedly back down Compton and another heave by Down'ards turned it down King Edward Street.

The ball was played down the brook, under the arches and past the station, right to the arches of School Lane bridge, but here a group of Up'ards stalwarts successfully prevented further progress. Following a hug the Up'ards threw the ball up to a confederate on the bridge and the latter dashed off, hotly pursued. He was caught at the church gates and the hug with the crowd moved slowly back along Church Street and down Dig Street and into Shaw Croft again. The ball again passed under the arches of Compton bridge and Station Road bridge to just behind the station. At the bottom of Bank Croft, however, a runaway was attempted but the holder of the ball was hunted down and Church Street again became the scene of the struggle. As before, the hug turned down Dig Street and over Compton bridge to where the Down'ards pushed it once more down King Edward Street.

Just as dusk was falling the hug was still moving slowly by Bank Croft. Slowly, however, the hug moved towards Church Street and Mayfield Road and at about 7.45pm was only just past the church, but faster progress was made and Green Lane reached before 8.30pm. The ball was finally goaled at Clifton Mill after 9.00pm by George Sowter.

1931

Second Ball Goaled by the Son of the Turner-up

Sir Ian Walker turned up the Tuesday ball from the site of the knoll. Snow was blowing horizontal with an icy wind. The ball was quickly in a hug and water play was at a minimum. The Up'ards forced play into Park Road but the ball was not released and pressure forced play into The Park. Slowly the hug was pushed right to the edge of the Fish Pond before backing away. Eventually the players found themselves against the barbed wire and the bog at the top of the pond and the ball landed in the middle of it. Players who went in pursuit sunk deep into the slime, sometimes up to their waists as some hefty throws were made. After a tremendous throw, Clowes left everyone behind and managed to reach the Green Road before passing the ball on to W Bell. Suddenly the ball had disappeared but turned up thirty minutes later in a garden. The Up'ards had the advantage and forced the game on towards Sturston. The mill was reached at about 4.30pm and the ball was goaled by Norman Burton.

A second ball was turned up before 5.00pm by Sam Sowter who had been playing the game for about 50 years. The Down'ards quickly forced play through the gates into Compton, along Station Street and on to Clifton via Clifton Road. Here the ball was goaled after some ninety minutes play by Sam Sowter Jnr.

A King Edward Street merry-go-round

On Wednesday L A Clowes turned up the ball. It was hugged up against the Bath House corner of the Croft before leaving the field into Compton. Play was somewhat slow until sudden pressure at Malbon's Yard found the ball going down the Yard and on to the Mission Room in King Edward Street. The Down'ards tried to get through the flood arches but the opposition forced play into King Edward Street again. The game went into Bank Croft and then the river as C Colclough headed downstream. However, a good throw landed the ball back into the field and the hug crashed through the railings near the hotel. Play then did a circuit and went back through the gate into Bank Croft. Yet again the ball went over the railings and into the street before play returned to Shaw Croft and on to The Park.

The hug forced its way to the Fish Pond but there was no enthusiasm for water play. The Down'ards pushed the game back into Park Road and the ball was soon at Sturston Road. Here the hug remained for some time before moving off in the direction of Clifton at about 8.00pm. The opposition remained strong and it was after 10.00pm before it was goaled there by J W Gadsby JP, chairman of the Urban Council.

1932

Another Game Abandoned

At the Tuesday Green Man Hotel lunch, Committee chairman Joseph Harrison paid tribute to the late John Edge of Ballidon. For about 35 years both men had supported on their shoulders the person who was turning up the ball.

Mr John Hall JP turned up the first ball. After a trip to the Bath House gardens the ball was kicked into the river and about thirty players dashed into the ice-cold water. On returning to the Croft it was hugged into Compton with fairly fast progress down the street. After reaching the cross roads the play returned and the ball was thrown into the Henmore. Redvers Wibberley and others played the ball upstream. A water-hug developed but play slowly moved towards Sturston. Passing under Back Bridge there was a break and the ball was then kicked about in Fish Pond meadow. Several huge throws saw the ball land on the north side of the river and one by S Griffiths nearly caused a runaway. Upon being thrown back near to the pond, play moved back towards the town. Down'ards kept the hug moving across Shaw Croft, down Compton and along Station Street.

Progress continued down Station Road and on passed the Church gates before there was a runaway from the railway bridge. The dash brought play along Church Street and St John Street before the Down'ards forced play up into the Market Place. It was then hugged along St John Street, down Park Road and back into Shaw Croft where the game was abandoned at 10.45pm.

Ladies Injured as Bridge Parapet Collapses

A blinding snowstorm welcomed Lt Comdr G S Williamson who turned up the Wednesday ball. Within five minutes a dozen players had the ball in the river but it was not for long, for within another five minutes play was in Compton. The game settled down in King Edward Street before returning to Compton via Malbon's Yard. The Down'ards pushed the hug down Station Street but the Up'ards forced play down Station Road. Moving towards the railway station, the Down'ards forced play through the double doors leading to the siding. Play crossed over the railway lines with players tripping up on wires, points bars etc. The Up'ards prevented play from entering the Goods Yard and the ball found its way into the river.

School Lane Bridge was lined with spectators when the whole of the parapet collapsed outwards in one piece. Several people went with it into the water and the falling coping stones missed the players by inches. The injured were carried to the Young Mens' Institute and then on to the Cottage Hospital. Ten people were treated at the hospital, the majority of them being women. Once the hug got on the move again Wright's mill and the sidings were visited but movement was slow. The Up'ards pushed play away from the river and into Clifton Road. There was a tremendous struggle around Nestlé's factory with play returning to Wrights via the railway. The ball even found its way almost to the bar of the Railway Hotel. The ball was then played through Church Street and Dig Street to Sturston Road where the game was abandoned around 11.00pm. This was the first recorded time when no goals were scored on either day.

1933

A Battle Royal

After Capt Evan Baillie had turned up the first ball, the Down'ards forced the play over the new bridge belonging to the Green Man Garage and into Compton. The Pathe News, Paramount and Gaumont Cinema companies were all filming the proceedings. After forty minutes, the Up'ards pressured and play passed back through Shaw Croft and on to The Park. Play crossed over to the railings bordering the public footpath. Over the railings went the ball into the field containing the Fish Pond. The Down'ards kicked the ball onto the frozen surface and although the ice held initially it eventually broke immersing one or two players. Upon returning to land the game returned to Shaw Croft and then Compton. After some play in the street, the ball broke free and was kicked at a fast speed up Dig Street, along Church Street and down School Lane to the railway.

After some play among the coal wagons, the ball was played across the river to the Church field where it was kicked around for a while before reaching Mayfield Road. Here Redvers Wibberley did a runner with the ball up Dark Lane but he was caught and the ball was hugged in Belle Vue Road before descending Church Banks. Over to Clifton Road the ball now went via the Church field and the railway coal wharf. Despite determined Up'ards opposition the ball continued on its way to Clifton where it was goaled at about 8.00pm by Jim Allsop.

A Hug Beneath a Railway Waggon

On a bright and occasionally sunny Wednesday, the ball was turned up by Walter Banks, the secretary of the Derbyshire Royal Infirmary where the Committee maintained two beds. Mr Hawksworth was ill and not at the lunch where it was noted that he had raised over £600 in the last 20 years for the Infirmary. The ball was hugged over to the Bath House corner before it went along Park Road to Sturston Road. Here there was a battle before the ball was pushed down Compton and back into Shaw Croft. A good kick lifted the ball into Park Road where it was kicked to the top of Hall Lane. Progress was not sustained and the ball returned to Back Bridge and then Shaw Croft. After being thrown into the river, it was scrambled out again into Dig Street. Here it was hugged for a considerable period before play moved down Church Street to The Ivies.

Here the ball was dropped and it was kicked at full speed down School House Lane to the goods station where there was some lively kicking among the coal wagons as on the previous day. Suddenly the ball vanished, puzzelling the spectators for a moment until it was spotted under a waggon. Here

The Ashbourne Game: Early Days

Mrs Elizabeth Woolley, who turned up the ball in 1860; she avoided the police by hiding the ball up her skirt

Selling oranges at Shrovetide was a popular custom. This lady is selling them on a beach (possibly in the Isle of Man) but the photo could have been taken in many places, especially at Scarborough, where oranges were thrown into the sea at Shrovetide

The 1862 painting, with Luke Faulkner seen holding the ball next to the bull ring, where balls were turned up. Betty Blore, an orange seller is on the far right. Bulls were baited in Ashbourne at Shrovetide

Above: Two views of Joe (Ninety) Burton, with a ball goaled in the boy's game and taking a kick in Dig Street

The man on the cart is Sam Smith, who scored nine goals

Play in the Park in 1903, looking towards Belper Road

The Ash Wednesday Fancy Dress Ball 1922. This probably grew out of the temperance meetings also held on Ash Wednesday

Two photographs taken c. 1900 showing Shaw Croft and goaling at Sturston Mill (the door gave access to the mill wheel)

Probably the oldest surviving Ashbourne Shrovetide photograph. Taken prior to Wednesday 1890. Top row: Mr Chell, John Barker, William Connell (he had just scored at Clifton), Mr Barker, ? Jack Hawksworth. Bottom: 2nd left ? Frank Tomlinson, 4th Mr Sherwin

Play outside the Station Hotel, opposite the railway station in 1907. The Tuesday ball was turned up by John Prince, landlord of the Green Man. On the Wednesday, his brother Bill turned it up. Bill ran Ashbourne Hall Hotel

River play in 1915. Many players had gone off to war and the sides were unusually depleted in players

Players on leave from the Great War joined the game. The ball is held by Private W. Fearn who scored at Sturston in 1918

The 1916 ball, which was sent to Ashbourne soldiers in France, held by Matty Thornley and Mrs Cresswell, the ball's owner

The Prince addresses the crowd

The commemorative postcard produced to mark the event

The Prince of Wales talking to Joseph Dudley, a cobbler in Dig Street who served in Egypt. He also recognised an ex-soldier from his own Regiment (Mr J. Rudge) and stopped to talk to him too. To his right are disabled soldiers to whom the Prince also spoke

The Prince turns up the ball to start the game on Shaw Croft

Another view of the Prince's party and the special platform erected for the turn-up

During the visit of the Queen in 1985, she was shown the ball turned up by the Prince. The event was in the Town Hall, used by police to try and prevent the game in the 1860s

The Mills

The tailrace and overshot waterwheel of Sturston Mill. Clifton wheel was undershot

The rear of Clifton Mill and the tail race, which was in the corner of the mill behind Jack Smith

Three photos to show the design style of earlier balls –
Top left: Mr Hugo Johnson with his ball. Top right: The two 1956 balls held by Arthur Froggatt, Committee secretary. Above: Jack Smith with his collection of balls and holding the 1954 ball. The middle of the three front balls is the 1925 ball turned up by Billy Meredith

The Balls

Arthur Chadwick, ball maker, with painter Tim Baker

Stuart Avery painting Mr Shield's ball, 1994, goaled by P Robson

Peter Gadsby's ball being passed around at the lunch, 1996. It was goaled by S Wright

Above: Dr Roy Bennett (left) chatting to the Duke of Rutland. They display the two main footballs of 1993

Left: The Wednesday ball with Barry Greenwood, 2002. It was ungoaled

Below: John Hanson's ball being admired by lunch guests, 2000. It was later goaled by M Spencer

The 2000 balls with Joan and Philip Tomlinson (left) and Barbara and John Hanson

Jack Smith presenting a ball to the German Football Association in 1966. The West German team were based at the Peveril of the Peak Hotel, Thorpe, during the World Cup

Balls hanging at the British Legion, Shrovetide 2000

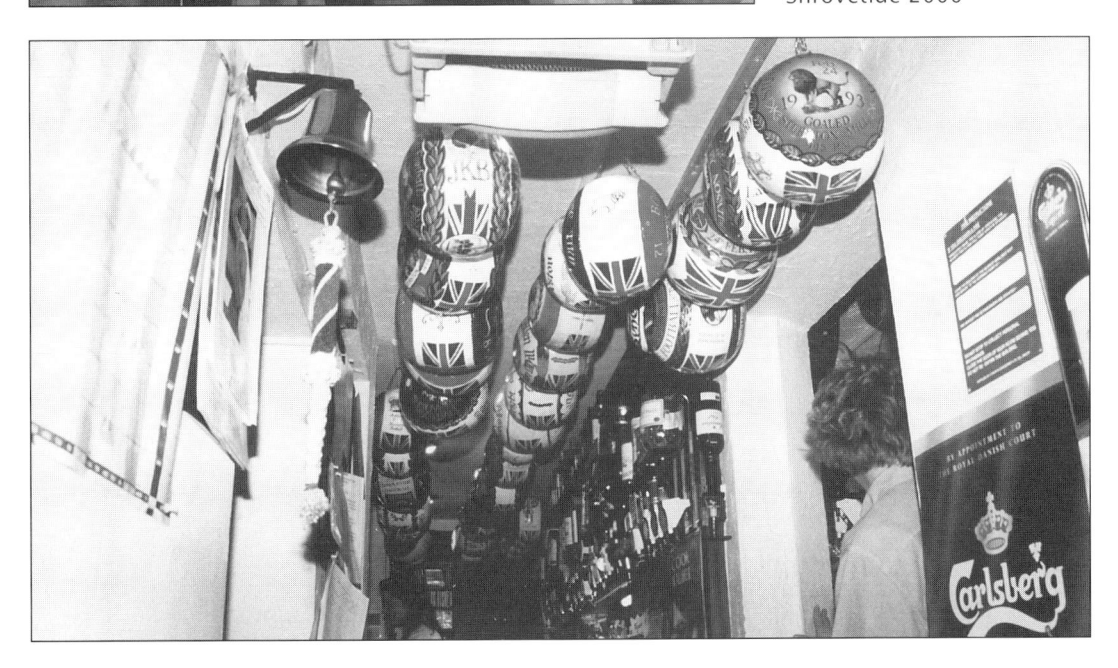

The pre-game lunch and visitors

The 9th Duke of Devonshire KG (mid-front) with the Committee, at The Mansion, 1924. The ball was goaled by J Harrison

The Committee in 1921 with Inspector Burton (holding the ball). Note the collecting tin for the Derby Royal Infirmary. The photograph was taken on Shaw Croft

The Marquis of Hartington with Committee members in 1922 at The Mansion in Church Street. The ball was the one presented to Princess Mary, who was married on Shrove Tuesday of that year

Tim Baker with the ball he painted for Lord Lieut., Mr Bather. It was goaled by N Fearn

Brell Ewart's ball, goaled by Darren Waring, held by Tim Fearn (Up'ard), Ash Wednesday, 1996, with Frank Lomas (Down'ard)

Alec Smith (left) and Tim Baker (right) with the 1928 Tuesday 2nd ball goaled by H Sowter & J Bill

Ellis Grimshaw addressing guests at the 1958 Wednesday lunch. The ball was ungoaled

Philip Tomlinson bringing in the Wednesday 2000 ball to the lunch, goaled by P Harrison

A pre-lunch photo of Don Lowndes, Arthur Chadwick, Arthur Birch (turner-up), Arthur Froggatt and Jack Gadsby (all left to right) in 1971. The ball was goaled by J Tomkinson

the players lay, flat on their backs on the railway in a hug! From here play returned to Church Street and on to Park Road, eventually reaching Compton via Sturston Road. After further fruitless wandering all over the town in the darkness it was agreed to abandon the game at about 10.30pm.

1934

Down'ards Breakaway Turns the Tide

Mr Harrison was ill and Mr Plumbly presided at the luncheon. He recalled that Mr Harrison had been Chairman for 15 years and a player for over 50 years. Supporting Mr Plumbly were Capt E Unwin VC of Wootton Lodge and Capt T R Pearson of Ednaston Hall who were throwing up the Tuesday and Wednesday balls respectively. The Tuesday ball was soon in the river followed by about thirty players before being landed in the Fish Pond meadow. The ball was thrown into the pond and floated unmolested for some time, when Stanley Phillips of Calton Moor plunged in and retrieved it. After a struggle the ball re-entered the lake and Harry Wigley plunged in and swam with the ball to the Sturston side. The ball criss- crossed between the Henmore and the meadow before the Down'ards forced the game under Back Bridge. It was played across Shaw Croft and through the gate into Compton where it was turned down Malbon's yard and King Edward Street. After returning to Compton the ball disappeared. Leslie Moon, racing at top speed dashed up Compton and along Station Street to the coal wharf and was only stopped near the signalman's box. After play around the river and Mayfield Road the game went downwards and the ball was eventually goaled at Clifton Mill by Stanley Harrrison at about 8.00pm.

Down'ards Do It Again

Wednesday was another brilliant day and the ball was quickly in the Henmore. It was out in a flash but back again after being played into Park Road. The play went upriver before being quickly transferred to the Green Road but it came back as quickly as it had gone. There was a considerable amount of play in and around the river and it seemed to sap the Up'ards strength. The Down'ards forced play through a hedge, and across the fields until Shaw Croft was reached at about 5.00pm. The ball went on along Compton and via Station Street to Clifton Road. From there it returned to the river and into a field at the rear of the Gas Works. It was now dark and many of the spectators had gone home. After being played here for a while, the ball suddenly vanished. It had been taken away by a young player named Atterbury. The ball was subsequently passed to Charlie Sowter who goaled it at Clifton at about 9.30pm.

Other News

The paper also reported that at Chester-le-Street in County Durham there was no Shrovetide football in the streets for the first time in centuries. The ball had been seized by the police. The game was quite different from the Ashbourne game and only played in the streets.

Before the games the Committee had agreed to assist the police in clearing the streets of football at 7.00pm each evening. To this end it was proposed by Mr J Barker that £1 be paid to the man who goaled the ball on either day between 6.00 and 7.00pm if it was the first ball thrown up.

Each year one hears comments that the game isn't played like it used to be. A letter to the local paper by Jack Hawksworth (AT 12/1/1934) indicates that the problem is nothing new. In fact it has been a regular criticism by old stalwarts for nearly a century. Jack's letter stated:

"It is up to those who take an active part in the game to assist in keeping our traditions as of old: by playing the game, I mean 'football' not 'hugball'. Let us have a good kicking, good play with good fellowship. Let's have the old shout: 'play for the water, boys', 'down with it' or 'up with it'. Let us see more of the ball and give the visitors a chance to see that the leather, as Ashbournians know, will stand the punching, our old friend Trevor sees to that, it does not require cuddling like a child three weeks old. Give it plenty of boot."

That year the committee offered £1 to the goaler, should it be a first ball, scored between 5pm and 7pm. The intention was to try and keep play out of the streets in an evening. This offer was repeated a year later. Given the lack of goals prior to 5pm these days, a similar incentive relating to goals scored before 5pm sounds like a good idea!

Several old stalwarts died this year. They included George Roome of Kniveton in March. He was a formidable water player. William 'Trip' Connell died the following month. He had once risked his life to rescue a girl, Marion Ellis, from drowning in the Henmore when the water was bank high. He was another of the game's stalwarts.

Other News

The exploits of Captain Edward Unwin have recently been documented. (See "VCs of the First World War: Gallipoli", by Stephen Snelling, pp 29-49). Snelling describes him as being "among the outstanding personalities of the Gallipoli campaign". He was recommended for the VC not by the Navy, but by the Army, for his bravery in trying to get troops ashore and then bringing wounded back to his ship. He did this several times, pulling them in an open boat under very heavy close-range rifle and machine gun fire. Apparently he only stopped when he was pulled from the water in a state of collapse.

The Unwins had lived at Wootton Lodge for almost 200 years when Edward left in 1936. He was deputy Lord Lieutenant of Staffordshire from 1929-39 and president of the Ellastone branch of the Royal British Legion. He retired from Navy Service in 1909, but was recalled in 1914. In 1950, at the age of 84 years, he died and was buried at Grayshott.

1935

By River To Each Goal

For the first time the day's play was broadcast by the BBC. Their journalist Mr John Stone attended the game and the broadcast went out that night. Mr Charles Turpie turned up the Tuesday ball. After a few moments the ball was in the river with Charlie Walker running with it up into The Park. He was stopped but Up'ards pressure prevailed. One man had his trouser legs torn right off him before the play continued upstream after a short diversion into the fields. Mr H Plumbly had possession of the ball with Tom Waterfall 'playing a rare game'. Play went passed the old bathing place which was now quite shallow and through the deeper Cantrell's Hole. After a final struggle with the Down'ards, Herbert Plumbly goaled the ball at 4.50pm.

A second ball was turned up at 5.30pm by Mr H Excell Thomas of Derby. As was usually the case following an Up'ards first goal, the ball was quickly played into the river and went downstream under Compton Bridge. Play soon reached the Church Field and after being played here, the ball returned to the water. Only on one occasion did the Up'ards make any real efforts and play went down the river to Clifton where the ball was goaled at 7.00pm by George Peach.

Mr Turpie's advert for his hams appeared in the local papers

Up'ards Denied A Goal

Mr Joseph Hayes turned up the Wednesday ball. The ball reached the river near to Back Bridge and Redvers Wibberley threw it first onto the bridge and then into Park Road. Back into the water it went with about forty players after it. The Up'ards got it under the bridge and it was eventually landed into the fields where it was kicked about. More than one lady got a kick as the ball was played at a remarkable speed. Jim Burton made a good run with it before there was a tedious hug in the river.

For quite a while the play roamed about the fields and the river as first one side and then the other took the advantage. All of a sudden a runner had it and made off towards the Green. A large crowd waited for the ball to appear at Sturston but they were to be disappointed. Some Down'ards obtained possession and took the ball by a circuitous route to Clifton where it was goaled at about 9.00pm by A Armstrong.

On 26 June, the death occurred of Joseph Harrison, who was 65 years old. He ran the Green Man Garage and Transport Company in Dig Street. He had been a player for 40 years and was Chairman of the Shrovetide Committee. He was replaced by Mr J C Prince who had retired at the beginning of May 1935 after being the landlord at the Green Man Inn for 28 years (he had previously kept the George and Dragon). Mr Prince had definitely been on the committee since 1908 and was to be the Chairman until 1946. Mr Harrison had been Chairman since 1924, when he had succeeded William Coxon.

1936

Riotous Scenes at Sturston Spoils Up'ards Day

At a Committee meeting in January 1936 the death was recorded of Jack Hawksworth, the Secretary, who had served on the Committee since 1897. After the lunch the Duke of Rutland got the first ball away. The ball was quickly played into The Park and there was then some lively play in the river before Tom Allen threw the ball out for the Up'ards. The ball almost reached the Fish Pond but the Up'ards were away with it at their feet. Fred Gallimore dribbled well before dropping the ball over a hedge to Charlie Russell who was gone like a hare. He made off to Bradley Wood with others. Arriving at Sturston Mill, Russell and Tom Allen entered the water with the ball, followed by the mill tenant, Mr Dethick. It turned out that after Russell had touched the wheel once, the ball was taken from him by Dethick who gave it to Allen. The latter then goaled it at 3.35pm.

The crowd resented the fact that Allen, Dethick's nephew, had been allowed to goal the ball. There was a scuffle and Allen went into the house. Dethick then appeared with a gun with which he threatened the crowd. The gun was taken from him and he was then alleged to have used a stick. The report then stated that a youth had his head cut. The players were now incensed and a general disturbance followed in which Mr Dethick was badly handled. Women members of the family then appeared waving hatchets and hammers but did not use them. However, another woman did throw boiling water over the crowd and some fell on small children. This was a signal to start breaking glass and soon every window in the house was broken. The police were called but the trouble had subsided when they arrived.

Understandably, the ball was not produced in the town and a new ball was not turned up until 4.55pm. Mr John Etches had the honour of doing so. The ball was soon in the Henmore but a throw by Les Moon landed it in Park Road and after returning to the Croft it eventually reached The Park. The ball went into the Fish Pond and Walter Stevenson followed it in. When it came out the hugging was the fiercest of the day. A dash across the Croft saw the Down'ards getting as far as Bank Croft down the river. Play then went via Malbon's Yard and into Compton which was reached at about 6.00pm. The leather went loose and got as far as Dig Street. It was deposited on a lorry turning into St John Street, but it rolled off. Jim Hackett was detected slipping away with it but a mighty effort carried play to the bottom of the Market Place where Horace Sowter collapsed and was carried away. In Cockayne Avenue it was discovered that the ball was missing from the hug. Neville Gettliffe had slipped away with the ball under his coat and calmly walked through the gardens near the Hall flats. A party of Up'ards got away with the ball via Windmill Lane to Sturston Mill (apparently by car) where Jim Burton, Neville Gettliffe and Redvers Wibberley shared the goaling at 8.30pm. This was the first time since 1911 that the Up'ards had scored two balls in one day.

Up'ards Make It Four

Mr J W Gadsby started the Wednesday game commenting that he hoped the previous day's scenes would not be repeated and asserting that the problems were no fault of any of the players. The Up'ards were determined to add to the previous day's success. A hug one hundred strong soon reached the Fish Pond and time after time the ball entered the lake. A good throw saw the ball land in the middle of the pond and it was some minutes before Walter Stephenson dived in from the opposite bank. Reaching land he made a dash for it but was stopped. A little later there was a runaway towards The Green Road with the ball being kicked up the fields. The ball was hugged in Green Road but the Up'ards were turned into the old tip field. Herbert Plumbly set things going with a powerful throw but it still took nearly an hour to reach Ashbourne Green post office. Tom Allen had possession nearly all the way. Crashing through a hedge the hug reached the Henmore and Down'ard's opposition faded away. The ball was goaled at Sturston at 4.45pm by Fred Hallam. Despite heavy rain hundreds of people swarmed into the mill yard but the large police presence was not required.

The second ball was thrown up by Mr Trevor Yeomans. Play went out into Compton reaching Station Street before returning to the Terrace near Compton Bridge. The Down'ards pushed a way into Malbon's yard and on to Clifton Road via King Edward Street. Here the ball went loose and was kicked all along Station Road. It was picked up and carried towards Mayfield. Near the cemetery the ball went missing. Someone had picked up the leather and quietly walked off with it towards the town in all the confusion. It was taken across Mayfield Road football ground and after refreshments in Smith Street, Tom and Ernest Brown and Jack Allen took the ball to Sturston where it was goaled by Ernest Brown at 10.20pm. After two days play the score was Up'ards 4, Down'ards 0. This was a record since the 1891 match reports were started. It was noted that the play on both days was almost entirely in the hands of young men. Allowing for a few years in the 19th Century when records are not available, no note of four balls in one day are recorded for any year from 1850.

Other News

Mr John (Jack) Hawksworth passed away on January 14th. He was 62 years old and was the popular landlord of 'Ye Olde Vaults'. His obituary states that he had been the Shrovetide Secretary for 28 years. If this is true, he was certainly on the committee prior to 1908 and had previously written to the paper which quoted him as being the secretary since 1897. (AN 8/3/1912) Perhaps that is when he joined the committee. If so, at the age of 23 years he must have been one of its youngest members ever.

In his early years he was employed by Smedley Bros and Mellor and then ran the local office of Pratt's motor oils. He was a keen angler and member of the Ashbourne Rifle Club and the Air Rifle Club. He had organised the Prisoners of War Aid Committee until he was called up during the Great War. The paper (AT 17/1/1936) stated that it was 'doubtful that no one has raised so much money for hospitals and other charities as Mr Hawksworth has done'. He left a widow, three sons and three daughters. Shrovetide lost one of its most dedicated supporters in the death of Jack Hawksworth. His grave may be seen near to the south door of St Oswalds Church, at the side of the path and just a little nearer to the alms houses.

1937

Down'ards Shy Of The Water

Mr J F Compton Inglefield turned up the first ball and it was soon being tightly hugged in Park Road. His party of guests watched the start from the rear of Messrs Burgon's shop where the Prince of Wales had thrown up the ball. George Peach got the leather at one point and turned, his face set for Clifton but he got no farther than six feet. Play moved into Cokayne Avenue. The ball was passed over the hedge to Stan Harrison of Mayfield who was in the Memorial Grounds. He raced away but was stopped. Some players were indignant at play in forbidden ground and the ball was passed to a policeman to be thrown into the road. It was snatched away and was soon in the river and being carried upstream. After some play near the Fish Pond, several Up'ards raced away with the ball at their feet. By the time the crowd caught up, the ball had been goaled by George Sellers just before 3.00pm.

A second ball was turned up by Charles Doxey, a former local footballer. It was soon in the water with Wilfred Bell heading upstream, with the Down'ards reportedly shy of the water. It seemed that a repeat of the earlier game was likely when the ball was thrown into the Recreation Ground where it was hugged for thirty minutes. After some free play which crossed the river, the ball was hugged in Cokayne Avenue. Tremendous pressure from the Down'ards forced the hug to Dig Street. It then went the length of Compton before returning to the entrance to Shaw Croft. The ball had been invisible for an hour. Eventually play reached Church Street but it quickly turned around and by 7.30pm it was in The Park. Someone dropped the ball into Belper Road which gave the Down'ards a break, but they were stopped by the police station and the ball went loose near the railway station. It was then kicked quickly to the bottom of the Market Place via Church Street where Jack Edge was stopped. The hug then made its way back to Dig Street and at 10.00pm the ball was outside the post office. Play continued into Belper Road and at 11.25pm a 'no ball' was declared.

It was rather ironic that play went on to 11.25pm as the Committee had agreed not to allow a second ball unless the first ball was returned for inspection before 5.00pm.

Two Balls Goaled In Three Hours

The weather was kinder on the Wednesday but there was mud and plenty of it. Two balls were scored at Sturston making seven in two years without reply from the Down'ards. The paper put it bluntly: 'they will have to do better than this'. Mr George Gather turned up the first ball. It was soon in the river but was thrown out at the Recreation Ground where an Up'ard ran off with it. It was kicked and ran with virtually all the way to Sturston where William Belfield goaled it at 2.40pm. However, there was some dissent when the ball returned to town as it was claimed that Belfield was a Down'ard. The second ball was turned up by Mr W L Foster and the play made off up the river and then over to the Fish Pond where Jack Burton threw it out. There was very little opposition as play made for Sturston. About 100 yards from the mill progress halted with a row over who should goal the ball and some Down'ards reinforced it. However, the journey resumed and Joe Wibberley goaled the ball at 5.06pm ending the day's play.

The question of whether a player was an Up'ard or a Down'ard was raised in the paper's editorial. (AN 18/2/1937). This was clearly blurred – Mayfield players were Down'ards, but where did this leave residents of Mayfield Road? This issue still crops up and brings to mind the controversy when Doug Sowter goaled at Sturston in 1972.

1938

Life Again At Clifton

The Tuesday play began with Brig-Gen. E C W D Walthall of Alton Hall turning up the ball. There was plenty of water play before play was forced into Park Road. The Down'ards seemed to be holding their own and prevented play entering The Park. At the Belper Road corner the battle was on in a hug at least 100 strong. All of a sudden there was a break with Bill Mainwaring, Bill Allen, Les Hall and Bill Twigge hairing off towards Sturston. They could not be stopped and Bill Twigge goaled it at 3.30pm.

A second ball was turned up by Mr J B Tomlinson, formerly of Ashbourne. A surprise move by the Down'ards swept the ball into Compton, a place little visited in recent years. However, the Up'ards recovered and forced the hug under Back Bridge. At about 6.00pm there was another runaway when George Cundy slung the ball out onto the north side of the river. Redvers Wibberley who had not previously touched the ball set off across the fields towards Green Road with spectators heading for Sturston anticipating a goal. However, the ball was thrown over a hedge and Ivor Moon got it, goaling it at Clifton just after 8.00pm.

A Last Minute Surprise

Mr S H Bagshaw started the Wednesday proceedings and play was soon underneath the arches of Back Bridge and in the Fish Pond where Wilfred Bell waded waist deep to retrieve it. There was further hugging in the river before the ball was landed and there was some thrilling open play before the Down'ards relented and Leslie Bull scored at Sturston at 4.30pm. A second ball was turned up by

Sam Sellars and the play turned out to be some of the fiercest and roughest for years before it was run away with over six hours later. Play went out into Compton but returned after some hard play and the ball then crossed the Croft into Park Road. It was then hugged down the road and ended up in Compton again. Here the ball was loose for a few moments for the only time in 6½ hours. For the next three hours the play went up and down Compton and the din was terrific. Just after 11.00pm there were suggestions that the ball should be given up and the hug was pushed up Dig Street. It ended up outside the locked doors of the Green Man Hotel and opinion was divided whether to end the game or not.

The ball was dropped and whisked away down Dig Street in the darkness. However, Bill Allen knew the way to Sturston without lights and he goaled it at 11.57pm.

1939

No Street Play

'Does the Henmore no longer run to Clifton Mill?' asked the paper. (AN 23/2/1939) The article lamented the collapse of Down'ard opposition, recalling four balls at Sturston in 1936, three in 1937 and again in 1938. However, despite the occasional goal, they did not find renewed vigour much before the 1950s. The first ball was turned up by Mr Dave Burnaby, a music hall star. There was a dash across the Croft with the ball being kicked towards the Henmore. Tom Allen set off upstream but fell full length and dropped the ball. He recovered things but changed tactics and threw it out. It was back about thirty minutes later but there was little progress to be made in either direction and the ball was taken out into Fish Pond Meadow. However, after a while the Up'ards, who seemed to have control, started to make progress as both opposition and spectators thinned. Among the players heading up river were Len Lowndes, Phil Slater, Norman Burton, Joe Wibberley, Bertie Birch, and Jack Roberts. At 5.15pm Len Lowndes goaled it to end the day's play.

A Close Call, But Down'ards Make It

There was a slight drizzle as Mr A E Ellaby, a Rugby League international, started the game. Three minutes later the ball was in the Henmore with Harry Hubert in possession. When he was challenged by George Peach, he threw the leather to Bill Allen. When Tom Allen, Joe Harrison and others dropped in, fists were flying for a few moments. Meanwhile Bill Allen was legging it upstream until he was sent full length by a Down'ard grabbing his ankle. A hug formed before Tom Allen threw the ball into Shaw Croft. So began an exciting day's play. After thirty minutes, the ball was in The Park where some fifty girls were pushing the hug. Play eventually came back to the road and the hug reached Belper Road before Jack Edge ran back with it down Park Road, dodging a pram which was thrust across his path. He was collared by Jack Brown and a hug formed and play returned to both the Fish Pond and the river. Jack Dethick threw it out and then made off with it but he was caught by Bertie Birch, who was tackled as he turned for town. Jack Bagnall, Maurice Spencer, Miss Plumbly and a few others then had the game to themselves until other players arrived.

Heavy rain thinned the crowd but the Down'ards held on until reinforcements arrived after work. Play then left Fish Pond meadow and went through Shaw Croft and into Compton at about 6.30pm. The play was tightly fought down the street and then it came back to Church Street. At 10.30pm the hug had reached the Church field and was still there at 11.00 o'clock. However, the Down'ards got a move on and Ernest Hellaby goaled the ball at 11.55pm. This was to be the last of the 'usual' games for a while. The outbreak of war again saw many stalwarts fighting another battle. It was to the younger lads and the women that the mantle of maintaining the custom now passed.

1940

Ball Given Up After Three And A Half Hours

Against the fear that a temporary lapse in the game would see its end, the Committee decided upon a shorter game. There was of course a precedent, for the game had continued during both the Boer War

Game Reports 1892–1949 135

and the Great War, let alone The Crimea. It was therefore decided that play would end at 5.00pm. There were many who expected the game to be a fiasco but despite the absence of visitors, there were plenty of spectators and local villages were well represented. The luncheon was not held, however. The traditional mound had gone but the ball was thrown up by Mr Joseph Dean from somewhere near to it.

There was a reluctance for water play although Bill Sowter maintained traditions by following the ball in. However, it was soon out and played into Compton. Play reached South Street, but just like so many times before, returned down Compton to the Shaw Croft gate. There were one or two older players but it was almost a ladies day. Dozens of girls, including schoolchildren, heaved at the hug. Evacuees from Manchester, both children and teachers were enjoying the old custom. The Down'ards got the ball to Bank Croft but it was recovered from the river and pushed back to Compton past the Auxiliary Fire Station. Play continued into Park Road via Sturston Road but time had slipped away and it was agreed to give the ball up. A policeman refused it saying it was the Committee's responsibility and so it was given to Mrs Doris Mugglestone at 5.25pm. Escorted by the crowd she carried it along Sturston Road and down Compton to the sounds of 'Tipperary'. The Green Man gates were closed and Mr H G Plumbly received the ball at his house in Victoria Square.

Mr Sidney Mugglestone of the George and Dragon Hotel turned up the Wednesday ball. There was a lot of kicking about before the hug made off down Park Road. The Down'ards managed to turn the corner into Sturston Road, slipping and sliding on snow and ice. The hug pushed and carried Les Bull, who had possession, down Compton. At 4.00pm the play was back in the Croft where some fifty players had several minutes of kicking again. The ball reached The Park where several Up'ards did a runner as best they could in deep snow. There were soon no challengers with them and they walked to the mill. At the toss of a coin, Frank Edge goaled it at 4.30pm and returned with the ball to the George and Dragon Hotel. Drinking hours were apparently more liberal there!

1941

Do We Carry On Or Don't We?

A large crowd saw Mr F B Birch, an old player, turn up the ball which was unpainted. Six soldiers joined in the water play although some quickly decided that it was not for them! With girls helping out in the hug, The Park was reached. Things seemed to be going the Up'ards way as had become the norm, but the Army took a hand again near the Fish Pond. One soldier enquired which way was Down'ard. An Up'ard told him. Ninety minutes after leaving the Croft, play returned there. Youth was having its day and old men and the girls did their bit. Play returned to The Park and the ball ended up in the pond and the three Allen brothers, Bill, Charlie and Tom, waded in after it. The Up'ards were proving best in the water and the Down'ards out of it and play moved in and out accordingly.

It was now past 5.00pm, and there was no agreement to stop play. There was almost a public meeting with Tom Allen standing in deep water holding the ball under his arm, conducting a discussion with players lined up in the water. With no agreement and no Committee member present, Allen walked out with the ball and asked a policeman, who was unable to advise if the goal would count after 5.00pm. During the debate there was no attempt to continue play. However, Allen resumed the game at 5.40pm, taking the Down'ards by surprise. There was no further opposition and Charles Allen goaled at Sturston a little before 6.00pm.

A Hug For A Lady

Wednesday's ball was turned up by William Spencer (Chairman of the Urban District Council). The afternoon saw him in the thick of it playing for the Up'ards. The ball was kicked across the Croft, but Herbert Wibberley, guarding the Park Road gate stopped the gallop. The leather went into the Henmore with Bill Sowter and Herbert Plumbly after it. Play eventually reached The Park where at one point a 17-year old girl was monarch of all she surveyed. She snatched the ball and held onto it as the players circled around her, but this was one hug she could manage without! A few minutes later the ball rolled out onto the thin ice on the pond. Tom Allen retrieved it from chest deep water and both sides formed a chain to assist him ashore before allowing him to toss the ball into the crowd. The ball edged towards Sturston but the Down'ards fought right to the mill yard. Charlie Etches of Roystone Grange and Jack Edge of Ballidon tossed for the honour and Etches won it, goaling the ball at 5.40pm. The paper's editorial reported that a lot of evacuees played in the game.

1942

A Late Start

The schools and many shops were closed but during the morning the Committee decided to postpone the game from 2.00pm to 4.30pm. This was due to representations made regarding the danger of men leaving their work to play. Another emergency meeting took place in the afternoon and it was evident that there was considerable feeling in some quarters against the game being played. A compromise was reached and it was decided that play should be allowed from 5.00 – 7.00pm on Wednesday. No attempt was made by the police to influence the discussions. This was how the paper reported the late start, but the Committee minute book gives the true story. There were several hundred Irishmen working on the building of the Ashbourne Aerodrome and they had stated their intention to play. After discussions with the Ministry of Labour it was decided to turn up the balls at 4.00pm (sic). In this way building work could continue for most of the day.

After all this, play only lasted half an hour on Tuesday. The ball was turned up at 4.25pm by Mr T Marsden of Youlgreave. It was played towards Compton but the efforts of women in the hug turned it back and it was soon in the river. Bill Allen handed the ball on to his brother Tom who set off under Back Bridge. So after only five minutes the ball began a speedy trip to Sturston Mill. One of the players was hauled out in an apparent half-drowned condition. There had been other casualties and allegations that a knife was used in the hug, as one or two players were bleeding from gashes on their hands. Your author has heard comments that it was not unknown for a cry to go up 'the knives are out', but this is the only documentary evidence of this. The Up'ards left the Henmore and quickly set off across the fields. Progress was stopped in order to determine who should goal the ball and there was a struggle as Down'ards joined in. Tom Allen who had the ball with brothers Bill, Charles and Jack, Joe Wibberley and others made it to the mill where Jack Allen goaled the ball at 4.55pm.

Twenty Girls In The Hug

Mr John Etches threw up the Wednesday ball announcing that play must finish two hours later at 6.30pm, and that if the ball was goaled after time it would not count. More of the usual players were there and some strangers had signed on as Down'ards. The hug was pushed out into Compton and straight over into King Edward Street. Windows were flung open in Compton and the street resounded with the old battle cries. There was another strenuous battle at the Clifton Road corner and at one stage it looked like Ashbourne versus Ireland. Progress was maintained to Nestlé where the Down'ards were held for a long time. About twenty girls had a hand in the play and it was here that Hubert Connell, who had held the ball all the way from the Croft over an hour previously, lost his grip when he went down in the hug. Once over the crest, play quickly reached the mill and the ball was goaled by Leslie Moon at about 7.00pm. Despite the late timing the goal appears to have been allowed.

1943

Doris Mugglestone Goals At Sturston

For the first time in recorded history, a woman goaled a ball. Mrs Mugglestone, of the George and Dragon Hotel, along with her daughter Mrs Wilson and several other women had played strenuously in the River Henmore. She was the daughter of Joseph Burton who goaled seven times for the Up'ards. The ball had been turned up by Group Captain the Lord Hamilton OBE AFC. Play gradually progressed upsteam with a digression towards The Green Road despite Down'ards resistance. At the top of the Fish Pond meadow there were some forty people in the hug including quite a few women. The paper speculated that their reserves of coupons would be severely tested as their silk stockings and dresses were saturated and torn. The women forced the hug across the river but the men bore things with fortitude. However, Douglas Silcock did a runner towards Belper Road and was joined by Les and G Moon. They turned for town and then changed their minds and headed for Sturston. Arthur Chadwick and Frank Godfrey intercepted them but after more spirited play between both sides the ball swept down towards the Henmore at abot 5.20pm. There was still some strong opposition and it was at about 6.20pm when Doris Mugglestone was given the honour of goaling, having played hard in the water. With a male escort she waded through water and mud waist deep to reach the wheel.

Schoolgirl Goals At Clifton Mill

An 11-year old school girl, Doris Sowter, goaled the ball for the Down'ards at Clifton Mill, on Wednesday. Her father, Sam Sowter, had played hard all the afternoon, and carried the ball down the Henmore for the last mile to the mill. Down'ards were present in force on Wednesday when the ball was turned up by Capt W E Newlands. Sam Sowter, gripped the leather and the Down'ards were grimly determined to turn the tables this time. Slowly they forced their way across the Croft and out into Compton. Hemmed in by the crowd the scrum progressed slowly up Compton until it shed the ball and there was a wild scramble. Twice they were repulsed but with a mighty effort, they gained Station Street. It was taking on the aspect of an international match for Ireland was again strongly represented in Down'ards ranks. A faulty throw sent it over the railings of the Methodist Church. It was rushed down the yard and into The Paddock. The crowd was just catching up when the leather was thrown over the wall and carried back to Station Street by the way it came.

It was swept along at a great pace as far as the police station where Jack Edge, of Ballidon snatched it up and was away along Station Road in a flash. He would have got clear away had not a railway employee collared him near the station. Down'ards meant business and they pushed a way into Clifton Road. Sam, Bill and Jack Sowter and Ike Beresford were the chief Down'ard stalwarts. Two hundred yards in about ten minutes was the rate of progress with only four Up'ards, Len Lowndes, Peter Etches, Bill Allen and 'Hockey' Ford fighting hard in a delaying action. It seemed a forlorn hope and at the Gas Works the opposition withdrew just after 5.00pm. For the last mile Sam Sowter carried the ball with Albert Rowe as escort, alternately wading, sometimes waist deep, and cutting across the fields. The arrival at Clifton Mill was greeted with cheers, and Sowter handed the ball to his daughter, Doris. Thus 11-year old Doris Sowter goaled the ball for Down'ards at 5.45pm. Unprecedented in the history of the game, this action was the Down'ards reply to the goaling of a ball for the Up'ards by a woman on the previous day. That had cut deeply into the pride of some players. So for the first time all the goaling was done by the fair sex.

1944

As Virile As Ever

In 1944 and 1945, it was agreed to confine play to the hours of 2.00 until 6.00pm with one ball on each day. The British Legion had been invited to nominate two people to turn up the balls and their President, Major G W Bond DSO and Management Committee Chairman, Mr J Wood started the games.

Shortly after play got going Tom Allen joined the hug and was soon off with the ball up the river. Leaving the water on the Hall Farm side, he was caught by Jack Spencer and George Bradley and a hug formed that soon dropped into the river. Down'ards pushed play towards the Fish Pond which had been drained and two traction engines were at work dredging out the deep mud. The hug thought better of it and went back to the river. The cries from the followers were almost drowned at times from the noise of aircraft overhead. Joe Wibberley fell flat on his face in the river on top of the ball. 'Want a drink, Joe?' someone asked. 'No, I've just had one' came the reply. After 2½ hours play resistance faded at the top of Fish Pond meadow. Peter Etches set off up the river for Sturston and goaled the ball at 5.10pm. The paint of the Union Jack was still on it.

No Play To Be Seen

Wednesday was a disappointing day. After the turn up, the ball was not seen for over two hours play chiefly up the river. Then Joe Wibberley got his hands on the ball and kept them there all the way up the river to the mill where he goaled the ball at 4.35pm. There had been some Down'ard's opposition with old stalwarts like Charlie, Bill, and Jack Sowter and Sid Taylor in the thick of it, but the Up'ards had them outnumbered two to one.

1945
Till The Boys Come Home

After weeks of bitter weather, conditions were good for the two days play. Mr T Pountain JP, Chairman of the town council turned up the first ball and his deputy, Mr A Hulme turned up the Wednesday ball. Mr Pountain said 'we want to keep the old traditions going until the boys come back'. There was little danger of that as the players soon slipped into the icy and chest deep water. Play as usual worked its way towards Back Bridge. The ball came out into the Park fields and broke loose ending up in the now very deep Fish Pond. No one was keen to retrieve it and an unknown airman swam into ten feet of water to reach it. In and out of the river play went, slowly moving towards Sturston until the mill was reached. After the last resistance in the mill yard, Tom Allen reached the wheel at 4.20pm. The river had proved as much an opposition as the Down'ards.

Goaled At Clifton In The Dark

Throwing up the Wednesday ball Mr Hulme said 'I hope you will keep the ball loose today'. He need not have worried. It was kicked more in the first hour in the Croft than in the whole of the previous day's play. After being tossed from the river, play swept through the fairground and the Green Man Garage yard into Compton where a hug developed. Slowly it moved to the top of Compton and into Station Street. It was forced through the gateway and onto The Paddock from where the ball was carried to Station Road. Down Clifton Road play proceeded and there was a tremendous fight for possession on the hill beyond Nestlé. The ball went through the hedge and Neville Harrison ran off with it down to the railway where he was caught. It took a further two hours for it to reach the mill and a goaler to be chosen. The honour went to Malcolm Chell at 7.45pm.

1946
A Goalless Tuesday

For the second time within 20 years a day went by without a goal and the Tuesday ball was handed in at the police station at 11.55pm after being hugged for nearly 6½ hours. The ball was turned up by Lt Col J P Stanton. The ball was quickly caught and the first hug began with H G Plumbly dispensing with his duties of accompanying Col Stanton. There was a rush for the river but it was noticed that many old stalwarts were now watching instead of playing. Some loose play took place in The Park and the ball was eventually kicked onto thin ice on the pond. The game had been in progress for about two hours when the Down'ards, now reinforced, made an effort to break away. The ball was forced into Park Road and on into St John Street. It was swept on down to the Green Man Hotel where there was a halt before there was another breakaway down Church Street and over to the railway bridge. Incredibly, the Up'ards forced the ball all the way back to Park Road and on to the Machine Inn. The huge hug was then moved as far as Nestlé where it went backwards and forwards in the dark. It had been agreed that play would terminate at 7.00pm, but there was no desire to end the game. One or two tentative suggestions by the police that the ball should be given up were ignored and play continued right up to the deadline of midnight.

Mobile Scorers

Good crowds turned out on Wednesday, to see Mr F S Bromage, of the Elite Cinema turn up the ball. This was goaled at Sturston after only two hours play. A second ball turned up by Mr F P Birch allowed the Down'ards to draw level soon after 6.00pm. The first hour's play was chiefly around Shaw Croft and then there was a runaway towards Sturston. Down'ards were in pursuit but might just as well have stayed on the Croft. While the chase was on Bill Allen jumped in a car, travelled up

Belper Road, ran across a field to meet fellow players and then goaled the ball. Up went the second ball and away went the Down'ards. With a plan in mind they gradually worked their way to the station. Denis Clewes made off on a bike and after making a headway came up with a better idea. Jumping on the back of a motor bike he was heading for Clifton before the Up'ards realised what had happened. The second ball was the unscored Tuesday ball.

1947

Brave Play Amid The Snow And Ice

The early months of the year saw the worst snows for a generation. Two weeks before the game a Halifax plane bringing food to the snow bound villages of North Staffordshire, crashed on Grindon Moor and killed the crew. Another plane, a little Auster-Arrow, landed on its skis in Biggin-by-Hartington carrying parcels of food. Nearer Ashbourne, some 600 men working with snow ploughs and bulldozers were used to free the Derby road. A way through was made a week before the game but the police advised the Trent Bus Company not to use it. In Ashbourne there were six inches of ice in the town's streets. Mr Winston Churchill and Air Vice Marshall Jones had been asked to turn up the balls this year, but both had been unable to attend. Air Vice Marshall Jones did visit, however, in 1949, the year in which the Duke of Edinburgh had been invited but was unable to come.

A good crowd waited for Mr E H Wheatcroft and Committee members including 83-year-old Jack Barker who was still painting the balls. Within a minute the ball was in the river despite the conditions with Joe Wibberley and a few more after it. However, water play did not last long. The ball was pushed right over Shaw Croft but deep drifts prevented play going up Park Road. There was even a fierce hug on the frozen pond before play went back to the river and then back into town where there was a circuit of the streets. Along Church Street, down to Station Street and then back down Compton went the ball. It was now dark and it was very difficult to see who had possession. The game made its way down to Nestlé before the Up'ards staged a recovery. The last Down'ard resistance was at the Plough Inn and after that it was simply a procession to Sturston Mill. Arthur Beresford won the toss and honour of goaling the ball. A car came along and the goaler and others rode to the mill, goaling it at around 10.00pm.

Stalemate

Contary to tradition there were fewer spectators when Mr H Wardle turned up the Wednesday ball although there were some German prisoners of war. The ball was soon out into Dig Street but it was forced back into the Croft and eventually reached Belper Road. It was seized by Bill Blake who dashed away with it. However, a Down'ard jumped onto a lorry, caught him and a hug began again. Play returned to town and out to Nestlé where a stalemate developed, neither side giving an inch. At midnight the ball was handed over to the Ashbourne police.

1948

Surprises

Mr S H Elkes of Uttoxeter turned up the first ball. As an Up'ard he said he hoped that it would be his team that would win! The ball was soon in the Henmore and twenty young men followed it plus Mrs Meg Gallimore. Don Lowndes caused some amusement as his trousers repeatedly slipped down and had to be adjusted just as often! The ball was played up to the Back Bridge and then carried down in a rush to the Green Man Garage where it was forced into Compton. There was a lot of play in the street before the game was gradually moved to within sight of Sturston Mill. Here, the Down'ards impressively recovered and by 8.30pm the ball was back in Church Street. Play moved on into Dig Street and then on to Clifton Road where Guy Harrison had the ball as it was hugged backwards and forwards. Midnight was drawing closer and eventually the Up'ards agreed to a suggestion that the Down'ards be allowed to score. As Ashbourne church chimed midnight, Guy goaled it for the Down'ards.

Even More Surprises

The Wednesday ball was turned up by Mr G W Casson and was soon in the river. There a long hug took place before it was agreed to throw the ball back into the Croft. Suddenly the ball was flung over a high wall and into Birch's yard. The crowd rushed out of Shaw Croft only to see the ball disappearing on the back of a lorry. It took the ball as far as Nestlé, where the players took it down to Clifton and Lew Bill goaled it incorrectly. Sam Sowter took the ball and goaled it in the prescribed manner. A second ball was thrown up just after three o'clock by Mr Cyril Heathcote. Open play continued throughout the afternoon, with first one side and then the other taking the advantage. Much of the play was confined to Compton and Shaw Croft. As time went by, the Up'ards seemed to be getting the better of the play and it came as no surprise when they broke for Sturston. At about 6.00pm, the mill was reached and Fred Dethick goaled the ball.

A Unique Record

Among the spectators on the Tuesday was Mr John Barker who was 84 years old and had been painting the balls for 70 years. He had painted the first one as an apprentice with Messrs Sellors. He had painted over 100 balls, including that sent to Princess Mary, and those turned up by the Prince of Wales, the late Duke and the then present Duke of Devonshire, and the Duke of Rutland. No two designs had been the same. In his Shrovetide days, he had goaled more than one ball and was one of the runners. He felt there was more kicking in the old days and the play was much rougher then. Sadly, Mr Barker died later that year. The job of painting the balls was taken over by his grandson, Jack Roberts.

1949

Don Lowndes' Day

The first ball was thrown up by one of the town's distinguished sons, Air Vice Marshal R O Jones CBE, AFC. After moving about the Croft for a while, the ball went into the river. Don Lowndes was well to the front trying to force the ball upstream. Meg Gallimore was in there along with her brother, Jack Roberts, checking how his paint was wearing and doing a considerable amount of pushing. At the end of the Recreation Ground, when the ball was moving fast, Norman Burton and several more Down'ards jumped in to stop the forward play. Eventually, the ball was forced to land and hugged but the move towards Sturston resumed. Finally, when near to Sturston, the opposition gave way and it was agreed that Don Lowndes, who had played magnificently, should have the honour of goaling and up the race he went. He returned the ball to the Green Man Hotel, reported that the ball had been goaled and requested another one.

Mr J E Gadsby, a prominent local tradesman and local NFU chairman, turned up a new ball which was kicked around the Croft for a while. This was followed by some good waterplay before the ball was hugged across Compton and down King Edward Street. A long push down Clifton Road began with the Up'ards occasionally forcing a reversal. Backwards and forwards went the game and at about 8.00pm between Wright's mill and Nestlé the ball was found to be missing. It later transpired that it had broken loose in the darkness and was picked up by Arthur Beresford who took it to Sturston and goaled it at his leisure.

Ball Missing For Three Hours

Capt S D Player turned up the Wednesday ball and some exciting open play followed. The Down'ards appeared to be out in greater force than on the previous day. The ball was eventually forced into the water but it was soon out again. More play took place on the Croft before the game was forced towards the Fish Pond. Around 5.00pm the ball was in the fields with a lot of open play, the ball being kicked and thrown about. It moved about the field very quickly. In the midst of it all was Coun. W G Goodall from Ednaston complete with his bowler hat. The Down'ards then forced playback through Shaw Croft and eventually into Clifton Road where there was a repeat of the previous night. The ball was hugged up and down before being thown over a wall near to Nestlé. Several players followed it, but Keith Smith had disappeared into the darkness with it. The ball was missing for some three hours but around 11.30pm, Smith was detected close to Clifton Mill. He was dispossessed after a short struggle, by Sid Taylor junior, who then goaled the ball for the Down'ards.

Game Reports 1950-2002

1950
An End Of Day Goal

The first ball was turned up by Brig C B Harvey DSO. It was soon in the water and going downstream but it was landed near the Green Man Garage and ended up in Compton. Play went down King Edward Street but the Down'ards could not reach Station Street. Playing hard at this point were Jack Bagnall, Hugh Connell, K Renshaw, T Potter and Joan Lomas. At the second attempt the ball reached Station Road and then began the journey down Clifton Road. All evening was spent in trying to get to the ball, or stop it from reaching Clifton. At 11.00pm the ball had been forced past Nestlé and down onto the railway lines. Guy Harrison and Don Lowndes were in the thick of it along with Sam Chell and Jack Higgins. At 11.30pm the ball reached the Clifton Mill and Sam Chell took the honour.

Jimmy Grant Chin Deep In The Water

Mr F J Edge, chairman of the town council, turned up the second day ball. It was kicked about the Croft for a considerable time and after some hard play, it was thrown over into the Horse and Jockey Yard. Some play took place in the Market Place before the ball was worked over to The Park. However, it returned to the town and play moved down Church Street and there the ball was run away with by Peter Ward, who dashed up the railway tunnel. He did not appear at the other end and it became clear that the ball must have been hidden in the tunnel. It was retrieved and went down the line towards Clifton. The ball was forced into the water which was chest deep in places. At one spot, when Jimmy Grant had the ball, he went into a hole and the water level rose up to his chin. He was undeterred and carried on downstream to Clifton where he goaled the ball just after 8.00pm. This year's balls had been made by Trevor Yeomans and Percy Chadwick. They were painted by Jack Roberts.

1951
Fastest Ever Goal

On the first day, the ball was turned up by Mr Frank Highfield and on the Wednesday by Col D G Ridout. It was noticed that this year many of the older players were content to leave the play in the hands of younger men. At 2.00pm there was a furious snowstorm. The Down'ards moved towards the water but the new flood banks now made this more difficult. In the centre of play were Don Lowndes, one of the Etches, Joe Wibberley, Jimmy Grant, H Tomlinson, N Harrison, Condon McGuinness and John Knight. The ball reached The Park and was carried across the weir at the Fish Pond. However, it soon moved over to the Henmore, gradually moving up towards Sturston. There were quite a few young ladies taking part in the game at this point. Once clear of The Park, there was little chance of a recovery and opposition gave way at the mill. Four players tossed for the honour of goaling which went to J Mansfield just before 5.00pm. Mr J Wedd, a local cattle dealer turned up the second ball which was quickly played into Compton. It was in Station Street before most of the crowd could get out of the Croft. Neville Shemilt led the breakaway, handing it to Cecil Challinor upon reaching the railway line. The ball was goaled at Clifton at 5.35pm, within 25 minutes after being thrown up and could well be the fastest ever goal. Challinor was reported to have ridden a bike to Clifton but he denied it two weeks later. (AN 22/02/1951) However, his contemporaries assert that he had taken the bike – from outside Nestlé's offices in Clifton Road! He was 14 years old.

Almost There

Regrettably, the report gives no detail of Wednesday's play prior to 5.00pm, when play was in Station Street. From here the ball was played along Sturston Road and brought back to Compton. After a short period in King Edward Street, the Up'ards forced play upriver as far as the tennis courts. Then play continued in Fish Pond Meadow and then Park Road. By 8.00pm it was back in Compton where it stayed for a while, eventually moving down Station Street, Station Road and into Church Street. By 11.00pm the ball had reached the Hanging Bridge Institute with rain falling heavily. Among the main players were N Waring, Bill Knight, Joe Wibberley, Colin LeGrice and Albert Evans. When the clock struck midnight, the ball was still being hugged by a large group of players some 20 yards from Clifton Mill. It was then handed over to waiting police officers.

1952

Duke Defends Ancient Customs

Ancient customs, such as Shrovetide football, were defended by the Duke of Devonshire when he spoke at the luncheon and again in his short speech before turning up the ball. His father had turned up the ball in 1923 and his grandfather in 1924. Both had been President of the Ashbourne Shire Horse Society, the same as the current Duke. For the first time in 50 years the crowd sang 'God save the Queen'. Play moved around the Croft for 30 minutes or so and then reached the Henmore. The ball was played down the river to the railway station. 'No trespassing' signs were ignored but there were only four or five trains a day now. The ball reached the Church Institute before crossing the field to reach Mayfield Road. Up'ards pressure then began to tell and the ball came back to town where the Labour Exchange reportedly had its biggest crowd since the depression and nearly lost a window. There was then some good open kicking which brought play to Dig Street before a long stay in King Edward Street heralded the story of the rest of the day's play. The ball was pushed into Church Street for another stay. Then it returned down the road to reach Clifton Road, being out of sight for much of the time. It took over three hours to reach Nestlé but there was then a break and J Mansfield ran off with it. He was stopped and another hug formed. However, there was a repeat of the previous year's play and at midnight the ball was given to Sgt Thompson.

Riding To The Goal Again

Major F D Ley turned up the Wednesday ball. Unfortunately the *Ashbourne News* did not carry a report of play. However, the ball was goaled at Sturston before 5.00pm, carried there by motor bike across the fields. A few Down'ards anticipated this action and Malcolm Chell, Tug Bradley and Ken Wood formed a token of resistance. Riding to goal apparently were Stan Cope and Don Lowndes and the former goaled the ball.

The second ball was turned up by Mr Albert Jones. At 10.00pm Kenneth Renshaw equalised at Clifton. After the games there was a threat of legal action against the Committee for damage to a car and Mr Plumbly was asked to deal with it.

1953

Exciting Water Play And One Goal Each

With the words 'I wish you a good and fierce game', Lord John Manners turned up the Tuesday ball, deputising for his brother, the Duke of Rutland. At first the ball was played towards the Henmore, swollen with melting snow. However, it was taken to the opposite end of the Croft and into a corner by Park Road, where it was hugged for a considerable time. The ball went over into The Park and eventually reached the river via the Fish Pond overflow. Beyond the Memorial gardens the ball was flung out and play centred for a long time on the Grammar School fields. After a desperate struggle which lasted for close on three hours, Don Lowndes scored for the Up'ards. A second ball was turned up on the Shaw Croft at about 5.30pm by Mr Sam Sellers. Play soon reached Compton and went up to the corset factory and back several times. The ball was kicked and hugged slowly but surely to Clifton via Dig Street, Church Street, Mayfield Road and finally Green Road. John Mansfield, D Clarke, Sam Chell and others played hard until it was goaled by Jack Higgins, just after 11.30pm.

Three Rescued From The Water

Mr R S Bury turned up the Wednesday ball. Three men had to be rescued from the swollen river during the day. An off duty policeman from Derby was secured by ropes and brought to safety by an Ashbourne policeman. Only a few moments later, another player was carried from the hug by a companion to the Shaw Croft bank. The third player to make the onlookers gasp was Raymond Tunnicliffe. He had swum out of Shaw Croft and under Compton Bridge only to loose his grip on the ball which was borne away by the current. He was in obvious difficulties as he approached Bank Croft, where he was assisted from the water by Jimmy Grant.

The ball shot from one end of Shaw Croft to the other and was played for sometime without a hug. It had an outing to South Street before returning down Compton to Shaw Croft and then went on to the Memorial gardens where it went into the river. It was during this period that the three rescues took place. After the nerve racking incident concerning Ray Tunnicliffe, the ball was landed into Bank Croft and play moved to King Edward Street. In the action at this point were Joe Wibberley, Mr Briggs, Brian Burton, Stuart Hellaby, Jack Grant, Sam Chell and Don Lowndes. Play moved back to the Fish Pond and then went through the new housing estate and into Sturston Road. Here the ball was picked up by John Mansfield who then rode his motor bike to Sturston where he goaled the ball at around 4.30pm. A fresh ball was then turned up by Mr T Brown. Play rarely went beyond a 150 yard radius of the Church Street/Dig Street corner. There was very little open play and at midnight the players gave the ball up to Sgt Thompson outside the Labour exchange. After singing the National Anthem the crowd dispersed.

1954

Huge Crowd Watches Tuesday's Turnup

Prior to the game the Committee chairman, Mr F P Birch wrote to the *Ashbourne News* stating that the Committee would not accept any liablity for any damage caused and included a plea for restraint.

The crowd was stated to be the largest since 1928. However, the play did not live up to expectations during the afternoon, although it picked up during the evening. The ball was turned up by Sir George Kenning and for a while it was hugged around the Croft. Play then entered the river and progressed upstream all the way to Sturston where the ball was goaled by Jack Clarke just before 5.00pm. Other players seen in the thick of it were 'Dinky' Shepherd, Albert Evans, Don Lowndes, Malcolm Chell, Bob Chell, Tom Allen, Charlie Etches, Tony Eagan, D Waring, John and Jimmy Grant. The new ball was turned up by Jack Roberts, the painter of the balls. At 6.00pm neither side seemed to have the advantage and the ball was in Compton. Then it reached Sturston Road and Church Street where play moved up and down. The hug then moved into Church Lane and down towards the Railway Bridge before it was brought back to Church Street by a runner. Having been stopped, play went down Mayfield Road to Green Road where there was very little opposition. The Down'ards carried on through ankle deep snow to the mill where Jack Smith goaled the ball at about 9.30pm. The players were given two gallons of ale in the village before wending their way back to town. In the latter stages of play also were Guy Harrison, Bill Hanley, Keith Smith, Alec Robinson, Mike Bradley, Ken Renshaw, John Waring, Dennis Carter, B and G Gadsby.

Stern Struggle in The Water

Mr Hugo Johnson of Tatton's Mill, Mayfield, turned up the Wednesday ball. There were several attempts to get the ball over the wall and into Compton before it actually made it. It made off up the street and was soon in The Paddock. It remained here for about thirty minutes when a good throw saw the ball sailing over the railings and into Station Road. The ball was then hugged into Mayfield Road. However, the ball returned down Station Road and entered the river. Here there was some hard hugging, both in and out of the water. However, the Down'ards started off down the river with five players continually in the water. It looked as though the ball was going to Clifton but it came back to town. Play went round and round the town all evening and the ball eventually disappeared from the hug in the railway goods yard. There was a lamp on the wheel at Sturston and a few patient folk waited at the mill. At 12.05am the ball had not been goaled but shortly afterwards there was a cheer from inside the mill. The report states that the ball had been brought from out of its hiding place by literally underground means to the very hub of the wheel, where it was goaled by George Mansfield. The way to the wheel had not been used before. The goal was allowed to stand despite strong Down'ard's criticism. In reaching its decision, the Committee decided that from 1955, if the ball had not been goaled by midnight it became the property of the Committee and anyone keeping it would be committing an offence.

An editorial comment the following week also carried a note highlighting the wedding of Doris Sowter, who scored the Wednesday goal in 1943. She married Mr Leslie Harrison (AN 11/03/1954).

1955

Down'ards Score After A Tense Struggle

A snow storm on the Tuesday did not deter a big crowd as Lt Col P V Gell turned up the ball. After hugging it for a while, play ventured down to Staffordshire Farmers in Park Road. However, it was soon back and was thrown from the river into one of the yards where it was gathered into the arms of a patiently waiting player. There then followed some two hours play in the streets before the ball returned to the river via Horse and Jockey Yard. After a break, play moved into Compton and then Clifton Road by way of Station Road. As darkness fell the ball was played down onto the railway line and into the fields near to Clifton Mill. However, it was fought for until late in the evening when George Challinor goaled it for the Down'ards.

Up'ards Even The Score

Mr Justice Callow turned up the ball on a dull and bitterly cold day. There was soon some thrilling play on the Croft before the ball reached the river. Only Bob Chell entered the icy water and had made fifty yards before Don Lowndes went in to stop him. The ball left the river for Compton and play did a circuit down the street, round to Park Road and then back to Compton via Shaw Croft. This time play veered off onto The Paddock where it was kicked, thrown and hugged for about 15 minutes. The ball was then pushed back to Compton. Also in the play in addition to Don Lowndes were Michael Betteridge, Bob Chell and Charles Allen. The move away from The Paddock was in vain and back it went. Jimmy Grant and Don were seen to be sitting down in the centre of the hug for ten minutes or so! Play reached Church Street as heavy snow fell and it grew dark. At 6.16pm, John Mansfield ran the ball to Sturston where there was a hug close to the mill. After 30 minutes, Billy Hellaby goaled the ball for the Up'ards to end the day's play.

1956

Mike Betteridge's Fine Getaway Brings A Goal For John Gadsby

The 1891 Shrovetide song was put to new music by Daly Atkinson and sung at the lunch by Arthur Froggatt and Fred Grime. It has now become a tradition for part of the song to be sung at the lunch by two people.

The game was started by Capt Waterhouse and the ball swiftly disappeared into Park Road. It was hugged around into Compton and then broke loose. Then it was kicked about in front of the post office before returning to Shaw Croft. Here it went into the river and the Down'ards quickly took the ball downstream to Nestlé. However, in the manner of Shrovetide football there was a reversal and play came back to town. Mike Betteridge made a great getaway when the ball was near to Back

Bridge. He managed to get it through Dr Madge's surgery and into the garden of Miss Rigby, next door. He obtained permission to go through her house and into St John Street. By way of an entry, garden and a yard, he emerged into the Market Place. Here, with John Gadsby, Ian Bates, and Gerry Williams, he found a car owned by Arthur Birch who drove them to Clifton. There was a struggle at the mill before John Gadsby goaled the ball just after 5.00pm.

Down'ards Make It Two

Dr R Ogley turned up the second day's ball, explaining that he was not there looking for work. The leather was quickly played over to the bus station. It moved on to the railway station and came out into Clifton Road through Frank Wright's yard. A hug was formed and the ball slowly reached Nestlé. Here the ball went into the water and was followed by Jimmy Grant, Don Lowndes, Charlie Burton and Betty Cundy. Play came out after a while and Jimmy carried the ball down the railway line to Clifton. Having scored the year before, he gave the ball to Charlie Burton who goaled it. As it was still before 5.00pm, another ball was demanded and this was turned up by Percy Wibberley of the Wellington Hotel. This was goaled by Cecil Challinor at Clifton.

The use of a car by Mike Betteridge and John Gadsby caused a stirring of discontent in the town, although history shows that the Up'ards had little to complain about. Whether one used a motor bike or a car seems to be immaterial. The following year there were even rumours (unfounded) that a horse had been used (see below)! In 1957, there was further controversy on another matter. It all went to show that the strength of the game was that it could (and still can) absorb irregularities in its stride. The year also saw the retirement of Mr F P Birch as the Committee chairman. He was succeeded by Herbert Plumbly who did a considerable amount of work in successfully raising the profile of the game through the people who he pursuaded to attend and speak at the lunches. One of his first tasks in 1957 was to advise the press that the use of any form of mechanical propulsion was no longer allowed.

1957

Miss Wibberley Goals At Clifton

The first ball was turned up by Frank Dalton, chairman of Silkolene Lubricants Ltd of Belper, and was soon in the river. It went up the valley almost to Sturston but was thrown out and turned back towards the town. It was around 4.30pm and a tough struggle took place, which saw the ball return to town and reach Clifton Road. During the evening, the ball was played several times in the Market Place and up and down St John Street and Church Street. The Up'ards regained the upper hand and play moved to the Fish Pond. Here Pop Robotham, George and Sidney Handley broke for Sturston but upon getting there found the mill well surrounded. It was getting late and they returned to town and found Nora Wibberley, the girl friend of George. They gave her the ball and took her to Clifton where she was able to goal the ball without opposition.

The above newspaper report is, however, contested. Alec Smith wonders whether this ball was actually goaled. He stood with Sgt Thompson and half a dozen others by the goal from 11.00pm to 1.00am and it was not goaled in that time. Frank Harrison who lived at the mill was sure that it was not goaled earlier. Another player is certain that there was insufficient time to have got the ball to Clifton before 11pm.

After a meeting of the Committee, the goal was allowed to stand as it had been scored prior to midnight. There was uproar at this as the two men were clearly Up'ards and had been playing as such. However, despite this, presumably Miss Wibberley was entitled to goal the ball wherever she pleased. Perhaps the editorial comment in the paper (AN 14/03/1957) summed up the situation best: 'Let's not take ourselves too seriously', it said. Sensitivity over using means other than on foot to reach the goal was evidently still high. There was a rumour that a horse had been used to reach the goal. In fact it was only the vicar's daughter, Miss Margaret Trendell, out on her pony!

During the game, two American Army ambulances drew up in Clifton Road when they saw the big Shrovetide crowd. The officer dismounted and enquired if there had been a train accident and if they could help! They were informed by the police that there was nothing to worry about; it was only an old English custom.

Another Lady Deprived Of A Goal

On the Wednesday, the ball was thrown up by Councillor G W Rose of The Firs and a director of Messrs R Cooper Ltd. It was goaled by Bob Braddock at Sturston, just before midnight. The ball became lost at about 6pm after leaving the river thanks to Mike Betteridge Snr. He threw it to Harrison, the sweep, who past it to Peter 'Pop' Robotham. 'Pop' took the ball past the gasworks and sewerage works to Bell's Pastures near Callow Hall, then climbing up the valley side to drop down to his home 65 Mayfield Rd. His mother was unhappy with the ball under the family's settle. Players were searching her garden and looking in her dustbin.

Pop went to Sid Handley's house on Buxton Hill at about 6.30pm, had a drink and arranged for his mother to bring the ball to the top of Church Steps. His intention was to go back to Sturston via Bell's Pastures. In the fog, the ball was hidden as others came by and their ruse was discovered by Alec Smith who found the ball behind the National School in a brown paper bag. He and Peter made for Clifton with the ball up the latter's jumper, but they were discovered. A hug formed in the street before the ball made its way to Sturston. It had been the intention of some Up'ards to allow a woman to goal the ball and she was actually sitting on the wheel with her father as the ball reached the mill. She was Barbara Hellaby, of Hulland, the 1956 Miss Derbyshire Young Farmers.

Don Lowndes gave her an assurance that he would not stop her from scoring, should she gain possession. However, Bob Braddock was determined to have the ball. He too was at the wheel and with the assistance of Don and George Nichols of Meir, Braddock goaled it. It was described in the paper (AT 1/3/57) that the ball was goaled after a bitter struggle in which no quarter was asked and none was given. Apparently that did not describe the half of it.

1958

Ball Missing For Two And A Half Hours

Mr Reg Parnell, the racing driver, turned up the first ball in glorious sunshine. After being hugged for fifteen minutes, the ball left Shaw Croft for Fish Pond Meadow. It was soon in the pond and Dinky Shepherd and Jack Clarke plunged in to retrieve it. The ball moved between the pond and the river gradually working upstream. Suddenly it was thrown out and Brian Mellor, a Down'ard ran off through a couple of fields towards Sturston and was dispossessed before he could turn for town. A hug formed and Down'ard pressure achieved where the runner failed. By 6.00pm the ball was in the bus station, having come down Sturston Road and Compton. The hug did a circuit down Station Road, along Church Street and back into Compton. It was now 8.30pm and the ball disappeared, with Birch's yard and the condemned houses in the street being thoroughly searched to no avail. The ball had in fact been played towards the railway lines where Roger Geeson managed to get hold of the ball. It was recovered from the mud at the side of the river. He hid it under the platform and then recovered it at about 11.00pm, proceeding down the railway lines to Clifton. Although there were Up'ards at Clifton, they were out looking for the ball rather than guarding the mill. They consequently allowed Geeson to reach the mill and goal the ball without opposition. It was goaled jointly with Ron Crookes and the goal stands in their joint names.

No Ball For The Church

On the Wednesday, Ellis Grimshaw of Bond's Mill turned up the ball. After twenty minutes, play broke away through Birch's yard and another hug formed in Compton. Down'ards forced play down the street to Station Street, but John Mansfield, for the Up'ards, broke away back down Compton. He crossed Shaw Croft and was going well with Sturston only a mile away when he was stopped. Tony Rose, Les Torr and Peter Robotham crossed the river and adjoining fields to reach Green Road. They returned to the Market Place where another hug formed. This proceeded down to Dig Street where the ball entered the river around 3.30pm. Ivan Handley took it 100 yards downstream where he handed it to Cecil Challinor who hid for some ten minutes at the Methodist Chapel until he was found. Play resumed down Church Street and back to the river in Dig Street. This time the play went upstream with Don Lowndes, Tom and Charlie Allen but they were to be denied a goal. The ball, by custom, was given to Mr Grimshaw. The parish church had asked if they could have it to auction it off for its roof fund.

At the Tuesday lunch, one minute's silence was held in memory of Trevor Yeomans who had died on the eve of Shrovetide, aged 84 years. He had asked to be relieved from the job of making the balls after the 1957 games. It is not clear when he made them for the first time but he certainly made one of the balls in 1907. He was a master bootmaker and had not retired from that until he was 73 years old. Like John Barker before him, it was a noteworthy achievement. He had even made them when the Committee could not afford to pay for them, taking his expenses later when the Committee had the money. He was succeeded by Mr Percy Chadwick, Arthur Chadwick's father. Also at the lunch was Joseph "Ninety" Burton then aged 83 years. He was the son of John Burton and had scored his first ball when he was eleven which would have been in 1885. He lived until he was 96-years-old. He had goaled a total of seven balls, the last in 1913. The Ashbourne paper stated that he held the record number of goals. However, Mathew Cleaver is held to have scored eight and Sam Smith scored nine.

1959

A Goal In Thirty Minutes

Mr J Peer Groves of Groves and Witnall, who were brewers and then owners of the Green Man Hotel, turned up the Tuesday ball. He had offered a pint of ale to the goaler of the ball. However, it was somewhat ironic that the winner was a teetotaller! After five minutes the ball was in Park Road and after a few minutes, the crowd surged into Fish Pond Meadow, soon to be followed by the ball. The ball was kicked around for a few minutes before Cecil Challinor made off for Sturston with the ball, John Mansfield accompanying him. The two runners were soon clear of opposition and at 2.30pm, Cecil handed the ball over to John who claimed the goal. The local paper stated that it was thought that Herbert Sowter held the record for the fastest goal in 22 minutes, but the records do not bear this out. The fastest on record was just under 25 minutes in 1951, by Cecil Challinor.

Just after 3.15pm the second ball was turned up by Mr Charles Botham, an old Ashbournian then living in Canada. The hug gradually moved into Dig Street and then into St John Street. From here, play moved up one of the yards into Union Street and then on into the fields bordering Mayfield Road. By 4.15pm the ball had reached Clifton and for 45 minutes was only inches from the goal. It seemed that the Down'ards would triumph again, but Don Lowndes and other Up'ards had other ideas. Gradually the ball moved away from the goal and was suddenly kicked into the river. Back to the goal went the ball and a second attempt at 5.30pm was successful. Tom Allen junior ran off with the ball accompanied by Cecil Challinor. Over the top of the Golf Course they went and on to the airfield. Unhindered by anyone they continued through Bradley Wood and across the fields of Sturston Hall Farm to reach the mill, where Tom Allen goaled the ball at 8.15pm.

With A Rope And Plank to Recover The Ball

On Wednesday, Squadron-Leader Peter Balean of The Green Hall turned up the ball. Only five minutes had passed before the ball went into the river. Behind it went Jimmy Grant, Pop Watson, Johnny Eacott and Eric Taylor. Seconds later, teenager David Wibberley took a terrific leap into the river to stop one player running upstream with the ball. However, the ball quickly moved under the bridge and upriver through The Park. Suddenly the ball was landed and went rolling onto the ice covered Fish Pond. After ten minutes some of the players appeared with a short plank which had a rope attached. However, 25 minutes later the ball was still there in the middle! Then the boys with the rope trick tried again. This time they had the plank tied in the middle of the rope which was stretched across the pond. Slowly but surely they slid the ball to the narrow end of the pond and play restarted. The local paper's report ends at this point, but the ball was not goaled and was given to Mr Balean. At the lunch, he offered a pin of Double Diamond, he was a director of Ind Coope, to the man who goaled the ball. If he was at the lunch he would receive two pins.

1960

Damage and a Disappearing Act

The Tuesday game was started by Donald Carr, Captain of Derbyshire Cricket Club. For 30 minutes the ball was hugged over the Croft and then kicked loose. Play went into the river before ending up in the bus station. At least that was what the crowd thought, although it was actually being played in the Butchery. The game then proceeded up St John Street where the window of Wigley's shop was broken. After some 30 minutes play, the ball returned to Dig Street and then to the river via the bus station. Into the river went Jimmy Grant, Jack Spencer, Bill Warrington, Eric Taylor, Don Lowndes, Tony and Gordon Sowter to follow the play down river. The ball was being thrown about in the water when Bob Chell passed the ball to Cecil Challinor, who started overland for Clifton. However, near to Doles Farm the ball returned to the river and the players were shoulder deep in water as they came in sight of the mill. Five players drew straws and Peter Harrison goaled the ball at 4.55pm.

A second ball was turned up by Mr S Froggatt. It was played in the Croft for a while and then went into the streets. At this point the players, pressed by the crowd, burst into Woolworth's shop. Play continued in the darkened shop, leaving by a back window in the basement. Damage was done to some of the stock and fittings, but by followers rather than the players. For most of the early evening, the ball was hugged up and down Compton and Dig Street. Shortly after 10.00pm, the ball was lost. It had in fact been kicked up Derby Road, chased by a few players. The ball was somehow taken around to the back of The Firs, where two players threw the ball to one another and then made off.

Alec Smith relates that two lads took the ball up onto the airfield. Eventually they brought the ball down to Clifton about 11.45pm. They were spotted and approached by Alec and friends. The two didn't know what to do with the ball. Alec knew what he was going to do with it, but the two objected and straws were drawn. As it happened, Alec drew the short one but the ball was thrown into the river in the mistaken belief that the act would deny the ball to one and all.

Alec fetched the ball out, but on regaining the bank, he was deliberately kicked on the chin. It was at this point that the ball disappeared and was taken to Waterfall, being retrieved by a Mr Ratcliffe the following Friday. One Up'ard was so sure that Alec had the ball, he threatened him with a police warrant to search his house for the ball!

Committee Allows Sturston Goal

Mr Roger Wright turned up the Wednesday ball. At first the Down'ards looked destined for an early goal as the ball was pushed towards Clifton at high speed. The ball went downstream but failed to clear Shaw Croft. However, once under Compton Bridge there was a break and Peter Robotham went off with the ball, running as fast as the river would allow. He managed to get as far as the Methodist school's field before the ball was forced out of the water and a hug formed. Play reached a stalemate and despite the efforts of such stalwarts as Don Lowndes, Bob Chambers, Eric Taylor and Cecil Challinor, play remained opposite the bus station for well over an hour. The report ends at this point but a late goal was allowed to stand despite allegations that it was goaled after midnight. The goaler was J Herridge at Sturston.

1961

Ten Hours Play Brings No Goals

Prior to this year's game, the Committee took the unusual step of threatening to resign if the wilful damage of the previous year continued. Mr John Moores, the Chairman of Everton Football Club, turned up the first ball and Mr Michael Sadler had the honour on the Wednesday. In the event, there was virtually no damage at all.

The Tuesday ball was in the river for a while, going nowhere, when it was kicked into the Wellington Yard and found its way into St John Street. Ian Bates made a rush with the ball but was soon stopped. A hug formed that went down the street and into Dig Street. The ball reached the river and went upwards. It was in the water for 30 minutes but the Down'ards took the advantage and landed the ball near to the bus station. Play went down the railway lines and into the church field. There was a break by Cecil Challinor, a Down'ard despite his habit of accompanying runners to either goal. He got no further than Peach's farm on this occasion. A hug reformed and play moved back to town via Green Lane and Mayfield Road. The ball reached the bus station from Dig Street and then Clifton Road having gone back into Compton. From here it returned to Church Street and the street play continued until 11.20pm when the hug lurched into Fish Pond Meadow. Play moved into the gardens in Park Avenue and stayed there until midnight when the ball was returned to the Green Man Hotel and handed over to Sgt W Turner. Only four times this century had the first Tuesday goal remained ungoaled, in 1932, 1940, 1946, and 1952, yet the same thing was to occur in the following two years.

No Goals On Wednesday Either

Once the ball had been thrown up, play moved quickly in the direction of Sturston. The hug moved out into Park Road and reached the river by the bridge. Despite Down'ards opposition, the play moved under the bridge and through the recreation ground, still in the water. In the thick of it were Pop Watson, Ivan and George Handley, Sid and Eric Taylor, Dennis Clarke, Roy Bennett and Spike Hollinshead. However, as on the previous day, the ball was ungoaled. This was only the second year since 1891 that there were no goals on either day. The other year was 1932.

1962

No Goal Makes It A Hat Trick

Mr Ted Moult, farmer and TV personality, turned up the Tuesday ball. It was to be one of the tamest games for years. There was an initial two hours of water play, with players including Mick Miller, John Clarke, George Handley, Pop Watson, Peter Robotham and Simon Plumbly. After lumbering up and down the river, the ball was brought out and hugged around Fish Pond Meadow. After ten minutes loose play, the ball went missing near to the Recreation Ground. It reappeared just as mysteriously around 5.30pm and proceeded down to the Almshouses in Church Street. From here it moved to the police station before ending up at the bus station where someone was heard to remark that never before had so many people been seen waiting for a bus. At 10.00pm the ball was in Compton when there was a break in the direction of Belper Road, followed by some open kicking in Park Road. However, the play returned to Compton and was in the area of the bus station again when midnight saw the end of play. It was reckoned that the evening was possibly the coldest for 25 years.

Ball Goaled In Forty Minutes

Mr Hamlet Yates, another farmer, turned up the Wednesday ball. This was goaled by Peter Harrison in 40 forty minutes at Clifton. The second ball was then turned up by L A Andrews of the Wheel Inn. The ball was played hard all day but in the early evening it was hidden down a yard by the Up'ards who intended to goal it later. On their return the ball had vanished. It had been found by Peter Shearsmith of Wootton who took it down to Clifton and goaled it. There were claims that the ball had not been struck three times on the mill wall. Mr A Froggatt was called to adjudicate and allowed the goal.

The Wednesday ball created a late night disturbance concerning whether it was goaled or not. Although the goal was granted by Arthur Froggatt, Alec Smith asserted that it had not been goaled. It was taken to the mill, but Alec was standing by the wheelhouse and stated that the ball had not been carried inside. He was convinced that the goaler didn't know what to do with the ball having reached the mill. An argument developed at the Green Man Hotel and glasses were thrown. Although not involved, Alec found himself explaining the position first to the police at the station and then to his wife who was sick in bed. Many Ashbourne women can ruefully testify that twice a year they take a back seat; their men preoccupied with the fortunes of a leather, often to the exclusion of everyone else.

1963

Ball Goes Missing After Hard Play In Bitter Weather

Prior to the start of this year's games, the weather had been the worst since 1947. At least 32 degrees of frost had been recorded at Clifton school in the third week of January. Bread parcels had been taken by train to Hartington where the village was cut off. Icy weather prevailed during Shrovetide and there was a lot of ice and snow on the Henmore.

At the Tuesday lunch, history was made when the Council Chairman, Mrs Doris Grimshaw, spoke to the guests. She said that Mrs Woolley was one of her ancestors and that her mother was one of the first women ever invited to a Shrovetide lunch, in 1930.

The ball was turned up by Mr G R Jackson and after some 15 minutes went into the water. Despite being bitterly cold, several players followed the ball in and water play continued for another 15 minutes before they decided to land the ball. Play quickly went into Compton and then around into Park Road where there was a break away. The ball appears to have gone up Belper Road where John Gadsby obtained possession. He crossed the fields and the river and the ball eventually reached the bottom of Buxton Road via Green Road. It was then pushed down the Wellington Yard and thrown over the wall into the river. Once it had been retrieved, it was played into Compton again. Eventually, play turned into Station Street and at 6.15pm was pressing against the doors of the corset works. Having reached the Railway Tavern, the hug ground to a halt for 90 minutes.

It then moved back to the police station where the ball and hug broke through the railings and went down the bank and onto the railway lines. Incredibly, the ball was then forced back up the bank and into the street, going all the way back to Compton. At 10.00pm there was a breakaway and the ball was kicked along Station Street and vanished on to the railway lines. The ball was missing until Friday when it was handed over to the police. It had been taken to Clifton but there were too many people about for the people with the ball. Those with it hung around until after midnight and then took the ball home to Waterhouses.

Hug Delays the Train Again

On the Wednesday, the ball was turned up by F H Thomas, the Clerk to the Ashbourne Urban and Rural District Councils. The game ended shortly before 8.30pm when Billy Bennett goaled the ball at Sturston. It was played hard throughout the afternoon in the streets and the fields. Early in the evening, play reached the railway line and entered the tunnel, delaying the departure of the Buxton train. Eventually a truce was called and it was agreed to bring the ball back into the open. It was then thrown up in Station Street.

Billy Bennett added the following (per. comm.): The ball was played through the tunnel and was being hugged on the line near to the north portal of the tunnel. The quarry train arrived and was held up for a time at the hug's convenience. From the tunnel, the ball was played back to Shaw Croft, where John Tompkinson threw him the ball. [Bill's great grandfather was William Bennett, one of those fined for playing the game in 1891].

Bill ran across to Park Road and into Fish Pond Meadow. The exceptionally cold weather had frozen the fishpond and he ran across, the ice cracking under him. No one followed, which gave him a lead and he continued on across the field to reach the river. Here he hid the ball under a tree root. He continued upriver before climbing out onto the bank.

For fifteen minutes people searched for the ball before someone said, 'it's gone off up the rec'. The crowd took off and eventually Bill retrieved the ball and went up the fields to Struston. He had a couple of lads with him, including fellow fireman Mick Baldy. They waited for a lone figure to move away from the mill and walked along the wheel axle to score. The other two went to fetch Mr Dethick from the mill house to act as a witness as Bill banged the ball three times.

Returning to town, he called at his father's house and threw the ball onto his chest as he sat in the lounge. Father William was not amused owing to the high number of enquiries he had received about the whereabouts of his son and a missing ball!

The ball was later repainted by John Roberts, who charged 30/- (£1.50).

During 1963, Princess Margaret visited Ashbourne and was presented with a miniature Shrovetide ball for Viscount Linley.

1964

Up'ards Scrape Home With A Last Minute Goal

After nearly ten hours play, the Up'ards ended a rather unexciting day with a last minute goal. Mr Sam Ramsden started proceedings and the ball was quickly in the river where it stayed for 30 minutes. There then followed about an hour's play in Compton before play returned to the river. Here play stayed for another hour before Bob Chambers threw the ball out. Play had been below the hoardings near to the bridge and was soon back in Compton. Play moved around into Sturston Road where an uncharitable lady doused the hug with a bucket of cold water. Encouraged to move on, play went into Park Road and back to Compton through Birch's timber yard. There was a repeat performance as play retuned to Park Road (except for the lady with the bucket!) but play moved down Park Road to Dr Madge's house. After further street play, the hug found itself in the river at 10.30pm. Later, when it was obvious that the hug would not reach either goal, it was decided that Bob Chambers, Winston and Tom Allen should toss for the goal. It was won by Tom Allen who handed the ball over to his brother John. The latter headed for Sturston and touched the wheel just before midnight.

Down'ards Make It With Three Minutes To Spare

Wednesday saw lots of fast moving play and plenty of excitement. Mr A E Dawson started proceedings on a mild and fine day. The hug quickly forced play into the river at Back Bridge and play steadily moved up the river. Here there was some exciting play as the ball was thrown about in the water for about an hour. Play then went back into the town without leaving the river and at 6.00pm was on the railway lines. It continued towards Clifton but at Nestlé, the ball was landed and at 10.00pm, play was in the fields near Mayfield Road. As Down'ards pressure eased, the hug moved back up the road towards town. An increasingly impatient hug saw the ball return to the river at Back Bridge at 11.20pm. Here there was a breakout at last. Reg Purdy was relieved of the ball by Graham Woolley who became exhausted at the top of Fish Pond Meadow. Cecil Challinor took it over and accompanied by Charles Coxon and John Mansfield, the three crossed the fields to Green Road. John Gadsby was just returning home and the three asked him to go to Clifton in his van. The three then went down Union Street, Belle Vue Road and over the fields to Clifton where John Gadsby was waiting to witness that the ball was goaled prior to midnight. It was 11.57pm and the goal equalled the score for the year.

1965

Youngest Goaler Of The Main Game

Major J W Chandos-Pole started the proceedings and saw the ball quickly leave the Croft for Fish Pond Meadow. The play went into the river and turned downstream. There was a break and when the crowd caught up, the play was down by Nestlé. However, John Mansfield obtained possession and accompanied by Gerald Connell and Barry Cooper, they crossed the snow covered fields beyond Clifton Road and made for the Secondary Modern School. They headed on towards Sturston and Mansfield, who already had three goals to his credit, gave the ball to Connell who touched the wheel at 3.15pm. Mr Percy Chadwick, the maker of the balls, turned up the second ball. John Mansfield returned to town declaring that he was off to milk his cows. Six hours later, he was back helping his 13-year-old son to goal the ball. The second ball was played around the Croft for a while before heading for the streets from Compton. Three hours later, at 7.30pm the ball was back in Compton but at 8.00pm it was spirited away by Cecil Challinor. He usually worked in concert with John Mansfield and the two met up, this time with Frank Mansfield. They proceeded to Clifton via Bell's Pastures and Seven Arches Bridge but found the plinth surrounded by people. They therefore withdrew and skirting Ashbourne, proceeded to Sturston where the two men agreed to let Frank goal the ball. His thirteenth birthday had been the day before.

Another Up'ard Goal, Another Teenage Scorer

On Wednesday, the ball was turned up by Mr John Archer of Yeldersley. It was goaled just before midnight by 16 years old Peter Gadsby after many hours of street play. At about 5.30pm, Gerald Vandenberg did a runner with the ball towards Belle Vue Road, but was caught by Peter Gadsby, his uncle, J J Gadsby and others. They hid the ball in a coal shed but there were too many people about and the ruse failed. There was more street play in the early evening. After some water play and at about 10.00pm, Peter and others managed to get the ball away from behind The Wheel Inn and the corset factory yard. Proceeding via the fields behind Old Derby Road, they went to Clifton and Peter Gadsby won the toss to decide on the goaler. On revealing that he was an Up'ard the young players went through the fields to Sturston where the ball was goaled.

Prior to this year's play, one of the balls was taken from the Green Man Hotel where it was being displayed. It was returned after several days by students, claiming that it was only a rag day stunt and that theft was not their intention.

1966

Town Honours A Great Sportsman

Sir Stanley Mathews turned up the Tuesday ball in the middle of a quagmire. A hug formed and after a while left for Compton where play went into the river by the side of the bank. The river was in spate and play quickly went downstream. Pouring rain made little difference to the players and play reached Nestlé. In the water at this point were Ian Bates, Philip Tomlinson, Nick Miller, Mick Bailey, Jim, Joe, and Ernie Grant, Bill Warrington, and others. After swimming through deep water by Nestlé, Guy Harrison and Ken Renshaw helped the players out of the water. The ball was then played across the fields by the sewage works to reach Mayfield Road. By Dark Lane, there was a sudden break and Peter Harrison, Ray Storer, John Croucher, Mel Godfrey and Robert Crane made off to the hospital. They dropped down towards Mappleton and then doubled back towards Clifton but were intercepted by Brian Mellor and other Up'ards. Play was forced back to town via Green Lane as the rain stopped and the crowds came out to watch again. The ball was played around the streets until midnight when it was handed over to the police.

No Goal On Either Day

On a fine day, Coun. Sam Flower turned up the Wednesday ball. The ball was soon in Compton on what was to be a rather active day. Play moved quickly past the bus station and on through the old railway station where the ball was kicked about for a while before reaching School Lane. Play was soon back in the town and went up into the Butchery. Here there was a breakaway and the ball was taken up one of the yards to Union Street. It returned to the Market Place and then went up to Windmill Lane. For most people, the ball was lost, but play was exciting for those that had stuck close to the leather. Play went down to Seven Arches where the ball had its first dip, but in the Bentley Brook just for a change. The players went down the brook until they reached the River Dove. From here, the ball was played around Upper Mayfield and down to Tatton's yard. However, the Down'ards were to be thwarted again. Upon reaching Clifton Mill, they were overwhelmed by Up'ards who forced the ball back to Mayfield Road. Play ended in the streets of the town at midnight with no goals scored this year. At the Committee meeting in the following October it was agreed that in future play should end at 10.00pm.

Other News

During the World Cup, the West German football team were based at the Peveril of the Peak Hotel at Thorpe. Mr Jack Smith presented a Shrovetide ball he had made to Herr Ludwig Franz Meremberg. He also gave three new leather panels cut to size, cork, wax, thread, needles and awl. The gifts were to be housed in the Football Museum, Zeppelinalle, Frankfurt.

1967

Three Balls In One Day

For the first time in 71 years, three goals were scored in one day and all at Clifton. This is the only time in recorded history that three goals have been scored in one day at the same goal, although an old player stated that five goals had been scored in one year in Victorian times.

Things started off when Mr Sam Longson turned up the ball. It quickly reached the river near to Back Bridge. Play went downstream and the ball was thrown out at Dig Street. It then went up Victoria Square and Union Street to Shakespeare Court where Ray Storer took possession and did a runner, goaling the ball within 40 minutes of the delayed start of 2.15pm. Jack Smith turned up the second ball and this went up into Fish Pond Meadow. It went into the pond and 17-year-old Roger Kornychy swam across the pond with it, throwing it clear at the other side. The hug continued up the valley when the ball became loose and was kicked and played back to the town. Peter Harrison took the ball down the old railway and scored the second goal at the alleged time of 4.55pm.

It was noted that the ball had been seen passing through the bus station at 4.52pm, but the Committee allowed another ball because of the late start. Mr Ken Wood turned up the third ball which went into Park Road and then Cokayne Avenue. The ball became loose and Bill Hellaby dropped it over into the Recreation Ground. It was picked up by Alec Smith who managed to get away undetected. With other Down'ards in support, he went via Seven Arches and Bell's Pastures to Mayfield Road and Doles Farm. Scouts went ahead to create a diversion and a hug crowded around what they thought was the ball. When the coast was clear, Alec Smith went to the goal at about 8.00pm according to the local paper, but see below.

The third ball of Shrove Tuesday was the last to be scored that day at Clifton. It was the last to be goaled by hitting the structure of Clifton Mill and the first time the church was depicted on the ball when it was subsequently painted for the goaler, Alec Smith. Alec asserts that he goaled the ball at about 7.40pm – earlier than reported. Three goals in 5 hours and 40 minutes was a great day by any standards. Much of Clifton Mill had been demolished by Nestlé prior to the game and only the back wall of the wheel pit remained. After Shrovetide, the wall was demolished and Herbert Plumbly provided the stone for the plinth which still stands on the site of the wheelpit.

A Goalless Day

The Rev F J H Lisemore, the Ashbourne vicar turned up the Wednesday ball. It was played over a wide area and had not been goaled by 10.00pm when it was handed in. After being turned up the ball soon went into the Henmore. It went under Compton Bridge and was played in the water for 30 minutes. It was then landed but was thrown back into the river off the bridge. Play then went back into Shaw Croft where eventually there was a break and the action moved into The Park. However, both sides were evenly matched and the ball remained ungoaled.

1968

Mini Shrovetide

The games for this year had been cancelled because of foot and mouth disease restrictions. However, Don Lowndes of Kniveton organised a game within the bounds of the recreation ground football pitch. Shortly after 2.00pm Lowndes and other stalwarts walked from town up to the pitch. The north goalpost would be the Up'ards goal and the south goalpost would act for the Down'ards. If there was no score by 5.00pm he would reclaim the ball. After the usual singing, the ball was turned up. The game was confined to the bounds of the pitch and many youngsters took part. At 3.55pm, four players got the ball to the Down'ard goal. Here, Frank Mitchell goaled the ball by knocking it on the post three times. He was assisted by Terry Weston, Derek Bullock and Louis Godfrey. After the goaling, Mitchell said that he would give the ball to be thrown up again on the Wednesday, to be played for in the same manner as on the Tuesday.

A true Shrovetide ball was used, made by Percy Chadwick and for which Don Lowndes had paid £7.00. The police and the Committee had been consulted prior to the game. Don made the point that it was a pity that the Committee had not done this themselves and went on to suggest that 'this might have been done if some true Shrovetiders had been members'. He was elected to the Committee a few days later. He had scored three goals in his time and was to be referred to later by Jimmy Grant as 'Mr Shrovetide himself'. After the game, Committee secretary Arthur Froggatt stated that he did not think the goal could be officially recorded. The Committee took the point about new members; at the meeting on 06/03/1968 they also appointed John P Gadsby and Alec Robinson.

The Committee's decision to abandon the game had been made in the light of the *Foot and Mouth (temporary restriction) Order 1967* which did not expire until 31/03/1968 and which effectively did not give the Committee any choice. On the Wednesday, the ball was turned up and a considerable number of goals were scored.

The full story of the alternative game has never been fully told: Ernie Grant refused to accept that a game should not be played. He was minded to turn up a ball and had arranged to turn up one from the upstairs window of The Vaults in the Market Place.

Ernie had to conceal his ball. He upturned the spare wheel in his car and increased the space beneath to create enough space to hide the ball. Incredibly his car was searched twice by the police. It seems it was well known he had the ball concealed – possibly in his car – but its whereabouts remained undisturbed. A week before Shrovetide, Ernie was still going ahead, but was persuaded to let Don Lowndes turn up his ball on the football pitch at Boothby Meadows (pers. comm.).

Initially, Don met with some reluctance from the Committee to assist him in organising his mini-Shrovetide. Percy Chadwick had initially declined to make a ball because the Committee had not sanctioned it. Don asked Alec Smith if his brother Jack would be prepared to help, but in any event, he (Alec) assured Don that he had one he could use if necessary. The local paper carried no report of the play on Wednesday. Jack Smith had made a brief note, which indicates that the Tuesday ball was turned up again by Jack Atkinson (an insurance agent of Spen Lane, Thorpe). It was goaled again by Frank Mitchell. It was thrown up again and this time goaled by Joey Waring for the Up'ards, who afterwards threw the ball back into play, to be turned up again. Play continued until 4.45pm when Frank Mitchell gave the ball back to Don Lowndes, who said he would hang it in his pub at Wirksworth.

1969

Goal Null And Void

The first ball was turned up by the 7th Earl of Yarborough, past president of the East Midlands area of the British Legion. The paper (ANT 13/02/1969) stated that it was the centenary year of the use of Shaw Croft, but this is now known to be incorrect. Within minutes the ball was in the water and lost. In actual fact it had been spirited away up the White Hart Yard and into Church Street. Ray Storer gained possession in Smith's Yard and the ball went up to Belle Vue Road and on to Dark Lane and the fields opposite the cemetery. It was hugged on the old railway line before a break saw the ball arrive in Clifton at about 3.00pm. Indecision as to who should goal the ball saw too many Up'ards arrive and it was 90 minutes later before the goal was scored. In the meantime, the ball took an outing as far as the Council Estate and the golf course. The goaler was Ray Storer. This ball remains largely with its elegant paint work intact.

A second ball was turned up by Harry Blow, British Legion Derbyshire Chairman. It was played in the streets between 5.00 and 6.00pm and then vanished. At 10.00pm Peter 'Pop' Robotham arrived in town claiming a goal at Clifton. However, mechanical transport had been used by "Pop" during play, and the goal was declared null and void by the Committee. He had not used the transport to get to the goal, but was penalised whether or not. He had lost a ball in 1957 in the Sturston wheel pit. Now he had lost another. However, 'Pop' was to get his ball in 1997, see below.

Two Balls Again

Coun. Dennis Moore turned up the Wednesday ball which was quickly hugged into the icy river. It was landed but was soon in the Fish Pond. Among those in the water were Don Lowndes and Jimmy

Grant with many younger men including John and Jim Grant, David and George Handley, Reg Purdy, Ian Bates and Philip Tomlinson. Well, at least the paper called them all younger men! A break saw the ball heading for The Green. Frank Lomas had it and with two other players, he took it up the Punch, with four Down'ards in pursuit. It was nearing 4.30pm and there was insufficient time for the Down'ards to get to Clifton. It was decided to allow a Sturston goal and claim another ball. Frank Lomas then goaled his first ball. Mr Jack Atkinson turned up the second one. Throughout the evening it was played in Compton and near to the bus station. Stalemate continued and at 10.00pm the game was abandoned, the ball being handed in at the Green Man Hotel.

1970
Ernie's Effort Gets Its Reward

Lord Cullen of Ashbourne – Charles B M Cokayne – turned up the Tuesday ball. Twenty minutes after starting play, the ball reached the Henmore in Fish Pond Meadow. Waterplay was short lived and the ball returned to Park Road and then St John Street. By 3.20pm, the hug was against the Coach and Horses in Dig Street. A break came with the ball taken quickly to Clifton Road via Station Street. The ball was taken down the old railway line to within 200 yards of Clifton goal where the Up'ards were waiting. In the play at this time were Ray Storer, Peter Gadsby, Jimmy Clarke, Mick Betteridge jnr, Paul Armstrong and Herbert Smith. Play left Clifton and was carried off, reaching Okeover Park before returning to Mayfield Road. Attempts to hide the ball in a barn and then a house failed and in the early evening the ball was played down Dove House Green, through the Market Place to Victoria Square. Ernie and John Grant and the two Etches brothers from Aldwark took to the river and stayed there – all the way to Clifton. Landing the ball near to the goal a hug ensued before Ernie Grant was allowed to score at 9.35pm.

The above local newspaper report of the Tuesday goaling is incorrect (pers. comm. Ernie Grant). In the evening, a group of players were in the water near Compton. There were some 22 players in all. Ernie Grant enquired loudly "how many Up'ards are there?" There were three and the Down'ards were hugging against themselves!

The Down'ards set off down river for Clifton, with Ernie carrying the ball. The main obstacles, other than the river itself, were the temperature (it was -7°F) and the weir at Nestlé. This was/is a notorious obstacle. Clearing this cost Ernie seven cracked ribs one year (and he played the next day). The Etches brothers left the river at this point, re-entering below the weir. Four Down'ards kept to the river the whole way, with Ernie carrying the ball to Clifton. It was, in fact, the last time this happened. No one has carried the ball from Shaw Croft along the river course to the goal since then.

Arriving at Clifton, the river was full and the mill weir had not been removed. There was no alternative than to swim across the former mill pond – and this was after they had been wading chest deep through silt and water, ice forming on layer of ice each time as they surfaced from beneath the water. It was arranged that the last man to hold the ball should goal it – and it was Ernie Grant. Having swam across the former millpond, the last few yards was a solid mass of people, including not a few Up'ards. Ernie's uncle – Jimmy Grant and Guy Harrison punched their way through the opposition to allow Ernie to reach the goal.

Unfortunately, although the goal was allowed by John Gadsby, it was subsequently queried on the grounds that the ball had not hit the plinth three times. Objections were, however, over-ruled by the Committee and the goaling prevailed.

Another Runaway Brings A Goal At Sturston

Mr Arthur Parry turned up the second day ball, throwing it towards the water. Play moved upriver before the ball broke free with Pip Plumbly and Jim Boden in the forefront. The ball was played in Park Road before Don Lowndes threw it over Back Bridge and into the river. Eventually, a break occurred with Paul and John Armstrong taking the ball to Sturston via Bradley Wood. Some 200 yards from the goal, they were dispossessed and Down'ards set off for the Ketch. They were almost there when Paul Armstrong reclaimed the ball. The Derbyshire AAA 800m and 1500m Youth Champion quickly turned for Sturston and before only a dozen or so spectators, goaled the ball at 4.30pm. A second ball was turned up by George Bradley, a Committee member. It was played around the streets until around 6.45pm when it was taken upstream to the top of Fish Pond Meadow. Play came back and was up against the fire station doors when the alarm went off and the crowd parted to allow the fire engine to leave. Play continued in the streets until just after 10.00pm, when the ball was handed in at the Green Man Hotel.

1971

The Shaw Croft Culvert

Col Peter Hilton, High Sheriff of Derbyshire, turned up the first ball. It was the first game since the river had been culverted across Shaw Croft as part of a £60,000 flood prevention scheme. Shaw Croft, now owned by the Ashbourne Council and part of their proposed central area redevelopment proposal, was a sea of mud. The ball headed for Park Road, which had been realigned, including the loss of Back Bridge. The ball was soon in the river, followed by Don Lowndes, Joe and Guy Harrison, Jim Boden, Andrew and Keith Birch, Charles and George Handley, Ernie Grant, Pip Plumbly, Barry Whittle and others. Water play ended with a rush downstream and into the right hand culvert for the first time. Although play reached Bank Croft, it quickly returned through the culvert and upriver to Sturston. Paul Armstrong had the ball as the players reached the mill, but this year he had opposition ahead of him. A decision was made to back track from Sturston. Down'ards then obtained the ball and brought it back to town via Corley and close to Kniveton. The ball came into town along Green Road and was played through the town for the remaining four hours of play, without being goaled.

A Late Break And Goal For The Down'ards

Mr Arthur Birch started Wednesday's proceedings. A break saw the ball go to where the river used to be – was this habit? – before it moved off to the Fish Pond. The ball crossed the waterfall between the two ponds and went through a garden to reach Park Avenue. The ball went on to Belper Road but returned to Shaw Croft via Park Road and Birch's yard. Play went up Dig Street and went through town to reach the Henmore from the Recreation Ground. Although some progress towards Sturston was made and there were several breaks, play returned to town. Here it remained for most of the evening. The ball was pushed along Compton and up the old Derby Road and at about 9.30pm there was a break. David Coxon passed the ball to John Tomkinson who ran with John Gregory through the Dockey Fields with the ball. They went down the old railway track to Clifton only to be met by John Mansfield, Pete Robotham, Mike Betteridge and others. However, the two Johns were allowed to toss for it and John Tompkinson took the honour at 9.52pm, eight minutes before the deadline.

1972

Power Cuts And A Sowter Goal At Sturston

There was plenty of news about this year's games. Play only lasted until 7.00pm on Wednesday so that people could get home before the expected power cut at 8.00pm (during the notorious three-day week). A Sowter goaled a ball for the first time in 22 years. It was the family's 21st ball since 1898. However, Doug Sowter goaled at Sturston, leaving old stalwarts shaking their heads with disbelief. His grandfather, father, sister, uncles and second cousins all scored theirs at Clifton!

Shaw Croft was now surfaced and a car park. The ball was turned up by Mr A E Sevier of Hulland Hall and within thirty minutes was in the Henmore near the top end of the culvert. It left here for a while and went via the recreation ground and Park Road to return to the icy waters of the river. The ball was thrown out at about 3.15pm and suddenly a group had hared off across the Grammar School fields, up to Windmill Lane and on to the Seven Arches. They emerged at Sandybrook and proceeded across the top of Punch, eventually reaching Sturston where lots were drawn to decide on the goaler. Doug Sowter pulled the shortest stick. He had carried the ball for most of the way. His father, Sam, declined to make any real comment when interviewed afterwards only to say he would never have done it!

Another ball was turned up by Albert Slingsby, licensee of the Meynell Arms, Kirk Langley. It was pushed up Madge's Hill and down to Compton. From here, it went to the Paddock with Pop Allcock, Brian Harrison, Philip Tomlinson and Philip Chell in prominent play. The ball returned to Compton and there was a break along Station Street and then up the Dockey Fields. The runners swung around towards Clifton Road and headed down the old railway track towards Clifton. At 9.33pm Jimmy Clarke, who had played hard all day and had been in the chase to Seven Arches and beyond, goaled the ball at the plinth.

Down'ards Within Yards Of Two Goals

On Wednesday J H Wheeldon started play. The ball moved to Belper Road via Park Road and Park Avenue. Play pushed on to Compton and reached the river at Bank Croft. It was thrown out and reached Station Street by Cooper's factory. The ball was carried down to Nestlé where a hug occurred. From here, play returned to the river across the site of the railway sidings at about 4.40pm. The ball was soon banked and ran by David Bates to Clifton. Although he was brought down at Cleaver's Crossing on the old railway, he regained possession and after drawing lots with Ian Bates goaled the ball with five minutes to go, helped by George Handley (an Up'ard). Mr Gordon Wheatcroft turned up the second ball at 5.45pm and it was moved into Compton. Daylight had gone and a break occurred leaving many people unaware of what had happened. The ball was whisked away up Church Street past the parish church and down the railway line to Clifton. A group of players were within yards of scoring when the ball was taken back towards the town again. At 7.00pm it had still not been scored and was returned to the Green Man Hotel at 7.30pm.

1973

Another Goal Disallowed

There was a last minute drama on the Tuesday when a Clifton goal was disallowed. Sgt Walter Turner had seen the ball in Coxon's Yard at 9.57pm and that was enough for the Committee. Mr Charles Harpur-Crewe turned up the first ball, which was pushed over into the recreation ground and then into the river. Progress was made slowly upstream with the ball being thrown from player to player. Play went up the valley to within 400 yards of Sturston Mill. However, Paul Armstrong and Ron Astbury ran off with the ball in the direction of the town. Play went up into Windmill Lane before the players emerged halfway down the Punch. Here Peter Gadsby obtained the ball by leaping from a van to seize it. The ball came back to the Market Place at about 5.15pm and it was played down Dig Street to The Paddock. The hug pushed the leather (claimed by some to be softer this year) down Station Road and Church Street and into Dig Street again, having taken 2½ hours to make the circuit. Further street play saw the time tick away towards 10.00pm and the close of play, after which the dash to Clifton was made.

Up'ards Foiled In An Attempt To Equalise

The Wednesday ball was turned up by Councillor George Peach, and had to be turned up twice. Having been turned up without the singing of the National Anthem or 'Auld Lang Syne', it was returned and thrown up again. This time, the ball got away and reached Park Road past the foundations of the new Council flats and into Fish Pond Meadow. However, it soon came back to reach the bus station and the old railway station site. It moved on behind Nestlé to reach Mayfield Road where it was hugged towards Clifton. There was to be no quick goal and the ball entered the river for 90 minutes. Here, Nigel Wright, Andy Birch, Billy Webster, John Grant, George Peach Jnr., Doug Sowter, Peter Gadsby and others were in the thick of things.

George Peach Snr., was pushed into the river at this point and stayed there to join the game. However, he was not the first thrower to join the water play as the paper indicated – that used to be a frequent event 75 years previously. At 4.15pm the struggle had reached Clifton and was only ten yards from the goal. Straws were drawn – despite strenuous opposition from Simon and Pip Plumbly and Jim Boden, John Grant won and took the honour.

Bill Knight turned up a second ball and this also went upwards, reaching the river near to the playing fields. It nearly reached Sturston Mill before there was a breakaway and the ball went over to Bradley Wood. After staying here for a while, it went off again but time ran out before the ball could be goaled.

Overheard during this year's game (ANT 08/03/1973):

In Fish Pond Meadow: 'Mummy will all those men in the water get into trouble when they get home?'

In St John Street: 'Do they have to stop when the light is on red?'

On the fringe of the hug: 'If you go in there you will be knocked down, trampled on and crushed.'

1974

Down'ards Thwarted Thirty Feet From Their Goal

On a very mild day, Lt Col JRG Stanton of Snelston turned up the first ball. It quickly disappeared into the culvert for 30 minutes, reappearing by Compton Bridge. At Bank Croft the ball was landed and went up Tyler and Coates' yard to Church Street where a hug formed. Play went back into town and returned to Shaw Croft via the new path down Horse and Jockey Yard. It left for St John Street through a garden and then the hug visited the conversion work at Boots' shop. From here, play went to Fish Pond Meadow where Pip Plumbly stumbled into the pond which was chest deep. Others followed and they all swam along the bank until Colin Morfitt struck out for the opposite side. As 5.00pm drew nearer, play crossed through gardens in the Park estate and a break came at 6.40pm when Mike Betteridge Jnr, John Smith, Ron Astbury and another set off at a pace and reached Nestlé undetected. They hid for a long time before proceeding to Clifton via the golf course. Through the garden of Mr and Mrs Pugh they went and reaching the plinth, managed to strike the ball once only. Up'ard pressure forced the ball up Cock Hill and then on to Cross Side, where it was returned to the goal. It was ten yards away when the 10.00pm deadline was reached.

Play At The Ketch

Don Lowndes proudest day arrived on the Wednesday as he turned up the ball. It was the crowning moment of a distinguished Shrovetide career. The ball was soon in the culvert from the upper end and passed quickly through. Play carried on down until the church field was reached. Here, a little before 5.00pm, the ball was thrown out. It was quickly taken from the field up Church Banks and over to the Tissington Trail. By a circuitous route the players reached the Ketch. In the play were Doug Sowter, Ron Astbury, Ray Storer, Frank Lomas, Robin Gallimore, Mick Bailey, John Stubbs, Bill Hellaby, Don Startin, Bob Bates and Brian Thornley. There was a break away from the Ketch at 6.00pm. Various ruses were made to throw others off the scent and eventually Robin Gallimore, David Bates and others went with the ball over to the Buxton and Mappleton Roads, around the sewerage works and onto Clifton golf course. Other players now included John Tomkinson, Bob Bates, Jim Massey, David Coxon, Bob Crane and Philip Walwyn. They were thwarted in their attempt to score and a hug formed at the goal at 9.00pm. Robin Gallimore and Ian Bates tossed for the goal. The latter won at his sixth attempt to win a toss or draw the right straw and it was his third in successive years. Robin had carried the ball all the way from the Ketch but dropped it within sight of his goal!

During the year Mr J E Gadsby retired as chairman and was succeeded by his son J P Gadsby.

1975

Successful Up'ards Break From Mayfield Road

Brian Clough the Derby County manager turned up the first ball before an enormous crowd. The ball went up before the usual ceremonies, Mr Clough being anxious for the safety of some young children. The ball was not returned as in 1974 and was soon in Park Road and then into the culvert. It appeared at the south end and went on down stream, going under Station Road at 4.30pm. In play at this time were Philip Tomlinson, the Hardy brothers – Robert, Jim and Peter, Jim Grant, Jim Breeze, Jim Boden, Derek Griffiths, Robert Bott, Robert Todd, Mick Baldy, Ernie Grant, Pip Plumbly, Frankie Mitchell and Nigel Wright.

The ball left the water at The Mansion and was taken through the garden into School Lane. It was then ran up into Mayfield Road, heading for Clifton. With others in pursuit, they were caught prior to another break towards Clifton. This was turned and players were strung out over 100 yards. A hug reformed on Mayfield Road and in the dark and rain after 6.00pm, yet another break occurred. Doug Sowter and a mate hid with the ball in the Bentley Brook until the coast was clear. Crossing the Dove, they proceeded around by Mappleton Wood, Callow Wood and Tanyard Farm to Sandybrook. Proceeding up the valley, the dozen or so players reached the top of The Punch and dropped down towards Sturston Mill. Here they were met by George Handley who was allowed to goal the ball.

Girls In The Hug

Drama ended a day that had started when Mr John Shemilt turned up the Wednesday ball. The ball made its usual course in recent years to Park Road and into The Park. The ball was soon in the pond where Andy Birch pushed it across. It then reached the river and culvert, the Down'ards pushing it quickly through. In the hug briefly were Julie Edge, Cathy Fourtune and Shirley Avery. Play continued down and was soon at Nestlé where play continued in waist deep water as the lock gates were approached. However, Bob Hudson and John Grant stopped the surge down stream and there was a large number battling it out in the river. Ian Bates landed the ball at 4.00pm when it moved into School Lane. There was a break at 4.20pm and the play soon transferred to the front of the Clifton Hotel (now Beresford Hotel). Colin Burton raced away after 30 minutes to reach the fields beyond The Park. His hope of reaching Sturston was thwarted by Down'ards who returned to town via the airfield and Derby Old Road. Play moved around the streets and the ball was ran off at 9.45pm and goaled at Clifton. However, it was taken by car and the goal was disallowed.

An excess of enthusiasm on the Wednesday was to have consequences more profound than anyone could have realised when the ball was in School Lane. The ball went over into the garden of Miss Kathleen Hollick. She was prevented from throwing the ball back and the people who invaded her garden caused damage, which she found unacceptable. The Committee had always regarded itself as not being responsible for any damage caused during play and repeated this message annually in the local paper. Miss Hollick's solicitors called for the regulation of the game so that the damage to her garden and the invasion of her privacy did not happen again.

1976

Public Meetings

After the problems of the previous year, a public meeting was called by the Committee on 11th February. At an earlier meeting called by the West Derbyshire District Council, the Chief Constable made a statement to the effect that unless a stricter control was maintained over the behaviour of the footballers, steps would be taken, if all else failed, to apply for an injunction to prevent football being played at Shrovetide. John Gadsby made the point that: "if we are to continue to enjoy the goodwill of the various authorities, it is incumbent upon us to respect the attitudes of everyone concerned, irrespective of our agreeing with them." He went on: "This of course, does not mean that we should in any way surrender the right to maintain our wonderful heritage, indeed we should be failing in our duty to our predecessors if we allowed the game to change basically from the way it has been played for centuries. Both players and spectators should at all times conduct themselves in a sportsmanlike and civilised manner, causing as little interference and obstruction as possible and no damage whatsoever."

A good cross-section of views were heard but the consensus seemed to be that the responsible majority would ensure that the game was not jeopardised. This in fact proved to be the case. This public meeting, called by the Committee, was followed by another called by the District Council. Some 150 supporters were present plus George Peach, Chairman of the District Council and a goaler in 1935, Mr R Bubb, the Council Chief Executive and Mr W Stanfield, the Chief Constable. The latter made it clear that he did not want to be put on record as making threats against the game. Indignation was expressed that the St Oswald's Parochial Church Council had written asking the police and those playing to keep the game out of the churchyard. The indignation was understandable.

The very essence of the fact that the players were responsible people was indicated by the fact that the unwritten rule concerning no play in the churchyard, cemetery or memorial gardens was always respected. Coun Moore expressed the view, as a member of the PCC, that they should not have taken advantage of the situation to write the letter. Later the police opposed the granting of pub liquor licence extensions for the two days, but their objection was overruled by the Bench.

Down'ards Denied by Indecision

The Tuesday ball was turned up by Lord Hives. Although the ball was only feet from Clifton goal within 30 minutes and there was a last minute break also, the day remained goal-less. It also remained damage free; the lessons and the appeals were heeded. The ball went into Park Road, with Grace Sowter pushing hard for the Up'ards along side the men. There was a break at 2.20pm and the ball was run to Clifton down the railway line. Steve Challinor drew the straw to goal the ball, but a dispute arose and the ball was thrown into the Henmore.

Despite efforts of the Down'ards, the ball started moving back towards town, if only slowly. At 4.10pm the ball was back near to the goal, but then the pressure increased and at 5.30pm play was in Mayfield Road on the outskirts of town. At 7.00pm there were over 500 people crammed into the road and the ball was slowly pushed to Church Street and then St John Street. An hour later the hug reached Shaw Croft before veering into The Park. The break occurred at 9.00pm. Peter Harrison gathered the leather from the pond and ran the ball back to Clifton. Incredibly the same indecision happened again and the deadline passed with the ball ungoaled.

No Goals Again

For only the third time since 1891 there were no goals on either day (the other two years were 1932 and 1961). Norman Moore turned up the ball. It was pushed into the river near Park Road and slung into the culvert at 2.37pm. It came out at the Sturston end. The play was in the river for 30 minutes and then moved over to the pond. The ball had an outing across the water and after being landed was brought back across the pond before returning to the river. Just after 5.00pm there was a break and the ball went through a garden and into Beresford Avenue. Fortunately only a few followed, the rest kept to the adjacent stile. The ball was, however, stopped in Park Avenue and hugged back to Shaw Croft and then through Dig Street to Church Street.

Here Keith Smith emerged from the hug to report that he had smelt whiskey, rum, silage and cow manure in the hug before, but never after-shave! Soon afterwards, he looked down to see the ball at his feet. Picking it up, it seemed that only a couple of girls knew he had it. With Barbara Brindley on one side of him and Helen Chadwick on the other he was moving away nicely but was rumbled. The ball did break loose in the last hour and was lost. It was still there – Bill Hellaby was sitting on it but Guy Harrison spotted it. Play continued in Clifton Road until the ball was tipped into the river by Gordon Cresswell. He and Paul Armstrong ran the ball up Belle Vue Road and onto Windmill Lane before they realised that the deadline had beaten them and they returned the leather to the Green Man Hotel.

1977

Fourth Successive No Goal

The first ball was turned up by Mr Anthony Bamford, Chairman and Chief Executive of J C Bamford Excavators Ltd. A relative, T H B Bamford, had turned up the ball on four previous occasions. The ball was closely hugged into Park Road and over to the fire station before going into Fish Pond Meadow and then the pond. In the water were Robert Woolley, Jim Breeze, Tom Poxon, Pop Robotham, Harvey Brown and Billy Webster. Just before 3.00pm, the venue changed to the river, which was in flood and waist deep. Play went down with the current and into the culvert. Upon reaching the Compton end, the ball was thrown into the White Hart yard and for many that was the last they saw of play. From Church Street, Stephen Challinor obtained the ball and it was run via Dove House Green and North Avenue down to Seven Arches where it was hugged for a while. Play crossed over to Sandybrook and then to the top side of Fenny Bentley, where the players with the ball hid, awaiting darkness, when they made for Sturston.

The pre-game lunch and visitors (continued)

Guest of Honour at the lunch with their ball: Sir John FitzHerbert in 1980 (above) and Viscount Tamworth in 1987 (below) with Lord Lieut., Col. Sir Peter Hilton & Lady Hilton

Turning up the ball

The 1933 ball rising in the air, explaining why it is traditionally referred to as 'turned-up'. The ball appears as though it is above the trees. Balls were smaller and lighter then. Behind is the Bath House, once the town's public bath for those who did not have one at home

Charles Turpie on the knoll where the ball used to be turned-up. It was situated (roughly) where the entrance to Shaw Croft car park was constructed. It had been removed years before, however

Darren Waring showing his ball, goaled the day before, to the lunch guests, on Ash Wednesday, 1996

Middle: Mayor of Ashbourne, Alan Hodkinson with his wife, Angela, and the 2000 Wednesday ball prior to the lunch where he introduced the turner-up, Philip Tomlinson

John Hanson addressing lunch guests. His player-escort stand patiently behind him. The mobiles record scorers and turners-up

The Chief Constable, Mr John Newing, leaves the Green Man Hotel, 1998 for the plinth with the Tuesday ball. It was goaled by A Etherington

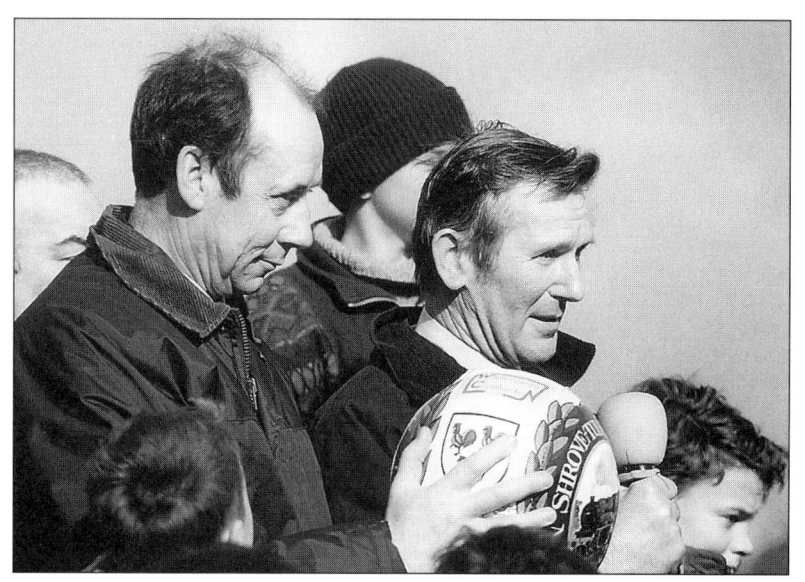

Two views of the old plinth with George Ward and his ball in 1995 (above) and Brell Ewatt (left) a year later. The balls were goaled by J Tomlinson and D Waring respectively

Turning up the 2nd balls: above: Harold Sherratt in 1990; below: Gerald Shepherd in 1993

Goaling

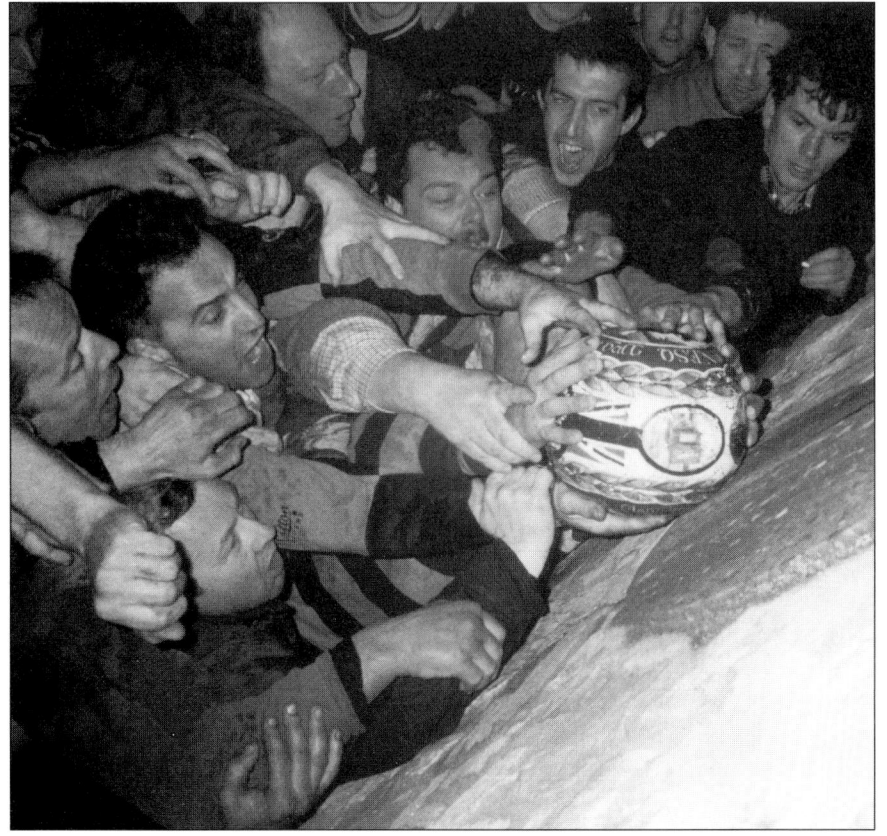

Photographs of goaling are not common. Here in this section are a few. Above: Steve Hudson at Clifton, 1989, goaling on the wooden post below the footbridge. Below: The Ash Wednesday goal, 2000, scored by Paul Harrison, the last goal of the millennium

The new plinth opened in 1999 by Lady Hilton. The plinth bears the date 1998. With Lady Hilton is the Shrovetide Committee and the Ashbourne Mayor, Mr A Birch

John Hanson and Philip Tomlinson, turners-up for 2000, on the plinth on Shrove Tuesday of that year

The atmosphere of the Ash Wednesday, 2000, goal is captured on this view from the Clifton footbridge

Andrew Etherington goaling the 1998 Tuesday ball turned up by the Chief Constable Mr John Newing

Nick Fearn goaling at Sturston. The ball was turned up by the Lord Lieutenant, Mr J Bather on Tuesday 1999

2001

Foot & Mouth Disease caused the cancellation of the games in 2001. The traditional singing was symbolically held at the plinth and is recorded here on Shrove Tuesday

Above: Paul Harrison and Down'ards after goaling the ball on Ash Wednesday, 2000

Two views of Mark Spencer upon returning to the town after scoring his ball on Shrove Tuesday, 2000

A large number of people turned up for the event

Keith Lomas, Ashbourne News Telegraph photographer, Simon Plumbly, 'Pip" Plumbly and Arthur Chadwick on the plinth on the Tuesday

Mayor Simon Spencer, Arthur Chadwick and Mick Betteridge lead the singing on the Wednesday

ASHBOURNE ROYAL SHROVETIDE FOOTBALL

LUNCHEON

TUESDAY, 27th FEBRUARY, 2001

12 noon for 12.15 p.m.

*

TICKET : £15.00

OFFICIAL Announcement

Royal Shrovetide Football 2001 has been.... CANCELLED 26th February....

Tuesday lunch ticket (above); cancellation notice in the Ashbourne News Telegraph window (right). The efforts of these youngsters (below) selling T-shirts were thwarted by the cancellation of the game. More general disappointment even brought tears to some hardened players

Mr F Boden by the former Coach & Horses in Dig Street in 1930

Middle: Mr Mallinson of Cressbrook Hall, a year earlier. He was the Liberal Party candidate for Parliament, for West Derbyshire

Mr Hayes of Froghall who turned up the Wednesday, 1935 ball

Heading for the Plinth

Top: Bill Prince addresses the crowd in 1905 or perhaps 1907. The buildings beyond have largely gone

Middle: A large crowd in Dig Street all sporting hats!

Inspector Burton with the Committee in 1921. It was said that this was the first time that a Burton gave a ball to a Sowter, as Sam Sowter scored it at Clifton!

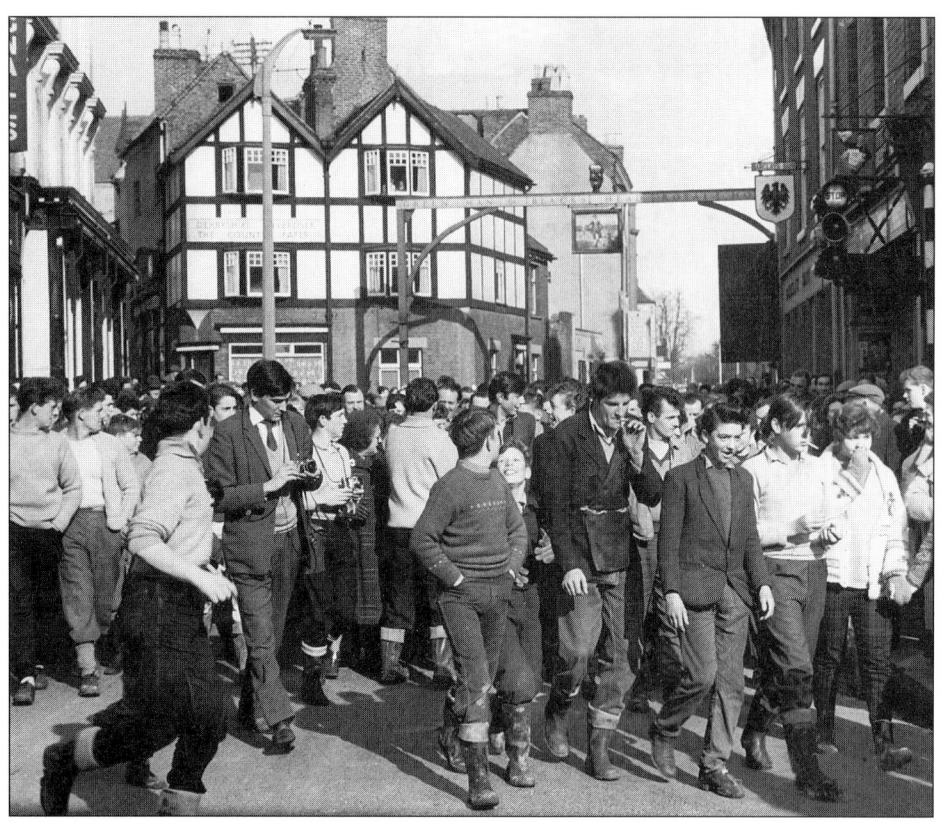

The crowds in 1962, ahead of the ball in St John Street (above) and (below), in Dig Street, heading for Shaw Croft

Despite diversionary tactics, attempts to goal the ball by Harvey Brown and Barry Handley were thwarted and the deadline passed with no goal and for most spectators, no sight of play after 3.50pm either.

A Sturston Goal Breaks The Duck

There was some tremendous play on the Wednesday but the day ended with controversy over the goaling by John Grant. The day started with Fred Hyde turning up the ball, followed by both hugging and open play. After 30 minutes a fast chase took the ball into Park Road and up to St John Street. From here, play moved down to the Green Man and around to Compton Bridge where the ball was tipped into the river. The water was still in spate and play inevitably went down river. The water became deeper, chest deep in fact, as play moved below the swimming pool. Water players included Jack Jones, Steve Kent, Mick Louth and Melvyn Moore.

Near Nestlé, the Up'ards managed to land the ball and a huge hug formed. Some loose play saw the ball reach Mayfield Road just before 5.00pm. The ball started to return to town and at 5.30pm the ball swept down Station Road and into the swimming pool car park. Play continued on to the police station and could have gone both Up or Down at this point. Play moved in favour of the Up'ards and at 6.00pm emerged into Compton where it stayed for over an hour. There were ideas of getting the ball back into the river but at 7.30pm the players realised that the ball was no longer under the hug. The ball was taken by 'Pop' Robotham, who raced for Sturston with Sid Sellers, Herbert Smith, Paul Armstrong, Steve Challinor and others.

'Mechanical means' moved opposition to Sturston as quick, if not quicker, than the players, who of course were denied such a convenience. A hug pushed and heaved outside the mill. There was a diversion and all of a sudden the ball was gone. Two lads named Bates and Tomkinson had run the ball to Clifton. There was a tustle at Clifton and at the goal were Cecil Challinor, John Grant Snr., and John Grant Jnr. There was a dispute and it was agreed that Philip Tomlinson should goal the ball. However, Philip lost possession and it was picked up by Ian Bates and John Grant.

The ball was then goaled, but who goaled it? John Grant came away from the goal with the ball and as John Gadsby put it – possession was nine parts of the law. There was an opinion amongst some players that the goal should be declared void, because no one had sufficient control of the ball. The Committee decided to award the goal to John Grant, after considering all the factors. As on many other occasions, those who brought it from Sturston felt somewhat aggrieved at being denied a goal. However, Shrovetide football is an individual game, not a team effort. Even a runner may get stopped by his own side, let alone the opposition. It can be every man for himself. There can be few other games where friends in 363 days of the year, can spend the other two days in a desperate struggle to help their 'team' win and yet in the moment of triumph, deny the worthy victor a goal in the pursuit of self interest.

1978

Sportsmanship from Paul Armstrong

Capt Peter Walker-Okeover turned up yet another of Sandra Church's distinctively painted balls, made by her father, Arthur Chadwick. Some 40 minutes later, the ball reached Dig Street and went up to Church Street. Someone opened the closed gates to the White Hart yard and in went the hug, down towards the Henmore where the ball was eventually tipped into the water. Up'ard's pressure saw the ball go into the culvert, but it soon returned only to be thrown up into Dig Street. Play returned to Church Street and Station Road where the break came at about 6.00pm which resulted in the Down'ards scoring their first Tuesday goal since 1972.

Harvey Brown picked up the ball near to the bus station and ran a short distance before passing the ball to Paul Armstrong. With him were Stephen Challinor, Steven Mitchell and Perry Weise. The latter dropped out above the Fish Pond. Approaching Sturston they drew for the right to goal the ball and Paul won. Stephen reminded him that he had already goaled a ball and Paul sportingly agreed to take it to Clifton. Taking tea at Bill and Marion Abbott's en route, they continued to Clifton via Seven Arches and Bell's Pastures. The ball was hidden near to the old coal yard at Clifton's former station.

Steven Mitchell went to look for Stephen's father Cecil, who returned with Jimmy Clarke. Cecil walked to the goal with the ball up the back of his jumper and with Jimmy behind him. At the plinth, out came the ball and Stephen Challinor tapped the stone three times at about 7.30pm. Much of the ball's paint work was still intact. Sportsmanship prevailed as a seasoned Up'ard helped a young Down'ard to goal rather than score himself.

Armstrong Denied Again, This Time by The Deadline

Mr Ken Ward turned up the Ash Wednesday ball and Steve Kent was hoisted high by fellow players to grab it down into the hug. However, within minutes, the ball had broken loose onto Park Road before being pushed into the river at about 3.00pm. The ball was hugged and then broke downstream before Philip Tomlinson, Mick Hydes, and Stephen Gallimore ran it into the culvert. The ball was thrown into Bank Croft where it was hugged for 30 minutes before returning to the river. Another break saw the ball thrown into a yard, emerging near to the Corner House. Paul Armstrong had the leather and along with Doug Sowter and others, the ball was quickly taken via Dove House Green to the fields behind North Avenue. They were met as they headed for Sandybrook and a hug formed. The Up'ards, still in possession, headed for Mappleton Road and then on to Okeover.

Another hug formed which heaved its way down Birdsgrove Lane to Swinscoe Hill. In the darkness, the ball was hugged down to the bridge and along Mayfield Road towards town. With snow falling, the hug went into the fields towards Clifton before rejoining the road. Just after 8.00pm the ball went loose and was found only several hundred yards from the Clifton goal in George Peach's fields. It was turned 9.30pm when an Up'ards break came. Peter Gadsby and Terry Weston had the ball and hid in Fred Harrison's yard, undecided as to what to do. Time ticked on and even though Cambridge Blue Paul Armstrong took the ball, he could not reach Sturston before 10.00pm, arriving 15 minutes too late.

1979

So Near Yet Again

Mr Denys Johnson started proceedings on an icy day with the river swollen. The hug made for Dig Street after about 30 minutes, proceeding around to the old railway bridge in Church Street. Here the ball was thrown over on to the former line where a few players stood anticipating the move. A break was foiled and the hug went into the tunnel. However, play moved back to the Henmore and Stephen Bott threw the ball into the river. Down by the church the river was chest deep, but Reg Purdy, Steve Kent, Stephen Bott, Mick Pepper, Andrew White, Melvyn Moore and Ernie Grant were undeterred. Steve Kent was dragged out of the water near to Nestlé with his shoulder out of joint. The water pulled both ball and players along until a visitor jumped into the water and landed the leather.

Children kicked the ball back into the river and Up'ards runners seized their chance, Geoff Harrison, John Stubbs and John Easton running to Mayfield Road where they were stopped. The hug made towards Clifton once more, down Mayfield Road and then across the fields to Green Lane. There was a break at Doles Farm when Doug Sowter and Don Startin were involved in working the ball clear. The ball was taken by a small group including Harvey Brown, Perry Weise, Stephen Challinor, Jeff Harrison and Anthony Bates, over to the Lichfield Road and up to the old airfield where a draw was made for who was to goal the ball and Perry Weise won. Although they reached Sturston Mill, George Handley told Weise he was a Down'ard and to hand the ball to an Up'ard. In the confusion that followed, most of the players ran off to The Green Road and later made their way to Clifton Golf Course. Their final strategy failed for there were too many Up'ards between them and the goal and Don Lowndes called time denying Anthony Bates' assault with the ball, just a yard short of his target.

Paul Armstrong goaled at Sturston on the Wednesday. It was the first Wednesday goal there since 1971. Mr John Kenny had turned up the ball and play went steadily upwards. In Fish Pond Meadow, play reached the river and went down the culvert. The ball was landed at Bank Croft and play moved around into Compton. Steadily, the hug moved into Station Street, but Up'ards pressure forced things back into Sturston Road. Eventually, play went through the Park estate, surviving various ruses in an attempt to break away. The latter did come when Nick Thornley threw the ball across the river. Paul

Game Reports 1950–2002

Armstrong obtained the ball after running with Martin Keeling and Nick Thornley. The latter passed it on to Paul who ran it towards the river. A newcomer retrieved it from the water, but he was dispossessed quickly and Paul turned for Sturston. With opposition still in the fields and away from their cars, the sprinter quickly brought the ball in to the wheel and goaled the ball around 6.45pm.

1980
Down'ards Run Out Of Time

The Tuesday ball was turned up by Sir John FitzHerbert, of Tissington Hall. It took some time before the ball moved from Shaw Croft and into Fish Pond Meadow, where it went into the river. Play returned to Park Road and worked its way via Sturston Road to Compton and the bus station before heading back to Fish Pond Meadow. After a few breaks in the field, play transferred to the north side of the river. There was then a break and play moved to the grammar school playing field. From here, the ball was hugged along Green Road to Hall Lane and down to Park Road, where it disappeared. Up to this point, the ball had been visable for much of the day. It was rather ironic that it had gone missing for Sir John had expressed the hope over lunch that the ball would not be hidden this year! Still it was 9.30pm, with only 30 minutes to go. What happened to the ball is not reported, but at 9.55pm, it was at the top of Park Road, in the hands of Anthony Bates. He realised he could not get to Clifton and handed the ball in at the Green Man at 10.00pm.

The Wednesday ball was turned up by Charles Etches. He had goaled at Sturston in 1941 and his father, John and uncle, Edwin had goaled in 1900 and 1895 respectively. His father had turned up the ball in 1942. After 20 minutes, the play passed into Park Road and then into the river. Here it stayed until nearly 5.00pm. In the water were Philip Tomlinson and his son John, Andy Birch, Jimmy Breeze, Eric Coates, Mick Baldy, Keith Birch, Ernie Grant, Andrew Adams, Ken Renshaw, Andrew Woodroff, Bob Hardy and Jack Jones. With the 5.00pm deadline only ten minutes away and Sturston Mill only a few fields to go, the ball was landed at last.

The ball went back towards town and at 6.30pm was in Park Road. It was played in the open down Compton before crossing past the bus station to reach Station Road and Clifton Road. A lorry driver mistook the crowds for pickets and enquired who was on strike! There was a break at 8.25pm and Stephen and Charles Mansfield ran the ball from near to Clifton, over the top of old Derby Road and down through Bradley Wood to Sturston Mill. Once inside the mill, they were deprived of the ball after being punched up. Andrew Lemon saw the ball bobbing up and down in the water and tapped it on the wheel three times to claim the goal. Needless to say the Mansfield's felt they should have been allowed to goal it. They clearly felt that having run all the way from Clifton, their claim to the goal was greater than those who arrived by car.

1981
The End Of An Era

Ashbourne had a shock when Sturston Mill was demolished on the eve of Shrovetide. It had last worked in the mid-1940s. Nestlé clearly felt the burden of a potentially unsafe building too great with so many people milling around. The building had only recently reverted to the company on the death of the tenant. The action caused widespread condemnation in the town none-the-less.

The ball was turned up by Bob Taylor the Derbyshire cricketer. The hug moved towards Compton and into the Henmore via Bank Croft. Some 15 players braved the cold water, including several girls. In the middle of things were Andrew Birch and Peter Gadsby. Play remained fairly static in the water until just before 5.00pm when the play entered the culvert. At 6.20pm the ball left the river for the recreation ground. As darkness fell, play had moved on to the football ground, but around 7.00pm it moved back across the gardens to Madge's Hill and into St John Street. Play halted outside the Green Man Hotel when suddenly the ball broke with Geoff Harrison running it down Church Street. He took it all the way to Clifton, maintaining possession despite a hug at the plinth where he eventually goaled it.

The Wednesday ball was turned up by Mr Roger Stevenson of the Green Hall, who had praise for the Committee and its work:

"As far as I can see the Shrovetide Committee has no legal standing, yet they can advise the police to introduce all these young constables – it must be a great education to them to learn that a crowd of people across the centre of the road is not a riot but simply Ashbourne enjoying itself."

His ball was caught by Mike Betteridge who became the centre of a hug. After ten minutes, play had reached Park Road where it entered the Henmore. Among the men was teenager Fiona Parker of Mayfield for the second day running. The game went in and out of the water as it became colder and snow began to fall. By 5.00pm, Up'ards pressure had told a little and play had reached the end of The Park estate. By 6.45pm the ball was within half a mile of the goal when Doug Sowter tunnelled out of the hug with ball, on his hands and knees. The ball broke from the Offcote side of the river, with Gordon Cresswell receiving the ball from Steve Challinor. The former ran with the ball to the top of Bradley Wood before returning to the road with Steve and Paul Armstrong.

Gordon approached the new plinth from Sturston Hall farm with the ball up his jumper, but was rumbled only inches from the goal. A hug was formed which spent the rest of the evening going round and round the plinth until 10.00pm arrived. There was much heated discussion as to whether the ball should be goaled jointly in the name of the rugby club. There was opposition to this – the next goal could be in the name of the WI for instance – but the 10.00pm rule ended play and debate. In the Green Man afterwards a group of the players including Peter Harrison, Colin LeGrice, Bill Hellaby and Doug Sowter all agreed that the evenings play had been the best for years. It was something of a consolation.

1982

Down'ards Delay Spoils Goal Chance

The spindle from the original mill wheel at Sturston was declared the official goal for the Up'ards. The spindle had been erected vertically and surrounded by a stone plinth. 1982 saw the tenth year that Sandra Church, daughter of ball maker Arthur Chadwick, had decorated the balls in their distinctive style. Also during the past year, the Roll of Honour boards in the Green Man Hotel had been erected, having been donated by Mr Anthony Bamford.

The Tuesday ball was turned up by Roy McFarland, the former Derby County Football Club captain. After 30 minutes' play on the Croft, play moved across Park Road and into the water. An hour later the ball was thrown from the river into Fish Pond Meadow. It was picked up by Up'ards runners including Andrew Lemon, Steve Challinor, John Dodd and Gordon Cresswell. They quickly ran it to the mill spindle, where Down'ards had arrived by car. However, after a final hug and a Down'ards break, Gordon Cresswell made it to the spindle.

A second ball was thrown up by Mr Bill Hellaby of Offcote, who had goaled the ball himself in 1955. The play moved off to Compton in what became a series of hour-long hugs, interspersed with water play and some running. From Bank Croft the play proceeded down river after a diversion into Tyler & Coates' yard. The ball left the river, crossed the carpark to Clifton Road where the ball went missing on Leys Bank before being dribbled back down to the road. After an hour-long hug around the old Goods Warehouse, Steve Challinor and Bob Bates broke with the ball up School Lane. After a run along Mayfield Road, a hug formed at Clifton. The Down'ards could not agree on who should goal the ball and the 10.00pm deadline passed, ending play and the debate.

A Distinguished Record

The Wednesday honour of turning up the ball went to Mr Herbert Plumbly who had been on the Committee for 51 years. John Gadsby pointed out that out of a total of 270 Committee meetings in the 51 years, Mr Plumbly had attended all bar twelve. It was a remarkable record. A total of 380 diners were present that day and Mr Plumbly recalled that there were twelve at his first lunch!

On a fine and dry day he turned up the ball considerably late at 2.17pm. The play soon made off to Park Road before it returned to the Croft and emerged into Dig Street, eventually reaching the river at Bank Croft. Waterplay ended at the church fields for a while before returning to the water. The decisive break occurred when Dave Roberts tossed the ball out and Andy Bates kicked it across the lorry park. Down'ards runners took it to Clifton where there was a lot of opposition from Up'ards who had arrived by car. In the darkness, the ball was hugged away from the plinth into the adjacent field. Unknown to the hug, the ball rolled free and Ged Weston picked it up, crossed the bridge and banged it three times without opposition. What a contrast to the farce of the previous day.

1983

Bitterly Cold And Bitterly Concluded

The Tuesday game was played in very cold weather and ended with a bitter dispute as to whether a goal had been scored. John Gadsby and Marion Abbott were adamant it had not and no goal was allowed.

The ball had been turned up by the Marquis of Hartington, several minutes early. He said he had never performed a public duty with such a feeling of trepidation. He went on: "Only the British and I dare say the English, would give up a winter's afternoon … to attempt to goal this beautifully painted leather ball, filled with cork, chasing through mud and mire, wasteland, woods and water in order to touch the goal which disappeared a long time ago; their only reward, and a very remote one, the chance to carry home the battered remains of what is now a beautiful ball." It was 31 years since his father, the Duke of Devonshire, had turned up the ball. His grandfather had done it in 1923 and his great grandfather in 1924.

Late arrivals at 2.00pm found that the ball had already left Shaw Croft! It stayed outside the fire station for nearly an hour before heading to the river and the culvert. Play progressed down to the church where the ball left the water for Mayfield Road. However, it became stuck again for $3^{1}/_{2}$ hours, repeating the pattern of the day's play. Eventually the ball edged back towards the town where a break occured down School Lane late in the evening. Geoff Harrison and Steve Challinor ran the ball to Clifton and crawled through the crowd to bang the ball three times on the steps to the plinth just before 10.00pm. A goal thought the lads, but the steps were not near enough. There was much bitter comment about the decision, but what rules there are remain rules.

Runaway Success For Down'ards

The honour on Wednesday went to Tony Wright of Frank Wright Ltd. He made an appeal for a woman to be allowed to be accorded the honour. By 2.30pm the ball had reached Compton and after a diversion to the bus station, it lurched towards Old Hill. While in King Edward Street, a nice ruse by Pip and Simon Plumbly, Bill Hellaby, Dick Marsh, and Andrew Adams saw most of the crowd rushing off down Compton until the ball was spotted behind Pip's legs! The ball slowly returned from the end of Compton and at 4.45pm, Stephen Bott tipped it into the river. It was soon returned to Compton and play went up into Church Street, the ball going back into the water at the end of Tyler and Coates' yard. It was landed for the second time at 6.25pm. This time, however, Steve Mitchell ran it across Shaw Croft with David Hollingworth. At Park Road, the latter took possession and ran it via Manor Road, and Windmill Lane gardens to Sandybrook. Proceeding behind the hospital he eventually reached Peach's farm where he hid the ball under silage. Having found fellow Down'ards Johnathan Dodd plus Bob, David and Anthony Bates, the ball was retrieved while Bob Bates went to the goal to see if the crowd would allow the ball through. Bob and Ian Bates escorted David to the plinth and a successful goaling.

The 1883 ball was exhibited at the lunch on Wednesday. It was goaled at Clifton by Henry Hurst and is probably the oldest surviving ball. Henry obtained possession at Buckholme, north of Hanging Bridge and swam down the river with it passed Bond's Mill. When the mill owner saw Henry and colleagues passing through, he fetched his whisky decanter to thaw them out!

In the Ashbourne paper of 03/03/1983, Mr Alec Smith suggested that to prevent the goals being swamped, they could be moved to the water. He argued that in the days of the mill wheels, the goaler had to wade up the mill race to hit the wheel. The suggestion was a good one and eventually found favour with the Committee in 1985. Alec Smith scored the last of the three Tuesday goals in 1967.

1984

Too Many Strangers

A day of fine weather and some fine play was hindered by perhaps too many strangers. The guest of honour was the town's MP, Mr Matthew Parris, who later took part in the game. The lunch, with 412 people, heard that it was 30 years since the town's bandmaster, Mr Arthur Chadwick, had been making the balls. At 2.20pm the ball had reached Park Road and after a diversion to Madge Hill and a hug in St John Street, it returned to the river and disappeared down the culvert just before 3.00pm. Emerging at the lower end, the play moved slowly down the river with Jim Boden, Tony Kaye, John Tomlinson, Jimmy Breeze, Melvyn Moore and Alan Kingstone in the middle of the hug.

Around 4.00pm, Ernie Grant threw a long ball to David Burton on the wall and he took it up Tyler and Coates' yard to Church Street. The hug reformed and eventually moved towards Dig Street, with a diversion into the White Hart yard. Just before 5.00pm the ball was back in the river and over several hours wended its way to Nestlé. A hug on the opposite side of the river brought the ball to Mayfield Road and it slowly made its way back into town, conveniently reaching the Green Man as 10.00pm brought play to an end. A measure of the closely fought play were the five casualties taken to hospital.

Highly Charged Atmospheres

Wednesday's honour fell to Czechosovakian-born Mr Karel Zouhar, the founder of Tyremiles Ltd. Following the turn up, the ball was quickly spirited away by Up'ards runners to Sturston. One of the runners being Janice Clowes accompanied by several lads. The ball reached Sturston at 2.22pm, but several Down'ards had arrived by car. There was a spirited and sometimes angry resistance around the spindle before Steve Bott claimed the goal at 2.48pm. Unfortunately, Simon Spencer, nephew of Mr Zouhar, had claimed he had goaled it just after 2.30pm and also had his hands on the ball when it was goaled. In the heat of the hug, one has to allow for consensus and it was Bott's day.

The second ball was turned up by Mr Alec Robinson of Clifton, at 3.30pm. The ball left the Croft for Dig Street and reached the bus station and the Henmore at 5.30pm. It slowly progressed down river, with Mark Harrison swimming through the deep weir pool at Nestlé with the leather and three other players. Below the weir, the ball was soon thrown clear of the water and play went across the field to Mayfield Road. Against such resistance, it eventually edged beyond the cemetery and became wedged against a thorn hedge. With typical foresight Marion Abbott called for the ball to be passed through the hedge. Down'ards runners were soon rewarded as Marion passed on the trophy. However, by the time the ball reached Clifton with time running out, it proved impossible to penetrate the opposition to reach the stone plinth by 10.00pm. The highly charged atmosphere being reminiscent of the earlier incident at Sturston.

Clearly something needed doing to prevent the stifling of a goal. This was especially the case at Sturston, where the runners had been thwarted by Down'ards arriving by car. There was nothing new in this – the 4.20pm train to Clifton had been used some 90 years previously, but the two plinths could be changed. The Committee responded the following year. The goal was to be a piece of wood suspended from the bridge at each goal. The bottom 12 inches would be painted and the painted area would represent the goal. To goal the ball the player had to be in the river and strike the painted area three times. Although a player could be supported in the goaling, the other person also had to be in the water. The scorer could not have any part of his person on land or on the bridge.

1985

A Bomb Hoax

In addition to the new rule concerning goaling, the Committee introduced a new rule on the number of balls that could be turned up in any one day. Three balls could be turned up prior to 5.00pm but none after 5.00pm.

This year the game's fine tradition was spoilt by a bomb hoax at the dinner and the ball being spirited away by four strangers. Mr Phil Drabble turned up the Tuesday ball, which left the Croft shortly before 3.00pm, being hugged in Park Road before breaking down the road and into Park

Avenue. Bob Bates was playing with a bloody nose, having inadvertently met Bill Ratcliffe's fist. Play returned back towards Shaw Croft with Ernie Grant, Steve Kent, Mark Harrison, Stephen Bott, Robert Todd, Nigel Brown, Alan Kingstone and others in the middle of it.

At about 4.00pm the ball reached the water and the above mentioned players were joined by Kevin Grime, Mick Pepper, Tim Fearn, Mick and David Dudley, Melvyn Moore and Peter Skelton, while Reg Purdy stood guard over the culvert entrance. Slowly the hug progressed down river, but it was going dark before Bank Croft was reached. Progress was maintained with much of the river frozen over. At about 7.30pm, the ball broke towards Mayfield Road but stayed in the fields for a further hour. Around 9.00pm the ball disappeared and later the police heard that it was in the Belle Vue Road area, before apprehending four youths with the ball behind the hospital. They were from Harwick in Scotland and did not know what to do with the ball! It was now after 10.00pm and many people drifted home feeling both cheated and chilled.

Appreciation, Anger and Anguish

Guest of honour on the Wednesday was Mr Arthur Chadwick BEM, who had the distinction of turning up his own ball, painted by his daughter, Sandra. It was an opportunity for the town to express its appreciation not only to the ball maker, but director of the town band for nearly 40 years. The ball was hugged into Park Road and up Madge's Hill from where it progressed down St John Street. Play turned into Dig Street and Andrew Adams tipped the leather into the river at about 3.00pm. For about an hour there was much activity and kicking about below Bank Croft. Across the river, police gathered in the gardens and a large notice read 'J P Gadsby and the police request please do not enter private gardens'.

Despite slow progress towards Clifton, it was upriver when the break came, with Brian Allen speeding away. Before the followers could catch up, the ball was landed near to the Health Centre, across Shaw Croft and on to Green Lane. Geoff Harrison had taken the ball up the Cattle Market before being dispossessed by David Calladine, with Richard Ryman kicking a loose ball down the hill to King Street. The leather was then run down Hall Lane, back over Shaw Croft, through the bus station, past the church and over the footbridge into Nestlé's yard. As Clifton was approached, further players arrived by car, with some taking to the water, including Melvyn Moore. Paddy Kerr was about to goal the ball when a cry went up for straws to be drawn. Paddy, on leave from Germany and the 9th/12th Lancers as usual, was not even given a straw. Melvyn Moore won and goaled the ball at 4.35pm, the first to do so on the new style goals. There was some anger expressed about the manner of the goaling, with straws drawn when there was a player in the water, ball in hands and in front of the goal. For Paddy Kerr disappointment was short – he was to goal on the Tuesday of the following year.

The second ball was to be turned up by Mr Arthur Attenborough. The ball soon went into the river at Park Road but stayed there for three hours with no movement for 45 minutes at one stage. Players withstanding the bitter cold included Mark Harrison, Kevin Grime, Alan Kingstone, Paul Astle and Paul Holmes. At Nestlé's weir, thick ice had to be broken. Below it, a dozen Up'ards waited and the ball was landed at about 8.30pm. However, it continued on towards Clifton. Mark Slater was seen to be crushed and was stretchered away to hospital, to be followed by Richard Sowter a little later. The ball eventually broke away to Clifton beneath Harry Fowler's sweater. There was controversy as to whether the ball had been goaled three times or not. Triumph turned to anguish and a petition was handed to the Committee asking that the evidence for goaling be considered. Several days later, the honour and ball went to Harry Fowler.

1985 saw the first of the now annual videos of the game, prepared by Yvonne and Harry Hithersay. From early beginnings, they now have five cameras filming each game to produce their video.

1986

Paddy's Day

Ashbourne strengthened its link with Kirkwall in the Orkneys – where street football is played on Christmas Day and New Year's Day – when the Tuesday ball was thrown up by John Robertson, the author of a history of the Kirkwall game, *Uppies and Doonies*.

For an hour or so, the hug wandered around the carpark. At 3.00pm Doug Marron suddenly realised that the ball, having been hurled high out of the hug, was heading straight to him. He turned in an instant, but was soon caught. From 3.30pm things really began to move and there was a fast break towards the Fish Pond. Players included Kevin Grime, Mick Pepper, Jim Breeze, Steve Kent, Alan Kingstone, Melvyn Moore, David Chell and Jim Boden. The game made a quick trip through the culvert. The ball continued downstream, and at one point Kevin Grime put on 200 yards before he was stopped. Play lodged by Tomlinson's field for an hour or so. It then continued down river and was eventually thrown out. Paddy Kerr took the ball and ran onto the golf course where he waited alone for about an hour. He then hid the ball and then went 'to get some muscle, such as Ernie Grant who was in The Plough.' He went back and was helped by Steve Challinor, Johnathan Todd, David Hollinshead, Graham Lemon, and David Yeomans who went in as decoys. Paddy walked to within six feet of the bridge and jumped straight into the river, reached the goal and hit it three times before being jumped on by several people. Kevin Grime reckoned Paddy deserved the goal 'for his spectacular flying leap from quite a few yards away.'

Several people maintained that the ball had not been goaled three times, but John Gadsby had no doubt. Some players continued to play the ball for some time after the goaling, with much open play in Mayfield Road. However, the ball was eventually retrieved by John Gadsby, supported by Don Lowndes and two burly policemen.

Down'ards Do It Again

The Wednesday ball was turned up by Councillor Bertie Birch. His family had a history of turning up the ball – his cousin F B Birch in 1941, great uncle Tom W Birch in 1908 and uncles, Bill Prince* –in 1905, 1907 and 1910 and John C Prince*in 1906 and 1907. Also Henry Prince* turned up the ball in1909 and Mr R Prince* in 1908. Those marked * were all pub landlords.

After 20 minutes there was an unexpected surge and the ball was kicked between the ambulance station and the flats. It was picked up by Steve Mitchell who passed it to Paddy Kerr. He took it across Derby Road, over Peak View Drive to the back of the golf course. With him were Steven Challinor, Gordon Cresswell, David Hollingsworth and Geoff Harrison, all past scorers. Others caught up and it was decided that Anthony Bates should goal the ball. However, he grew tired and gave the ball back to Paddy Kerr. Clifton was given a wide berth, coming in via Colley Croft before cutting across Snelston Lane and dropping down the steep bank to the coal yard. Paddy dropped into the water some 20 metres from the goal, but just short of the bridge, handed the ball to Ernie Grant. He passed it on to Mark Harrison who goaled the ball a little before 3.00pm.

Don Thornley turned up the second ball. He had never goaled one himself, but a no-goal saw the ball going to him. There was 2½ hours of water play in bitter conditions, with the pond frozen over. At 4.45pm the ball went into the culvert, stopping by Compton Bridge for some time, before a break downstream. Here it was landed and hugged onto Station Road. For over three hours the ball was hugged around the town, travelling down Station Street and Compton to reach the bus station. Despite a break at 9.25pm with runners going down Mayfield Road, both this and a final Up'ard attempt by Gordon Cresswell were thwarted as the deadline past.

1987

By Car To Clifton

The Tuesday ball was thrown up by Viscount Tamworth, the heir of the 13th Earl Ferrers and a member of the Shirley family. He lived at Shirley where his family had owned land continually since the Conquest, over 900 years before.

In the first hour the ball was played around Shaw Croft, and Park Road before the hug plunged into the Henmore. Early players were the Birch brothers, several members of the Bates and Harrison families, Kevin Grime, Doug Marron, Tim Fearn, Alan Kingstone, Jack Jones, Ernie Grant, Tony Coulton, Melvyn Moore, Kenny Renshaw, Tony Millward, Alistair Fuller, Ged Weston and Reg Purdy. The ball was played up and down the brook before entering the culvert at 4.20pm. Most people then rushed to reach the other end, only to find disappointment and no ball. After a few minutes Mark

Harrison emerged at the Park Road end where Doug Marron and Kevin Grime were waiting for him. Passing the ball between them, they ran up Hall Lane, but were tempted into a Ford Fiesta, which took them and the ball to Dark Lane. Here they set off through the fields to Tatton's Mill and on towards the Clifton goal. However, the ball was repossessed by Philip Tomlinson on behalf of the Committee, declaring that the use of a car was against the rules. He returned to Ashbourne where he restarted the game by Compton Bridge.

The ball made slow progress toward Fish Pond Meadow where it stayed for what was described as 'two very cold and boring hours', as night fell. Movement eventually came as the players realised the ball was no longer there! It had in fact been spirited away by Darrel Mansfield. Players and spectators divided, some heading for Sturston. The lucky ones went to Clifton, waiting in a bitingly cold east wind. As 10.00pm neared, the ball appeared and there was a debate as to who should goal it. It had been run most of the way by David Mycock but eventually straws were drawn by David, Kenny Renshaw and Mick Betteridge. The latter won and struck the goal three times at two minutes to ten, with an authoritative nod from John Gadsby just before snow began to fall. The game had been covered by an Australian TV crew and spectators had the unusual treat of seeing the goal being scored under the bright lights of the camera team. There was also a German TV crew present and their viewers were welcomed in their own language by John Gadsby.

In The Nick Of Time At Sturston

The Wednesday ball was thrown up by local magistrate Mr Sid Taylor who goaled at Clifton the ball turned up by Captain S D Player on Ash Wednesday in 1949. His father goaled the Ash Wednesday ball in 1914 and the Shrove Tuesday ball in 1922. He had also served on the Royal Shrovetide Committee for the previous ten years, but could not decide which was the greater honour: goaling the ball or turning it up.

Ash Wednesday saw a welcome thaw. Within five minutes the ball had crossed Park Road and was in the river. The play moved up and down until there was a break a little after 4.00pm and the ball disappeared down the culvert. As the 5.00pm deadline approached the ball broke down river from below Cary's Wine Bar, with John Tomlinson and Tim Fearn running it a good distance to the Station Road Bridge. The ball left the water near the Flying Club and reached Clifton Road at about 6.15pm. It was hugged up the side of the former Railway Tavern, through the gardens and emerged into North Leys before returning down the road to Station Street and then Clifton Road again. Play nudged on to the bottom of Highfield Road and then up Hinds Barn Hill before returning to Clifton Road at about 9.15pm.

If a goal was to be scored, a break had to come soon. Suddenly, it did, with the ball loose and being kicked along the road by Sean Breeze to Steve Bott who passed it to Paddy Kerr. The ball was taken across the river, up Dark Lane, behind the hospital and on to Belle Vue Road, reaching Northcliffe Road after going through someone's house. In the running with the ball were Paddy, Johnathan Dodd, Paul Armstrong, Gordon Cresswell, Steve Challinor, Dave Hollingsworth and Michael Wright. Progress continued via Windmill Lane and the grammar school to the mill where Johnathan Dodd goaled it. It was the first goal to be scored at Sturston since the introduction of the new style goal and it was 9.53pm.

During his lunch speech Mr Taylor recalled that his Grandfather, Sam Sowter, had collected thirteen summonses in the space of two days at the time of the prosecutions.

1988

Two Minutes To Go

The Tuesday ball was turned up by Judge Brian Woods, who spoke of his experience not being of turning up but sending down. He said it was 'cheering to find Ashbourne and its friends thronging together for a feast and a game played since a time where of the memory of man runneth not to the contrary'. John Gadsby told the 430 people gathered for the lunch that it was 60 years to the day since HRH The Prince of Wales had thrown up the ball. The Wednesday ball of 1928 had been brought along for people to see. It was also noted that it was Tom Webster's fortieth luncheon.

Early play was marred by too many outsiders being involved. One regular player said he had not seen anyone he knew in the first half hour of play. There was therefore no rapid play until after 5.00pm. The ball left Shaw Croft and was hugged into Park Road and up Madge Hill where it was pushed over the park railings. It was then hugged into the river by Melvyn Moore, Robert Todd, Tony Millward, Mark Hellaby, Mark Harrison, Ged Weston, and Mick Pepper. An oriental film crew hovered above the hug in a helicopter but saw little spirited play. By 2.30pm the ball was locked at the culvert entrance and stayed there until 4.20pm when it disappeared inside it. It was 5.00pm before the crowd saw the hug again, but they were rewarded with some good open play outside Cary's Wine Bar. The ball then left the river via Nigel's Yard and was hugged into St John Street. The closed doors to the Green Man Yard yielded to pressure. However, the ball was lost amid the new Shaw Croft development. It had been taken by Johnathan Dodd with Darrel Marshall, Paddy Kerr and Mick Wright through Town Hall Yard and on to Seven Arches, the Royal Oak at Hanging Bridge and down to Tattons. Here they swam across the river to goal the ball at Clifton. However, the goal was declared void by Philip Tomlinson on the grounds that it had been out of sight for over two hours.

Philip turned the ball up again off the Health Centre steps at 8.45pm. Lively street play followed with the ball going down Compton and into Station Street, where it was hugged from end to end. Around 9.30pm the ball broke towards Derby Road. It was run across Shaw Croft where Paddy Kerr took it up Horse and Jockey Yard and onto Union Street via Tiger Yard. It ended up behind the hospital where players included Martin Farr, Geoff Harrison, Kevin Clark, David Lemon, David Calladine, Steven Mitchell and Andy Keeling. The ball moved via Doles Farm towards Clifton. Here Anthony Bates drew the winning straw to goal it, accompanied by his father, Bob and his uncle, David Bates. It was goaled on the second attempt with only only two minutes of play remaining, exactly as in the previous year.

Two Minutes Too Late

The next day it was two minutes too late when Paddy Kerr reached Clifton and it was returned to the Green Man Hotel for Jimmy Grant who had turned it up. It had taken nearly eight hours for the break to come, with a lot of vigorous play but without the frantic pace of Tuesday's late play. The ball had been played around the car park before reaching Dig Street. The hug then pushed into St John Street and down the Green Man yard before returning to Dig Street. At 3.45pm the ball was thrown into the river but became static at the first bend below Cary's Wine Bar for 30 minutes. It slowly reached Station Road where it became stuck before a burst took it on to The Mansion. Here the hug included Tony Millward, Dave Chell, Jim Breeze, Alan Kingstone, Andrew Lemon, John Tomlinson, Pip Plumbly, Brian Moss, Darren Waring, Mark Harrison, Roger Jones, Doug Marron, Simon Spencer, Mark Hellaby, Tim Fearn, Melvyn Moore, Stephen Bull, Craig Slater, Stuart Radford and others. The ball continued on slowly down towards Nestlé's weir, with the runners having a lean time on the bank. By 8.00pm the ball had left the river near the Henmore Trading Centre to reach Mayfield Road and slowly return to town, eventually reaching the railway bridge.

At 9.40pm a few players darted out of the hug and it was unclear if they had the ball or not. It was a good five minutes before the majority realised that the ball had indeed gone. Stuart Radford made the break, followed by Malcolm Fernyhough, David Lee and Paul Armstrong. The ball was run up Church Banks, over Belle Vue Road and into the fields. Coincidentally, Paddy Kerr followed the others and caught up with them near to the cemetery. Paddy took the ball from David Lee, running alone to Clifton only to find that he had arrived just two minutes too late.

1989

Controversy At Sturston

Controversy raged at the end of the first day and the Committee was called to adjudicate. They found that on balance, Bill Ratcliffe had scored at Sturston without the use of a car. The ball had been turned up by the 12th Marquis of Lothian and at 2.10pm it entered Fish Pond Meadow. The ball was soon in the river and in the hug were seen Jim Breeze, Tommy Poxon, Steve Bott, Russ Simpson, Stuart Gerrard, John Lemon, Billy Webster, Philip Chell and Doug Marron. The hug was to remain there for a long time, slowly moving upriver, with only occasional views of the ball. In fact at 4.00pm it was still only 300 yards from the plinth. The ball was then suddenly banked and the hug carried on heaving away on the recreation ground.

There was a break and the Down'ards headed for town. In the bus station, as the crowd flooded through, Doug Startin sat on the ball, watching them go by. He then went up Dig Street to the Market Place, on up the Channel, and around through the fields north of town to Offcote. With him were Mick Wright, Rob Godfrey, and Neil Donnelly. At Offcote they were joined by Dave Calladine and Mark Spencer. At the goal was Bill Ratcliffe who was chosen to score the goal, which was accomplished at about 6.30pm.

Sturston's Year

For the first time in 24 years, the Up'ards scored two goals in one year! The ball was turned up by Philip Binder. It was played around Shaw Croft for half an hour, often visible as it bobbed about. It reached Dig Street and then Church Street. There was a break up Church Banks and Dave Lee and Chris Fearn made off, only to be stopped by Mick Wright, Rob Godfrey and Gordon Cresswell.

The ball moved on at a rapid pace down Bell's Pastures, across the fields to Sandybrook Hall and back over to the Tissington Trail. From here, the ball's trip to the countryside continued through Mappleton and Okeover Park before coming back to familiar territory near to Clifton. Upon seeing Up'ards approaching, Steve Hudson, Geoff Harrison and Gary Baker swam across the River Dove and came back into Clifton through the yard of Mayfield Yarns. They reached the goal from the top-side and at the third attempt, Steve Hudson goaled the ball. It was about 4.20pm.

A second ball was turned up by Ron Ford. It headed for Park Road this time and was eventually pushed into the Fish Pond Meadow, where the ball went into the pond. Out it came and play veered over and into the culvert. However, it came back out again in the hands of Paul Clarke. However, his throw was miss aimed and it went to Chris Fearn who ran off over the playing fields, passing the ball to Mick Wright. However, they were stopped by Pete Harrison, who held onto the ball until a hug formed. The ball returned to the river but there was another break and Alex Shipley picked up the ball by the Fish Pond. A group of players – both Up'ards and Down'ards – hid for a while in a garden on the Park estate. A coin was turned up to see which side should have the opportunity of goaling. The Up'ards won and the Down'ards withdrew. Mick Wright, Chris Fearn and Alex Shipley went up the Stepping Fields and around the airfield via Peak View Drive and the school playing field. Crossing Bradley Wood to Sturston, Mick Wright drew the correct straw. He brought the ball in and was assisted by Bill Ratcliffe, who hid the ball under his jumper before Mick jumped into the water to bang the ball three times at 7.40pm.

The year 1989 saw Stuart Avery's painted balls being turned up for the first time. Stuart has also enlightened the lunches with his cartoons on the menu and painted both the recent paintings of Ashbourne people at their Shrovetide game, in St John Street and in the Henmore.

1990

Another Close Run

Councillor Fred Elliott turned up the Tuesday ball on a bitterly cold wet and windy day. A late goal for the Down'ards ended an otherwise dull game, when Paul Clarke scored at 9.50pm. For the next seven hours the ball stayed relatively close to Shaw Croft. After ten minutes, play crossed over to the Fish Pond and the hug moved between the pond and fire station as hail lashed like gravel. There was a break after half an hour and the ball sailed into the pond before reaching the river where it remained for 90 minutes. Play moved gradually towards the culvert and disappeared for thirty minutes, reappearing at the Compton end.

The ball was landed and taken up Tyler & Coates' yard and on to Belle Vue Road. Play visited Bright's fish and chip shop in Union Street – the hug going in the front door and leaving through the back. Eventually, the action moved back to Shaw Croft and into Park Road, slowly moving around via Sturston Road into Compton. At 9.15pm the ball disappeared, in fact it had gone through the Henmore Place flats up Park Road and on to the Cattle Market. From here the ball was taken across the fields north of the hospital. Straws were drawn and Paul Clarke took the honour at Clifton goal.

Accompanying him on the run were Steve Challinor, Paddy Kerr, Adie Webb, Andrew Bates, Tim Sears and Dave Calladine.

Two Goals and Maybe Two Records

Councillor Ian Bates turned up the Wednesday ball. He made a plea for a two hour armistice by the runners to allow the followers to see open play. It was a plea in vain. After appearing at head height several times, the ball was loose and quickly kicked into Compton and then into the bus station. It became wedged between the Trent Garage and the bowling green, with heavy rain falling.

Just after 2.30pm the ball entered the Henmore near the Henmore Centre. In the water were Jim Lemon, David Chell, Tim Fearn, Doug Marron and Ernie Grant amongst others. However, after 15 minutes, the ball was pitched up onto the old railway bridge where it was picked up by Paddy Kerr. Accompanied by Steve Challinor, Steve and Geoff Hudson, he then headed for the railway tunnel. Progress north of the tunnel was stopped by Up'ards players including David Calladine, Robert Godfrey, Andrew Lemon and Gordon Cresswell. Play made towards Buxton Road and 30 minutes after leaving the Henmore it was at Sandybrook, eventually being kicked back up the A515 where it re-entered the fields. It was then run down to Seven Arches and across to the large weir over the Dove at Hanging Bridge.

Safely across the weir, the ball progressed towards Mayfield Yarns. Amongst the hug were Jim Lemon, Tim Fearn, Mick Pepper, Bill Ratcliffe, Steve Bott, Doug Marron, the Hellaby brothers, Jason Clowes, John Tomlinson, Billy Webster and Andrew Bates. Four of the runners decided that they would like a river player to goal the ball and Jim Lemon drew the longest straw. After 20 years his first chance had arrived, but play was still in Staffordshire! After being hugged across the swollen River Dove, tragedy almost struck when a fence gave way at the goal, toppling players into the water. Jim Lemon recalled afterwards that he owed his life to Dave Chell who pulled him from under the water. Undaunted, Jim allowed the current to carry him under the bridge where he goaled the ball at the second attempt. It was 4.30pm.

The second ball was thrown up at 5.07pm by Harold Sherratt, in pouring rain. At 81 years old he is possibly the oldest person so honoured. An hour later it had been goaled at Sturston and the game was over. It may have been the fastest goaled second ball. Upon being turned up, the ball was immediately kicked towards St John Street, emerging from Prince's Yard, where HRH The Prince of Wales had left after turning up the 1928 ball. Partner's plate glass window unfortunately gave way, despite a plywood covering, before the ball was hugged through Upper St John Street, down Park Road and into the Henmore. The ball entered the culvert but quickly reappeared and was collected by several Up'ards including Michael Wright, David Calladine, Lenny Lyon, Steve Challinor, Tim Sears and Robert Godfrey. They approached Sturston in a blinding snowstorm and Robert Godfrey drew the right straw. After a final skirmish, he goaled the ball with Paddy Kerr by the post but graciously making no final attempt to prevent it. It was just after 6.00pm.

Regrettably over £1,000 of damage was caused but fortunately the warnings for the game's future were heeded the following year. Unheeded was a plea at the Wednesday's dinner from John Gadsby. Could a woman turn up the ball in 1991 to celebrate the centenary of the ball being turned up by Mrs Wooley? It was not to be. Later investigation by Carol Frost and John Gadsby upturned the tradition that Mrs Woolley had thrown the ball up in 1891. This effectively spiked the idea of a committee set up by Mrs Trilby Shaw and others. Its object (ANT 30/08/1990) was to try and persuade the Shrovetide Committee to allow a woman to throw up the ball in 1991, which was also the 750th anniversary of the church.

1991

Honours Even

Following the outbreak of war in the Gulf, some Ashbourne lads had been refused leave from the forces, being on stand by yet again for a more dangerous battle. There was also a change in what rules exist for the game. If the ball was missing for more than one hour, that ball shall be declared void and the game restarted at Shaw Croft.

On a cold and snowy day, Bob Chambers turned up the first ball. Within 30 minutes it was in The Park, heading for the river. In the water went Dave Chell, Jim Breeze, Doug Marron, Jim Lemon,

John Foster, Tim Fearn, Darren Waring, Mel Godfrey, Mark Hellaby and Mick Betteridge. After some movement around the river, play settled down and the hug gradually worked up the fields towards Sturston, on the north side of the river. Doug Sowter threw the ball over a hedge where the runners were waiting, spaced out up the fields. Harvey Brown, Mel Godfrey and Lenny Lyon were involved but eventually it was just Dave Calladine and Mick Wright who legged it to Sturston where the former goaled it at 4.50pm.

Mr Ken Hunt turned up the second ball. A sudden break sent the ball towards the Horse and Jockey Yard. It turned left at St John Street and Anthony Bates and others made for Union Street, Belle Vue Road and down to Mayfield Road. Involved this time were Dave and Anthony Bates, Adrian Webb, Andy Cox, Jim Lemon and Mark Harrison. Bob Bates was waiting at Clifton with Tim Fearn, Dave Chell, John Webb and Billy Webster. Lots were drawn and Bob Bates won, goaling the ball at about 7.00pm and ending the day's play early.

Down'ards Run From Sturston To Score

Speaking at the Wednesday lunch, Councillor Mrs Esme Plumbly apologised for her husband's absence. It was the first time he had not been present at one of the two annual games for 62 years. At the dinner also was Canon Lytle with his Grandfather's ball – goaled exactly 100 years ago to the day. His greatgrandfather was Supt Lytle, well known to players, especially summonsed players!

Mr John Allsopp turned up the ball, which was soon heading for the pond before veering up to the Memorial Gates. Play passed down St John Street, with Steve Kent, Steve Bott, Jim Breeze, Nigel Brown, Jim Hogg and Les Hainsworth prominent in the hug. There was a break at Prince's Gate and the ball went down the yard and back to Shaw Croft. After visiting the Henmore flats and deep snow in Fish Pond Meadows, the hug reached the river at 3.04pm. Waterplayers, some as usual in wet suits, included Doug Marron, Steve Bott, Stuart Lees, John Tomlinson, Eric Taylor, Andy Breeze, Phil, James and Anthony Spencer, Nick Smith, Pete Dunn, Alistair Fuller, Mark Hudson, Tim Fearn and John Foster.

After nearly an hour in the river, play transferred to the ice covered Fish Pond. Thin ice in the centre gave way and four players were quickly pulled out of the water. Play went back to the river, going downstream to the culvert as darkness fell. Emerging at the Compton end, the ball was landed near Cary's Wine Bar and Andy Keeling took the ball up the Market Place and through Town Hall Yard. Chris Fearn and Lenny Lyon took it on towards Green Road and the school field.

Gordon Cresswell attempted a runaway, but he was stopped by Paddy Kerr, one field from the Sturston goal. Down'ard's runners, mindful of the new one hour rule made off for home territory, via Windmill Lane, North Avenue and Belle Vue Road. Martin Holland was accompanied by Paddy Kerr, Steve Challinor, Geoff Harrison, Steve Hudson, John Hemstock and Dave Hollingworth. Down Dark Lane, and over the fields to Clifton they went, deciding that the honour would be divided between Martin and John Hemstock the only ones who had not goaled a ball. Martin won but then had to win a further draw with three water players. Lady luck favoured him and he walked the ball in to the goal at 8.27pm, with many people at the wrong goal, waiting disappointedly at Sturston!

1992

Changes

The Tuesday lunch had a common theme: change, although much of it was not of the Committee's making. Just a matter of days prior to the game, the Green Man closed its doors having gone into receivership. Although it reopened its bars for the game, the kitchens remained closed. Lunch was arranged in a 120ft-long marquee sited on the fairground site off Park Road. Over 400 people sat down for lunch under canvas on both days.

There was change in personalities too, with John Gadsby recalling the loss during the year of Herbert Plumbly, a Committee member for 53 years, including two periods as chairman. He had goaled at Sturston in 1935 and had turned up the Wednesday ball in 1982. For the late Marion Abbott there had been no such honour but she too had been a staunch supporter. Recalled John Gadsby: 'I always felt whenever the ball was missing that if I could find Marion she would know where it was and, half the time, who had it'. Also recalled was the loss of Chris Daly Atkinson. In 1956, he had composed the melody to the Shrovetide song of 1891, now adopted by the Committee and sung at every luncheon. A quiet, well-respected man, Daly was the organist of St Oswald's Church.

The Chairman of the Committee had changed too during the previous year. After 17 years as Chairman, John Gadsby had retired. A presentation to him by the players had been made previously and the Committee made another at the lunch. There had been some difficult times during his term of office but he had left with the game in good shape. The new Chairman, Philip Tomlinson, introduced his predecessor. Change was the theme of John Gadsby's speech prior to turning up the ball. He speculated on the forthcoming bypass and what change, if any, it would mean. He felt that so long as change was accepted 'Ashbourne Royal Shrovetide Football will go on forever'. He even nudged his fellow Committee members again by remarking 'but the Committee don't like ladies'.

After being carried across Park Road onto Shaw Croft he implored the waiting players to get the ball onto The Paddock and kick it about for half an hour. Within 15 minutes however, it had entered the culvert and was heading downstream. After some play around Compton Bridge, the ball was thrown up onto the pavement and was kicked and hugged over Shaw Croft. It was kicked towards Cokayne Avenue by Dave Brown with Chris Fearn but a hug formed before any break was made. Slowly the ball returned to the water, entering the Fish Pond briefly before reaching the Henmore just before 5.00pm. Here it stayed, slowly moving upriver as light fell. It was virtually stationary for 30 minutes before Ernie Grant banked it amid grunts and shoves from the hug. With spectators on either bank, the ball was suddenly gone at 6.45pm, disappearing into the darkness, leaving the majority of spectators on the wrong river bank.

The players, including Paddy Kerr, Dave Challinor, Nick Wright, Rob Godfrey, Dave Calladine, Lenny Lyon and Phil Woolley hugged the ball past the school and up to Windmill Lane. Dave Hollingworth ran with the leather down Windmill Lane and hid in a garden to throw off his pursuers. He then returned the way they had all come to Cokayne Avenue. He crossed Belper Road and proceeded through the fields to the south of the town to Clifton. It had been agreed that Tim Fearn should goal the ball and Paddy Kerr – who must be one of the Down'ards most tenacious players – dropped into the water with the ball for Tim to goal unopposed at nearly 8.50pm. So ended a game played in brilliant sunshine until night fell.

Up'ards Even The Score

Mr Stanley Bury turned up the Wednesday ball at 2.07pm. His father had turned up the first Wednesday ball in 1953. The ball quickly reached Compton and turned over the bridge into Dig Street and then St John Street. However, the ball suddenly went missing, having been taken up the entry at the side of Eddowes, Simm & Waldron. The ball was passed on to Doug Sowter and then Terry Brown who went across Belle Vue Road and on to Northcliffe where it was thrown over a wall and into the street. From here it was quickly taken along North Avenue and via the cattle market to the fields beyond the old maternity home.

It was turned 4.00pm as the ball was landed on the south side of the river and kicked towards Belper Road before returning towards the river. Down'ards had possession through Darren Waring, Nobby Clarke and Tim Fearn. Five o'clock passed as the ball remained tight in the hug, which lasted for some 45 minutes. Police in town had no idea where the ball was. The ball eventually reached Sturston at about 6.15pm. Five names were drawn for the honour of taking the ball and Mark Hellaby's name was drawn by his brother Simon. Helping him towards the vertical post serving as the goal– and through a sea of humanity, which kept moving the goal post – were brother Simon, Andy Harrison, Terry Brown, Derek Seed, Phil Chell, Simon Spencer and others.

1993

In January the committee gave notice that it would consider declaring a goal void if extensive vandalism occurred, not withstanding that vandalism was more likely to result from followers rather than players. Further, the ball would be declared void if it was kept out of active play for more than one hour. The headquarters for the game this year was to be the Town Hall, as the Green Man Hotel was still closed.

A Lot Of Shoving And Panting

'What's happening?'

'Nothing, just a lot of shoving and panting.' This comment between two girls at 6.45 pm seemed to sum up Tuesday's play.

Over 400 people had sat down to lunch in the old Meridian Knitwear factory on the edge of The Paddock. Guest of honour was the Duke of Rutland who commented that his father had turned up the ball in 1936 and his brother in 1952 (actually 1953). In fact his father had also accompanied the Prince of Wales in 1928. His Grace commented "what fun to have a football cum rugby game without an umpire and virtually no rules". The loss of Jimmy Grant in January was marked by a moment of silence. He had served on the committee for some twelve years and had been one of the game's best players in his day.

Philip Tomlinson, chairing the proceedings, highlighted that Mr Tom Webster was at the lunch for the 45th year, having been to both lunches each year. There were 14 at the 1948 lunch and it cost 3/6d (17p). Referring to the new book on Shrovetide's history ("a very good book too", he said), he commented that both his grandparents had been fined in 1891. These were John Tomlinson and John Sellers. He had also noted in the book comments about two new water players. One was himself and the other was the town Mayor, Ian Bates. Councillor Bates and his brother Brian had just purchased the Green Man Hotel sign to ensure its preservation. 'I did tell him had he bought the Green Man Hotel, he could have had it for nothing,' he continued.

After Auld Lang Syne and the National Anthem, the Duke turned up the ball. It made for the park and was in the Henmore within thirty minutes. Despite a lot of effort, play stayed in the river alongside the memorial ground until 3.21 pm, moving just a few yards in one way or another. Beneath the rising stream were Doug Marron, Billy Webster, Darren Hooley, Mark and Simon Hellaby, Pip Plumbly, Alan Kingston, Alistair Fuller, Richard and Steve Bott, Simon Spencer, Derek Seed, Darren Waring, Jim Breeze, Jim Lemon, Mick Betteridge, Bob Hudson, Mel Godfrey, Nigel Brown, John Foster and Peter Gadsby.

The ball was soon back in the river and at 3.35 pm started moving downstream, entering the culvert just before 4 pm. Emerging at the lower end, play progressed just beyond the railway tunnel. It then returned along Church Street to St John Street before ending up on Shaw Croft and becoming lodged up against the flats in Park Road.

Moving on once more, play re-entered the park and reached the river by the culvert at 6.25 pm. A repeat of the afternoon's play resumed with a lot of shoving in the river before being banked on Fish Pond Meadow. The ball went through the culvert once more to reach St John Street and the Green Man Hotel, still boarded up and awaiting a buyer. A late run up Belper Road was stopped and the deadline passed with no goals. Other than in 1940 when play ended after 3 hours, it is probable that this game was played the shortest distance from the plinth since 1891. The extent of play was just past the railway tunnel and at the other end, as far as the recreation ground.

An Up'ards And A Family Double

Wednesday saw two goals for the Up'ards and a goal for Chris Fearn, whose brother goaled in 1992, albeit at Clifton.

Some 450 people sat down for lunch, prepared by Ridgeway Catering of Stoke-on-Trent. Philip Tomlinson commented upon the previous day's play, stating that there had been too much hugging and pushing against buildings and riverbanks. As expected, popular Roy Bennett gave a witty speech. Saying he was so delighted to see so many former pupils, he teased them by saying as a teacher, he had been confident 'that by the age of 45, adolescence would be safely behind you.' He drew an analogy between the transformation of the Meridian mill for the lunch and the 'transformation' of solicitor John Hanson's clients, which he read about each week in the local paper. He could no longer pass the steps up to John Hanson's offices at Eddows, Sims and Waldron without thinking the steps had witnessed 'more seeing of the light than there had been on the Damascus Road', prior to cases reaching the Court!

Being asked to turn up the ball was 'official recognition that he was no longer good enough to be a player.' It was vintage Bennett at his best, remarked one listener. He alluded to his family's Shrovetide tradition – the roll of honour was like looking at his own family tree (he is a Burton). Even the ball he was turning up was painted by one of his family – Tim Baker was also descended from the Burtons.

He concluded by saying if the game was to succeed, 'it will be because of the players and the way they play the game.' It was not a game for the spectators and the game would manage without the lunch, press reports and even 'books on Shrovetide'. However, it was the manner in which they played the game which would determine whether or not it survived as a tradition. It was a good omen. Play that afternoon was the game at its best.

Just after 2pm, Dr Bennett released his ball to the players. At 2.20pm it crossed Park Road to reach the river. Play went into the culvert and came out of the lower end at 2.30pm. Spectators were making for Bank Croft as the ball was thrown out into the White Hart yard where Andrew Lemon grabbed it. Play went out into Church Street and down Dig Street and towards Bank Croft. At 3pm it reached the Henmore yet again. The ball was frequently loose, to the pleasure of the crowd. Police patrolled the bottom of Tyler and Coates yard. They were not needed however, for the ball broke down river, with frequent views of the ball for the play then surged down stream about 100 yards, just after the Mayor, now suitably dressed, joined the edge of the hug.

It was now 3.45pm as the ball was thrown into the Church Field. In the play were Roger Jones, Ernie Grant, Steve Bull, Eric Taylor, Peter Skelton, Graham Hill, Julian Burton, Tim Fearn, Mark Hellaby, Phil Chell, Andrew Harrison, Darren Waring, Billy Webster, Peter Mellor, Doug Marron, Kevin Grime, Bob Hudson, Philip Williams and Harry Bennett, Dr Bennett's son who had travelled from Exmouth for the game.

There was some rough and determined play in the field before Stuart (Lenny) Lyon ran for much of the length of the field, vaulting the gate to reach School Lane (and nearly missing his foot on the top rail as he did so). He was stopped in Church Street by Pete Millward and Tim Fearn before the ball was kicked the length of Church Street and to the end of St John Street. Some hand to hand play amongst Up'ards' Simon Hellaby and Darren Hooley and Mick Wright resulted in the latter running with the ball from the recreation ground to Parkside School. The ball headed for Sturston via Paper House Farm. In the running were David Jones, Paul Burton, Andrew Lemon and of course Mick Wright plus Harvey Brown, Barry Handley, Chris Fearn and Bill Ratcliffe who had the ball up his jumper as they approached the goal. Chris Fearn took the honour at 4.13pm with only token opposition.

As players and spectators streamed back down to town it became apparent that another ball had been turned up. Gerald "Dinky" Shepherd had turned up the first decorated ball at 4.44pm. Previous second balls had usually been just plain white.

Feelings were running high with some Down'ards describing the Up'ards tactics of using vehicles and fresh runners as 'absolutely disgraceful'. There was further disquiet that a second ball had been allowed. However, the Committee Chairman had taken his decision to pacify a growing crowd in the Market Place (he was at the Town Hall). Despite the feelings of some people, there were plenty of precedent for both decisions.

For well over a century, players have been still on their way back to Shaw Croft when a second ball was turned up. It was often more convenient for Down'ards to get back – via road or train – and they have traditionally had an advantage here, plus the advantage of travelling with the current rather than pushing against it in the Henmore. The Up'ards tactic to score a goal was also perfectly legitimate. The ball had been continually in play. How players kept it that way was pure tactics. Some Up'ards felt that the goaler deserved his moment of triumph in being carried into town shoulder high. Although this is a recent trend, the argument that it shouldn't be allowed to interrupt the flow of play is persuasive.

Following the second turn up, the ball soon passed Park Road to the area between the Fish Pond and Fire Station. At 5.12pm the ball entered the pond and in the middle, Jim Breeze and his sons Shaun and Andrew, Mark, Anthony and Andrew Slater stopped to throw the ball amongst themselves. Continuing on at length, they crossed the Fish Pond Meadow and went up the rugby field, the ball being kicked back to the Henmore at 5.23pm.

The ball became stuck for about ninety minutes in the field adjacent to Brookside. It had moved the length of the field to the town end as it went dark. Paddy Kerr had the ball but inadvertently threw it to Stuart Lyon who made it off towards Sturston, losing the Down'ards in the dark. As he moved up the fields he passed the ball to Mick Wright who offered to keep it for a while as Stuart made for the mill.

Eventually a group of Up'ards including Bill Ratcliffe, Steve Bott, Johnathan Moss, Mark Hellaby, Andrew Lemon and Stuart Lyon converged upon the goal. As they dropped into the river, on the mill side, Johnathan Moss pulled the ball from up his jumper and Stuart Lyon goaled the leather just after 9pm with only light opposition. It was the 200th goal since 1900.

On the eve of Shrovetide, the town's Mayor, Mr Ian Bates and his brother Brian purchased the gallows sign of the Green Man Hotel to ensure its preservation on behalf of the town. It was reported that the swinging section of the sign hanging from the top was to be repainted by Stuart Avery, with the traditional Green Man on one side and a Shrovetide feature on the other. However, this idea was rejected by the town planners. Another feature of Ashbourne's heritage had been in the news two months earlier, when a planning application to rebuild Sturston Mill was announced. (ANT 17/12/1992) Mr K Pegg wished to restore the remaining machinery to working condition and rebuild the mill. However, although the pit wheel was intact, the waterwheel seemed damaged beyond repair and the wallower seemed to be missing. The building itself was reduced to ground level but the structure below ground level had been excavated and the walls appeared intact.

Tom Webster & Mrs Woolley

The local paper (ANT 4/3/1993) carried a reference to Tom Webster's long-held assertion that his great grandmother turned up the ball by throwing it out of a window in the Market Place in 1878. Her name was Slater. The similarity to Mrs Woolley in 1860 is readily apparent, especially as her maiden name was Barnes and Tom Webster's grandfather was Joe Barnes. One is also tempted to question the accuracy of this, mindful of the article in 1955 (AT 25/2/1955) which gave details submitted by old players about the whereabouts of old balls. James "Tug" Bradley said he goaled his ball in 1898 (it was 1899). He had said he had goaled a second ball in 1913 (it was 1911). Mr J W Walker said he had goaled his ball in 1902 (it was 1903). Mr G E Leese, said his was goaled in 1905 (it was 1904)!

In Mr Webster's defence a second ball was turned up on the Wednesday. However, if much detail of the 1878 games is denied us, there is plenty of evidence about the townspeople and their associated activities that year. 1878 was the year of the riots and excessive drunkenness. There was so much fighting that the police had to call in assistance from local tradesmen. Two days later, several people were charged with being drunk and assaulting the police.

The inquest into the death of J W Barker was also reported. Significantly, there were no charges for playing football in the streets. The evidence for or against a second woman throwing up the ball turns on this point. If the ball had been thrown out of a window in the Market Place, there would have been play in the streets and certainly prosecutions for doing so.

It has been demonstrated that happenings in the town were widely reported – the riots, the prosecution of those drunk and the drowning. It is inconceivable that prosecutions of players would go unreported. Consequently one is drawn to the inevitable conclusion that there was no play in the streets and therefore the assertion that the ball was turned up in the Market Place in 1878 is illfounded. The link between Mr Webster and the lady who turned up the ball must be through the Barnes side of his family; the mists of time having drawn a veil over the truth.

Second Balls

Although "Dinky" Shepherd's ball was the first fully painted second ball with motifs etc, it is possibly not the first second ball to bear more than white paint. It is understood that the second ball turned up after the Prince of Wales may have been painted red, white and blue.

During this period, total goals scored were more even: 115 Down'ards; 111 Up'ards. However, since 1950, the position has become somewhat academic, for a second ball is rarely goaled. From 1950-1993, there have been only 16 of them. Since 1970, they have become rare. In the 1970s (1970-79) there was only one and in the 1980s it was the same, despite 12 second balls being turned up in that period. Clearly there is a good chance that anyone turning up a second ball will find it being returned to him. Third balls were scored in 1896 and 1967.

1994

Nestlé's Nest Egg

Shrovetide got off to a good start on February 15th. Mr Jim Heslop, manager of Nestlé's Ashbourne factory announced that the company had agreed, after two years of negotiation and waiting for head office approval, to donate the site of Clifton Mill and land containing the goal to the committee. He handed over the deeds to John Gadsby at the Tuesday lunch. The last legal difficulty being resolved the previous Friday.

The latter was being held again in the old textile mill – a splendid venue really; it was just a pity that the building was due for demolition. The lunch, for about 430 people, was of good quality and tickets were £12.50 each. John Gadsby deputised for Philip Tomlinson, who was ill.

Councillor Fred Elliot introduced Mr Shields whose hobbies of shooting and fishing were represented on the ball along with the Shields coat of arms. Mr Shields felt it was wonderful that this old tradition was being maintained and noted that the bells had been pealing since 10.00am, thanks to the vicar. He speculated that the bypass currently under construction wouldn't stop the game, especially as it hadn't been stopped in 1860! Finally he addressed the players gathering at the back of the room – "be it up or down, play up and play the ball".

John Gadsby drew attention to two goalers from Kirkwall who were present. In the past year, the game had lost Arthur Birch, who scored the 1928 Wednesday goal (his ball had hung in the Green Man for years and was currently hanging in the Royal Oak at Hanging Bridge with the much larger 1989 ball goaled by Bill Ratcliffe). Mrs Esme Plumbly, wife of the late Herbert Plumbly, had also recently died. Along with Joan Chadwick and Olga Gadsby, she had made and maintained the mobiles hung at lunches, which gave details of turners-up and goalers.

He considered that the lunch could be described as a retirement luncheon. Mr Alan Smith was leaving the Grammar School, having organised half term at Shrovetide; Judge Brian Woods was about to retire (he turned up the ball in 1988). His Lordship always did his best to ensure Ashburnians were back following sentencing in time for Shrovetide. Sir Peter Hilton, the County's Lord Lieutenant (a regular top table guest) was also about to retire. Other guests this year included the Chief Constable, the Derbyshire Dales Council Chairman and the Ashbourne Mayor.

Mr Shields was the Chairman of Longcliffe Quarry, near to Grangemill. He was a Deputy Lieutenant of Derbyshire and he had been the county's High Sheriff in 1989/90. He was also the current President of the Ashbourne Shire Horse Society. Mr Chadwick, the turner-up on the Wednesday, had recently retired as officer in charge of Ashbourne Fire Station. He had been associated with the restoration of an old Shand Mason appliance, which was often seen at special events around the town. Mr Chadwick said he regarded being chosen as an honour not only for himself, 'but for what the fire station lads stand for'.

The balls were made by Arthur Chadwick and painted by Stuart Avery (Tuesday) and Tim Baker (Wednesday). The latter had also decorated the second balls, to be turned up, if required, by Ken Renshaw and Peter Robotham.

Unannounced was the appointment to the committee of Mike Betteridge, following the vacancy created by the death of Jimmy Grant and Ian Bates who replaced Colin Clayton, as one of two council representatives on the committee.

Arriving at the plinth on Shaw Croft, John Gadsby ensured a prompt start; Mr Shields led the singing before he turned up the ball, shouting 'best of luck, are you ready?' whereupon hundreds of arms shot up. Yes, they were ready. By 2.15pm the ball had left the Croft via the Wellington yard for St John Street. John Gadsby was left diplomatically fielding another radio interviewer's statement: 'of course it's a violent game'. Only Ashbourne would disagree and maybe the two lads from Kirkwall, lost from view in the hug.

By 2.30pm the heavy snowfall which had greeted lunch guests had abated and it started to warm up. The ball broke outside the Green Man yard and reached the traffic lights before turning into Dig Street. Twenty minutes later, the ball was in the river below the bank. Play was tediously slow for a while and it was 4.15pm before the ball reached Bank Croft. Much of the paint seemed intact as it occasionally bobbed about above the players. An occasional female voice shouted 'come on you Down'ards'. 'Ginger dan it', her great grandmother would have shouted. Water players included

Andy Hill, Andy and Jimmy Breeze, Dave and Phil Chell, Albert Evans, Mark Johnson, Donald Blenkinsop, John and Ernie Grant, Johnathan Moss, Steve Bott, Dave and Duncan Waring, Andrew Etherington, John Webb, Steve Evans, Doug Marron, Kirk and Scott Maskell, Billy Webster and Mike Betteridge.

The ball left the river unexpectedly up Tyler and Coate's yard to Church Street. A plate glass window wobbled a little and four vehicles took the brunt of the hug as the Down'ards broke down the street to Station Road and towards the swimming baths.

At 4.55pm the ball broke again up to North Leys carried by Mark Allsop. Paul Robson got to it on the edge of the Dockey Fields, but the ball came back to Station Street via the field behind Tidy Hire Ltd, half way along the street. The leather was then kicked down the street, passed Station Road and almost to the lorry park beyond the swimming baths. It came back a little and was picked up by Paddy Kerr and carried up the steps to North Leys with Paul Robson behind him. The ball was thrown into the field where Paddy was challenged by Mick Wright. 'Robbo' picked up the ball and headed off towards the fields at Clifton. He was caught up with and joined by Steve Hudson and Geoff Harrison, together with Dave Hollingworth, Johnathan Henstock, Martin Holland, Gary Baker and Up'ard Mick Parker.

After passing the bypass construction site and one more field, 'Robbo' passed the ball to Steve Hudson and he carried it almost to the golf course before dropping down to Green Lane and the old railway line. Running down the line towards the goal, there was hardly anyone to be seen, but the water was entered early, near the sharp bend above the goal. The leather was passed back by Steve Hudson to Paul Robson and they made for the goal aided by river players including John Tomlinson, Doug Marron, Billy Webster, John Parker, John Webb, Chell, Fearn, Steve Bull and Pete Millward.

The ball came down with about 50 players in the water to the goal where a lone Up'ard hand offered a token resistance before the owner thought better of it. The honour went to Paul Robson who goaled it cleanly first time around, despite a repeat for good measure. It was 5.17pm and only a 100 or so people witnessed the goaling from the bank or bridge. Fortunately, someone had a camera to hand and the owner came forward after an appeal in the paper!

A visitor to the game was Bruce Grobellar, the Liverpool F C goalkeeper.

A Day For The fireman

A record 520 people sat down for lunch with Philip Tomlinson in the chair. Mr John Chadwick ascerted that tradition, custom and sport were what Shrovetide was all about. It was also good training for firemen he contended. Only one of the Ashbourne firemen had goaled the ball (Bill Bennett on Ash Wednesday 1963 when the hug had stopped the train near the tunnel). Looking at his colleagues he said 'how about it. There's one here'. Little did he know what they had in mind that evening. His colleagues had rushed out of the lunch to answer a call at 12.55pm, returning forty minutes later, in time for the sweet course.

Mr Chadwick drew attention to Tim Baker who was 21 years old the following Monday and had painted the days ball, including a picture of the restored Shand Mason fire engine. He felt the game must be the spirit of Ashbourne and ended with the comment 'good luck to the brave who play the game and good luck to the game.'

Philip Tomlinson, commenting on the Nestlé's windfall, dryly remarked that it was just as well Mr Heslop wasn't present, as no Ashbourne water was on the tables. It was a 100 years ago to the day that the first outsider in recorded history had turned up the ball – Mr Harrison of Macclesfield. John Hanson and his wife Barbara were complimented on the organisation of the lunches. He has done everything but had nearly forgotten the balls!

The record number of people attending the lunch would have impressed the former secretary, Arthur Froggatt. It was his idea to issue invitations to enlarge the interest in the game, especially amongst people of influence. The greater the degree of respectability afforded to the custom, the better. The local paper (ANT 24/2/1994) listed the people attending the 1948 lunch, which was Tom Websters first. They were: Sam Flower, Arthur Birch, Harry Wheeldon, Harold Holbrook, Jack Hawksworth, L Harris, J Etches, F Edge, J Edge, Jack Gadsby, Arthur Froggatt, Fred Grime, Bertie Birch (who was also at the 1994 Wednesday lunch) and Tom Webster.

It was exactly 2pm as the ball was turned up by Mr Chadwick. Play moved to Park Road and up to St John Street. The hug moved up and down the street and at 2.12pm moved back once more towards the centre of town. Ten minutes later the ball moved down the Wellington yard and across Shaw Croft. Many people thought the ball had gone up to Sturston in the hands of Up'ards runners, but this was not the case.

The ball was taken through the Park Estate and slowly down Belper Road, reaching the traffic lights at 3.28pm. It was seen several times in Sturston Road and progress was beginning to quicken. Play was outside Cooper's factory in Station Street at 3.50pm and moved inextricably towards Clifton. However, the Down'ards were thwarted as the end of Station Street was reached at 4.01pm, for the ball was run down Station Road to Church Street by Simon Hellaby and other Up'ards. They progressed along Church Street to Smiths Yard before Gary Baker tackled them quickly aided by Steve Hudson and Geoff Harrison.

The ball was worked down Dig Street and between Penny's and the Electricity showroom on the cul-de-sac leading to Shaw Croft. Play continued on to Fish Pond Meadow where the ball was played by Up'ards through the pond itself. It was now 4.30pm and play progressed slowly over to the river. In the Fish Pond were Phil Chell, Darren Hooley, Sean and Anthony Breeze, Pete Mellor, Steve Robotham, Graham Hill, Brian Johnson, Scott Maskell and Jim Breeze.

The 5pm deadline saw play in the rugby field before it returned to the river in the dark. It stayed here for some time before moving back up the fields to Cokayne Avenue. Down'ards pressure saw play proceeding down the road towards town, with a diversion to Shaw Croft before heading down St John Street. The firemen were called away yet again during this period. The Green Man was passed at 7.55pm and Station Road twenty minutes later. Play moved very slowly along by the church and a break by the Down'ards runners seemed inevitable.

However, Up'ards pressure held the hug by the church until play entered Church Fields (close to 9.30pm) where it stayed until 10pm. The firemen had returned and were determined to ensure the day remained goal-less so Mr Chadwick would see his ball returned to him.

At the 1994 annual Ashbourne parish meeting Councillor Jack Moore suggested that the Shrovetide plinth be improved, being 'very poor and uninspiring', with one of the steps broken. (ANT 5/5/1994) The step was repaired before the next game.

The local paper reported that the 1995 games would be held over two months: February 28th and March 1st. George Shaw revealed that the last time this happened was 1933. (ANT 17/11/1994) A new locally-produced ale was announced in December. It was brewed by Bill Allingham at the Bentley Brook Hotel and called *Tearbrain*. The name was taken from the 1821 poem about the game. Fenny Bentley's other pub, the Coach and Horses was already selling another local ale, made at Ashes Farm in the village and sold from pumps showing the game being played at Compton Bridge. It was called *Old Shrovetider*.

1995

At the end of 1994, the committee announced the names of the two guests of honour for 1995. Mr Jim Heslop of Nestlés was to turn up the Tuesday ball and Councillor George Ward MBE, JP, the Wednesday ball. Mr Heslop's invitation was in recognition of the gift of the Clifton Mill site to the committee. The honour was nearly soured by an ill-judged attempt to link it to redundancies at the factory just prior to the game. Mr Heslop rode above suggestions that it was insensitive after 25% of the factory's workforce was cut. (ANT 09/02/1995) The game has consistently avoided indirect linkage with anything and the lack of comment from the committee was only to be expected.

The decision to return to the Green Man Hotel for the lunches was announced in January.

When You've Got Hold Of It, It 'Wunner' go Anywhere

This year saw the Cooper's mill demolished and more importantly, the Barnes Wear/Meridian building gone where the lunch had been held in the previous two years. It was good to be back at the Green Man Hotel after three venues in four years, even if the 407 guests had to be shoe-horned in. Chairman Philip Tomlinson mentioned that Jim Heslop was turning up the 250th ball since 1900 (he said 'this century' but that began in 1901). He also referred to Frank Tomlinson, his great great uncle, who had turned up the ball on the Wednesday of 1895, for the first of nine times. He noted that Arthur Chadwick had been making balls for the game for 41 years – a tremendous achievement and typical of the long term commitment many Ashbourne people had given to the game.

He recalled the Nestlé gift of the Clifton Mill site and noted that no one could stop play on their own ground. He clearly didn't have the same faith when he referred to the decision by Derby County F C to ban swearing and hoped that Shrovetide players would remember it. The two balls for this year's games and the two decorated second balls lay before him on the table, included Ken Renshaw's ball, the first of the second balls. Philip Tomlinson referred to this. It had a view of the local church and a football on it. Philip, in his dry way, referred to the time Ken had lost control of a horse belonging to his (Philip's) farm. It had been stopped by the gas works and a tedding machine minus a wheel might have been more appropriate, he thought.

Mr Heslop said that he was 'grateful, thrilled and excited'. He referred to Stuart Avery, the painter of his ball and described its decoration. It included a loco, a symbol of Workington Iron and Steel Works where he served his apprenticeship as a fitter mending locos. He was a member of the Institute of Mechanical Engineers and their Coat of Arms featured on the ball too, together with the Nestlé logo.

He moved on indirectly to the recent redundancies at Nestlé's. It was, he said, nice to make the donation of the Clifton Mill site and other donations to local charities on behalf of his company, but his most important contribution was to maintain a healthy business in the town, even if that meant making difficult decisions.

He held up the ball, which had been sent to the Ashbourne lads serving in France in 1916. The owner, Mrs Creswall, was present at the lunch. At least seven, perhaps 11 men from Nestlé did not return from the Great War. (See detail under 1916 for more on this).

Finally he concluded by saying that he hoped that 'long may they prosper – Nestlé, the game and the town.'

If ever there was a potent symbol that it was 'business as usual', it was the sight of the ball being brought down the steps from the first floor into the Green Man yard. At the plinth, Philip Tomlinson reminded players to keep the ball out of the churchyard, cemetery and memorial garden – and all other gardens. He was not amused about events the previous year when there was play in gardens in the Park Estate and a fence brought down on Belper Road.

The ball was turned up at 2.07pm and after veering towards the Health Centre, left Shaw Croft for the fire station at 2.20pm. Five minutes later, the second of the two fire engines left for Thorpe, threading its way through the massed supporters in Park Road. Tom Donnelly, Dave Sellers, Stuart Leese, P Holmes and Alan Maher had left the game to answer the call. Play moved into Park Avenue and at 2.51pm the ball was thrown high and into Peter Street. Shortly afterwards, a helicopter on hire to Central TV, which had been overhead for an hour, made off for the last time.

Play moved back into Park Avenue, eventually reaching Cullen Avenue before breaking across the fire station at 3.12pm, ending up on the fairground in Fish Pond Meadow. The game was still progressing only slowly, but at 3.35pm the ball appeared again and movement started across the field, reaching the pond. It kept clear of both the pond and the river becoming lodged against the memorial ground wall at 3.48pm. At this point, the following were in play (per the ANT report) Tim and Chris Fearn, Darren Waring, Mark Harrison, Doug Sowter, Steve Bott, Bill Radcliffe and Nick Jones plus many more of course.

Movement only meant a cross over the road to Madge House where one player was heard saying, 'when you've got hold of it, it wunner go anywhere!' It seemed to sum up play very well. Play wandered back down the road towards Shaw Croft and by 4.40pm had reached the school playing fields adjacent to the river, having crossed the pond and river to get there. Mark Johnson had gone into the pond with the ball and with about fifteen players in all floating about, including Scott Maskell, Jason Clowes, Mick Fearn, Jim Breeze, Bobby Brown and Steve Robotham who threw the ball out to Duncan Collins.

Although the weather had been fine, a cold wind started to make itself felt amongst supporters anxious for some action. The ball reached the river again as the 5pm deadline passed and play was virtually stationary (and very boring) until a break at 5.18pm when the ball was landed. This was toiled after about 50 feet or so and play returned to the water. Amongst the players were John Tomlinson, Julian Burton, Nick Adams, Dave Chell, Billy Webster, Doug Morran and Ernie Grant. Another attempt to land the ball was successful for only ten minutes and at 5.45pm play was still in the river. Another break saw a determined effort to leave the Henmore and the hug reached Parkside School and Cokayne Avenue.

The ball was stopped by the Down'ards at the junction of Cokayne Avenue and Green Road. It then broke back to Parkside and then back into the Grammar School playing field before crossing the recreation ground to the swings. Play crossed the river into Fish Pond Meadow before re-crossing over the footbridge and onto the Wellington Pub football pitch.

It crossed the river at least three times, in fact ending up on the school playing fields again. In the dark, three Down'ards walked away from the hug. Brian Thornley had the ball up his jumper and had Garry Baker and Martin Holland with him. However, it appears he didn't get far and David Calladine took the ball off him. Included in the play at this part of the evening were Stuart Lyon, Mark Harrison, Geoff Harrison, Billy Webster, Dave Bolt, Paddy Kerr, David Wright, Brian Thornley, Steve Hudson, Jim Boden, Andrew Adams, Nigel Wright, Pete Bettany and Rob Godfrey.

Action crossed the river once more, moving up a field before coming back again over the Henmore on to the north side. It was at this point that play broke up to Sturston. David Calladine ran up the hedge side and hid the ball. There was controversy at this point with allegations of the ball being moved towards Sturston by car, which the Up'ards denied. Although serious consideration was not given to this claim, at least one Down'ard claimed he saw the leather in a vehicle. The ANT reports that David Calladine proceeded to Sturston after retrieving the ball and passed it to Andrew Etherington but George Handley had already called time and the goal was disallowed.

Play At Sandybrook

At the Ash Wednesday lunch attended by 408 guests, Philip Tomlinson admonished the players for their short memories – relating to the play in Alec Smith's and Mrs Ruby Gregory's garden the day before. 'Tie a knot in your ties ... or something' he suggested. The day before, the emphasis had been on Nestlé and the Clifton Mill gift. He referred on this day to Mr and Mrs Pegg of Sturston Mill who had had the hug and followers in their back yard the night before. 'They do not complain', he said as he thanked them for their tolerance. He also thanked the ball painters – Stuart Avery (the Tuesday ball) and Tim Baker (the Wednesday ball), the caterers (the Green Man Hotel had retained Ridgeway Caterers from Stoke-on-Trent who had done the job in the previous three years), the Green Man staff and Whitehouse Construction for repairing the Shaw Croft plinth.

He mentioned that it was apparently 200 years since the goals were moved to the two mills (see comments above), raising a laugh saying that Tom Webster had been to that many lunches he was probably there then! Councillor Bertie Birch introduced Councillor Ward who had been a councillor for 30 years and was part of the Burton family of Shrovetide players. Between them they could account for 22 goals. Councillor Birch ended by urging the players to 'play it up and down, like you ought to. Let's see some rough play and no damage'.

Councillor Ward then rose and gave an impressive speech. He referred to his ball, painted by his nephew – 'a Down'ard and proud of it'. His family were part of Shrovetide history. His mother was 97 years old and was on School Lane Bridge when it collapsed in 1932, pitching her into the river, but it hadn't dampened her enthusiasm. To goal the ball you needed to be hard and tough and display stamina and courage. The stalwarts of the game were men of a rare breed. He had a memory of water play from beneath the arches of Compton Bridge to Back Bridge when the ball was hugged and thrown up and down the river beneath the former hoardings that bounded the former course of the river. He hoped that this sort of play would be seen again, for the benefit of spectators. He needn't have worried.

The game, he continued, should never be allowed to die. There was a community spirit evident every Shrovetide, drawn together by a common bond. He was proud of the council, of Ashbourne and Royal Shrovetide Football. After being carried from Dig Street to the plinth, where he was joined by Tim Baker at his (Mr Ward's) request. Councillor Ward turned up the ball, which moved towards the Health Centre before doubling back to Fish Pond Meadow where it was quickly in the pond with six players close behind. In the water were Adam Stubbs, Mark Robotham, Nick Fearn, Graham Hill, Chris Russell and one other player.

However, by 2.15pm play left the water and moved over to the fire station, as on the previous day. The game moved into Park Avenue before making for the traffic lights and reaching Belper Road about 2.30pm. At 2.51pm play was going through the traffic lights at the end of Compton after the ball had been pitched high in the air in Sturston Road. The hug turned down Compton and the ball broke free, reaching Dig Street at 3pm. Down'ard pressure told again and the ball was hugged towards the church, reaching School Lane at 3.26pm. Play was soon in the river. It became stuck just below the bridge, bringing back thoughts of Councillor Ward's comments about his mother falling into the river from the bridge in 1932.

After twenty minutes of little movement, the ball was worked loose and with two good throws, Up'ard Terry Brown was off up the river with it. He handed the leather to his brother Alan who headed into the tunnel. Play continued into the fields east of the river and upstream of Seven Arches. There was much kicking going on and plenty of opportunity to see the ball. Following a trip to the river, it was thrown out at 4.30pm. It was kicked across a field, thrown over a fence and broke away up to the Buxton Road and on up the drive to Hurtswood. Many stragglers had no idea where the ball had gone. Some, like Ken Dakin, were wet to the waist.

The ball had been taken to Windmill Lane and dropped into a compost heap. It was 'lost' for twenty minutes before being found by Down'ard Geoff Harrsion, accompanied by Steve Hudson. It had been hidden by Tim Brown's nephew. Geoff's discovery was rumbled and the ball taken by Up'ard Mick Parker. He ran into John Tomlinson and Pete Mellor.

After being hugged for five minutes, it broke with Mick Parker taking it again and passing it to George Ditchfield. Mick Wright took it across a small ravine north of Windmill Lane and without agreement, the ball was released. Amongst the players at this time were Mark Hellaby, Steve Wright, Mark Harrison, Nobby Clarke and Pete Mellor. Others arrived including Adrian Webb, Mark Wesson, Richard Wyman, Jim Leemon, Lenny Lyons, Richard Whieldon, Nigel Bailey and others.

It was over an hour before the ball broke and headed for the rear of Sandybrook Hall. David Hollingsworth made the initial running before Paul Robson and Nigel Bailey run it to behind the hall where three Down'ards and two Up'ards were with the leather. Play reached the Buxton Road at about 6pm with Steve Bott in possession. Play returned to the fields at about 6.20pm and Charlie Birch had the ball on Callow Top Drive at one point. The ball was thrown over a fence and picked up Paddy Kerr who headed over the Tissington Trail with Steve Challinor. Paddy acted as a decoy and Steve headed for Clifton via Mappleton, having to swim the River Dove at one point. The ball was out of play for nearly an hour (not missed by the Up'ards) but the issue was not seriously contended. Paddy met up with Steve at a pre-arranged point and drew lots for the goal. Paddy won and jumped into the river, but was prevented from scoring, as much by Down'ards as others. Lots were drawn and Doug Renshaw won, but objections were then raised that he had not been playing long enough.

It was agreed that John Tomlinson should take the honour and after eventually overcoming the last of the opposition, it was goaled at 7.55pm before a good-sized crowd.

This was the first time that the ball had been run the whole way from Ashbourne to Clifton since Geoff Harrison did it 1981.

The reference to the bicentenary of using the two mills as goals stems from a reference in the ANT to this effect, but see pp 44/45.

Other News

In April the old house of correction was put up for sale. It had been built in 1815 and details of its sale in 1830 have been given above. Here past Shrovetiders were incarcerated during the 19th century disturbances. They included Luke Faulkner in 1879 as a result of the Compton Bridge riot. He is the man holding the ball on the 1862 painting. It is situated near the bottom of Derby Road.

On 30th May, Col Sir Peter Hilton, the former Lord Lieutenant of Derbyshire, died aged 75 years. He had been awarded the Military Cross three times, was President of the Normandy Veterans

Association and had taken the Norwegian surrender in 1945. He always maintained that turning up the ball in 1971 was the greatest moment of his life, after his wedding. He was knighted in 1993 and Lord Lieutenant from 1978-94. Each year both he and Lady Hilton came to the Shrovetide lunches. The day before, Mr Charles Etches died, aged 76. The Etches had been formidable players – his father and uncle had goaled in 1900 and 1895 respectively and he had followed them in 1941, turning up the Wednesday ball in 1980.

On 27 October, the new store plinths on the riverbank at Sturston and Clifton were topped out. Sixty tons of concrete and limestone were used at Clifton and 74 tons at Sturston. The new rule for goaling required the scorer to hit the millstone (incorporated within the plinth) three times whilst standing in the river. The stone was given by Longcliffe Quarry and built by Whitehouse Construction Ltd.

1996

The 4 January *Ashbourne News Telegraph* led with the news that Brell Ewart and Peter Gadsby were to turn up the balls. Both were described as being generous supporters of the game. Brell had constructed the two plinths the year before, Peter's grandfather, J E Gadsby goaled at Clifton on Ash Wednesday 1931; his cousin John Gadsby had scored in 1956 and Peter himself in 1965 – one of the youngest ever to score.

At the Tuesday lunch, Brell had turned up with his workers who had built the plinths, a far cry from his initial days in the town when he had refused them permission to have time off for the two games (they went anyway). He raised a laugh when he explained that he had had an unfortunate experience with both the current and the previous Committee Chairman. He urged caution for anyone with a vision of becoming Committee Chairman 'because Whitehouse Construction is coming and sewerage is involved!'

A Rumble In The Rec

The ball went up after the usual singing on a bitterly cold day. After closing on the wall by the Shaw Croft flats, the hug moved over Park Road and into Fish Pond Meadow. The ball quickly headed for the Fish Pond, but only one player went after it. However, play swung around to the river and for an hour or so the hug circled around between the river and the pond.

Just after 4pm, the game made off towards the rec and the rugby pitches, remaining in what is to be the new school playing field until after darkness fell. Eventually, the Down'ards pushed play back towards the town reaching Shaw Croft. An attempt to reach St John Street via the Wellington Yard failed before the ball eventually was to be seen in the street. After a deviation into Dig Street failed to see the ball reaching the river, play went down Church Street and into Station Road.

A break saw the ball thrown down onto the railway line. The ball eventually headed for Clifton, reaching the plinth in the arms of Andy Hill, accompanied by Darren Waring, Paul Clarke and brothers Paul and Mark Harrison. Steve Bull drew straws for those in the water; Darren won and he goaled the ball at 8.47pm. It was the first one to be scored on the new plinths.

Peter Gadsby Does It Twice

On Ash Wednesday, Peter Gadsby told the lunchtime guests that the game had taught him many qualities for his business life – motivation, economics and opportunity. Amongst the guests were players from Derby County F.C., (where he was vice-chairman) along with the team manager – Jim Smith. The team had to face six matches in three weeks and Philip Tomlinson wondered how they would fair if they had to play for eight hours at a stretch as at Ashbourne.

If the game had taught Peter Gadsby the meaning of 'opportunity' he took the chance of displaying this by turning the ball up twice. After turning it up in the usual manner, it was hugged for five minutes or so at the plinth. John Grant managed to get it back onto the plinth but before he could turn it up, Philip Tomlinson passed it to Peter Gadsby who turned it up for a second time. George Peach had done the same in 1973.

This time play got under way and quickly reached Park Road via the flats and Ashbourne Taxis' premises next door. Within minutes, the ball broke across Fishpond Meadow, across the rec and on towards Parkside School. It returned like a yo-yo to Fishpond Meadow before heading back to the school. A break by Terry Brown, David Hollingworth and John Hemstock saw the ball heading for Cokayne Avenue and then up the footpath to the Green Road.

The ball was then ran along King Street and into Union Street before being hugged through the Market Place and via Victoria Square into St John Street. The fast pace wasn't over either for the ball headed into Shaw Croft before returning to the top of Dig Street, by the Corner House. There was much for the spectators to see and the weather was much warmer than the previous day.

From the Corner House, the ball reached the river via the White Hart yard. After a time in the culvert, play went into Compton and Belper Road before going missing – allegedly being rested in a house in St Oswalds Crescent. Wherever it had been, it was found after 5pm being hugged at the top of the Crescent, before it broke and reached the river via Brookside. An hour later play was in the fields near Paper House Farm. The Up'ards held the advantage now, players including Simon Hellaby, George Ditchfield, Terry Brown, Andrew Etherington, Martin Hellaby, Algie Fearn, Alan Brown, Mark Hellaby, Joe Moss, Kirk Maskell, Rob Godfrey, Andy Hill, six of the Spencers, Doug Sowter and Mick Wright.

Bill Ratcliffe drew straws and Steve Wright hit the plinth at 6.45pm.

1997

Four hundred and thirty people booked the Ash Wednesday meal but there were a lot less on the Tuesday, well below 400 guests. The balls were made by Arthur Chadwick and painted by Tim Baker (Tuesday) and Stuart Avery (Ash Wednesday).

The Tuesday turner-up was Roy Spencer, of Ashbourne Biscuits Ltd. A player in his youth, he could remember the Prince of Wales coming to Ashbourne in 1928. He commented that his ball incorporated the Lions organisation logo of which he was a founder member. 'At the present time they are hoping to raise £100,000 for the new Community & Sports Hall complex,' he said. To celebrate the invitation to turn up the ball, Mr Spencer had given his employees half a day off.

Philip Tomlinson commented on the death of Committee member Arthur Parry. The pre-game disco had raised over £400 for charity. It was now emulating the work of the Committee under Jack Hawksworth in the early years of the century. Handing over to the town Mayor, Harold Maddocks, the latter commented that Mr Spencer now employed over 50 people, and over a third of their output was exported. He was glad of the opportunity of seeing the ball without being pushed and shoved all over Ashbourne.

The Up'ards Assert Themselves

Mr Bill Kent, a local farmer with a long association with the Rugby Club, turned up the Wednesday ball. It rose into the air at 2.02pm and was quickly played through the area of the flats and on to Park Road. After a diversion into Fishpond Meadow, the hug went up Park Road to Belper Road. Here it turned right, reaching the top of Compton at about 2.30pm, being hugged against the Social Club wall. From here, play moved down Compton and the ball went over the wall into the river by the bridge. Played down to Bank Croft, the ball was hugged outside the Empire Club before returning to Bank Croft. In the rain, the hug eventually proceeded down Station Road and Station Street (with a diversion up North Leys), before returning down Compton to Dig Street. Play was static at the traffic lights for some time before moving along St John Street. A sudden break occurred, leaving most people not knowing where the ball had gone to. It was hugged in the fields near Green Road, slowly heading for Sturston where Simon Hellaby ended play at 8.28pm after drawing for it at the goal.

This was the first time one side had scored on each day since 1990 (two at Clifton) and the first time the Up'ards had scored one on each day since 1989. Their previous success at this was back in 1965 when they had achieved three goals in one year.

Another Second Ball For The Up'ards

Following the traditional turning, it took ten minutes before play crossed Park Road to the river. The ball went through the culvert and down the Henmore to Bank Croft where it was landed at about 2.40pm. Play progressed into the Bus Station and at about 2.50pm the ball was thrown clear of the hug by Ernie Fearn. Taken initially by Roy Gibbs, the ball was passed to Mick Wright who ran with it across the rugby pitches towards Paper House Farm. Various other Up'ards helped to carry the leather even closer to Sturston. It reached the goal in the hands of Terry Brown, who crossed the river to reach the goal at about 3.15pm. It was two goals in the two days for the Up'ards and the local paper rightly pointed out that it was one of the fastest goals in recent years, the ball retaining much of its paint.

Another Second Ball For 'Pop' Robotham

Although Ken Renshaw was down to turn up the next second ball required, he was in hospital and the honour went to Peter (Pop) Robotham, who turned up the leather at 3.45pm. Another quick goal would have given us the first third ball for 30 years but it was not to be.

Play circulated a lone red Peugeot before the ball went over the wall past the flats and on to Park Road, being slowly hugged along to Belper Road. Here the usual pause occurred; each side trying to ensure the ball went their way. The Down'ards overcame the opposition and play went along Compton and into the Bus Station, ignoring a downpour of rain. Eventually the Down'ards reached the river after spirited opposition on Bank Croft.

Although the ball went down the river, eventually reaching the bypass, the Up'ards pressure saw a change of direction and play headed back towards town after about an hour of near stationary hugging. From Clifton Road, the ball was hugged down Station Street and Compton and on to Park Road via Shaw Croft for the second time.

It was turned 9pm when the hug, now in Park Avenue, realised that the ball was missing. The Down'ards had hidden it in a phone box before quietly moving away. They were caught out However, and although making a good break, they were stopped on Derby Road where it was hugged back to Sturston Road as 10.00pm saw the end of play.

Peter Robotham had been denied the ball he had thought he had goaled in the second game of 1969. This year, the second ball went home with him. Terry Brown's goal was the third in a row for the Up'ards. Only Peter Gadsby had achieved that since 1949. However, the sun was rising for the Up'ards. The local paper recorded the following amongst the hug: Up'ards – John Hughes, George Ditchfield, Doug Sowter, Phil Chell, Andy Hill, Mark Hallam, Andrew Lemon, Andrew Etherington, Nick Fearn, Steve Bott, Bill Ratcliffe and Alan Brown. For the Down'ards – Pete Millward, Steve & Andrew Bull, Dave Chell, Darren Waring, John Tomlinson, Billy Webster, Tim Fearn, Mark & Paul Harrison, Doug Marron, Craig Slater, Eric Taylor and Peter Mellor.

Ernie Grant was accredited with supplying on-site refreshment, as usual, from a bottle in his pocket.

The honour of turning up the Wednesday ball went to Bill Kent, a local farmer, member of Wyaston Show Committee, former chairman of the Ashbourne Farmers' Ball and enthusiastic supporter of Ashbourne RUFC. He was introduced by Councillor P Brindley, Chairman of Derbyshire Dales District Council. At the lunch, Philip Tomlinson announced plans for a new plinth on Shaw Croft, hoping that quotes for its construction would begin with a nought, rather than ending with one!

1998

Civil Liberties

The Chief Constable of Derbyshire, Mr John Newing, was the guest of honour on the Tuesday, attending the game under different circumstances than some of his 19th century predecessors or from 1976. The only previous policeman to turn up the ball was Ex-Inspector John Burton in 1921. He had then joined the hug only to be injured in the face. It was the 75th anniversary since the 'Royal' appendage was first used by the game, following acceptance of a football by Princess Mary the year before. It was also 150 years since the first reported upset between the police and the players, when a constable tried to stop the ball from being cut up and was thumped for his trouble (see page 51). Philip Tomlinson advised the Chief Constable that he imagined there would be some people around with the same name as those involved if he cared to look them up!

After the Mayor, Coun Vince Ferry, had proposed the toast to the game, Mr Newing rose to respond. Having been a London police officer he was used to civil unrest and riots. Ashbourne's game was neither he said. "I believe these events are part of the British tradition and must continue", he continued.

Citing the analogy of the Notting Hill Carnival, which brought two million people onto the streets, he said: "I think that demonstrated what this is about. It is about people exercising their civil liberties and the police officers are here as referees and observers. I expect them to exercise discretion and a good sense of perspective. I know they do that because I have seen them do it."

A car parked by the plinth and definitely in the way turned out to belong to the manageress of Ridgway Catering, who provided the Shrovetide lunch!

The ball rose just before 2pm and after being pushed around Shaw Croft for over twenty minutes, play moved to Park Road and slowly progressed along to the traffic lights and into Sturston Road. The ball rose in the air from time to time and cameras clicked on a sunny day to record it.

Turning into Compton, the ball broke, but only as far as King Edward Street, being hugged tightly against the Council offices and then Lloyds Bank. Play looked as though it was heading for the river, but the Up'ards turned it over the road to the side of the Health Centre. A long throw along the flats perimeter wall saw play go out of sight and off to Park Road. Going through Fishpond Meadow, as 4pm passed, the ball was pitched into the pond and broke quickly across the river and up the playing fields towards the car park.

Play returned to the river however, slowly moving downstream towards the culvert with spectators covering every inch of available viewing space. It was getting close to 5pm when the ball was thrown clear at 4.50pm, but a break was thwarted just before the fields, south of the river. Up'ards Alan Brown and Lenny Lyon pulled the ball clear to Nobby Clarke who threw it to Algie Fearn. In the dark, he hid it up his jumper and walked away. Simon and Mark Hellaby took over, passing it to George Ditchfield. A draw was made, favouring Andrew Etherington, who received the ball brought in by Mark Hellaby and Tony Goldstraw. Touching the plinth, Andrew maintained a family tradition – his grandfather was Arthur Froggatt, Shrovetide Committee Secretary from 1953-74.

It was good to see Andrew getting his ball. However, with the Rugby Club playing Up'ards *en masse*, contrary to tradition but in exercise of their civil liberty, one wondered if the Up'ards needed to 'exercise a bit more discretion and good sense of perspective,' as the Chief Constable had put it.

A Good Afternoon In The River

Chris Trafford turned up the Wednesday ball, the last to be lifted from the old-style plinth in the middle of Shaw Croft. He had been attending lunches for some 35 years and most of his Company's employees were present at the lunch, or expected to be on Shaw Croft for the turn up. Amongst the guests of honour were Mr & Mrs Pegg of Sturston Mill, who regularly had to put up with the players and spectators visiting them at Shrovetide. Mr Trafford was introduced by Alan Hodkinson, Chairman of the Derbyshire Dales District Council. Alan said the choice was very fitting. Mr Trafford was a successful businessman, running Dove Valley Poultry. The Company employed over 300 people, with a turnover of £35 million. He had been an active supporter for many years. His ball had a leghorn cockerel on one of the side faces and a shire horse on the other. Mr Trafford had held various positions in the community and had been a past President of the Ashbourne Shire Horse Society.

The ball rose at 1.57pm and was soon in the Fishpond Meadow. It quickly broke in the hands of Roger Tomkinson and then Mick Wright, who was stopped by Gary Baker. The ball soon went into the River Henmore but the Up'ards held the initiative, carrying the ball via Terry Ball and George Ditchfield across the playing fields. The ball was then hugged for some time with continual Down'ard pressure pushing the ball towards the river. The Up'ards however, hugged the ball into the Grammar School playing field where the play remained for some time.

Play inevitably reached the river and despite exertion by both sides and some hard play, the ball did not leave it until just turned 5pm. It then went into Fishpond Meadow, but it soon broke over the river, reaching The Green Road from the school playing field, using the narrow access point adjacent to 100 Green Road.

Play proceeded up the road to Old Boothby Farm – Up'ard Alan Kingston's home and the former Boothby Arms pub. The pace quickened as play broke with Simon Hellaby legging it towards Sturston. He passed the ball on to Wayne Travers and a succession of Up'ards maintained the run towards the goal. Although there was some Down'ard opposition, Sturston was reached with the ball in the possession of George Ditchfield who jumped into the river to reach the plinth.

It was another two goals for the Up'ards over the two days and five Up'ards goals in a row at Sturston. An excess of bad language on the march back to town and in the Green Man earned the Up'ards a strong admonishment from Carol Frost the following week in the local paper. To their credit, the Up'ards have not repeated it.

In September, work started on the construction of the new plinth. Initial thoughts were to place it in the south west corner of Shaw Croft, but photographs would have placed the turner-up in shadow or even silhouette. It was officially opened on 1st February 1999 by Lady Hilton.

1999

The turners-up for the year were announced on the last day of 1998 as the Lord Lieutenant of Derbyshire, Mr John Bather and Brian Bates. Mr Bather had succeeded Shrovetide enthusiast Col Sir Peter Hilton. Brian had recently retired and the well-known Bates' Bakery in Compton had finally baked its final loaf. The balls had been made by Arthur Chadwick; Tim Baker had painted the Tuesday ball and Stuart Avery, the Wednesday ball.

Family Records

At the lunch, the Lord Lieutenant and Committee Chairman both did a creditable performance showing their grasp of the game's history. The former highlighted the involvement of the Tomlinsons over the last 140 years, making a career with many of Ashbourne's finest at the Magistrates Courts, picking up a string of convictions for playing Shrovetide in the street. After the last of the prosecutions, succeeding generations had turned up the ball and Philip had become chairman in 1991 (he was to turn the ball up too in 2000). Moreover, his son, John, had scored in 1995. As family support for the game goes, the Tomlinsons' record is second to none. However, what Mr Bather did not realise is that the record of their involvement goes back to 1797 and the switch to the two mills as goals. No other family can match that, purely (and only) because the early records are incomplete. Nonetheless, it does show the allegiance the game commands over the generations. (see p 196)

The Chairman referred to the work undertaken by various businesses in supplying materials for the new plinth and to Mr Barry Wibberley who had given two days of his time to build it. He went on to advise guests that is was 100 years since a serving Shrovetide secretary had goaled a ball and 75 years since a serving chairman had goaled it (J Hawksworth and J Harrison respectively).

After the turn-up, the first one from the new plinth, play moved into Fishpond Meadow. It remained there for a while before moving up Park Road to Belper Road. It was now 3pm as the play moved Up'ards towards Sturston. It reached the top of the ridge just beyond Park Avenue by 5pm, but play was very slow and predictable. Near the top of Sturston Lane, play was in the field and it was getting dark. The Down'ards introduced a dummy ball and for a while the ruse worked.

Despite spirited opposition, the real ball slowly headed towards Sturston, reaching the bridge just prior to 7pm. At 6.59pm Nick Fearn lifted the ball for another Up'ard goal. For him it was a family hat trick, for brother Tim scored at Clifton in 1992 and brother Chris scored at Sturston in 1993. It had probably been the first time this had happened for many decades. Nick's family has other Shrovetide connections; his wife Colleen's father, Colin LeGrice was a well known stalwart too. It was another fine family record.

A Ball For Brian

At the Wednesday lunch, prior to introducing the turner-up, Brian Bates, who really did not require an introduction, Philip Tomlinson remarked on the Up'ards goal of the previous day and the 'Shrovetide-free zone south of the bypass'. Certainly the Down'ards needed a new strategy to overcome the Up'ards superiority.

Brian was introduced by the chairman of Derbyshire Dales District Council, Alun Thomas, a member of the Winster Morris Men. He sang their traditional song too. Brian talked about the rivalry between the two sides before declaring his support for the Up'ards. After further singing – 'Land of Hope & Glory' by Arthur Chadwick, Barry Greenwood, plus the diners – Brian was escorted down the hotel's back steps, down Dig Street for the traditional photographs outside the Coach & Horses and then on to the plinth.

It was to be a day of spirited play despite the rain and another bout of prolonged play near the Sturston goal in the dark. It ended without a goal too, an event becoming increasingly common.

After the traditional singing of Auld Lang Syne and the National Anthem at the plinth – the last to be lead by the turner-up; Arthur and Barry were to lead it in 2000 – the ball was turned up early and by 2pm was heading along Park Road. Some of the Up'ards had been badly caught out and were only just reaching Shaw Croft. At the traffic lights and after some hesitation, the hug moved to the top of Compton.

Following attempts to pull the ball clear at the Social Club, play moved on to the corner of Lloyds Bank, where the ball was lifted into the air a couple of times. It did not reach the river and became fast again against the Health Centre at 3pm. A good throw saw the ball being taken through the flats and on to Park Road once more. After a lull in Fishpond Meadow, a surge saw the leather bobbing along in the Fish Pond.

This did not produce a break, however, and after further hugging in the Meadow, a Down'ards initiative saw more water play, this time in the river. It was now 3.30pm and the ball slowly made its way downstream. The Up'ards took advantage of the area of the Fish Pond overflow to force play back into Fishpond Meadow. However, nearly an hour had passed and the 5pm deadline once more seemed to be slipping away. Several Down'ards initiatives came to nothing, but at least they kept the ball on the move, delighting the crowd as it sailed up above outstretched arms.

If a break to Clifton could not be achieved, a change of tactics could stop an Up'ard goal and as time ticked on, the ball was hugged around fields and in the river, ending up near Paper House Farm in the rain at 10pm. The local newspaper carried a letter of support from Down'ard Davina Harrison (ANT 24/2/1999), urging her team on and expressing thanks for 'Stopping the boring play by the Up'ards clones on Wednesday'. Historians of social behaviour will be interested to note that the passionate support of female followers of the game, expressed vociferously over generations, is still extant.

2000

Records And Regrets

For the last year of the millennium the turners-up were Committee Secretary John Hanson and Chairman Philip Tomlinson. Not mentioned at the time was that it was John's 21st year as Secretary. Given the never-ending rumour and gossip about the Committee, it was perhaps inevitable that he would set the record straight on various issues. Perhaps the main ones being financial assets: "no amazing amount of money stowed in a churn in Philip Tomlinson's field; 'bungs' for turning up balls etc." He also reminded the guests, sitting in three rooms, linked by expensive CCTV, that in 1936, the Committee had invited a woman – Gracie Fields – who turned down the request. Introduced by the Mayor, Alan Hodkinson, the latter felt that the choice of turners-up was a popular move and indeed it was. John, in thanking various helpers, presented his wife, Barbara, with flowers for all the help she did annually in arranging the Shrovetide lunch. Apparently later, he asked her to jointly turn up the ball with him, but she declined. No doubt controversial had she done so, many would have felt it was appropriate and timely. However, as John Gadsby was to lament on the Wednesday 'the Committee don't like women'. John Hanson's speech, $17^1/_2$ minutes, created a record of its own, even if Barbara did not a little later!

Regrettably, just as the lunch proceedings were about to commence on Shrove Tuesday, Committee member Alec Robinson collapsed and died. He had been a Committee member for over 20 years. John Hanson's son, Dr Richard Hanson and others had endeavoured to revive Alec after he collapsed in his chair, but to no avail.

The tragic circumstances delayed the lunch and the turn-up was probably the latest since 1942. The reason was not officially given, however, until Ash Wednesday, when a minute silence was observed at the lunch. Alec had turned up the second Wednesday ball in 1984.

Philip Tomlinson did announce that play would be allowed until 10.45pm and the 5pm deadline for a second ball would be extended to 5.45pm. After the singing of the National Anthem, John Hanson said that 'as Scotland was bent on going it alone' Auld Land Syne should be dispensed with and the ball was turned up at 2.41pm with no further ado.

'From A Spectator's View...A Dead Loss'

The above was how the local paper described play in the afternoon, with play restricted to a few yards from Shaw Croft – with quick visits to Fishpond Meadow and Compton. Eventually play went back to Park Road and then up to St John's Street, at about 4.30pm. Play then went from Cokayne Avenue into the recreational ground and across the river. It was still in Fishpond Meadow at 7pm before the ball re-crossed the river for the inevitable hugging towards Sturston. Diversionary tactics kept the Down'ards at bay and Mark Spencer won two draws to score. His grandfather, William Spencer had scored in 1911.

Down'ards Stop Up'ards Equalling A Record

On the Wednesday, Philip Tomlinson was the recipient of the usual Derwent Crystal goblet, rather than handing it over. This was received from John Gadsby who was back in the chair for the day. He called for a moment's silence out of respect for Alec Robinson and also referred to the resignation of Sid Taylor after 25 years on the Committee.

At 2pm the ball rose in the air on time, Philip Tomlinson no doubt giving it an extra shove towards Clifton as he sent it on its way on a fine day. Play quickly moved through the flats and into Fishpond Meadow before moving on to Sturston Road and being hugged against the Social Club wall, where it was thrown onto the roof of the club extension before bouncing back into the hug.

Play proceeded down Compton to Lloyds Bank before crossing over the road to the supermarket where the ball was hugged against the building. The Down'ards were trying to reach the river and did so at 4.10pm. Slowly, they made ground, reaching the swimming pool car park just after 5.00pm. The Down'ards all-time record of a straight run of eight goals was in jeopardy with the Up'ards now on seven. Desperate times called for strategic planning which came in the form of a duffle bag.

Somehow, the ball was extracted from the hug by Mark and Geoff Harrison, hidden in the bag; then tied to a tree. The Down'ards kept hugging down river as Richard Wheeldon made off through Nestlé's yard and via the Shires Estate and Golf Course to Clifton. Hiding the ball in the coalyard, he went to summon aid, finding Billy Webster and Sean Kellow. Sue Bull shouted that the ball was being played in town and a lorry load of Up'ards roared off conveniently. Mark Harrison brought the ball upstream to the goal where brother Paul waited to goal it.

Returning via Mayfield Road, the victory parade stopped at the Cemetery, where Paul and Mark took the ball to their father's grave for a moment's reflection. Guy Harrison had goaled the Tuesday ball in 1948. Another generation of another family followed the time-honoured tradition of following footsteps.

Prior to the games, the players unveiled their own Roll of Honour Board. It had a carved oak motif of two hands holding a ball. Both the carving and boards had been made by David Cowen of Clifton. Belonging to the Committee, the Boards now may be seen in the hallway of the Green Man Ballroom. Other carvings – of the wheels and a player – are slightly different, reflecting the undershot wheel at Clifton and the overshot wheel at Sturston, which resulted in plain paddles at Clifton and bucket-type paddles at Sturston. It records goals since 1891. The existing Roll of Honour in the pub only records the turners-up.

2001

At the beginning of the year, as Mr Simon Plumbly was announced as the turner-up for the Tuesday, there was much speculation that the Prince of Wales would turn up the Wednesday ball and so it turned out, albeit late in the day. However, the intricacies of organising the event continued. The outbreak of Foot & Mouth Disease, which began on 19 February 2001 spread with a speed that was totally unexpected. Over the weekend prior to the game it was still hoped that something could be salvaged but it was not to be.

The decision to cancel the game was taken but it was clear that a good number of players were looking for the opportunity to have a game of some kind.

At the Green Man Ballroom, Ashbourne on 26 February 2001 (Monday night) a meeting was called to decide whether there should be a mini-Shrovetide. About 150 people were present including Committee member Mick Betteridge.

Mark Harrison started proceedings off, stating that he recognised that 'all were gutted'. It had been decided by several Down'ards (meeting at The Wheel Inn) to call a meeting to decide whether or not to hold a mini-Shrovetide on the recreation ground. The police had been approached who had said that a normal game, or one in the town, would be unacceptable. Options considered were from the weir at the top end of the Fish Pond to Nestlé's weir or from one street to another street, but it was felt that 'play on the recreation ground was the only avenue'.

The representative from the Police advised the meeting that there was an unconfirmed outbreak in Derbyshire 'which could jeopardise your standing.' Crucially many policemen had stood down. It was, he said 'entirely your thing, do what you like – the police are totally neutral. We are very sorry for the whole of Ashbourne.'. His advice was to 'keep the game off agricultural land – I implore you.' Another case had been reported on the Staffordshire border and care was cautioned. In an answer to a question, he advised that the police would not be happy for play to proceed through the streets, (there being insufficient men available now to police it). Contained on land it would be better, he said.

Paul Harrison enquired what would the position be if the Council said 'no' to play on the recreation ground. The police response found a warm reception: 'It is a civil matter and we are not interested' he said.

The police indicated that they would offer 'support and help'; 'we will assist but not officially sanction it,' but 'we will officially police it on the day.'

Mark Harrison, acting as chairman, made it clear that 'we are not a rebel against the committee; we support them.' He went on to suggest play on the Park between 2 & 5pm on Fishpond Meadow. At this point Jim Boden, Simon Plumbly and Pop Robotham were called in. Mick Betteridge, another committee member, was already present.

Simon Plumbly addressed the meeting, saying that it was all very sad, but he was relieved that he did not have to turn up the ball. He stated that 'there was no choice if you wish to continue playing Shrovetide.' The prospect of play continuing and then there being burning carcasses up the valley would give the media a field day against the game, he said. He continued: "Now is the chance to show how responsible you are. We want nothing to be done. If you want to signify the tradition of Shrovetide, I suggest that you turn it up and make a gesture, but that is a personal idea. You could play on the rec but who controls it all? It could antagonise people in Ashbourne and the farmers". There was a risk that people might say 'let them play it always on the rec.' He concluded by adding 'be responsible; the Committee cannot support it; we don't want anything to happen.'

Jim Boden stated: "a triumph for Shrovetide had been turned into a disaster. At the moment, we have made a sensible decision and we have what credit there is to be had out of it. We could not put us in the position which affects the goodwill. A 13th case [of Foot & Mouth disease] was expected to be confirmed. We owe it to ourselves to accept the decision." He was against even a token turn up off the plinth. The play, he said "would give the media a field day. It will go against us. We will never get the Prince of Wales to turn it up", he concluded. Simon Plumbly then added "when we had the meeting on Sunday, it was under difficult conditions. We feel we might get away with it if we restricted it in someway, but we were beaten by it. Had the game been totally within the town, we might have got away with it. We play from Sturston to Clifton thanks to the farmers. I am sure they will be more amenable in the future [if we are responsible]. This whole game is all in your players' hands. Over time you will have to help this game more and more – you have all got to try and help – the more and more critical it becomes as time goes on."

'Pop' Robotham added: 'in 1968, there were hardly any people there' [on the rec] and Jim Boden added that since 1968 the game had changed remarkably: people were more responsible [alluding to the invasion of Miss Hollick's garden]; 'we have tremendous goodwill'. Billy Webster thanked the Committee for what they had done. Mark Harrison made a passionate plea to play. 'If it went ahead in '68, why not in 01?'

A proposal was made that a mini-game be played on Fishpond Meadow between the river and the houses. The disease could not be spread by the river, it was stated. Someone asked about potential damage: who would pay for it?

Alan Kingston was against the idea; "we run the risk of stopping the game, not Hitler, [alluding to Hitler's lack of ability to stop the game, noted earlier in the meeting] because of the media presence.

The only people who could stop Shrovetide could be us. We all want to play, but we cannot always make compromises".

Ernie Grant noted that in 1968 it had only been a handful of players. Mike Betteridge – speaking as a player – recalled that the 1968 game was played mostly by kids; it was a devalued ball not a real game. The crux was that as players, 'it was our Tuesday and Wednesday; we give our whole for future operations. I'd rather you lose one year for my lad to have a lifetime'.

At this point Mark Harrison turned and said that he had changed his mind: 'I feel we don't have a game', he said. It was acknowledged that he was a big man to have said that. There wasn't anyone in the room who did not want to play, that was clear, but the inevitability that play could not proceed was also clear.

A vote was taken with 6 for play. Only about 50 people raised an arm to vote against play, but that did not reflect the overall desire to accept the Committee's recommendation. On the Tuesday morning, Steve Bull and his wife Sue of the Wheel Inn proposed that a singsong should take place at the plinth. Steve advised the *Ashbourne News Telegraph* and your author to bring their cameras and the latter rang Arthur Chadwick to enquire if he would lead the singing. Thus at 2pm, a large crowd of 400-plus people assembled at the plinth to sing a couple of verses of the Shrovetide song, Auld Lang Syne and The National Anthem.

The singing was repeated on the Wednesday. Prior to the singing, Simon Plumbly spoke to the crowd, reiterating some of the points raised at the previous night's meeting. On the Wednesday, Mayor Simon Spencer made a similar exhortation and noted that he understood that the players had been busy the previous night assisting the town's landlords out of their difficulty over the town's beer lake.

Foot & Mouth disease created a national disaster with some 2,030 cases and 4,068,000 animals slaughtered (according to Government statistics) or 10,849,000 according to the Meat & Livestock Commission (Sunday Telegraph 17th February 2002 p.14). Clifton goal was in a restricted area within a week of Shrovetide and the players decision had been the right one.

The Tuesday singing saw popular Keith Lomas, the local paper's photographer, on the plinth taking photographs as usual. Keith died in June after a short illness. There were many tributes to him; his passing came as a shock to many people including this author, who annually followed the hug with Keith, taking photographs of the game. He was good company.

2002

The whole town expected the guests of honour to be the same as in 2001 and although confirmation of the Prince's acceptance came late in the day, all was set for a grand day; the Prince apparently keen to attend. However, on the Saturday before the game, 9th February, Princess Margaret died and the Prince cancelled all bar the most essential of his appointments. The top table guests included the Earl of Shrewsbury, (the premier Earl of England), Sir Richard FitzHerbert Bt., and local politicians.

After the usual three-course lunch of soup, beef and apple pie, Philip Tomlinson rose to read a letter from the Prince of Wales. He (the Prince) had written to say that he was "utterly mortified that I cannot be with you … perhaps it will be third time lucky … should you be rash enough to invite me again." Referring to Simon Plumbly (whose choice clearly met with very popular approval), Philip's dry sense of humour found much hilarity when he referred to the fact that they had played against each other over the years 'but he played the other way; he was not a good player, so it didn't really matter!' He went on to point out that it was twenty years since Simon's father Herbert had turned up the ball and eleven years since Simon had joined the Committee. Philip did not mention that it was ten years since he had chaired the lunch, succeeding John Gadsby as Committee Chairman in 1991.

Simon's speech was both punchy and witty – perhaps the best since Roy Bennett's speech in 1993. He referred to the presence of his aunt, Esmie Stinson, who was 89 years old. She had been at the lunches in 1935 when Herbert Plumbly had scored Charles Turpin's ball at Sturston, and in 1982 when he turned up the ball. He presented her with one of the Royal Doulton Shrovetide plates.

He said that he accepted the honour of turner-up with a lot of pride; the Shrovetide Committee had done a lot to be proud of for Ashbourne.

Heading for the Plinth (continued)

Stan Bury addresses the crowd in 1992. The ball was goaled by M Hellaby

Simon Plumbly at the new plinth in 2002. The ball was goaled by K Maskell

Philip Tomlinson with his ball in 2000. His predecessor Frank Tomlinson turned the ball up nine times

Play in 2000. top: a break in Fish Pond Meadow and in Park Road (middle). Bottom: Mr Newing's ball rises above the crowd in Sturston Road, 1998

Play in the streets

Top: play in Park Road, 1996; the ball rises into the air in Compton, 1998 (middle)

Play at the traffic lights, 1999

Above: stalemate in the hug, 2002; below: play by the Shaw Croft flats, 2000, as the ball rises into the air

The ball rises above the hug on Wednesday, 2002 (left) and Madge's Corner, 2000 (below),

Waterplay

Keith Lomas's classic photograph of 1994 (above). Another view (below) of the river in Shaw Croft in 1933

Play outside the Health Centre (above) and Park Road (below), Ash Wednesday 1999. The ball is just visible in both photographs

Play at Back Bridge in 1962 (above). Looking towards the bridge (below) showing people on the metal arches of the adjacent footbridge. The year is unknown

River play at the Recreation ground with a break in progress (below), 1996

Play in the river at Sandybrook (above) and in the Henmore (below), both in 1995

Water play in 1925 (above) and 1920 (below). Photographs of this time show huge crowds watching the game

Play by the Rec in 1996, with the hug stuck against the bank (above) and by Bank Croft, 1999

The crowd lining the river bank in 1963

Play in the Fish Pond in 1996 showing the ball (above & top right).

Play by the Culvert, 1996

Play in the Fish Pond, 1996

The ball (circled) breaks away on Ash Wednesday, 2000 from the Fish Pond. The ball can be seen being kicked away

Before & After

St John Street, 2002, with shops boarded up to protect the glass windows. The flags and bunting were for the cancelled visit of HRH The Prince of Wales

Up'ard goalers of the 1990s. Back row: (L-R) Steve Wright, 1996; Mark Hellaby, 1992; Simon Hellaby, 1997; Andrew Etherington, 1998. Middle row: David Calladine, 1991; Terry Brown, 1997; Stuart Lyon, 1993. Bottom row: Chris Fearn, 1993; George Ditchfield, 1998; Nick Fearn, 1999; Robert Godfrey, 1990

He then announced a new problem the Committee had to contend with. From now on, they had to find £5,000 annually to operate Shrovetide. This was to comply with the requirement of a Derbyshire County Council 'Event Plan'. Despite Shrovetide having had a record of being trouble free over the years: 'why should we need to raise it?' he asked.

'This Bureaucracy will ruin rural activities,' he went on. 'Maybe this is the grand plan.'

He wondered whether it would jeopardise the future of Shrovetide, Golden Jubilee street parties, the town's Highland Gathering and Ashbourne Show. Even 'Sir Richard Fitzherbert's well dressing at Tissington, perhaps.' It was a chilling prospect. If the Council was interested in public safety [the cost was apparently to cover policing, safety issues and insurance], 'why not build a bypass rather than interfere with Shrovetide or plucking and dressing pheasants?' he asked. The latter referred to Hulme's Fish Shop being unable to sell pheasants without a butcher's licence.

His main point was still to come, however. He focused attention on the players [in much the same way as Roy Bennett had done]. It was they who organised the game. To them went great credit for giving up the game the previous year. They had raised £1,600 at a dance too.

Following 'Land of Hope and Glory', Simon was escorted from the room, down the steps to the Green Man yard and down Dig Street where he was raised shoulder height in time-honoured fashion for the traditional photograph before crossing Shaw Croft to the plinth.

Another Uneventful Day's Play

With a two-year gap between games, Shaw Croft was literally packed with enthusiastic players and followers. They were patient too; the ball was late. After Auld Lang Syne and The National Anthem, Simon Plumbly turned up his ball, one year and thirteen minutes late. There seemed to be camera crews all over the place. As the day wore on, a Japanese TV team, together with its noisy helicopter above, seemed to become even more intrusive.

After ten minutes of slow movement, the ball was hauled over the perimeter wall to the Shaw Croft flats. Moving across the road into Fishpond Meadow, the Up'ards edged the ball behind the fire station and towards Lakeside at 2.50pm. At 3.00pm play was in Lakeside, the ball being tightly hugged. It was the pattern for the whole day: by 3.25pm it had only moved about 50 yards, the ball appearing momentarily at 3.15pm – a rare sight as things turned out.

Moving slowly up Park Avenue, it passed St Oswalds Crescent at 3.28pm and Dovedale Avenue at 4.00pm. The Down'ards made a stand at Brookside at 4.23pm, pushing the Up'ards back to one side, but the move was thwarted and the relentless progress up the road resumed, eventually spilling into the field off Brookside at about 4.45pm. As darkness fell, play went down to and then across the river. The Down'ards held play in a water covered and marshy area near the old site of the swimming club pool for a long time – perhaps as long as 30 minutes – before the ball broke. Although it had been a fine day, it was now quite cold as the pace quickened towards the Sturston goal.

The reason was soon clear as Down'ards slipped away in the dark to form a 3-line defensive wall in front of the goal. The ball reached the bridge at 8.45pm. There was a long period of drawing straws until a visibly shaken Kirk Maskell realised the day was his. However, getting him to the plinth was another matter. No matter how hard the Up'ards tried to 'wheel' the mass of Down'ards away from the plinth, nothing moved. At 9.10pm it looked as though the stalemate could continue until 10.00pm. However, tactics then changed to charging the wall head on and at 9.15pm the leather rose three times to end the day's play.

The Up'ards took the goal but there were no plaudits for the style of play or its entertainment value. They were assisted by a contingent of Sherwood Foresters. With the Rugby Club playing to Sturston *en masse* as well, irrespective of traditional loyalty, the whole nature of play seems to have changed for the worst and many voices expressed this. This wasn't hug football, it was glorified 'shove' up the street. Another day of this didn't seem at all appealing. It was only as darkness came that the less hardy peeled away, helping to balance the struggle between the two sides.

A Good Day For The Mayor

Standing in for the Prince of Wales on Ash Wednesday was the popular Mayor of Ashbourne, Mr Tony Millward. Enjoying his year in office, his chance to turn up the ball came as double honour for him. Philip Tomlinson described him as 'a man for all occasions and that they were fortunate that he had stepped into the breach.' Councillor Spencer reminded the gathering that Tony had contributed many hours of community service plus his work for H.I.T. (Help Improve the Town) Society, knockout cricket, twenty years service to the Ashbourne Town Band including 15 years as chairman of it etc.

Tony's speech was commendable too, especially as it had to be written in a hurry – his invitation had come on the Monday. Reminiscing on past days, he felt a lot of people probably didn't take him seriously as a player (he is a Down'ard). Trying to get the ball off Philip Tomlinson was like trying to get it off an octopus. He spoke of Don Lowndes and his father playing down in the river near the former Ashbourne signal box, breaking ice on the surface as they went. His father had gone beneath the surface but the other players had fetched him back up again.

He mentioned other memories too: Jim Boden's boiler suit (it had 'JIM' on the back), 'the game's first sponsored solicitor', he said; Marion Abbot running up and down the river bank; Grace Sowter, always on the Green Man steps; John Allsopp's sweater etc.

Referring to his wife, he mentioned her habit of running by the hug with a bottle of rum in one pocket and whisky in another for the players. He found it upsetting that as you got older you still felt you could go in the river only to be told off by the wife when you went home wet through. Mrs Milward always checked his speeches, he said, so she should be blamed for what he had said. Much of it was in a lighthearted vein, touching just about the right note and it went down well. Amongst the guests were the Deputy Lord Lieutenant of Derbyshire; the High Sheriff, Miss Jane Walker-Okeover; Sir Richard FitzHerbert Bt; Lady Hilton; Mr P McLoughlin MP and local politicians. It was perhaps the first time that a Lady High Sheriff had attended the lunch, but not the first time an incumbent leader of the council had turned up the ball. Wednesday 1912 was perhaps the first time, although Alfred Hall might have contested this, from his days on the Local Board in the 19th century.

Tim Baker had painted the Wednesday ball and had to do some quick repainting on the Monday to put 'Tony Millward Mayor of Ashbourne' on the ball. Stuart Avery had painted the Tuesday ball.

The Best Play For Years

Crossing the Shaw Croft, it started to drizzle and after the traditional singing and an appeal to keep out of gardens to the game's followers, the ball rose at 1.56pm. Tony threw it backwards to project as far as possible. If the turn up was novel, the play was to be stimulating, reflecting the type of game played 100 years ago. A greater contrast with Tuesday's play could not have been imagined. The ball continually rose in the air, being thrown about and kicked all day long.

After wandering around Shaw Croft and seeing a break into the area of the flats foiled, the game returned to the plinth at 2.31pm, en route for Park Road. At 3.40pm it broke from Madge's Corner into St John Street, where several vehicles were trapped, including a tanker. Play moved along the street, reaching the top of Horse & Jockey Yard by 3.00pm. At 3.20pm, play was back on Shaw Croft, having gone down the Yard. Here play was brisk, the ball at one point bouncing off the gable wall of the flats nearest the plinth between a couple of first floor windows.

As the rain eased, the ball broke, past the Post Office into Dig Street at 3.25pm, quickly proceeding up to Church Street where the windows of Pretty Perfects took the pressure opposite the Green Man. Displays of ladies' underwear were no distraction as the ball rose repeatedly into the air. The Down'ards pushed the hug back to Dig Street at 3.46pm, but the Up'ards responded and play moved back into St John Street. Again the Down'ards pushed back to Dig Street and down towards the bridge. With both sides trying to gain the advantage at this point, there was spirited play before the ball broke down Compton. It soon came back down the street where the first serious break occurred.

Seizing his chance, David 'Roo' Hollingworth ran through the bus station and on to the swimming pool. Tiring, he tried to throw the ball across the river to Stephen Ford and Nick Hopewell, but it ended up in the river. A hug soon formed and at 4.00pm the ball was opposite the church. Mark Harrison threw the ball clear and play hugged the ball at the rear of the old railway warehouse (Peak Textiles). Another Down'ard throw was thwarted when somebody's back got in the way, spoiling the Down'ards best chance of a good break.

Spirited play ensued in Clifton Road. The Down'ards countered Up'ards pressure by freeing the ball and trying to get it over the heads in the hug. A good throw by Darren Waring showed what could be done. However, the game reached Station Street and quickly went to Compton by 6.15pm. Down'ards regrouped here to block concerted Up'ards pressure and the ball turned into Compton. At the bridge play progressed across to Shaw Croft and along Park Road. By 8.15pm it had passed The Cabin in Belper Road and went up to The Mulberry Bush (102, Belper Road) before returning to the phone box where the jitty allowed play to regroup on the open land at the top of St Oswalds Crescent. Time was moving on as the hug went down Dovedale Avenue to Park Avenue. As time ran out, the ball was adjacent to the Ambulance Station at the junction with Park Road. Lady Luck touched Tony Millward once more as the leather was returned to the Green Man. An indicator of the hammering the balls received this year was that they ended up devoid of paint. In 1998, George Ditchfield's ball seemed hardly touched in comparison.

Two other balls remain to be turned up. They are the second-goal balls standing in the name of Ken Renshaw and succeeding him, Alec Smith. Goodness knows when we shall see them in play!

A Final Look Back

In a materialistic age, what is the value or the point of our ancient game? We tend to look at our 'heritage' in terms of buildings or machinery, eg old steam railway locomotives. Our game reflects the way people pursued their recreation on the few days when they had time off from work on various Christian festival days. As described above (pp 9/12), these were the times when authority feared civic unrest – the only remedy being to call out the local militia, and then only if the commander felt moved to go. Allowing the local population to 'blow off steam' with the certain knowledge that all would be back to normal the next day was important.

Those days involved rough play and rough living; it is startling to think of the militia entering Winchester College with fixed bayonets (see page 11), but it happened. The Peterloo Massacre in Manchester is enough testimony of the militia's resolve to draw blood when necessary. Life was tough and rough compared to today.

Our game then, reflects those past days. It is as much a part of English history and our heritage as anything else. In fact because heritage so rarely expresses itself through recreational human social behaviour over such a prolonged period and on such a large scale of involvement, its value is so important. This is no re-enactment; the game banned in Chester in 1540 was little different from Ashbourne in 2002. It is an astonishing survivor.

When guests of honour at the Shrovetide lunches claim the game belongs to the players they are correct, but only partly correct. This game not only belongs to Ashbourne, it belongs to England.

Statistics: Goals at Sturston and Clifton

	S	C	Total
1901-10	19	11	30
1911-20	8	17	25
1921-30	9	18	27
1931-40	13	9	22
1941-50	12	9	21
1951-60	11	11	22
1961-70	7	8	15
1971-80	4	7	11
1981-90	6	12	18
1991-00	11	7	18
	100	109	209
Last half century	39	45	84

Maximum number of goals in a straight run: 8, 1918-22
Three goals in one a day: 1896 (W) & 1967 (T)
Four goals in one year: 1936 (all at Sturston)

Traditions & Reminiscenses — 8

An important article headed 'Some traditions and reminiscences of the Ashbourne Shrovetide Football' was published in the *Ashbourne News* of 12/02/1909. It was written by the Rev J F Tomlinson MA. The late Mr William Tomlinson of Bradley Pastures, the writer's father, died aged 82 years in 1900 and from him to his great grandfather (of Sturston Hall) he had first-hand traditional knowledge of the game. His article recalled some of the information handed down to him. It gives us a rich vein of material otherwise no longer available to us.

Prior to the use of the two mills as goals, the original custom, it was said, was to select for the goals the cowshed or stable door of two farms on the north or south side respectively of the river. These farms were usually chosen to be above the town one year or below it the next year, with the idea of distributing as far as possible the damage to fences etc. In those days, the river was the natural dividing line to settle which side a player should belong. The ball was turned up at the bull ring and often there would be a battle royal to see which direction the ball would leave town — via St John Street or King Street. This old system of goals was changed, merely as an experiment, about the close of the eighteenth century. The late Mr Thomas Tomlinson (his Grandfather) of Corley, Bradley Pastures and Hall Fields died in 1879 aged 90. He had stated that he could just remember the change. It was found as a result that an additional element of interest and strife arose from the increased amount of water play, this approximating the conditions and character of the game more closely to those prevailing at Derby.

Accordingly, the same choice was made in subsequent years until it came to be recognised as a settled custom to play to the two mills. However, this caused some dissatisfaction because some Down'ards suddenly became Up'ards. An example of this was Sturston Hall, situated adjacent to Sturston Mill, but ostensibly now Down'ard and playing to Clifton goal. A hundred years later, Jim Hooson of Bradley still played Down'ards and strongly maintained that he was right and his neighbours were wrong.

If this is correct, then the use of the Henmore rather than Compton as the boundary dates at least from the end of the eighteenth century, but also see comments below on the boundary.

The article continued with a note on what was considered to be one of the most stubbornly contested games ever, although no year is given. The Down'ards goal was Shaw Wood House at the top of Derby Road hill. By 4.00pm, the Down'ards had succeeded in getting the ball into the field to the south side of Sturston Lane, at the top of which was their goal. The steep hill gave the opposition an advantage and there was a furious struggle for five hours. During this time, the ball almost reached its destination several times before being rushed back down the hill. Eventually, at about 9.00pm, the ball was goaled by a Wheeldon of Wyaston, possibly either the Grandfather or father of the John Wheeldon in the 1862 painting.

The Rev Tomlinson's reminiscences were published in the issues of 12, 19, and 26 February 1909. Here are quoted some of the details which relate chiefly to Up'ards players and the 1862 painting. In the latter, 'the proportions of Luke Faulkner were far greater than depicted. He was undoubtedly the finest player of his time. In his earlier years he took charge of the bull for any baitings. Mr Thomas Tomlinson could remember going to a baiting at Bakewell and on that occasion, Faulkner had brought the bull. In the picture he is shown holding the ball and standing by the bull ring'. In 1909, the only survivor of the group, he said, 'was Black Harry – William Hawksworth', Black Harry was actually

Henry Hawksworth and he died on 27/02/1909 aged 82 years. The *Ashbourne News* of 05/03/1909 carries his photograph.

When the 1862 painting was reproduced in the paper (AN 22/02/1901), the Rev Tomlinson's father had recalled some of the other players:

'Frenchman' Etches was another good player, almost equal to Faulkner. The writer remembered him as a keeper employed in watching the Henmore at Sturston. He also remembered the excellent home-made ginger beer sold by Mrs Etches at a little shop in Church Street. Jack Wheeldon of Wyaston was a particularly fine player, but certainly no better than his father who had been the foremost player of his day. Most of the players depicted on the painting were good players, including Black Harry, and the two Shaws, Jack and Ned [who] were good water players."

The report continues:

"Here are two anecdotes concerning the late William Tomlinson. They are of general interest because they introduce the reader to two names which, in different ways, were at one time very prominently associated with the game. I once asked him if he had ever run off with the ball. 'No' was the reply, 'but I once had a long and futile chase after a man who got away with it'. Then he gave the following account of it. It was about the year 1840, and after very stiff play the Up'ards had got the ball passed Ashbourne Green and along the road nearly to 'The Grove'. There it was thrown over the hedge on the north side of the road, and was at once picked up by a Down'ards man named Frost (was he not a shoemaker in the Butchery?) who made off with it towards Kniveton. He started in pursuit, but though at the time a very good runner, lost ground for the first mile. However, as they neared Bradbourne Mill he gradually gained upon and caught his man when nearly at the top of the mill field on the way to Tissington. But they were both so beaten and breathless that all they could do was to hold each other while the ball lay on the grass a couple of yards away.

It was several minutes before anyone else came up. Unfortunately the next man to arrive was a Down'ards man who picked up the ball and ran off with it. He then gave it up, but Frost went in pursuit once more, and finally goaled the ball at Clifton. This man Frost was remarkably successful over a long series of years in running away with the ball. There had been no one since his day to quite equal him for speed and stamina combined, though Mathew Cleaver, at a later date, when once clear away was very difficult to catch.

The other anecdote is as follows: when Mrs Frank of the Hall began to oppose the game, the ball on several occasions got into the Park and was played there despite of all attempts to prevent it. On one of these occasions he happened to be following the ball and its fortunes as it careered about the field. Mrs Frank, brandishing a walking stick, or riding whip, came up to him as he stood some 20 yards from the footpath, engrossed in watching the game. 'Are you aware, Mr Tomlinson,' she said sternly, 'that you are trespassing? Allow me to remind you that you are not on the footpath!' 'Allow me to remind you, Mrs Frank,' he replied, 'that I am here in the pursuit of sport, and that when for the same purpose you come galloping over *my* land after hounds, I don't call out to you that *you* are trespassing'. This was a very shrewd hit. The lady was most enthusiastic in following the hounds two or three days a week, especially the Dove Valley Harriers, and these hounds crossed some part of his land on an average nearly once a week.

The writer saw the game for the first time at the age of seven, in the year 1870. In order to witness it, he, with three others gave school (in the country) the slip for the afternoon. A year or two later, along with a brother and several cousins, he began to attend the grammar school. All of us used to have our midday meal together daily at the old 'Horse and Jockey'. Whether with the knowledge of our parents or not we never learned or enquired, but annually on Shrovetide, Mrs Gallimore, our hostess at our united entreaty, consented to write letters of excuse to the headmaster (Mr Young) signed in our parents names, which enabled us to absent ourselves from school and to witness the game.

At that period, no single player was quite so conspicuous as 'Ninety' Burton – 'Young Ninety' then. He played a wonderfully hard and vigorous game and his red head was always noticeable in the thick of the fray. He was not over scrupulous in his methods — he would admit it — and was a decidedly 'high kicker', sometimes indeed, when the ball was not there! I have often seen him, however, by sheer hard kicking and strength, drive the ball through the scrimmage and out at the other side. What a fine Rugby forward he would have made at that time! But I doubt if John would have been amenable to any Rugby rules! 'Ninety' did not play unnecessarily in the water, but, when he did go in, the ball usually soon came out with a huge throw which sent it far on to the land high over the heads of the crowd of players who lined the stream.

John had several brothers, including Dick, Joe, and Neddy, who played most useful, if not quite such brilliant football. They all played well in the water, and were particularly clever on land at stopping rushes by picking up and throwing the ball – undoubtedly the most effective play of all in this Shrovetide game. One of them, who played under the disadvantage of a twisted foot, was particularly clever in that way. It was simply wonderful how smartly he did it. Two or three Shaws, including Jack and Arthur, were at that time (in the early 1870s) very quick and nimble in the water and usually played in scarlet. Tom Cundy also played a great game, both on the land and in the water and not seldom the Up'ards had to thank him for getting the ball out of the brook when it seemed almost passed hope. With his strong, tall, wiry figure and quick sudden attack, he would take his opponent or opponents in the water unawares and, before combined resistance could be organised, the ball was out.

At [this] time ... the Down'ards were easily masters in the water. Their supremacy was scarcely disputed. The only thought of the Up'ards was to get the ball out as quickly as possible. If it remained in the brook the game was 'up'. Certainly it was quite unknown for the ball to be carried upstream to Sturston Mill, as had happened several times in recent years. It was I think, on Shrove Tuesday in 1877 that for the first time something of that kind happened. In that year a number of Sturston and Ashbourne Green players in a body joined the usual 'Up'ards' watermen in the stream, with the result that their opponents, to their surprise and chagrin, found themselves worsted in their own element, and after their own particular game. The ball was rushed under the Back Bridge, and with, at first, many intervals of very even play on land, progressed chiefly up the river, and for the last mile never left it. But a ding dong struggle was kept up till the end, when the ball was finally goaled by the Sturston Miller himself.

About this time the 'Up'ards' side had several men who were great at running away with the ball. Matthew Cleaver and Tom Coxon (of Agnes Meadow) each achieved success on numerous occasions. Charles Coxon, the butcher, and Henry Holyoak, the auctioneer, were also at one time very quick in getting the ball away into the country, but generally after a time handed it to someone else. It was Matthew Cleaver, so I am told, who goaled the ball on the last occasion when it was turned up in the Market Place in 1862. (Or was it the one thrown from the window in 1860 which led to the litigation?) Tom Coxon, in the 1870s, goaled the ball in at least two successive years. He was no mean player in the melee. I recollect him on one occasion performing a really remarkable feat which had the effect of changing the whole fortunes of the game. The ball had got below the Station and was looked upon as almost a gift to the Cliftonians. By a sudden rush it was taken from the brook into Clifton Lane and thence into the Goods Yard. Here Coxon got possession and running up the wall which separated the Station Yard from the old Station Street, with a truly remarkable throw, he landed the ball clean across the wide street and over the opposite wall into the Paddock; and the Up'ards happening to be in the majority there it was quickly taken into Compton, and, after some heavy play, finally goaled at Sturston.

Other good players for the Up'ards at that time were the brothers Stone, of Ashbourne Green (three of them), a bearded butcher employed by Taylor, of the Butchery (whose name I forget, but he was a very fine player indeed), Gallimore the butcher, Jim and George Porter, Charles Coxon jnr., R Wallis, and others. Tom Webster of Kniveton, also played a good game, but Tom could box with or without gloves, even better than he could play football."

The articles by the Rev Tomlinson attracted another one on Down'ards players (AN 24/02/1911). An extract is included here and it was written by Mr W Abraham:

"Jack Shaw (an Up'ard), Frenchman Etches and Teddy Pearson once took the ball from the bottom of the Fish Pond to the widest part, buried the ball in the mud and left the water. It was recovered by five or six Down'ards who, after some trouble, found the ball and brought it out. It was afterwards goaled at Clifton Mill. Shaw's fondness for the Fish Pond was cured after Philip Brown waded in and met Shaw halfway up the pond. He took the ball from Shaw and held him (ie Shaw) under the water for a while, leaving him spluttering in the water. Will Frost (a fast runner) goaled two or three balls in a day [which has not been equalled since]."

The Rev Tomlinson's assertions on how the game was played prior to the switch to the two mills is interesting. However, stories do persist that games were played between goals in the town and that the goals were two pubs – The Plough at the end of Compton being one. However, this is further complicated by a frustrating article in the *Ashbourne News Telegraph* in 1961. It is frustrating in that the so-called evidence for the article was not given and cannot be evaluated. If it is true then the possibility of The Plough being a goal seems doubtful: it was on the so-called boundary between the teams. Perhaps the answer is that, as now, the game changed to meet specific circumstances.

The article (ANT 23/02/1961) concerned the boundary between the two teams. Mr Sidney Richardson suggested that the game originally took place between those who lived in the combined parish of Clifton and Compton and those who lived in Sturston and Offcote. Mr Richardson made the division on the basis of a line running down the centre of Old Derby Hill, down the centre of Compton, over Compton Bridge and down the centre of Dig Street, crossing St John Street to the Westminster Bank. The Bank was once the Wheatsheaf Hotel and there was a big carriageway in the centre. Mr Richardson claimed that the line ran through this carriageway and along a path which in those days ran up to Dove House Green.

The following week, the paper's editor stated that evidence had been produced to show that Mr Richardson was right. This evidence was not given, however. Another view put forward was that the game was played by those who lived in the hundred of Litchurch and those in the hundred of Wirksworth. The boundary suggested by Mr Richardson accorded with this other view, it was noted. However, perhaps of more relevance is the fact that the boundary between the parishes of Clifton and Sturston ran down the middle of Compton. Sid Taylor, a previous Committee member recalls being told that the game was played between Clifton and Sturston and was 'hijacked' by Ashbourne. There is perhaps a lot of truth in this. It would also account for the use of the two parishes' mills being used as goals.

Unfortunately all this raises as many problems as it solves. For instance, if the game was originally between Clifton and Sturston, was the ball thrown up in Compton? When was the switch made to include Ashbourne, and, did the reorganisation to include Ashbourne coincide with the change of goals to the two mills with a boundary change to the Henmore? It is possible that we will never know. John Gadsby in his booklet on the game states that the goals were at one time The Plough inn at the bottom of Spittal Hill and in Union Street. The latter goal, he believes, was a pub called the Ostrich but a wall there collapsed under pressure from the hug and the goal was then moved elsewhere. Was this when the goals moved to places out of town as related by the Rev Tomlinson or to the two mills? See however the detail on the proposed date for this move on pp 44/45.

Mr Corbishley's Reminicences

In 1958, G J Corbishley, then Assistant Editor at the *Ashbourne News Telegraph* wrote his reminiscences of the game, some of which are quoted below:

"Mr Hawkesworth [sic], was the first man to have conceived the idea that Shrovetide Football might make an appeal outside the town, and he did much to turn it into a real attraction. Another way in which Mr Hawkesworth raised money for the Royal Infirmary was by placing old Shrovetide balls in public houses. When visitors asked to be allowed to handle a ball, they were only allowed to do so if they put a sum of money in the Infirmary box.

The first year I remember Shrovetide Football the ball was thrown up, or turned up, as is the correct phrase, by an American. He was a director of one of the oil companies and gave £50 to the funds for the privilege of performing the ceremony. He asked that he should be allowed to throw it up in the same way as the Prince, and so, for the second time in Shrovetide history, a bridge was built across the Henmore at the bottom of Prince's Gate in St John Street and the ball was thrown up from there instead of Shaw Croft. The second day a Derby publican said he was not going to be beaten by any Yankee millionaire and raised the sum of £50 amongst his customers.

I think it was that year that the game was first filmed, and a number of well known Shrovetiders were persuaded to put on a mock display in the water on Tuesday morning for the benefit of the film cameras. The ball used on that occasion was subsequently thrown up as the second ball of the day and was, if I remember, painted white. I remember, however, the old custom that took place when the ball was finally goaled and the scorer, with a number of his supporters, set off on a tour of the public houses, where he was presented at each house with a gallon of beer. I suppose subsequent Chancellors of the Exchequer have put an end to this, more's the pity."

Ashbourne Years Ago

On 15/05/1935, the *Ashbourne News Telegraph* published an article under the above heading. It is reproduced because it gives a good insight into the Ashbourne of our forefathers and reflects the character of the town in which the Shrovetide game was played.

"Stage Coaches And Candles

Twenty five years ago the late Mr Robert Bull, of Compton, gave an interesting address at the Derby Road Social Union on 'Looking Back'. Mr Bull, who was then advanced in years, said one of his earliest recollections was watching his father using the flint and steel in order to obtain a light, as matches had not then come into general use. Candles were mostly employed for illumination, and he well remembered several chandler's shops in Ashbourne, whilst the streets were lighted with a very poor quality gas. In those days there was no Smithfield, and at the fairs all the cattle, sheep, and horses had to be displayed in the streets. He could well remember the sheep pens in Church Street, and the horses in Upper St John Street. The Market Place used to be packed with shows and various attractions, and for many years Wombwell's menagerie used to attend one of the principle fairs. The cheese fairs used to be important events in those days, the cheese, after being purchased in the Market Place, being conveyed to Bridden's warehouse, in Sturston Road, to await transmission to Derby. Large herds of cattle used to be landed at Liverpool for London, and there being no railway they used to pass through Ashbourne on their way, and he remembered seeing some of them being shod with small tin plates to protect their feet.

Opening Of The N S R Branch Line

With regard to travelling he had many times stood and watched the arrival of the stage coaches from Derby, one of which he recollected was called 'The Defiance'. He was present at the cutting of the first sod of the Ashbourne to Rocester railway line, the ceremony being performed by Mr Whitham, a chemist. When the line was complete a banquet was held in the goods warehouse on May 29 1852. His first railway journey was in an open carriage, which was something equal to the modern cattle truck without the top. The sports of those days were characterised by their crudeness. With regard to the old custom of bull baiting, although he could not remember it, his father used to march in front of the bull, playing the violin, as the animal was being brought to the Market Place.

Crude Sports

His memory of other sports took him back to the time when the Shrovetide football was turned up in the Market Place, the ox roasting, the bonfire on November 5, and the goose swarming, apple-ducking, treacle-roll eating, stir-pudding eating, sack racing, women's races, and grinning through horse collars, all at the Wakes festival. Another custom which was now defunct was Plough Monday. With regard to structural changes he could recall about 50 public houses in Ashbourne, many of which had since been done away with. He could also remember the old theatre in Dig Street, and also a chapel in the same street. There was no public hall at that time, and both the magistrates and guardians used to meet in the assembly room at the Green Man Hotel. In conclusion, Mr Bull referred to several well-known local characters, relating a few humorous incidents concerning them.

Among the relics which Mr Bull displayed were the original bull ring which was used in the Market Place, to which the bull used to be tethered while the dogs attacked it, and a panel taken from the old stage coach bearing the neatly-painted crest, 'The Swan with Two Necks', Lad Lane, [London]."

Traditions of The Game

Before the game on each day, the guest who is going to start the game is entertained to lunch, always held until 1992 at the Green Man Hotel. In its early days this was a small private affair, but due to the efforts of Mr Arthur Froggatt and Herbert Plumbly the numbers rose steadily and over 400 people now attend. Before lunch starts, the Shrovetide Song is sung. Immediately after the lunch the guest is escorted (usually carried shoulder high) to the Shaw Croft, where a special dias was erected by the people of Ashbourne in 1978. It has now been replaced by a more substantial structure. After a few words to the gathered crowd, 'Auld Lang Syne' is sung, followed by 'God Save the Queen' and then the ball is turned up, which is the local term for being thrown to the crowd. The game then commences, the ball being either kicked, thrown or 'hugged' until a goal is scored at either of the goals. The method of scoring is to strike the marker three times with the ball. The ball then becomes the property of the scorer. If a goal is scored before 5.00pm another ball is thrown up, (to a maximum of three) and this can be played until 10.00pm when, if it is ungoaled, it is returned to the Committee who give it to the turner-up.

To have goaled or turned up a ball is considered an honour in Ashbourne, and if one goes into many local homes, one may find a ball inscribed often with the name of some long dead member of the family who scored a goal for Up'ards or Down'ards in a battle long ago.

The Ball

A ball that is going to be kicked, pushed, pulled, trodden on, and generally ill-treated for eight hours cannot be just an ordinary ball. The Shrovetide ball is therefore exceptional and the making of it is a work of art. The leather used is ordinary shoe leather which has to be soaked for many hours, because it is extremely difficult to work. It is cut into three panels, two circular panels with a diameter of about 12 inches which are the outside panels, and a rectangular panel 33in x 5in which is the centre panel. These panels are sewn together with a waxed thread. Great care has to be taken as there must be no weak spots in the ball.

The ball is then stuffed with fine cork shavings, which after many years has been found to be the best substance. This job takes many hours and is very laborious, it being essential that the ball is tightly stuffed or it would soon be kicked out of shape. When finished the ball is sewn up ready to withstand the rigours of the play. The balls are always made locally and almost without exception have been made by just three men since1907. Until 2001, the maker was Mr Arthur Chadwick, following in the footsteps of his father Mr Percy Chadwick, and before him Mr Trevor Yeomans. The balls are now (2002) made by John Harrison.

A similar situation applies with regard to the painting of the balls. For more than seventy years, one of the balls each year was painted by Mr John Barker, with a variety of other people doing the other ball. Then for 22 years (from 1949-70) the painter was his grandson Mr Jack Roberts, followed by Mr Chadwick's daughter Sandra and now by Stuart Avery and Tim Baker. Ball painting is indeed the most transitory of arts, for very often within an hour or so of the ball being thrown up all sign of the design can be lost. However, as John Gadsby put it, Ashburnians believe that their historic game is worth a coat of paint. Moreover, with the use of modern signwriter's enamel, the paint work is surviving more of the rigour of play.

The actual painting is no ordinary job. The first thing to do is to kill the grease in the leather with knotting spirit. Then a coat of primer is applied followed by two coats of undercoat and two coats of enamel paint. The ball is then decorated with a chinagraph pencil. The design has a connection with the person who is going to turn up the ball. A coat of arms is used if this is appropriate, or something depicting the person's trade or profession. The Union flag is always included and the design is completed by the name of the gentleman concerned, and the date. Remember too, that the artist is painting on a curved surface. Tim Baker, remarkably, has not had a painting lesson since leaving school.

It takes up to nine months for the ball to dry out after play and most players then have their ball repainted – sometimes with the original design, often with a new one depicting the goaler's name.

Surviving Games at Shrovetide 9

Atherstone
Punchard (1) states that "the play at Atherstone does not justify the term 'game'." It is played between 1-6pm, but there is no throwing – the holder usually 'punts' and only carries in order to kick. There are no sides, the ball being kicked freely through the streets. Moreover, there are no goals and no scoring. The ball is about three times the size of an ordinary Association football, made of leather, enclosing rubber bladders. Only one ball is used during the day.

It is not easy to reconcile Punchard's view. The absence of a goal does not mean a lack of competitive spirit. The ball is smuggled away at the end of play, which presumably creates a degree of competitiveness.

Workington
This is not a Shrovetide game, but it is mass football, played at Easter. It has many similarities to the Ashbourne game. It is, in fact, the only English game, which survives with these similarities. It is also a game under threat – from the development of the land upon which the game is traditionally played. Unfortunately the game does not enjoy civic support in the manner of the Ashbourne game. Perhaps the time has come for Ashbourne and its supporters to try to change this.

It is played by the 'Uppies' and 'Doonies', the former traditionally representing the colliers and the latter, the sailors. The ball is 'hailed'; to score it. Both the names of the teams and the place of scoring (hails, rather than goals) reflect Scottish (? Celtic) terminology. Similarly at Alnwick, the ball is 'haled' despite being south of the border.

Alnwick
Details of this are given below and on p 27.

Elsewhere
A list of surviving games of 'folk football', as it was called, was published in the 1920s (by Punchard). In Scotland, nine places were mentioned and only two were not Shrovetide events – Kirkwall, which plays on Christmas Day and New Years Day and at St Boswell's which played on March 12th and seems clearly linked to Shrovetide. The places playing the game – some with dates just before or just after Fastern's E'en (Shrovetide) – were: Hawick, Jedburgh, Ancrum, Denholm, Hobkirk, Lilliesleaf and Yetholm.

The ball was only kicked at Ancrum and Yetholm. It was smuggled away or hidden at Hawick and Yetholm. Most places called the teams Uppies v Doonies or Eastenders v Westenders. The sides were generally drawn up by place of residence, but at Denholm, married men and the Doonies played the unmarried men and the Uppies, while at Yetholm, the married men played those unmarried. Most had a boys' game and all called the 'goal' a hail except Kirkwall which has goals.

All had a solid ball sizes $3^{1}/_{2}$ - 6 inches in diameter except Kirkwall, where it was 9 inches. Most were stuffed with hay, sometimes wetted first, although Kirkwall used cork, as at Ashbourne. Most were decorated with ribbon, some also with flowers as well as ribbons. The number of balls used was several (in each case except Kirkwall where there is one ball per game and a fresh one each day). Most were kept by the scorer. Outsiders were a regular feature and women seemed to join in only 'in a quiet way' except at Kirkwall where they played regularly.

In some places the balls were presented by newly married couples. The author noted that an attempt to suppress the game had failed at Kirkwall and also at Jedburgh, the latter in 1849.

There were only seven places listed for England including Ashbourne. Of these, excluding Ashbourne, only three played football (that at St Columb Major in Cornwall 'Hurls' a ball) at Shrovetide. At the latter place, the 2½ inches diameter apple-wood ball, covered with sheet silver, may be carried and thrown only. There is no hugging or kicking, so it's not strictly football.

At Chester le Street, the ball is not scored – at 6pm the side having forced the ball past the Middle Chase, up or down, is the winner. In this respect it has a similarity with Atherstone.

At Alnwick, there was no throwing, carrying or hugging, smuggling or hiding the ball. The Parishes of St Michael played St Pauls. The goals are ¼ mile apart (2 miles at St Columb Major), nowhere in the UK matching the 3 miles of Ashbourne. The ball at Alnwick is a normal Association ball and was undecorated. At the end of the game, there is a scramble for possession of it. The goals are posts about 5 feet apart and 10 feet high, decorated with evergreens. The ball is introduced by being thrown off the Castle Barbican. In 1928, there were no outsiders playing or women. There was no provision for a boys' game in the English games. No game survived in Wales. Of the survivors, two – Workington and Kirkwall are the nearest to the Ashbourne game, but neither are played at Shrovetide. Of the Shrovetide games played only two have a ball above handball size – Alnwick and Atherstone. Neither of these games are hug football, as at Ashbourne, but both are remarkable survivors.

This book has not covered games in Wales. It is understood that it was played in the South and Pembrokeshire, but it is unclear if this was more akin to hurling rather than traditional football. Hurling was hand, not football. There are no references to play in Wales in any of the sources of reference used in the compilation of this book and the subject needs further investigation. However see comments on page 43.

References
1 Punchard, F.N., Survivals of Folk Football, 1928, p3

APPENDICES

Appendix A
Football Songs and Poems

Ever since Charles Cotton's time, there have been verses written about the game and those located have been brought together here. Some recent ones have been omitted through space consideration.
Burlesque on The Great Frost, by Charles Cotton
Two Towns, that long that war had waged,
Being at Foot-ball now engaged
For honour, as both sides pretended
left the brave tryall to be ended
Till the next thaw, for they were frozen
On either part at leest a dozen;
with a good handsome space between 'em,
Like Rolle-rich stones, if you've seen 'em,
And could no more run, Kick or tripye,
Than I can quaff of Aganippe;

The same old game, with the same old name, played in the same old way on the same old day.
(AN 01/03/1895)

Ere two notes St Oswald's clock had uttered
You heard as if an army muttered,
And the muttering grew to a loud rumbling,
As out of the houses the people came tumbling;
Tall men, short men, lean men, brawny men,
Fair men, dark men, grey men, tawny men,
Grave old plodders, gay young friskers,
Fathers, mothers, uncles, cousins,
Men clean shaved, and men with whiskers,
Families of tens and dozens,
Brothers, sisters, husbands, wives –
Followed the leather for their lives.
(AN 14/02/1902)

The following is supposed to have been written in 1861:

Ye Anciente Gayme
In Ashburne town, long synne, uppon the daye
Of Shrovetide, did the men in stoutest shoon
And doubtlet well lyned with pancake, playe
At football vigourously alle afternoon,
By anciente custom of the manour done.
The ball was at the Ball Ring tossed away
And in the Market Place and streets the funne
Was seene, and in the brooke with frolick gaye,
And through the fields until the ball was goaled
At Clyfton mylle, or Sturstone mylle of olde.
(AT 03/03/1933)

This song was performed at the Ashbourne theatre in Dig Street in 1821 by Mr Fawcett, a comedian:

I'll sing you a song of a neat little place
Top full of good humour and beauty and grace;
Where coaches are rolling by day and by night
And playing at football the people delight.
Where health and good humour does always abound
And hospitality's cup flows freely around
Where friendship and harmony are to be found
In the neat little town of Ashbourne.

Shrove Tuesday, you know, is always the day
When pancake's the prelude and footballs the play,
Where Uppards and Downards men ready for fun
Like the French at the battle of Waterloo run.
And well may they run like the Devil to pay,
'Tis always the case as I have heard say,
If a Derbyshire football man comes in the way
In the neat little town of Ashbourne.

There's Mappleton, Mayfield, Okeover and Thorpe
Can furnish some men that nothing can whop
And Bentley and Tissington, always in tune,
And Clifton and Sturston are ready as soon,
Then there's Snelston and Wyaston, Shirley and all,
Who are all good men at brave Whittaker's call,
And who come to kick at Paul Getliffe's football
In the neat little town of Ashbourne.

The ball is turned up and the Bullring's the place
And as fierce as a bulldog's is every man's face:
Whilst kicking and shouting and howling they run
Until every stitch of the ball comes undone.
There's Faulkner and Smith, Bodge Hand and some more
Who hide it and hug it and kick it so sore
And deserve a good whopping at every man's door
In the neat little town of Ashbourne.

If they get to the Park, The Upwards men shout
And think all the Downards men put to the rout
But a right about face they soon have to learn
And the Uppards men shout and huzza in their turn.
Then into Shawcroft where the bold and the brave
Get a ducking in trying the football to save,
For 'tis well known they fear not a watery grave
In defence of the football at Ashbourne.

If into Church Street should the ball take its way
The White Hart and the Wheatsheaf will cause some delay
For from tasting their liquor no man can refrain
Till he rolls like the football in Warin's tear-brain.
Then they run and they shout, they bawl and they laugh,
They kick and huzza, still the liquor they quaff
Till another Football has been cut into half
By the unfair players of Ashbourne.

(Originally published in *The Reliquary* 1867, p254)

The following song was composed for the 1891 concert in aid of funds to pay the fines for playing in the streets. It was sung to the tune 'Englishman' but today is sung in part at the pre-game lunch to a tune composed by Daly Atkinson:

Ashbourne Football Song
There's a game that bears a well-known name,
Though foes do it deride,
For years and years it has been played,
And why should it now subside?
It's helped us conquer the Russians and French,
In days that are long gone by,
For many a gallant soldiers played,
Who under the sod doth lie;
'Tis a good old game, deny it who can,
Is football played by Englishmen!

There's a town still plays this glorious game,
Tho' 'tis but a little spot,
And year by year the contest's fought,
From the field that's called Shaw Croft;
Then friend meets friend in friendly strife,
The leather for to gain,
And they play the game right manfully,
In snow, sunshine, or rain
'Tis a glorious game, deny it who can,
And no weather daunts an Englishman!

There's a Champion of this well-known Game,
A Coachbuilder bold and true,
Who never will let the Game go down,
A regular good old Blue.
He nutures a deep and honest love

For his humble domicile,
Yet fights with the boldness of a lion
For the rights of this little Isle.
He's a good old Blue, deny it who can,
There's a good old Tomtyfuge, he's an Englishman!

For loyal the Game shall ever be,
No matter when or where
And to treat that Game as ought but the free,
Is more than the boldest dare;
Through the ups and downs of its chequered life
May the ball still ever roll,
Until by fair and gallant strife,
We've reached the treasur'd goal.
It's a good old Game, deny it who can,
That tries the pluck of an Englishman!

There was another song printed in the souvenir of the same 1891 concert, also by George Porter:

Lines on the Ashbourne Football
Shrove Tuesday, Ash Wednesday my boys are the days
When football at Ashbourne is then all the rage,
And the Upwards and Downwards strive hard with a will
The ball for to goal at the Up or Down mill;
From the North and the South, from the East and the West,
The sturdy lads come, in stout courdroys dressed,
With legs wrapped in hay bands, and hat tied to chin,
They come for to kick boys, and kick hard to win.
Chorus
Its Upwards and Downwards, Hurrah for the Game
They play in the snow, Hail, Sun or the Rain,
Through the brook and the Meadows, both play with a will,
Till the ball's touched the wheel, at the Up or Down mill.
Shaw Croft is the place, and Two is the time,
Where each side will gather, awaiting the chime.
Then the ball is thrown up, midst a mighty hurrah,
And the lads thay all kick both from town and afar.
Oh how the legs fly as the ball rolls about,
And every good throw brings a hearty good shout,
For now they will show you before they have done,
How battles are fought boys, and how they are won.
Chorus
To Clifton or Sturston, they shout and they roar,
The Down play for the water, the Up for the shore,
They kick and they hug till the leather rolls in,
And then in the water the duckings begin.
'Keep her in' cry the Downards, 'throw her out' shout the Ups,
Whilst many a player unexpectedly sups,
The Upwards then get it and throw it ashore,
Where many a sound shin will soon be made sore.
Chorus
Now they are all at the Ball, how joyous they play,

There's the Doctor and Lawyer, and soldier so gay,
Schoolmaster, Surveyor, and Parson and all
Are kicking together at the glorious Football,
Good tempered and cheerful each plays his own way,
Both the old and the young, the bald and the grey,
Each striving together with hearty good will,
Till the Ball has been goaled, at the Up or Down Mill.
Chorus

This poem was printed in the *Ashbourne News Telegraph* on 04/03/1982, and relates to Herbert Plumbly:

Shrovetide
I've attended some functions in my humble career
From dry as dust meetings to those filled with jeers
But Ash Wednesday's dinner for me beat the rest
The Company genial, the food of the best.
The spontaneous welcome to our guest was sincere
Applause and foot stamping made that point quite clear.
Then we heard of his record, his long association
Of 50 years work, now that's dedication.
Herbert's reply I found quite a delight
To a 60 plus follower who's seen many a fight
Recalling past years naming some names
Who also worked hard for our Shrovetide games.
I'm proud to have been in that happy throng
Proud to have joined in the Shrovetide song
While chuckling still over one or two items
Say 'Let our Shrovetide continue, *ad infinitum*'

ERNIE'S GOAL
Written for Ernie on scoring his goal

The day dawned chill, but bright withal,
Our Lord Cullen threw up the ball;
Three blood red cocks upon the sphere,
Denoted Lord Cokayne lived here.

And in the hug right in the van,
Stood Ernie Grant, a massive man.
He'd played the game for many years,
But never got the goal that cheers.

Would nineteen Seventy be the year,
That he would celebrate with beer.
Would this be the year of Grace,
For 'Erne' to win at last the race.

Tho' years fly by like yesterday,
The Grants they came from far away.
For ten long years they'd heard the call,
Would this be it - to goal the ball.

All the long day the battle rolled,
But still the ball had not been gaoled.
Until at last, somebody threw,
The ball into the Henmore Brew.

Then Ernie quick to seize his chance,
Tho'blood his face did not enhance.
Plunged into the icy pool;
His partners also 'played it cool'.

His shin was hacked, and down he went,
But Ernie Grant was far from spent.
And rising up from off his knees,
Gave portent of the years be.

With blood of foes upon his mouth,
He fought them off, from north to south.
As down the Henmore he did toil,
Covered in blood, and mud, and soil.

And he was helped in mighty force,
By cousin John- And dad of course.
As they did strive with might and main,
In the dark, And in the icy rain

Until at last, the goal **in** view,
None was left of the motley crew.
And tho' it took him ten long years,
Mong the Down'ards he had no peers.

At Clifton mill, his name was made,
Tho' years may go, twill never fade.
Three times he smote the rough hewn stone,
His Auntie's memory to atone.

The tumult and the Shouting Dies,
Above the town the standard flies;
Long may it live, and may it bide,
Ashburne's Ball Game at Shrovetide.

Dedicated to Ernest Grant, on his feat of Goaling the Ball at Shrovetide, 1970.

Appendix B
The Boys' Games

It seems usual for a boys' game to have been played on Ash Wednesday. This applied in Derby as well as Ashbourne. A children's game is also a feature at Kirkwall. It was rare for game reports to mention the boy's game and therefore it is difficult to be precise about it. However the 1860 Court hearing heard that Supt Corbishley had previously taken a ball from the grammar schoolboys and had been summonsed before Derby County Court to return it, (DM 07/03/1860). The ball was described as being filled with 'shavings' which clearly would not be a normal football. It is reasonable to assume that it was regularly occurring as part of the annual custom. Joe Burton goaled his first ball when he was eleven, which would have been in 1885, so the game was being played then.

The ball for the boys' game was thrown up at 1.00pm. In 1894, it was thrown up 'as in former years' according to the report. The ball was painted with the national colours. It was run away with by Fred Fowell and goaled at Sturston. In 1896, a ball was turned up on Shaw Croft by George Dakin and played into Sandy Lane, up Hall Lane and onto Ashbourne Green. It was then run off by four boys including Thomas Handley, who goaled it at Sturston Mill. In 1908, it was reported that a boys' ball would be turned up by J Hawksworth the Committee secretary. The ball had been made and presented by Trevor Yeomans, the boot and shoe repairer of Dig Street who made the balls for the main game. It was quickly played to Clifton Mill where it was goaled by M Johnson, F Chell, and H Sowter at 1.45pm. It was reported that 'the little chaps carried the ball down the river like veterans'.

In 1909, Mr Coxon turned up a ball on Shaw Croft for boys under 16 years of age. The ball was soon under Back Bridge and was then played across the fields to Sturston Road. Play continued in the fields on the other side of the road where a hug took place. After a good run, the ball reached The Park. G Hill ran off with the ball up the Old Hill, but Joe Wibberley overtook him and later goaled the ball at Clifton. In 1910, it was reported that Mr J C Prince turned up the ball for the lads and that it was eventually goaled at Sturston by a youth named Higgins.

In 1912, Karl Blank turned up the ball which was goaled at Clifton by George Sowter. It is likely that the game continued until 1914. Perhaps it was abandoned in 1915 after the outbreak of the Great War. However, the 1990 Shrovetide Souvenir (ANT, March) reproduces a photo of the Wesleyan School in 1918 with the boys holding three balls and the photograph captioned 'young footballers'. Had this anything to do with the boys' game? Today, Ashbourne schools have the Lent term holiday at a different time to much of Derbyshire so that it coincides with Shrovetide week. In former days schoolboys asked permission to leave school and play the game. It was apparently granted so long as the request was genuine.

Appendix C
Detail From The Law Cases

1860

The following persons were summonsed under sec 72 of the *Highways Act 1835* for 'obstructing the highways by playing the game of football in the streets of the town of Ashbourn [sic] on Shrove Tuesday and Ash Wednesday, February 21st and 22nd 1860'. Note this did not include the townships of Clifton or Sturston.

Joseph Brandreath, cordwainer (shoemaker) and maker of the footballs
Thomas Wallis, farmer, Sturston
John Hill, labourer
John Atterbury, bricklayer
James Brown, junior, bricklayer
Richard Brown, bricklayer
Charles Griffiths, brewer
George Yeomans, labourer
Joseph Bridden, timber merchant
Joseph Cundy, labourer
Thomas Waterfall
Henry Wibberley
Joseph Howell
Isaac Wright
John Fogg
Charles Hudson Hall, grocer
Charles Dean, innkeeper
John Millward
John Whitham, junior, chemist
Mark Faulkner, junior
George W Tomlinson, attorney
George Goodwin Brittlebank, attorney
John Smith, gentleman
Alfred Pearson, labourer
Henry Pearson, labourer
William Robson, labourer
Arthur Ball
Edward Pool
Henry Prince, farmer
George Peach, Clifton, innkeeper
Richard Chester
Samuel Wibberley, jun, blacksmith
George H Mountfort, grocer*
Robert Dawson, gentleman*
Allen Cox, vet. surgeon
Thomas Kennedy
Samuel Smith, Clifton
William Room
Thomas Yeomans
Charles Coxon, butcher
Thomas Lane, innkeeper
George Herp, butcher
Henry Hawkesworth [Black Harry]*
Joseph Greatorex, blacksmith
George Woolley, draper*
Edward Boam
George Getliffe, tailor
Edwin Goodwin
James Pearson*
Thomas Bridden
William Inge, innkeeper
John Bowler
Thomas Brinsley, builder*
William Smith, gentleman, Stanton

* These people appear on the 1862 painting. George Mountfort is called Mountford on the painting. Also, Black Harry's name on the painting description is given as William. He is referred to as Henry in other reports.

1861
The sentences were:
Fined forty shillings:
George Yeomans
Fined ten shillings:
Philip Brown
John Buxton
Thomas Waterfall
James and Sam Wibberley
William Room
John Miers, innkeeper
John Rowbotham

Fined one shilling:
James Larkin
Charles Furber
John Redfern
Edward and James Brown
Henry and Joseph Wibberley
James and Elisha Atterbury
Henry and Edward Prince
Joseph and Thomas Hill
Thomas Woodhouse
Alfred Pearson
Thomas Wood
George Brown
Joseph Cundy
Cases dismissed:
John Williamson
George Faulkner
Thomas Manlove
George Herp
John Bladon
James Dougherty
William Smith

Enoch Bill did not appear and a warrant was issued for his arrest. Costs were also imposed in addition to the above fines.

1879

John Tomlinson of Sturston was charged with playing football on the highway on Shrove Tuesday. The ball was turned up and apparently kicked across the Market Place. It was then taken down St John Street and then up Hall Lane. Tomlinson was in the front ranks of the crowd and shouting them encouragement. He was fined £2 and costs. James Larkin was similarly charged with playing the game in Church Street. He was fined ten shillings and costs along with George Salt, Thomas Sowter, Thomas Haworth and Charles Coxon. Thomas Woodhouse was fined £1, along with William Johnson, who appeared with a crutch and a stick having been injured on the Wednesday, and William Silvester, a rural policeman, dressed in a soldier's uniform. Both had incited the crowd to play. George Warner was also fined £1.

Fined ten shillings:
Walter Woodward
Henry Pearson
Mathew Cleaver
William Hodgkinson
Joseph Hill
Charles Waterfall
William Bennett.
Fined fifteen shillings:
Thomas Swinscoe.

Arthur Bill, James Larkin and Thomas Sowter, having been fined for playing on 25 February, were fined a further five shillings for playing on the 26th.
In all cases, costs were imposed on top of the fines.

1891
The names of the defendents under the first hearing were:
William Coxon (who caused a laugh by appearing in a butcher' smock — there was very little respect for the dignity of the Court)

Samuel Sowter
James Sowter
John Atterbury
William Johnson
Frederick Burton
Henry Atterbury
Frank Hollingshead
Albert Jones
George Plant
W H Oldham
Arthur Boden
Frank Clarke
John Barker
Frank Henstock
Henry Brown
Joseph Mellor
H Hand
George Peach junior

John Tomlinson
William Edge
Charles Woolley
William Purdy
Joseph Harlow
Robert Wigley
George Howson
John Palmer
Arthur Joyce

James Gilman
John Sellers
These men all pleaded guilty and were fined 2s 6d with 7s 6d costs
Other summonses were:
Frank Swindells
James Howson
James Gilman

The above were also fined ten shillings in total.
Frank Smith pleaded not guilty and the case was dismissed.
Rev Frederick Tomlinson pleaded that he had endeavoured to get the ball out of town and the court 'had regard to his station in life'. He was not fined but was ordered to pay costs of 7s 6d. One cannot help thinking that this decision was somewhat tenuous. It is beyond doubt that all the players were trying to get the ball out of town, as that is where the goals were situated.
Also fined ten shillings (including costs) were:

Joseph Harrison
William Ellaby
Arthur Bill
Trevour Tunnicliffe
Ralph Plant
John Sherwin
Thomas Burns
Arthur Udall
Francis Purdy
William Bennett
William Connell
John Hilton jnr
William Palmer

Joseph Hilton
Josoph Willerby
William Gossard
David Roberts
Henry Haywood
George Brown
John Palmer
Henry Atterbury
Lewis Goodwin
William Woodisse
Joseph Hilton
Charles Atterbury
William Lea
John Leason

Robert Lister was found not guilty (mistaken identity).
On a second hearing heard on 07/03/1891, the following pleaded guilty and were fined ten shillings:

Albert Jones
Henry Hand
Charles Wooley
John Jones
Joseph Massey
Thomas Purdy
Thomas Cundy
John Frost
Thomas Sowter

The following pleaded not guilty but were also fined ten shillings:
Thomas Purdy*
Henry Hawkesworth (Black Harry)
Alfred Hall
John Faulkner
Charles Wooley*
George Astle

* These two were also fined for playing on the Wednesday but their fines were remitted as they had already been fined for the Tuesday's play.
Cases dismissed: William Lytle and Charles Purdy.
Charles Coxon was also fined ten shillings and the case against John Burton was adjourned because of ill health. The case had not been heard by the end of June.

Roll of Honour

Date	Turned up by	Goaled by	Goaled at
1848	Not known	ungoaled, cut to pieces	–
1859 T	Not known	? Ungoaled	–
1859 W	Not known	Not known	C
1860 T	Not known	Not known	–
1860 W	Not known	Not known	–
W	Elizabeth Woolley	Mathew Cleaver	N/K
1861 T	G Yeomans	Not known	S
1861 W	Not known	Not known	C
W	Not known	Not known	S
1862-1869	Not known*	Not known	–
1870 T	Not known	Not known	C
1870 W	Not known	Not known	S
1871 T	Not known	Ball came to pieces	–
1871 W	Not known	Whieldon	S
1872 T	Not known	Not known	S
1872 W	Not known	Not known	C
W	Not known	Ball cut	–
W	Not known	Not known	C
1873-1875	Not known	Not known	–
1876 T	Not known	Not known	S
1876 W	Not known	Ball cut	–
W	Not known	Not known	C
1877 T	Not known	John Tomlinson	S
1877 W	Not known	Not known	N/K
1878 T	Not known	Ball cut up but goaled	S
1878 W	Not known	Not known	S
W	Not known	Not known	C
1879 T	Not known	Ball seized by police and cut up	–
T	Not known	Not known	C
T	No details available but ? kicked to pieces		–
1879 W	Dummy ball seized by the police		–
W	Not known	Not known	C
1880 T	Alfred Hall	Samuel Taylor	C
T	Not known	Not known	N/K
1880 W	?James Harrison	Not known	N/K
1881 T	Alfred Hall	Not known	S
1881 W	Not known	Tom Cundy	S
1882 T	Not known	Not known	C
1882 W	Not known	Not known	S
W	Not known	Not known	C
1883 T	Alfred Hall	Not known	C
W	Not known	Not known	C
	One of the above by Henry Hurst		

	W	Not known	Not known	S
1884	T	No details available		–
1885	T	Alfred Hall	Not known	C
1885	W	? Harry Gallimore	Not known	C
	W	Not known	Not known	S
	W	Not known	Not known	S
1886	T	Alfred Hall	Atterbury & Hurst	C
1886	W	Not known	Not known	?C
1887	T	Not known	Not known	C
	T	Not known	Not known	C
		One of the above by H Hind		
	T	Not known	?John Wibberley	S
1888	T	Not known	Not known	C
	T	Not known	Not known	S
1888	W	Not known	Not known	S
	W	Not known	- Heywood	C
1889	T	?Alfred Hall	Not known	S
1889	W	? Charles Coxon	Not known	C
1890	T	? Alfred Hall	Not known	C
	T	Not known	Not known	C
1890	W	?Charles Coxon	Charles Coxon	S
1891	T	E Burton	W Lytle	S
	W	Not known	Mr Avery	S
		Not known	J Barker	C
1892	T	R Wallis	(?) J Barker & T Burns	C
	W	C Purdy	(ball kicked to pieces)	
		J Winterton	C Howard	C
1893	T	J Marple		
	W	W Hall	T Cundy	S
		H Taylor	W Mellor & C Bretby	C
1894	T	Capt Matthews	Mr Chell	S
	W	Mr Harrison	G Everett	S
1895	T	(?) E Ball	G Everett	S
	W	F Tomlinson	C Etches	S
1896	T	F Tomlinson	J Handley & J Wibberley	S
	W	E Ball	J Burton	S
		R Wallis	W Allsop	C
		F Tomlinson	F Howard	S
1897	T	F Tomlinson	C Hill	C
	W	Mr Carter	T Waterfall	S
		L C Coxon	A Lymn	S
1898	T	F Tomlinson	J Faulkner & S Sowter	C
	W	G Gather	J Burton	S
		F Tomlinson	W Prince	S
1899	T	W Coxon	J Bradley	C
	W	F Tomlinson	J Hawksworth	S
1900	T	W Coxon	T Taylor	S
	W	F Tomlinson	J Etches	S
		T Waterfall	F Ashton	S
1901	T	F Tomlinson	J Burton	S
	W	J Hawksworth	G Hall	S
1902	T	W Storer	J Burton	S
	W	D Allsop	G Ainsworth	C
1903	T	J Winterton	J W Walker	S
	W	E Porter	G Roome	S
		G Derbyshire	G Ainsworth	C
1904	T	M Roberts	H Buckley	S
		C Tarlton	G Leese	C

W	S Boden	R Botham	S
1905 T	W Prince	Mr Tunnicliffe	C
W	F Evershed	T Botham	S
1906 T	P Morgan	T Waterfall	S
	F Ashton	(?) J Sowter	C
W	J C Prince	C Goodwin	S
	J Winterton	C Ainsworth	C
1907 T	J C Prince	T Waterfall	S
	T L Demery		
W	W Prince	A Buckley	S
	R J Cooke	J Chell	C
1908 T	W C Tomlinson	C Phillips	S
	T Finney	G Walker	S
W	T W Birch	G Handley	S
	R Prince	G Ainsworth	C
1909 T	R H Vessey	J Brown	S
	H Prince	C Eccles	S
W	F Glanville	J Harrison	C
1910 T	S Clarke	S Grindey	S
	W Prince	H Massey	C
W	G Derbyshire	F Ward	S
	W Coxon	N Etherington	C
1911 T	C C Busby	W Spencer	S
W	E Wood	J Bradley & H Massey	C
1912 T	Capt W Jelf	J Dethick	S
	S H Bagshaw	G Taylor	C
W	T H B Bamford	W Shakespeare	S
	J Hawksworth	G Ainsworth	C
1913 T	T H B Bamford	J Burton	S
	S H Bagshaw	C Sowter	C
W	E Stebbings	R Hall	S
1914 T	G Huntress	T Brown	S
W	T H B Bamford	S Taylor	C
1915 T	T H B Bamford	G Smith	C
W	B M Simms	T Sowter	C
	S H Beresford	J Bowler	S
1916 T	W Fowell	G Walker	S
W	J Eggleston	W Brunt	C
1917 T	J Harrison	H Sowter	C
	J Harrison	A Sowter	C
W	J W Chapman	F Harrison	C
1918 T	J Etches	W Fearn	S
W	J Barker	C Sowter	C
	A Bentley		
1919 T	Brig Gen R Jelf DSO	F Sowter	C
W	W Ludlow	T H Chell	C
1920 T	J Barker	C & W Sowter	C
W	S Bloomer	B Faulkner	C
1921 T	Mr Burton	C Sowter	C
W	E J Morley	G Sowter	C
1922 T	T Yeomans	S Taylor	C
W	A Holmes	O Hill	S
	M E Bland	W Birch	C
1923 T	The Marquis of Hartington	E Chell	C
W	Capt F E F Wright	G Peach	C
1924 T	The Duke of Devonshire KG	J Harrison	S
W	H J Newbold	R Wibberley	S
	Gunner Stone VC	H Connell	C
1925 T	W Meredith	F Moon & S Sowter	C

Roll of Honour

W	Mr Knowles	J Barker	C
1926 T	Mr Farmer	W Brown	S
	J Harrison	F Taylor	C
W	Mr Beardsley	C Colclough	C
	F Ward	W Sowter	C
1927 T	F Turner	J Sowter	C
	Mr Farmer	F Smith	S
W	C Holmes	R Wibberley	S
1928 T	HRH The Prince of Wales	G Ratcliffe	S
	S Dakin	H Sowter & J Bill	C
W	G T Riding	A Birch	C
1929 T	W C Mallinson	A Hill	S
W	J Lilley	F Atkin	C
1930 T	F Powell	C Mee	S
	G Roome	J Robinson & J Bagnall	C
W	F Boden	G Sowter	C
1931 T	Sir I Walker	N Burton	S
	S Sowter Snr	S Sowter Jnr	C
W	L A Clowes	J W Gadsby	C
1932 T	J Hall JP		
W	Lt Com G S Williamson RN		
1933 T	Capt Baillie JP MC	J Allsop	C
W	Mr Banks		
1934 T	Capt Unwin VC	S Harrison	C
W	Capt Pearson	C Sowter	C
1935 T	C Turpie	H G Plumbly	S
	H E Thomas	G Peach	C
W	J Hayes	T Armstrong	C
1936 T	The Duke of Rutland	T Allen	S
	J Etches	J Burton	S
W	J W Gadsby	F Hallam	S
	T Yeomans	E Brown	S
1937 T	J Crompton Inglefield	G Sellers	S
	C Doxey		
W	G E Gather	J Wibberley	S
1938 T	Brig Gen Walthall	W L Twigge	S
	J B Tomlinson	I Moon	C
W	S H Bagshaw	L Bull	S
	S Sellers	W Allen	S
1939 T	D Burnaby	L Lowndes	S
W	A Ellaby	E Hellaby	C
1940 T	J Dean		
W	S Mugglestone	F Edge	S
1941 T	F P Birch	C Allen	S
W	W Spencer	C Etches	S
1942 T	T Marsden	J Allen	S
W	J Etches	L Moon	C
1943 T	Gp Capt The Lord Hamilton	Mrs Mugglestone	S
W	Capt W E Newlands	Miss D Sowter	C
1944 T	Major G W Bond	P Etches	S
W	J Wood	J Wibberley	S
1945 T	T Pountain JP	T Allen	S
W	A Hulme	M Chell	C
1946 T	Col J P Stanton		
W	F S Bromwich	W Allen	S
	F P Birch	D Clowes	C
1947 T	E Wheatcroft	A Beresford	S
W	H Wardle		
1948 T	S H Elkes	G Harrison	C

	W	G W Casson	S Sowter	C
		C C Heathcote	F Dethick	S
1949	T	AVM RO Jones CBE AFC	D Lowndes	S
		J E Gadsby	A Beresford	S
	W	Capt S D Player	S Taylor	C
1950	T	Brig Gen Harvey	S Chell	C
	W	F J Edge	J Grant	C
1951	T	F Highfield	J Mansfield	S
		J Wedd	C Challinor	C
	W	Col Ridout		
1952	T	The Duke of Devonshire		
	W	Major F D Ley	S Cope	S
		A Jones	K Renshaw	C
1953	T	Lord John Manners	D Lowndes	S
		S Sellers	J Higgins	C
	W	R S Bury	J Mansfield	S
		T Brown		
1954	T	Sir G Kennings	J Clarke	S
		J Roberts	J Smith	C
	W	H Johnson	G Mansfield	S
1955	T	Col P V W Gell	G Challinor	C
	W	Mr Justice Callow	W Hellaby	S
1956	T	Capt C Waterhouse MP	J Gadsby	C
	W	Dr R Ogley	C Burton	C
		P Wibberley	C Challinor	C
1957	T	F Dalton	Miss Nora Wibberley	C
	W	G W Rose JP	R Braddock	S
1958	T	R Parnell	R Geeson & R Crooks	C
	W	W Ellis Grimshaw		
1959	T	J W P Groves OBE	J Mansfield	S
		C Botham	T Allen	S
	W	P Balean		
1960	T	D Carr	P Harrison	C
		S Froggatt		
	W	R F Wright	J Herridge	S
1961	T	J Moores		
	W	M R H Sadler		
1962	T	E Moult		
	W	H Yates	P Harrison	C
		L A Andrews	P Shearsmith	C
1963	T	G R Jackson		
	W	F H Thomas	W Bennett	S
1964	T	S Ramsden	J Allen	S
	W	A E Dawson	C Coxon	C
1965	T	Major J W Chandos-Pole	G Connell	S
		P Chadwick	F Mansfield	S
	W	J Archer	P Gadsby	S
1966	T	Sir S Mathews		
	W	S Flower		
1967	T	S Longson	R Storer	C
		J Smith	P Harrison	C
		K Wood	A Smith	C
	W	Rev F J H Lisemore		
1968 No official game
1969	T	Lord Yarborough	R Storer	C
		H Blow	Goal declared void	
	W	D Moore	F Lomas	S
		J Atkinson		
1970	T	Lord Cullen of Ashbourne	E Grant	C

Roll of Honour

W	A Parry	P Armstrong	S
	G Bradley		
1971 T	Col P Hilton		
W	A Birch	J Tomkinson	C
1972 T	A E H Sevier	D Sowter	S
	A Slingsby	J Clarke	C
W	J H Wheeldon	D Bates	C
	G Wheatcroft		
1973 T	C Harpur-Crewe		
W	G Peach	J R Grant	C
	T W Knight		
1974 T	Col J R G Stanton		
W	D Lowndes	I Bates	C
1975 T	B Clough	G Handley	S
W	J Shemilt		
1976 T	Lord Hives		
W	N Moore		
1977	T	A Bamford	
W	F Hyde	J Grant	C
1978 T	Capt P Walker-Okeover	S Challinor	C
W	K Ward		
1979 T	D John		
W	J Kenny	P Armstrong	S
1980T	Sir J Fitzherbert		
W	C Etches	A Lemon	S
1981 T	R Taylor	G Harrison	C
W	R Stevenson		
1982 T	R MacFarland	G Cresswell	S
	W Hellaby		
W	H Plumbly	G Weston	C
1983 T	The Marquis of Hartington		
W	A Wright	D Hollingworth	C
1984 T	M Parris MP		
W	K Zouhar	S Bott	S
	A Robinson		
1985 T	P Drabble		
W	A Chadwick BEM	M Moore	C
	A Attenborough	H Fowler	C
1986 T	J Robertson	P Kerr	C
W	B Birch	M Harrison	C
	D Thornley		
1987 T	Viscount Tamworth	M Betteridge	C
W	S Taylor	J Dodd	S
1988 T	Mr Justice Woods	A Bates	C
W	J Grant		
1989 T	Marquis of Lothian	W Ratcliffe	S
W	P Binder	S Hudson	C
	R Ford	M Wright	S
1990 T	F Elliott	P Clarke	C
W	I Bates	J Lemon	C
	H Sherratt	R Godfrey	S
1991 T	R Chambers	D Calladine	S
	K Hunt	R Bates	C
W	J Allsopp	M Holland	C
1992 T	J P Gadsby	T Fearn	C
W	S Bury	M Hellaby	S
1993 T	The Duke of Rutland		
W	Dr R Bennett	C Fearn	S

		G W Shepherd	S Lyon	S
1994	T	D Shields DL	P Robson	C
	W	J Chadwick		
1995	T	J Heslop		
	W	G Ward	J Tomlinson	C
1996	T	B Ewart	D Waring	C
	W	P Gadsby	S Wright	S
1997	T	R Spencer	S Hellaby	S
	W	W Kent	T Brown	S
		P Rowbotham		
1998	T	Chief Const J Newing	A Etherington	S
	W	C Trafford	G Ditchfield	S
1999	T	Lord Lieut J Bather	N Fearn	S
	W	B Bates		
2000	T	J Hanson	M Spencer	S
	W	P Tomlinson	P Harrison	C
2001		No game		
2002	T	S Plumbly	K Maskell	S
	W	A Millward		

Throughout the 1880s, each team had a Captain and it is probable that the Down'ards Captain turned up the ball on the Tuesday and the Up'ards on the Wednesday. For all of this time it appears that the Down'ards Captain was Alfred Hall and the Up'ards Captain was Charles Coxon.

Royal Shrovetide Committee

Chairmen

1909-1910	Mr G Derbyshire
1912-1924	Mr W Coxon*
1924-1935	Mr J Harrison
1936-1946	Mr J C Prince
1946-1947	Mr H G Plumbly
1947-1956	Mr F P Birch
1956-1969	Mr H G Plumbly
1969-1974	Mr J E Gadsby
1974-1991	Mr J P Gadsby
1991-	Mr P Tomlinson

Secretary

1897-1936	Mr J Hawksworth**
1908-1909	J F Spencer Joint Secretary
1936-1937	Mr F W Henstock
1937-1953	Mr H Sellers
1953-1974	Mr A Froggatt
1974-1975	Mr A Hill
1975-1979	Mr I Brett
1979-	Mr D J Hanson

*Mr Coxon was reported as being Chairman in 1912
** In 1912, Mr Hawksworth wrote to the *Ashbourne News* saying that he had been secretary for fifteen years.

The Committee adopted the name 'Royal' after Princess Mary accepted a ball in 1922.

CHRONOLOGY

Highlights of the Ashbourne Game

1683		Charles Cotton's reference to the playing of football
1797		Shrovetide game at the Grammar School
1798		Probable date for the first Shrovetide game played between Clifton and Sturston Mills
1821		Football song earliest specific reference to the game
1823		Webb Ellis picks up the ball at Rugby School where three Ashbourne boys are pupils
1840		Ball carried close to Tissington
1848		Earliest reference of a ball being cut; policeman assaulted
1858		Mass football game played in January to celebrate marriage of Princess Royal
1859		Vicar attempts to have game moved to Ashbourne Green
1860		Players fined for playing in the streets; fifty-four arrested. Earliest reference to the boys' game
1860	W	Mrs Woolley turned up the second ball
1861		Thirty-six players arrested
		Ashbourne Hall sold to Mr Frank
		Earliest known reference to the town band (playing after the game)
1861	W	First ball goaled in about thirty minutes at Clifton
1862		Over sixty summonses served. Football painting completed
1863	T	Ball turned up at Shaw Croft for the first time
1870	W	Play in the Market Place
1871	T	Ball kicked to pieces
1872	W	Play in the town's streets. Ball cut and another thrown up in the town. Ten prosecutions followed
1876	W	Ball cut to pieces, another turned up
1877	T	Up'ards wade upriver to goal for the first time
1878	T	Ball cut up. Game at its lowest ebb with much fighting and drunkenness
	W	William Barker drowned at Clifton
		Joseph Osborne awarded bravery medal for saving Jimmy Harrison's life in Clifton Mill pool
1879	T	Ball cut to pieces by the police on Shaw Croft
	W	Ball turned up in the Market Place when dummy ball seized by the police
		Twenty-one prosecuted for playing in the streets, eleven for drunkenness and nineteen warned for trespass on Shaw Croft
1880	W	Shaw Croft closed
		Battle with police at Compton Bridge. Ten people summonsed for drunkenness or assaulting the police. Possibly ninety-seven summonses issued for playing football. Mr Simpson intervenes with £100 surety
1881	T	Shaw Croft reopened, game played as usual after meeting
1885		Interest in the game 'in a great measure gone'. Three players summonsed for playing second ball in The Park
	W	Three balls goaled, one at Clifton, two at Sturston
1887		Ball played in streets, police application for summonses declined by magistrates
	T	Three goals scored, two at Clifton, one at Sturston

Year	Day	Event
1888		Game played in the Market Place and ninety-four summonses applies for but withdrawn. First Tuesday ball goaled at Sturston for first time in years
1888	W	Ball run to Dovedale; another turned up and two in play at once
1890		Last time ball goaled by the turner-up, Wm Coxon
1891		Summonses issued against eighty-four people Turner up of the Tuesday ball prosecuted and probably the same for Wednesday (Wm Coxon) First reference to a painted ball
1892		First invited guest
1892	W	Ball kicked to pieces
1893		First mention of carrying guest shoulder high
1893	T	Ball cut in two
1894/95		Consecutive balls goaled by same person (only record)
1896	W	Two balls in play at once; two goals at Sturston, one at Clifton
1898	T	Police prevent play in Sandy Lane; four balls cost 10/- – 12/- each
1898		Shaw Croft sold to F Stretton
1899		Last time Committee Secretary goaled a ball
1899	T	Ball kicked to pieces
	W	Game played in The Park again
1900	T	Game played through the streets
1900		Railway to Buxton opened
1901	W	Police barrier at Compton Bridge (and in 1902)
1902	W	Players fall down well in The Park
1903		Game stopped by a car for the first time
1906	T	William Tunnicliffe died at Clifton
1907	T	Ball kicked to pieces Balls turned up by two brothers, one each day
1908		First list of Committee members
1908	W	Goal at Clifton in 32 minutes
1909	W	6,000 alleged spectators
1912		Chief Constable a spectator
1913		Play to end at 5.00pm but Committee relented; first cine film of the game – at the Empire Cinema
1915		A near fatality
1916		Only one ball per day unless goaled by 4.00pm Ball sent to the men at the War Front
1917	T	One ball rule again but two goals at Clifton by brothers
1918		500 to 600 men play at the Front with an Ashbourne ball
1920		Clifton waterwheel removed since last game
1921		The only time a Burton allowed a Sowter to score! Inspector Burton turned up the ball which was goaled by Charles Sowter
1922		Ball sent to Princess Mary as a wedding present
1922	W	Two balls in play at once
1923		Game referred to as Ashbourne Royal Shrovetide Football for the first time
1924		Last time Committee Chairman goaled a ball
1928	T	HRH The Prince of Wales turns up the ball
1930	T	Game started by a foreign national for the first time
1931	T	Ball goaled by son of the turner up (both named Sam Sowter)
1932	W	Spectators injured as bridge parapet collapses No goal on either day for the first time in recorded history
1934		£1 award to goaler if first ball goaled between 6.00 and 7.00pm
1935	T	First broadcast on the BBC
1936	T	Riotous scenes at Sturston
	T	First time since 1911 that Up'ards goal two balls in one day
1936		First time that a side scores four goals in one year in recorded history
1938		Up'ards score ten goals in three years
1942	T	Shortest game on record – 30 minutes
1943	T	Doris Mugglestone goals at Sturston
	W	Doris Sowter goals at Clifton
1946	W	Goaler uses a motor bike
1947	T	Another goal by vehicle

1948	T	Down'ards recover from Sturston Mill to goal at Clifton
1948		John Barker died after painting balls for 70 years
1951	T	Perhaps the fastest ever goal – at Clifton in under 25 minutes by Cecil Challinor
1952	W	Motor bike used by Up'ards
1953		Three men rescued from the river
1954	W	Ball goaled at 12.08 am at Sturston
1956		Committee states ball their property at midnight
1956	T	Down'ards take a car to Clifton goal
1956		F P Birch resigns as chairman, H Plumbly takes over
1957	T	Nora Wibberley goals at Clifton
		Use of mechanical means to goal a ball disallowed
	W	Barbara Hellaby denied a goal at Sturston
1958		Trevor Yeomans died after making balls for 50 years
1960		Damage to Wigley's and Woolworth's shops
1960	T	Ball disappears and game abandoned
1961	T	Ball ungoaled for only fifth time since 1891
	W	Ball ungoaled; first year with no goals since 1932
1963		Princess Margaret came to Ashbourne and presented with a mini-ball, painted by John Roberts
1963	T	Ball disappears again and game abandoned
1965	T	Youngest goaler (except for the boys' games) – 13 years
1966		No goals on either day; Joe (Ninety) Burton died, aged 96 years
1967		Play ends at 10.00pm
		Three goals in one day for first time since 1896, all at Clifton. Last time a goal scored by hitting the masonry at Clifton Mill
1968		Game abandoned through Foot and Mouth disease; Mini Shrovetide
1969	T	Second goal disallowed; Clifton Mill now demolished
		HG Plumbly resigns as Chairman, JE Gadsby elected
1970		Last balls to be decorated by John Roberts
1971		John Roberts died; ball painter for 22 years
1971	T	First game since river culverted
1972	T	A Sowter goals at Sturston!
	W	Game finishes at 7.30 pm in three day week power cut
1974		JE Gadsby retires as Chairman; succeeded by son John
1975	W	Goal disallowed
1976		No goals on either day
1977	T	Fourth successive no goal
	W	Committee awards goal to John Grant
1978	T	Down'ards score first Tuesday goal since 1972
1979	W	Up'ards score first Wednesday goal since 1971
1981		Sturston Mill demolished prior to Shrovetide
1982		Roll of Honour boards erected in the Green Man Hotel
1984		Arthur Chadwick chalks up 30 years as ball maker
	T	First serving MP turns up the ball – Matthew Parris
1985	W	Committee awards goal to Harry Fowler
		Herbert Plumbly resigns from the Committee after 53 years
1987	T	Ball re-turned up after game declared void by use of a car
1988		Sandra Church (nee Chadwick) decorates her last ball after 16 years
1989	T	Committee awards goal to Bill Ratcliffe
	W	Up'ards score two goals in a day for first time in 24 years
1990	T	Possibly the oldest turner-up, Harold Sherratt at 81 years old
1991		New rule: ball void if missing for more than one hour
		Herbert Plumbly misses the game for first time in 62 years
		John Gadsby retires as Committee Chairman, succeeded by Philip Tomlinson
1992		Lunch in a marquee due to closure of Green Man
2000	T	Last goal of millennium by P Harrison, Clifton
2002	T	Premier Earl of England, The Earl of Shrewsbury, a lunch guest for the first time
	T	First ball of new millennium scored by Kirk Maskell, Sturston
		Was this the first time a person in the hug took a call on his mobile phone?
	W	First lady High Sheriff of Derbyshire attends lunch – Miss Jane Walker-Okeover

INDEX

A
Abstinence Union 61, 85
Alnwick 27, 39, 41, 202
Angel Inn, Kniveton 97
Ashbourne Aerodrome 136
Ashbourne Bathing Club 99
Ashbourne Grammar School 11
Ashbourne Green brickyard 76, 81, 95
Ashbourne Hall 56, 90
Ashbourne Band 56, 194
Ashbourne Zoo 102
Ashford-in-the-Water 33, 39, 103

B
Barnes 30, 35, 39, 53, 99, 177, 180
Bedworth 39
Beverley 33, 39
Bletchley 39
Bluebell Inn 74
Board of Guardians 84
Boothby Arms 83
Boys' Games 210
Bristol 19, 22, 23, 29, 39
Bromfield 25, 39
Bull ring 196
Bull-baiting 63
Bury 43
Bury, Lancs 39
Bushy 30, 39
Buxton 17

C
Camp Ball 15, 16, 22
Capt Parry 62, 66-69, 74, 77, 91
Carlisle 19, 28, 39
Cattle plague 57
Charles Cotton 11, 13, 23, 29, 44, 48, 57, 204, 221
Cheam 34, 42
Chester 10, 11, 17, 18, 22, 39, 49, 195, 211
Chester-le-Street 39, 129
cholera 79
Clifton Mill, history of 46
Clifton steeplechases 65
Coach and Horses Inn 75
Cock Inn 50, 60, 65, 77, 89, 92, 93, 95, 96
Compton brewery 71
Corfe 14, 19, 20, 40
Cornwall 40
Crown Inn, Parwich 97

D
Derby 12, 16-17, 24-25, 30-34
Devon 27
Dog and Partridge Inn 87
Dorking 34-38, 40, 42, 83, 84, 89
Duns 24, 40
Durham Ox Inn 73, 81, 88

E
Ely 16, 22
Empire Cinema 103, 104, 112, 119, 222
Epsom 34, 42
Ewell 34, 42

F
Fasten E'en 10
Finsbury Fields 22, 40
Foot and Mouth 153
Football Songs 204

G
Glasgow 18, 20, 21, 40
Green Man Hotel Sale 83
Guisborough 22, 40

H
Hampton-on-Thames 28, 30, 38, 40
Hampton-Wick 30
Hawick 25, 29, 40, 202
Haxey 40
Hornsea 40
Hug ball 9, 14-16, 39
Hull 30
Hurling 15, 27, 40, 203

I
Ickleton 40
Ilderton 41
Inveresk 14, 27, 40

J
Jedburgh 24, 40, 202, 203

K
Kingston-upon-Thames 27, 34
Kirkmichael 26, 40
Kirkwall 14, 18, 34, 45, 48, 67, 167, 178, 202, 203, 210
Knives in the hug 50

L
Landbeach 40
Leek 9
Leicester 11, 43

M
Machine Inn 104, 105, 116, 138
Manchester 21
Mansion 70, 88, 100, 112, 116, 159, 170
Melrose 41
Messingham 41, 43
Mini Shrovetide 153
Molesey 34, 36, 42
Mortlake 34, 35, 42

N
Ness 17, 41
'Ninety' Burton 87, 90, 92, 112, 197
Nuneaton 41

O
Olney Pancake race 9
Oxford 22, 41

P
Peebles 20
Prince of Wales 45, 99, 101, 112, 121, 123, 124, 132, 140, 169, 172, 175, 178, 185, 191-194, 217, 222
Princess Margaret 151
Princess Mary 116
Princess Royal 51

Q
Queen's Vaults 97

R
Railway Tavern 82, 108, 150, 169
Richmond 34, 35, 41
Ripley 34, 42, 91
Roebuck Inn 87
Rothbury 41
Rugby 11
Ruislip 21, 41

S
Scarborough 41, 43
Scone 26
Sedgefield 39, 41
Shrewsbury 21, 29, 42, 43, 192, 223
Shrovetide Festivities 61
Shrovetide song of 1891. 81, 144, 174, 192, 208
Snotch 15
Sous St Leger 109
Stag and Pheasant 97
Stonyhurst College, near Blackburn 33, 38, 39
Sturston Mill, history of 47
Supt Burford 85, 96, 98, 99, 103

T
Teddington 9, 30
Thames Ditton 34
The Ball, description of 201
The Tiger 97
Three Horse Shoes 95
Tideswell 12
Tissington 85, 91
Town Crier 37, 73, 95
Traditions 201
Twickenham 30, 42

V
Volunteer Corps 79

W
Walton-on-Thames 34, 36, 42
Webb Ellis, William 50
Weybridge 34, 42
Wheel, Hulland Ward 97
Whitby 41-43
Wirksworth Hundred 84
Women's Total Abstinence Union 85
Woodeaves Mills 65
Wooler 41

Y
Yetholm 42

224